AMERICAN NEIGHBORHOODS
AND
RESIDENTIAL DIFFERENTIATION

AMERICAN NEIGHBORHOODS AND RESIDENTIAL DIFFERENTIATION

Michael J. White

for the
National Committee for Research
on the 1980 Census

RUSSELL SAGE FOUNDATION / NEW YORK

The Russell Sage Foundation

The Russell Sage Foundation, one of the oldest of America's general purpose foundations, was established in 1907 by Mrs. Margaret Olivia Sage for "the improvement of social and living conditions in the United States." The Foundation seeks to fulfill the mandate by fostering the development and dissemination of knowledge about the political, social, and economic problems of America. It conducts research in the social sciences and public policy, and publishes books and pamphlets that derive from the research.

The Board of Trustees is responsible for oversight and the general policies of the Foundation, while administrative direction of the program and staff is vested in the President, assisted by the officers and staff. The President bears final responsibility for the decision to publish a manuscript as a Russell Sage Foundation book. In reaching a judgment on the competence, accuracy, and objectivity of each study, the President is advised by the staff and selected expert readers. The conclusions and interpretations in Russell Sage Foundation publications are those of the authors and not of the Foundation, its Trustees, or its Staff. Publication by the Foundation, therefore, does not imply endorsement of the contents of the study.

Library of Congress Cataloging-in-Publication Data

White, Michael J., 1953–
    American neighborhoods and residential differentiation.

    (The Population of the United States in the 1980s)
    Bibliography: p.
    Includes index.
    1. Neighborhood—United States—Case studies.
2. Neighborhood—United States— Statistics.
3. Social structure—United States.   4. Community organization—United States.   5. United States—
Census, 20th 1980.   I. National Committee for
Research on the 1980 Census.   II. Title.
III. Title: Residential differentiation.   IV. Series.
HN59.2.W52   1987   307.3'362'0973   86–42951
ISBN 0–87154–922–0

Cover and text design: Huguette Franco

10 9 8 7 6 5 4 3 2 1

Foreword

American Neighborhoods and Residential Differentiation is one of an ambitious series of volumes aimed at converting the vast statistical yield of the 1980 census into authoritative analyses of major changes and trends in American life. This series, "The Population of the United States in the 1980s," represents an important episode in social science research and revives a long tradition of independent census analysis. First in 1930, and then again in 1950 and 1960, teams of social scientists worked with the U.S. Bureau of the Census to investigate significant social, economic, and demographic developments revealed by the decennial censuses. These census projects produced three landmark series of studies, providing a firm foundation and setting a high standard for our present undertaking.

There is, in fact, more than a theoretical continuity between those earlier census projects and the present one. Like those previous efforts, this new census project has benefited from close cooperation between the Census Bureau and a distinguished, interdisciplinary group of scholars. Like the 1950 and 1960 research projects, research on the 1980 census was initiated by the Social Science Research Council and the Russell Sage Foundation. In deciding once again to promote a coordinated program of census analysis, Russell Sage and the Council were mindful not only of the severe budgetary restrictions imposed on the Census Bureau's own publishing and dissemination activities in the 1980s, but also of the extraordinary changes that have occurred in so many dimensions of American life over the past two decades.

The studies constituting "The Population of the United States in the 1980s" were planned, commissioned, and monitored by the National Committee for Research on the 1980 Census, a special committee appointed by the Social Science Research Council and sponsored by the Council, the Russell Sage Foundation, and the Alfred P. Sloan Foundation, with the collaboration of the U.S. Bureau of the Census. This committee includes leading social scientists from a broad range of fields—demography, economics, education, geography, history, political science, sociology, and statistics. It has been the committee's task to select the main topics for research, obtain highly qualified specialists to carry out that research, and provide the structure necessary to facilitate coordination among researchers and with the Census Bureau.

The topics treated in this series span virtually all the major features of American society—ethnic groups (blacks, Hispanics, foreign-born); spatial dimensions (migration, neighborhoods, housing, regional and metropolitan growth and decline); and status groups (income levels, families and households, women). Authors were encouraged to draw not only on the 1980 census but also on previous censuses and on subsequent national data. Each individual research project was assigned a special advisory panel made up of one committee member, one member nominated by the Census Bureau, one nominated by the National Science Foundation, and one or two other experts. These advisory panels were responsible for project liaison and review and for recommendations to the National Committee regarding the readiness of each manuscript for publication. With the final approval of the chairman of the National Committee, each report was released to the Russell Sage Foundation for publication and distribution.

The debts of gratitude incurred by a project of such scope and organizational complexity are necessarily large and numerous. The committee must thank, first, its sponsors—the Social Science Research Council, the Russell Sage Foundation, and the Alfred P. Sloan Foundation. The long-range vision and day-to-day persistence of these organizations and individuals sustained this research program over many years. The active and willing cooperation of the Bureau of the Census was clearly invaluable at all stages of this project, and the extra commitment of time and effort made by Bureau economist James R. Wetzel must be singled out for special recognition. A special tribute is also due to David L. Sills of the Social Science Research Council, staff member of the committee, whose organizational, administrative, and diplomatic skills kept this complicated project running smoothly.

The committee also wishes to thank those organizations that contributed additional funding to the 1980 census report—the Ford Foundation and its deputy vice president, Louis Winnick, the National Science Foundation, the National Institute on Aging, and the National Institute of Child Health and Human Development. Their support of the research program in general and of several particular studies is gratefully acknowledged.

The ultimate goal of the National Committee and its sponsors has been to produce a definitive, accurate, and comprehensive picture of the

U.S. population in the 1980s, a picture that would be primarily descriptive but also enriched by a historical perspective and a sense of the challenges for the future inherent in the trends of today. We hope our readers will agree that the present volume takes a significant step toward achieving that goal.

CHARLES F. WESTOFF

Chairman and Executive Director
National Committee for Research
on the 1980 Census

For my Parents

Acknowledgments

What can the 1980 census tell us about neighborhoods and patterns of residential differentiation? This book tries to provide an answer. The evolution of the settlement system is like a film with intricate cinematography. While some of the U.S. statistical system follows portions of the action continuously, the census freezes the action every decade and makes it visible at high resolution. It is only with the fine-grain snapshot of the census that we can look systematically at the nation's neighborhoods. The census snapshot gives us direct insight into the social and economic organization of the residential system.

This volume examines the neighborhoods of twenty-one metropolitan areas, chosen to be representative of the wide array of communities in which Americans live. Since we are interested in the settlement system generally, I have included some of the smallest as well as some of the largest metropolitan areas in the United States. By examining this group intensively, I hope to shed some light on the entire spectrum of settlement. To examine change in residential differentiation and the pattern of metropolitan organization, I compare the 1980 census with comparable information from past censuses, going back to 1940 in some cases.

At the outset of the census research project, authors were charged with the task of "authoritative description" about the United States. Our underlying question, "who lives where?," is premised on the notion that the pattern of residential differentiation offers a mirror to society. This book is a product of the (sometimes uneasy) compromise between the desire for representative description accessible to all and a desire to probe as deeply as possible into the structure of metropolitan residential differentiation. We very consciously examine a wide range of characteristics simultaneously, extending the focus beyond that usually encountered in studies of residential differentiation. At several points I have introduced new methods, suggesting further that we need new ways of looking at American cities and how the population becomes sorted into residential neighborhoods.

Although they are tied together by the theme of residential differentiation, the chapters of this book may be read independently. Chapter 1 discusses the definition of neighborhood and the role of neighborhood in public policy, and introduces the metropolitan areas of this study. Chapters 2 and 3 treat the issue of differentiation and provide a basic analysis of its sources and dimensions. Chapter 4 deals with segregation, a topic of long-standing concern. Chapter 5 follows with an analysis of spatial organization, a more direct treatment of "who lives where." Chapter 6 takes up change in the metropolitan system over the decades, including the evolution of individual neighborhoods. In Chapter 7 we try to pool the information of previous chapters and draw a picture of the metropolis as it looks in the late twentieth century. The concluding chapter discusses what light our results shed on some issues of public policy.

Several people and organizations were instrumental in bringing this monograph to fruition. Support for the research and the writing of the book was provided by the Russell Sage Foundation through the National Committee for Research on the 1980 Census. David L. Sills of the Social Science Research Council and Priscilla Lewis of the Russell Sage Foundation have helped and guided throughout. The Donnelley Marketing Information Company provided extracts of its small area data files and the shaded maps for use in this project. The cooperation of Gary Hill and Garry Meyer helped the research get under way. This monograph was written while I was at Princeton University, and several persons there assisted with its production. Throughout the entire term of the project, Ozer Babakol ably programmed his way through complicated data files. Melissa zur Loye and Beverly Rockhill performed a number of calculations. Andrew Foster was responsible for programming the metropolitan contours. Carol Ryner, Kathy Reynolds, Mary-Ann Prytherch, and Hieu Ly helped immeasurably in shepherding the words through various electronic media.

I would like to thank the members of the Advisory Panel for this project, John S. Adams, William Clark, Richard Forstall, and Omer Galle, for their suggestions at various points along the way. Charles Westoff, Chairman of the National Committee for Research on the 1980 Census, read the entire manuscript and provided numerous useful suggestions. Peter Mueser, Julian Wolpert, and Richard Nathan provided many comments and much encouragement.

Finally I would like to thank Jane for her patience.

MICHAEL J. WHITE
The Urban Institute

Contents

List of Tables

List of Figures

NEIGHBORHOODS
AND URBAN SOCIETY

O NE PARTICULARLY telling way in which contemporary society manifests its social structure is in the residential pattern of the settlement system. In addition to providing a window on society, the pattern of neighborhoods tells us about the form and function of the settlement system generally.[1] Where people live is also partly determined by the location of jobs and industry, by the technology of transportation and communication, and by the availability of (and selective preference for) local public services.

The concept of neighborhood is important in urban policy, social science, and everyday city living, yet the neighborhood is a difficult entity to define and to delineate. The neighborhood is at times an analytical unit and at times a rallying point for community sentiment. For us, neighborhoods are the *sites* of the sorting-out process, which is what we

---

[1]We use the terminology "settlement system" or "residential system" to describe in abstract terms the whole array of spatial locations of persons. We think of these as very general, encompassing all persons. As a practical matter we are limited to the residences within metropolitan areas, so we will speak of the metropolitan residential system as well. Almost all of our analysis pertains to differentiation within metropolitan areas, and we will describe them as metropolises, SMSAs, and cities equivalently. When we refer specifically to the core municipality, we will use the term "central city."

mean by residential differentiation.[2] Once we have an understanding of residential differentiation, or how the neighborhoods fit together, we can begin to make inferences about some of the forces driving the present settlement system and the changes that we see.

It is true that, whatever the social, geographic, and technological forces that bring neighborhoods into existence, once formed they begin to take on a character and life of their own. They develop institutions (or neighborhoods develop around institutions), local community organization, and even some internal economic structure. They may reach into the political system through grass-roots, neighborhood-based organizations, and in recent years neighborhoods themselves have become the focus of policy. A view into the sorting-out process for 1980 can give some hint as to the residential basis for local community life.

Notions of Neighborhood and Community

"Neighborhood" is a term at once common and vague. It is a physical reality, yet one laden with symbolism. The term arises time and time again in vernacular urban conversation. We speak, for example, of "living in a good neighborhood," or "the neighborhood where I grew up." Parents do not permit children to wander beyond the neighborhood, even going so far as to delineate precise boundaries. We speak also of neighborhoods in terms of their characteristics, such as a Mexican neighborhood, or singles' neighborhood, or even simply an "interesting" neighborhood. One may read a newspaper article that suggests that a place is a "city of neighborhoods." Even urban dynamics are implicitly invoked (often with a value judgment) with claims such as "the neighborhood has declined," or "the neighborhood has tipped." These notions have crept into the policy arena as well when politicians, bureaucrats, and private citizens speak of "neighborhood development," "neighborhood preservation," or "strong neighborhoods." Often the use of such terms belies an underlying controversy.

Neighborhood, and its position within the metropolis, has been the object of American urban sociology since the early part of the twentieth century. Robert E. Park emphasized the sentiments, traditions, and history that prevailed in a neighborhood's life. He argued that the neigh-

---

[2]From a time when the type of data used here was unavailable, and in a more anthropomorphic style, Adna Weber offered a description that is apt for our theme here: "The city is the spectroscope of society; it analyzes and sifts the population, separating and classifying the diverse elements." Adna Weber, *The Growth of Cities in the Nineteenth Century* (New York: Macmillan, 1899).

borhood is the smallest unit in the social and political organization of the city. Almost contradictorily, however, it exists, he states, with little or no formal organization.[3]

Roderick D. McKenzie, another early urban sociologist writing in the "ecological" tradition, linked the neighborhood more directly to the metropolis:

> The general effect of the continuous sifting and sorting of the city's population . . . is to produce a patchwork of local areas differentiated from one another by cultural, racial, or linguistic peculiarities. In common parlance such areas are usually designated as localities, districts, colonies, or neighborhoods.[4]

Although McKenzie appears to omit socioeconomic status and life cycle characteristics (save as they are embedded in cultural differences), we will include them in this study, along with other characteristics measured by the U.S. Census.

Most uses of the term neighborhood have in common the meaning of physically bounded area characterized by some degree of relative homogeneity and/or social cohesion. McKenzie offers: "The word neighborhood has two general connotations: physical proximity to a given object of attention, and intimacy of association among people living in close proximity to one another."[5] Implied is a sense of "inside" and "outside." Almost always, our notion of neighborhood carries the implication that it does not reflect the complete diversity of the city as a whole. Stated more formally, the neighborhood is not merely a random sample of the metropolitan population. From this point of (usual) agreement, disciplinary and practical applications begin to diverge. Suzanne Keller, emphasizing the sociological role of neighbor in the process, agrees that the neighborhood ("where neighbors reside") may either be clearly demarcated or only a vaguely defined part of the city.[6] In writing about neighborhood conservation, Robert K. Yin admits that "there is no standard definition of neighborhood."[7] The National Commission on Neighborhoods (NCN) points out that no level of govern-

---

[3]Robert E. Park, "The City: Suggestions for the Investigation of Human Behavior in the Urban Environment," in Robert Park and Ernest Burgess, *The City* (Chicago: University of Chicago Press, (1925) 1967), p. 7.

[4]Roderick D. McKenzie, "The Neighborhood," in R. D. McKenzie, *On Human Ecology* (Chicago: University of Chicago Press, (1921) 1968), p. 73.

[5]McKenzie, "The Neighborhood."

[6]Suzanne Keller, *The Urban Neighborhood: A Sociological Perspective* (New York: Random House, 1968), p. 12.

[7]Robert K. Yin, *Conserving America's Neighborhoods* (New York: Plenum Press, 1982), p. 121.

ment has a generally accepted definition and that there are no standard characteristics; it relies on a "sensible" one adopted by the City of Atlanta, which incorporates "distinguishing characteristics" and/or residents' common identity.[8] The commission states: "In the last analysis, each neighborhood is what the inhabitants think it is."[9] Albert Hunter tries to get out of this definitional quicksand by suggesting that, on the one hand, a neighborhood becomes operationally defined by a specific program or policy, and on the other, neighborhood definition is a problem for empirical social science inquiry.[10]

The neighborhood is to be distinguished from another of the sociologist's terms, "community." While community usually denotes common interests and values (and usually, by extension, some degree of homogeneity), it need not be physically defined. Many of the qualities of community are, however, carried over into the concept of neighborhood. Of course, "community" suffers from even more extreme problems of ambiguity, and many competing definitions exist.[11] Some communality of mores or interests is usually implied. A bond exists between the members of the neighborhood community. It may rest on mere physical proximity but usually extends to other social characteristics.[12] The use of the phrase "urban community" does come close to the idea of neighborhood; for example, Morris Janowitz argues that "the urban community . . . implies sentiments and attachments to a geographic area, no matter how transitory or complex."[13] To the extent that these characteristics become visible in census information, we can then peer into urban communities. It is here, too, that we find the discussion of "neighbor" and "neighborliness" as social roles and social norms, respectively.[14]

To the extent that neighborhoods take on a more formal existence, it is the planning profession that is charged with implementing and overseeing neighborhood-related policy. Most important, it is the

[8]National Commission on Neighborhoods, *People, Building Neighborhoods.* Final Report to the President and Congress of the United States (Washington, D.C.: Superintendent of Documents, 1979), p. 7.

[9]National Commission on Neighborhoods, *People, Building Neighborhoods,* p. 7.

[10]Albert Hunter, "The Urban Neighborhood: Its Analytical and Social Contexts," *Urban Affairs Quarterly,* 14 (March 1979):267–288.

[11]Colin Bell and Howard Newby, *Community Studies* (New York: Praeger, 1972), pp. 28–29.

[12]Keller also identifies physical and social components of neighborhoods, but finds the dimensions to be sometimes incompatible. Keller, *The Urban Neighborhood,* pp. 87–123.

[13]Morris Janowitz, *The Community Press in an Urban Setting* (Chicago: University of Chicago Press, 1967), p. vii.

[14]Keller, *The Urban Neighborhood,* and Herbert J. Gans, *The Levittowners* (New York: Pantheon Books, 1967).

planners who (often in the midst of community consultation or controversy) must draw the boundaries for service delivery or policy activity. Planners, too, help develop and maintain information on de facto (even de jure) neighborhoods. Even "neighborhood planning" has developed into a subfield of its own.[15]

Neighborhoods can be the sites of political activity and organization. While the ward or precinct can be treated as a de facto neighborhood, it does typically suffer from the constraint of equal population size and from periodic boundary realignment. Other definitions in political science ignore the fixed ward boundaries and emphasize patterns of association among residents and the possibility of political action. The neighborhood movement, whether deemed a success or failure, has been viewed as the urban grass-roots movement.[16] Conflict, latent or manifest, exists due to the competing interests between "downtown" and the "neighborhoods." Neighborhoods and neighborhood organizations have received considerable attention, for they both arise outside of the formal structure of the political system.[17] In recent years neighborhood organizations in many cities (including a few in this study) have achieved formal recognition from city hall and quasi-legal or legal status.

The economic literature on neighborhoods contributes the important concept of "neighborhood externality" and a good deal of empirical research. The phrase "neighborhood externality," or simple neighborhood effect, describes the economic reality that the behavior of an individual and a neighbor are not independent, even though the individual market actions of each may not reflect it. The degree of interdependence has a great deal to say about the character of policy activity within urban areas. Economists have attempted to develop and test models of the demand, supply, and dynamics of neighborhoods.[18]

The work of this volume on neighborhoods parallels most closely an earlier tradition of human ecology. Taking the ecological orientation

[15]For example, see the collection, Philip L. Clay and Robert M. Hollister, eds., *Neighborhood Policy and Planning* (Lexington, Mass.: Lexington Books, 1983), particularly chapters 10–13.

[16]Robert Bailey, Jr., *Radicals in Urban Politics* (Chicago: University of Chicago Press, 1974), p. 43; Milton Kotler, *Neighborhood Government* (Indianapolis: Bobbs-Merrill, 1969); David J. O'Brien, *Neighborhood Organization and Interest-Group Processes* (Princeton, N.J.: Princeton University Press, 1975); and Geno Baroni, "The Neighborhood Movement in the United States," in P. Clay and R. Hollister, *Neighborhood Policy and Planning*.

[17]Matthew Crenson, *Neighborhood Politics* (Cambridge, Mass.: Harvard University Press, 1983).

[18]See, for example, David Segal, ed., *The Economics of Neighborhood* (New York: Academic Press, 1979).

as our starting point, we argue that the neighborhood is the geographic manifestation of community in urban areas. Paralleling much ecological work that has come before, we will look at neighborhoods through their census data to get an idea of community structure. The ecological literature generally prefers the term "community" over the use of "neighborhood." Some of the traditional issues—diversity, segregation, succession—will occupy us here. Our ecological approach draws upon other social scientific notions of neighborhood and adds the more quantitative information available from census materials. Neighborhood as ecological community involves three aspects: (1) physical delimitation; (2) some degree of self-support and centrality; and (3) some degree of homogeneity. The third may derive from the other two in the general process of urban differentiation.

In subsequent chapters we will draw on the relevant theory and empirical research that predicts or describes "who lives where." This is an interdisciplinary literature, with roots in sociology, economics, and geography. Although this literature is enormous, several themes unify it. First is a concern with residential segregation and succession, the separation of social groups among the communities, and the process of change in social composition of neighborhoods. Second is a concern for the underlying dimensions of urban differentiation; that is, the part played by life cycle, socioeconomic status, and ethnic characteristics. A third concern is the explicit prediction of residential location from information about the characteristics of individuals. These writings also describe competing models of the residential structure of the metropolis, and our discussion will review them as well.

Neighborhood Size and Boundaries

Two issues regarding practical neighborhood definition have always been most vexing. They are, first, the absolute size and geographic boundary of neighborhoods and, second, the importance of neighborhood or community homogeneity.

There is very little agreement on a functionally appropriate or sociologically meaningful neighborhood size. Clarence A. Perry, an early champion of the neighborhood concept in city planning, suggested that neighborhoods should contain 6,000 residents and be identified with a local elementary school.[19] Jane Jacobs, in her well-known criticism of

---

[19]Clarence A. Perry, *The Rebuilding of Blighted Areas* (New York: Russell Sage Foundation, 1933).

city planning practice, claims that three levels of neighborhood exist: the smallest is the block, the middle is the community or district of about 100,000, and the third is the city as a whole.[20] An ecological approach might identify the service area of the lowest level of economic activity (usually a drugstore or corner grocery) as the neighborhood. Other institutions, such as the churches or local newspapers, can serve this definitional function as well.[21]

Herbert J. Gans's urban village in Boston's West End contained about 7,000 inner city residents at the time of the study, about one-third of the population present in the same area near the turn of the century.[22] Levittown, Pennsylvania, a growing, planned new suburb, subject of a subsequent study by Gans, contained about 12,000 persons and grew to 25,000.[23] Gans did not claim that these were unitary neighborhoods; indeed, the West End was inconsistently subdivided into smaller neighborhoods by the residents. Gerald D. Suttles and William Kornblum, in community studies of inner city areas of Chicago, identified both entire districts and outlined several distinct subareas within, defined by natural barriers and containing distinct population groups.[24] The long-established Chicago community areas rely on combinations of history, identity, trade, institutions, and natural features for their definitions.[25] Columbia, Maryland, a new, planned smaller city located between Baltimore and Washington, had neighborhoods defined a priori, with boundaries and names. These mesh into the overall community.

Residents themselves sometimes have difficulty describing the boundaries of their neighborhoods, and even these nominal boundaries can be inconsistent. A study of the "symbolic communities" of Chicago revealed considerable ambiguity in residents' perceptions of boundaries.[26] Other research has argued that most residents can quickly identify their neighborhood and some associated boundary.[27] Keller re-

---

[20]Interestingly, Jacobs's 100,000 cutoff is roughly equal in size to the entire metropolitan population of two of our study SMSAs, Bangor and Sheboygan. Jane Jacobs, *The Death and Life of Great American Cities* (New York: Random House, 1961), p. 117.

[21]Janowitz, *The Community Press in an Urban Setting.*

[22]Herbert J. Gans, *The Urban Villagers* (New York: Free Press, 1962), p. 8.

[23]Gans, *The Urban Villagers*, p. 22.

[24]Gerald D. Suttles, *The Social Order of the Slum* (Chicago: University of Chicago Press, 1968), and William Kornblum, *Blue Collar Community* (Chicago: University of Chicago Press, 1974).

[25]Evelyn M. Kitagawa and Karl E. Taeuber, *Local Community Fact Book* (Chicago: Chicago Community Inventory, 1963).

[26]Albert Hunter, *Symbolic Communities* (Chicago: University of Chicago Press, 1974).

[27]Roger S. Albrecht and James V. Cunningham, *A New Public Policy for Neighborhood Preservation* (New York: Praeger, 1979).

views some efforts to ascertain neighborhoods and their boundaries. The difficulty is not always one of size or scale. Frequently, major physical features such as railroad tracks, parks, landmarks, and arterial streets help.[28] Where these are absent, the neighborhood boundaries can become quite fluid. Major institutions (church parishes, elementary school districts, and the like) provide an additional source of delimitation and simultaneously competing boundaries. The old ecological notion of "natural area" draws heavily on physical characteristics as a starting point.[29]

The municipality itself or its delegate can adopt a recognized set of official or quasi-official neighborhoods, such as Chicago's 77 community areas, or Baltimore's 277 neighborhoods. Even then, these areas can be of widely varying size and disputed definition.[30]

There is equally little consensus on what role social homogeneity plays in neighborhood identification and definition. This extends to disagreement about whether social composition is inherently part of the definition or is the result of the workings of ecological differentiation, sorting people into preexisting neighborhoods. The dimensions (or characteristics) along which this homogeneity is measured are also not well established. Indeed, one runs the risk of circularity as one investigates differentiation with units of analysis defined with a particular type of differentiation in mind.

Out of practical necessity we introduce the phrase "statistical neighborhood." Unappealing or unromantic as it may be, the fact remains that if we are to perform quantitative analysis on neighborhoods, we must collect and tabulate information for discrete areas. The statistical neighborhood, then, is the small area established for the statistical tabulation scheme. The statistical neighborhoods provide our means of organizing data within cities and form the observational units of a study such as this one. The census tract, the statistical neighborhood used most extensively here, was developed in the early part of this century to respond to concerns for collecting local community statistics in a systematic way. Once the statistical geography is established, it becomes a sort of de facto social system, since all subsequent analysis

[28]Kevin Lynch, *The Image of the City* (Cambridge, Mass.: MIT Press, 1960).

[29]Robert E. Park, "The City: Suggestions for the Investigation of Human Behavior in the Urban Environment," in Robert E. Park and E. W. Burgess, eds., *The City* (Chicago: University of Chicago Press, 1968), pp. 1–46; Harvey W. Zorbaugh, *The Gold Coast and the Slum* (Chicago: University of Chicago Press, 1929); Paul Hatt, "The Concept of Natural Area," *American Sociological Review* 11 (August 1946):423–427; and Donald J. Bogue, "Ecological Community Areas," in Donald J. Bogue and Michael J. White, eds., *Essays in Human Ecology II* (Chicago: Community and Family Study Center, 1984), pp. 1–25.

[30]Chicago's 77th Community Area, for example, was separated out from another community area because of both increasing differentiation and community pressure.

proceeds from this set of boundaries. Despite all the rhetoric about proper neighborhood boundaries, it is these small-area data to which scholars, planners, and community organizers usually turn first to understand urban communities. We return to describe our "statistical neighborhoods" in more detail at the end of the chapter.

Neighborhood as the Focus of Policy

There has been substantial concern in recent years with the elements of neighborhood structure and dynamics that bear on policy. Some disillusionment with past urban policy and its perceived impact on central neighborhoods is undoubtedly responsible. Also important is a shifting consideration of the strategies for urban revival. The United States does not have an explicit neighborhood policy, nor does it possess a comprehensive urban policy per se. Nevertheless, a great number of policies affect neighborhoods.[31] Any activity aimed at changing the population distribution or composition within the settlement system, even if unwittingly, will have its effect on neighborhoods. We mention here a few of the most important.[32]

From the 1950s through the 1970s, several programs had a very dramatic impact on the face of cities and certainly on many individual neighborhoods. The urban renewal program allowed for wholesale clearance and reconstruction, and public policy could radically alter neighborhoods.[33] Urban renewal sought to revitalize cities, mostly by

[31]U.S. Department of Housing and Urban Development, *The President's National Urban Policy Report* (Washington, D.C.: Superintendent of Documents, 1983).

[32]A more comprehensive review of United States urban policy in the 1970s is contained in Committee on National Urban Policy, *The Evolution of National Urban Policy 1970–1980* (Washington, D.C.: National Academy of Sciences, 1982).

[33]The Housing Act of 1937 allowed for slum clearance and redevelopment. The 1949 Housing Act formally inaugurated the urban renewal program as it was known in the 1960s. Several modifications took place in the 1950s and 1960s. More extensive reviews of the program and attendant criticism are contained in James Q. Wilson, ed., *Urban Renewal: The Record and the Controversy* (Cambridge, Mass.: MIT Press, 1966); Ashley A. Foard and Hilbert Fefferman, "Federal Urban Renewal Legislation," in James Q. Wilson, ed., *Urban Renewal*; and Michael J. White, *Urban Renewal and the Changing Residential Structure of the City* (Chicago: Community and Family Study Center, 1981). The planning involved in these programs was not without criticism. Jacobs's work, mentioned earlier (*The Death and Life of Great American Cities*, 1961), was one of the first to attack contemporary planning practice of the post–World War II period and discusses neighborhood social patterns at length. For Jacobs the key to healthy urban neighborhoods (and hence cities) lay in diversity of activity. Mixture of uses and time scheduling differed from contemporary planning practice, which advocated the separation of uses. It certainly differed as well from the developing reality of suburban communities of predominantly residential character.

transforming the social composition of project neighborhoods.[34] The Model Cities program also operated in the 1960s, generally offering financial aid (through service delivery) to targeted low-income areas in major cities. Shifts in urban policy in the 1970s saw the arrival of Community Development Block Grants. These monies, made available mostly through revenue sharing funds, were much less restricted in application than the programs of the 1960s. Many municipalities did use these funds for neighborhood-related activity.[35] Urban Development Action Grants followed soon after and were intended to spur economic revival in targeted municipalities by using federal funds to leverage local investment. The effects of Model Cities on neighborhoods and internal urban structure are difficult to discern.

Several pieces of legislation and administrative policy have made available funds for rehabilitation and preservation in urban areas. Parts of the urban renewal program had such options.[36] In 1979, through the Neighborhood Reinvestment Corporation Act and the Neighborhood Self Help Development Act, grants became available specifically for neighborhood preservation. These entailed application by the neighborhood organization and provided some modest funds, often in concert with housing rehabilitation.[37]

Finally, certain programs are linked indirectly to the fate of cities and their neighborhoods. It has been argued in particular that federal tax deductions for interest, local property tax payments, and federally subsidized highway construction in metropolitan areas have given further impetus to suburbanization and helped to empty central cities of their middle classes. How much of the process can be attributed to the federal government is unknown, but the reality of decentralization is certainly known, and the changing internal population and socioeconomic balance between central city and suburb in many metropolitan areas is well established.

As of 1980 only limited aspects of these federal urban programs

---

[34]Between 1949 and 1975 about 2,000 urban renewal projects were undertaken in the United States, at a total cost of $10 billion [U.S. Department of Housing and Urban Development, *HUD Statistical Yearbook* (Washington, D.C.: U.S. Government Printing Office, 1976), Table 18]. The affected residential population is difficult to count, although we do know that as of 1971 the program had demolished over one-half million dwellings and replaced them with about 200,000 new units, with another 325,000 planned [John C. Weicher, "The Effect of Urban Renewal on Municipal Service Expenditures," *Journal of Political Economy* 80 (Jan./Feb. 1972):86–101].

[35]Paul R. Dommel et al., *Targeting Community Development* (Washington, D.C.: U.S. Department of Housing and Urban Development, 1980), p. 123.

[36]These appeared with the 1954 Housing Act.

[37]Rachel G. Blatt, "People and Their Neighborhoods: Attitudes and Policy Implications," in Phillip L. Clay and Robert M. Hollister, eds., *Neighborhood Policy and Planning* (Lexington, Mass.: Lexington Books, 1983), pp. 133–150.

were active in major metropolitan areas. Their physical legacy remains. Models of urban structure and assumptions about dynamics implicit in these policies also persist. Analyses of the residential pattern of 1980 can help inform public policy for the 1980s and beyond.

In recent years there have been several calls for a fundamental rethinking of American urban policy. But these calls have a variety of tones. They range from advocacy of the free market and population mobility as a means for revitalizing cities and the national economy[38] to a cry for further public sector intervention to redress perceived inequities (or bias in public policy itself) with respect to central city versus suburb or Sunbelt versus Frostbelt. The 1982 biennial report of the Department of Housing and Urban Development sounded a note far different from the 1980 report, emphasizing national economic recovery as the key to any improvement in the problems of cities, and more reliance on private sector activity within cities.[39]

During this period of rethinking, some argued for more focus on the neighborhood by policymakers. The National Neighborhood Policy Act of April 1977 established the National Commission on Neighborhoods. Its charge was to "investigate the causes of neighborhood decline, and to recommend changes in public policy so that the federal government becomes more supportive of neighborhood stability."[40] In March 1979, after fifteen months of research and field hearings in cities around the country, the commission delivered its report to President Carter.

Recognizing the dissatisfaction with previous federal urban programs and the recent tightening of the federal budget belt, the commission wrote that it did not want to throw more federal dollars at problems, and that it acknowledged the indispensable role of private enterprise in neighborhood problems and solutions. The commission organized itself into five task forces to investigate key issues related to its charge: economic development, reinvestment, human services, fiscal and legal obstacles to neighborhood revitalization, and neighborhood governance.

The commission described how the neighborhoods on which it focused had been the victims of public and private disinvestment, and how the poor and minorities bore a disproportionate burden of discrimination within their neighborhoods. The report described the present alienation of neighborhoods from big government and the growth of the neighborhood movement. Not surprisingly, the commission advocated a

[38]U.S. President's Commission, *Urban America in the Eighties* (Washington, D.C.: U.S. Government Printing Office, 1981).

[39]U.S. Department of Housing and Urban Development, *National Urban Policy Report* (Washington, D.C.: U.S. Government Printing Office, 1982).

[40]National Commission on Neighborhoods, *People, Building Neighborhoods*, p. vii.

11

position that the preferable, and less costly, policy option is to increase the livability of existing neighborhoods through local investment strategies and by improving the delivery of services.

Among its recommendations the commission argued for the cessation of financial discrimination against neighborhoods, and the introduction of funds and legislation to aid neighborhood rehabilitation. Subsequent recommendations stress notions of full community employment, property and income tax reforms that would favor residents of urban neighborhoods, restoring the neighborhood focus on human service delivery, and increased citizen participation in federal and local programs. The final report of the commission contains thirty-eight pages of specific recommendations for policymakers.

Equally interesting are some of the report's apparent assumptions about neighborhoods. The first is that neighborhoods are a big city phenomenon. Neighborhoods the commission describes tend to be located in the larger and older central cities, many of the same places that appear on a list of distressed cities. Even the sites of the commission's field hearings are revealing: Baltimore, Cleveland, St. Louis, Chicago, Los Angeles, Seattle. Neighborhoods are further identified with the residences of the poor, the elderly, and minorities. Although the commission makes note of the diversity of neighborhood types and composition, there is little mention of the middle class or well-to-do neighborhoods. To be sure, in its notion of neighborhoods, the commission has identified those places that possess some of the most severe social problems, and which have borne the brunt of inequities deriving from public and private urban policies. The commission also argues implicitly that the quality of life of the nation's urban populace is best improved through policies directed at small local areas, the neighborhoods themselves. This point of view stands in stark contrast to the view of several contemporaneous policy documents, which advocate a shift away from an "aid to places" policy.

A recent and growing literature on neighborhood revitalization and viability has many close parallels with the ecological conceptions of local community. This literature emphasizes the identification of boundaries, the existence of information flows, and the sharing of values and common interests. It differs in its advocacy of a particular set of policy prescriptions.

Roger S. Albrecht and James V. Cunningham argue for research and policy to build stronger neighborhoods through the maintenance and encouragement of "social fabric."[41] Social fabric provides the cohesion

---

[41]Roger S. Albrecht and James V. Cunningham, *A New Public Policy for Neighborhood Preservation*, (New York: Praeger, 1979) p. 199.

in a community and involves the networks of personal and informal group relationships within the neighborhood. James H. Johnson argues that an improved theoretical base for understanding neighborhood revitalization is needed.[42] Sandra Schoenberg and Patricia L. Rosenbaum speak to policy issues in their analysis of neighborhood success.[43] Their definition of the existence of a neighborhood emphasizes identifiable boundaries, the presence of a major name, of institutions and social ties, among the residents. They go on to develop propositions about the viability of neighborhoods, based on the presence of these traits.

Neighborhood change, neighborhood reinvestment, and neighborhood dynamics have all become part of the vocabulary of national urban policy. In 1979 the *Journal of the American Planning Association* devoted an issue to a symposium on neighborhood revitalization, with articles covering such topics as city–neighborhood relationships, the neighborhood movement, and gentrification and displacement.[44] More recently in the same journal, Rolf Goetz and Kent W. Colton have tried to link demographic changes in the housing market to changes within neighborhoods.[45]

Anthony Downs has provided an extensive analysis of "those aspects of policies that should be influenced by the links between individual neighborhoods and the urban development process."[46] He provides a detailed typology of neighborhood change along a reversible continuum. Downs's own policy recommendations are quite different from those above. He recommends a series of treatments, matched to the stage and direction of the neighborhood status, ranging from normal upkeep of stable and viable neighborhoods to emptying out and redeveloping nonviable neighborhoods. His approach stands in contrast to some earlier work by urban economists, which marked neighborhood evolution within a typology of increased density followed by emptying out and redevelopment.[47]

A more controversial set of options revolves around the notion of triage for city neighborhoods, borrowing a term from military medicine.

[42]James H. Johnson, "The Role of Community Action in Neighborhood Revitalization," *Urban Geography* 4 (1983).

[43]Sandra Schoenberg and Patricia L. Rosenbaum, *Neighborhoods That Work* (New Brunswick, N.J.: Rutgers University Press, 1981).

[44]*Journal of the American Planning Association* 45 (October 1979).

[45]Rolf Goetz and Kent W. Colton, "Dynamics of Neighborhoods: A Fresh Approach to Understanding Housing and Neighborhood Change," *Journal of the American Planning Association* 46 (1980):184–194.

[46]Anthony Downs, *Neighborhoods and Urban Development* (Washington, D.C.: Brookings Institution, 1981).

[47]Edgar M. Hoover and Raymond E. Vernon, *Anatomy of a Metropolis* (New York: Doubleday-Anchor, 1962).

It offers the prospect of choice among neighborhoods in a time of shrinking overall resources; some are designated for rescue while others are abandoned. The notion of triage has received a great deal of sharp criticism.[48]

Many of these policy arguments about neighborhoods extend to issues beyond the scope of this book. We can demonstrate here, however, the status of the metropolitan residential system as of 1980, shedding some light on the validity of claims about the status quo made by the writers. We can also provide some help with data and methods. Many policy arguments are notably bereft of information about individual neighborhoods and about the ecological character of the city generally, and lack methods for evaluating whether a claim or premise is true.

The Metropolitan Context

Neighborhoods are embedded in the web of the social and economic activities that constitute a metropolitan community. The fate of neighborhoods is bound up with the demographic and economic and social transformations of their surrounding metropolitan area. To some degree the future of any particular place within a city is determined by its ecological position, and its destiny sealed by the manner in which time wears at the outer shell of its metropolis. Indeed, one can view a great deal of the policy debate as disagreement about the degree of determinacy for individual communities within the metropolitan context. We sketch now some of the major forces that swept metropolitan America in the 1970s. This is merely an overview; another volume in the census series takes up this subject directly.[49]

We identify three general population trends in metropolitan processes that bear on neighborhoods: (1) diffusion; (2) regional redistribution; and (3) immigration.

Under the heading of diffusion we place a series of related trends involving population and employment distribution. Included here are the nonmetropolitan turnaround, decentralization, and gentrification. It is commonly known now that American metropolitan areas continued to

---

[48]Peter Marcuse, Peter Medoff, and Andrea Pereira, "Triage as Urban Policy," *Social Policy* (Winter 1982):33–37; and Julian Wolpert and John Seely, "Why Urban Triage Will Not Work," paper presented to the Association of Collegiate Schools on Planning, Atlanta, October 1985.

[49]William Frey and Alden Speare, Jr., *Regional and Metropolitan Growth and Decline in the United States,* The Population of the United States in the 1980s: A Census Monograph Series (New York: Russell Sage Foundation, 1988).

suburbanize or decentralize throughout the 1970s. In most major metropolitan areas, suburbs gained over central cities. In the 1950 census, suburbs contained 41 percent of the metropolitan area population. In 1970 the suburban share had grown to over half, and by the 1980 census it had climbed to 60 percent, continuing a well-established trend in American urbanization.[50] What is new, however, is the revival of growth in nonmetropolitan areas, outside the officially designated Standard Metropolitan Statistical Areas. Careful work by Calvin L. Beale,[51] Larry Long and Diana DeAre,[52] and others has documented that this is neither a statistical fluke nor a mere spilling over of metropolitan population into still more exurban locales. In the 1970s the nonmetropolitan growth rate exceeded that of metropolitan growth, reversing longstanding trends in American population distribution patterns.[53] Generally, the larger and more urbanized a place, the more slowly it grew (or even declined), a phenomenon apparent in virtually all regions.[54] Metropolitan neighborhoods, especially neighborhoods in larger cities, were at the other end of the population distribution spectrum. They withstood a great depopulation. It remains for us to document the net effect of this redistribution on urban diversity, segregation, and the relative position of neighborhoods within the sociospatial fabric.

Private market rehabilitation and resettlement of the old urban cores, dubbed gentrification, has acquired a great deal of notoriety. The phenomenon was certainly present in the 1970s, but it was far outweighed by the dominant movement of middle class families outward. The so-called "back to the city" movement involved renters or homeowners moving within city boundaries to improve their level of housing and neighborhood amenities.[55]

Collectively we call these intraregional trends "diffusion." We introduce the term to emphasize that the traditional outline of the urban economic and ecological structure is much less applicable in 1980 than it was in 1970, 1950, or 1920. The picture of a densely built-up core, the

[50]U.S. Bureau of the Census, *1980 Census of Population and Housing* (PC80-S1-5, 1981), p. 1.

[51]Calvin L. Beale, "The Population Turnaround in Rural Small-Town America," in William P. Browne and Don F. Hadwinger, eds., *Rural Policy Problems: Changing Dimensions* (Lexington, Mass.: Lexington Books, 1982), chapter 4.

[52]Larry Long and Diana DeAre, "Repopulating the Countryside: A 1980 Census Trend," *Science* 217 (September 1982):1111–1116.

[53]About one-third of the nonmetropolitan growth was "spillover," and there has been a post-1980 resumption in the larger metropolitan growth rate.

[54]Long and DeAre, "Repopulating the Countryside."

[55]Franklin D. James, "The Revitalization of Older Urban Housing and Neighborhoods," in Arthur P. Solomon, ed., *The Prospective City* (Cambridge, Mass.: MIT Press, 1980).

center of which contains institutions of commerce and industry, surrounded by residential areas, is breaking up. Industry, offices, and apartment dwellings are scattered through suburban areas and now even some rural areas. The pull of downtown has been diminished, and the rent and population gradients are much flatter now than they were a generation ago.

As diffusion within regions proceeded during the 1970s, so did the interregional movement to the South and West. Parts of this trend were evident in the 1960s and even in the 1950s, but the redistribution gained popular attention in the recent decade, partly because it was coupled with the continued stagnation of the large urban agglomerations of the Northeast.

In 1950 the Northeast and North Central Census Regions together held 55 percent of the U.S. population. This has decreased steadily, so that by 1980 their share had slipped to under half.[56] During the 1975–1980 period, there was a net loss of over 3 million people through migration from the North to the South and West.[57]

Almost 4.5 million legal immigrants entered the United States during the 1970s, the largest number since the first two decades of this century.[58] In comparison with past immigrant streams, the 1970s saw a heavier representation of persons from Asia and Central and South America, but large numbers continued to arrive from Europe. The shift in origin has produced a shift in entrepôt cities. Southern and western cities have become increasingly important as sites of first residence.[59] Of course, the decade also witnessed a great deal of undocumented migration into the country. Although the dense immigrant neighborhoods of the turn of the century period are not as prominent now, most of these newcomers to the United States have settled in metropolitan America.

The trends of diffusion, regional redistribution, and immigration together suggest several things worth looking for among American neighborhoods in the 1980s. First, we can look for diffusion processes. Contrary to the assumptions of many, we may well find that no more homogeneity exists within suburban communities than in central city communities. We expect to find areas of rental housing, low density, and social class groupings scattered throughout the metropolitan area.

[56]U.S. Bureau of the Census, *State and Metropolitan Area Data Book* (Washington, D.C.: U.S. Government Printing Office, 1982).

[57]U.S. Bureau of the Census, *Statistical Abstract* (Washington, D.C.: U.S. Government Printing Office, 1984), p. 15.

[58]Data are for the period 1971–1980, U.S. Bureau of the Census, *Statistical Abstract*, p. 88.

[59]Symbolically perhaps, Miami was the city with the highest fraction of foreign-born residents in 1980 (*New York Times*, March 1, 1983, p. A21).

The redistribution of population among regions of the United States and to places lower on the size-of-place ladder means that we will find great variation in growth rates in our sample between, for instance, a large northeastern and a small southwestern city. With growth we can see either new forms of variability, diversity, and segregation, or a reconsolidation along traditional lines. It will be of great interest here to determine whether the patterns of variability and differentiation in older cities are repeated in the growth areas. We can question whether the same patterns of differentiation will obtain throughout the United States. The decade of immigration just passed presents once again the promise and challenge of assimilation into the society. We can examine the patterns of diversity and segregation in cities in an effort to discern whether cities still continue to perform the role of melting pot that they were once accorded. The 1980 census also permits us to compare a great range of groups along this dimension.

The Study Design

The analysis of this book will itself be statistical insofar as we examine many neighborhood areas, simultaneously sorting through their characteristics and looking for patterns. Often we will be interested in how neighborhood structure (ecological differentiation) changes across the cities in our sample. We provide no case study of a neighborhood, nor do we undertake a historical review of developments of individual cities and their subareas. This choice may disappoint some readers, for it unquestionably sacrifices a look at some of the rich texture of urban social life. On the other hand, we hope that the drier statistical analyses presented here will help form a needed companion to these life histories of the cities, lending a greater understanding of how the pieces of the urban puzzle fit together.

Our approach and premises can be summarized as follows.

1. We link the study of neighborhoods to the study of urban differentiation generally. Rather than analyze individual neighborhoods, we look for urban patterns that exist through the window provided by information about neighborhoods in the census.

2. The process of ecological differentiation within the metropolis results in the development of smaller ecological communities; the geographical boundaries of these communities are the neighborhoods. This results in a degree of relative social homogeneity within the neighborhoods. Much of our effort will be directed toward measuring the degree of sorting and how geographically systematic that sorting is. Many pol-

icy concerns bear on the issue of neighborhood diversity and evolution of urban differentiation over time.

3. A consistent statistical system for the analysis is needed. We elect census tracts because they are comprehensive, contiguous, and try to be uniform. They are mutually exclusive and exhaustive units. The tract becomes our statistical neighborhood. This makes clear another premise. We believe that neighborhoods exist throughout the metropolitan area. Often the term is reserved for inner city areas and, even among those, places with a great deal of street life or community activity. Even though one may plausibly disagree about the accuracy of boundaries, we accept that neighborhoods are completely comprehensive with respect to metropolitan areas. It is important to point out that we work with the metropolis and its constituent neighborhoods as the analytical units. We do not discuss in detail central city versus suburb, but do look at "inner" versus "outer" residential districts.

4. We provide some analysis over time through comparative cross-section and limited longitudinal analysis, so as better to fix our 1980 portrait and help to show the way toward answers for theoretical and practical policy questions.

Neighborhood Statistics and Statistical Neighborhoods

Much description of neighborhoods and their social life is less concerned with the exact demarcation of neighborhood boundaries than with the quality of social life and communal attachment within. Formerly, even less attention was paid to the delimitation of a set of mutually exclusive and exhaustive boundaries, but in a statistical approach such a system takes priority at the start. In this section we explain the types of data and methods used in this book and introduce the twenty-one metropolitan areas to be analyzed.

We make use of census tract data most extensively. According to the Census Bureau's own description, tracts are:

> small, relatively permanent areas into which metropolitan and certain other areas are divided for the purpose of providing statistics for small areas. When census tracts are established, they are designed to be homogeneous with respect to population characteristics, economic status, and living conditions. Tracts generally have between 2,500 and 8,000 residents.[60]

[60]U.S. Bureau of the Census, *1980 Census of Population and Housing* (Washington, D.C.: Government Printing Office, 1982).

This is, of course, the ideal. Census tracts should have a modal population of 4,000 persons, a figure designed to be small enough to be homogeneous yet still large enough to avoid problems of suppression (see below). City block data provide a finer grain; however, they are too numerous, too often subject to suppression to preserve the confidentiality of individual responses. Average population size within the block can be extremely inconsistent as one travels within and between cities, for instance, from the Gold Coast of Chicago to the far suburbs, or from the city of Chicago to the city of San Antonio.[61]

Our group of twenty-one metropolitan areas contains nearly 6,000 census tracts altogether, with an average size of 4,200 persons. While there is a good deal of variability, the approximate norm of 4,000 holds. About 60 percent of the tracts fall between the sizes 2,400 and 6,400. Appendix B describes in greater detail statistical characteristics of the sample of tracts and the development and criteria of the tract system.

As defined for the 1980 census, census tracts completely comprise the metropolitan area. Standard Metropolitan Statistical Areas (SMSAs) are constructed from contiguous counties that are economically and socially integrated with a core usually containing a city of at least 50,000.[62] SMSAs, then, contain all of the aggregated county population. The outskirts of metropolitan areas (and thus individual tracts) may in fact be somewhat rural in character. This phenomenon occurs most often where counties themselves are very large, such as in the West. Tracts are established with the idea of being consistent over time. This differentiates them from other small-area data, and we make use of this feature in Chapter 6.

For our purposes, census tracts become the statistical neighborhoods. Thus, we have 5,995 neighborhoods in our twenty-one cities, containing a total of over 27 million people. Tracts offer the best compromise with respect to size, homogeneity, data availability, and comparability. Indeed, the definition of tract stands not too far apart from the notion of neighborhood (excepting values and attitudes) one finds in much of the literature. Since the tract is our desired unit of analysis, nagging controversy over the ecological fallacy is less relevant.

---

[61]Block group data and officially tabulated neighborhood statistics are other possibilities, but they have problems akin to blocks. Block statistics have been used quite successfully in other studies and are the only source of detailed socioeconomic and housing data for the very small areas so necessary in planning. For the 1980 census a Neighborhood Statistics Program was established. In essence, the program provided special tabulation of census statistics for established neighborhoods within municipalities and metropolitan areas, but for reasons explained in Appendix B we have chosen not to use the NSP data.

[62]SMSAs in New England are based on towns rather than counties. Some definitions changed after the 1980 census. Appendix A and a number of Census Bureau publications provide more detail regarding definitions.

We do *not* aim to make inferences from the census data about individual people (indeed, the Public Use Microdata Samples now facilitate that directly), but rather we strive to learn about the characteristics of communities themselves.

Virtually all of the tabulations available for states and the nation are made for census tracts. We have information about age, race, sex, marital status, education, ancestry, occupation, income, housing type, and housing quality for every one of our statistical neighborhoods. In principle, the richness of analysis permitted at the national level is available for neighborhoods. In practice, however, we are usually more interested in the spatial variation of basic characteristics than in the complete detail. In addition, suppression of data to preserve confidentiality eliminates many of the most detailed tabulations from consideration.[63]

Previous research that has employed census small-area data has varied greatly in geographic and subject matter extent. On the one hand, some studies, most notably of segregation, subject nearly every block and tract within SMSAs and major cities to analysis of one or a few characteristics. On the other hand, some researchers focus on one or a modest number of cities, subjecting a wide array of census subject characteristics to statistical treatment. This book takes a middle position. Since we want to generalize about differentiation in the national settlement pattern, we subject a fairly large number of characteristics to analysis for a modest number of metropolitan areas.

The Metropolitan Areas

Our group sample of twenty-one metropolitan areas was chosen to reflect a variety of regions, size groups, and growth rates, for which historical data were available with reasonably consistent tract boundaries, and to correspond to a sample of cities used in previous ecological research.[64] It is not, then, a random but rather, we hope, a widely

[63]Our work makes use of Summary Tape File 1 (STF1) and Summary Tape File 3 (STF3). These still possess extensive information. STF1 contains 321 cells of complete count (short form) tabulation for each tract; STF3 contains 1,123 cells of sample (long form) information. For the 6,000 tracts this makes 8.5 million pieces of information altogether. (We do not employ STF2 or STF4, which contain the respective detailed cross-tabulations.)

[64]The metropolitan ecology project of the Community and Family Study Center, University of Chicago, assembled census tract data for many metropolitan areas, extending back to 1940. We have used some of those data here. For a description of these data, see Donald J. Bogue, "Ecological Community Areas," in Donald J. Bogue and Michael J. White, eds., *Essays in Human Ecology II* (Chicago: Community and Family Study Center, 1984), pp. 1–25.

representative sample of cities, so that our findings will transfer to metropolitan America generally. For the 1980 census, the number of SMSAs grew to 318 with about 40,000 tracts altogether containing three-quarters of the American population, too large to work with alone.[65]

It may be useful to think of this book as a study of nearly 6,000 neighborhoods, which happened to be clumped into twenty-one metropolitan areas. The neighborhoods form the tiles of a variegated mosaic, a mosaic we call the American settlement system. We look carefully within the twenty-one metropolitan clusters to search for a pattern in the tiles. To the extent that we find the pattern repeated in a large number of our metropolitan areas, we have evidence that it is truly national.

In recent years the requirements for qualification as an SMSA have been relaxed, and several fairly small areas have been added, even areas that can only questionably possess metropolitan or big city status. We have elected not to impose our own definition based on a larger threshold size; therefore, we include representatives from the entire range of places with SMSA designation, in keeping with official recognition, and allowing a wider range of comparison. Moreover, we are interested in the settlement system generally, not just the largest localities in that system. Our smallest SMSAs, Bangor and Sheboygan, first qualified as SMSAs for the 1980 census and contain under 50,000 persons in the central city. When we do comparisons over time, we have elected to use SMSA boundaries as they existed at the time of each census. As a result, our over-time research is not based on exactly comparable geographic units from census to census but, rather, includes all metropolitan territory as defined from decade to decade.

Table 1.1 contains some basic information about our twenty-one SMSAs. The population distribution trends discussed earlier are visible here. Metropolitan growth rates in the 1970s were generally lower than in the 1960s, down from 17 to 10 percent nationally. Growth in northern and eastern SMSAs slowed especially, and Boston, Newark, and St. Louis SMSAs registered absolute declines in population. Growth of the so-called Sunbelt is evident in the upswing in growth of SMSAs such as Amarillo, Atlanta,[66] Salt Lake City, San Diego, and Stockton. The fraction of metropolitan population held by central cities declined, with

[65]There were another five SMSAs defined for Puerto Rico for the 1980 census. These tracted areas, plus many non-SMSA counties that elected to participate in the census tract program, account for the additional 2,000 tracts (Table 1.1).

[66]In some instances, SMSAs grow by the addition of new counties as well. The Atlanta SMSA, an extreme case, added ten new counties between 1970 and 1980. Lexington added five, and Salt Lake City SMSA added two. Allentown, Newark, St. Louis, and San Antonio added one.

TABLE 1.1

Basic Characteristics of Sample Metropolitan Areas

Metropolitan Area*	Region	SMSA Population 1980	Central City Population 1980†	SMSA Population Change 1970–1980	SMSA Population Change 1960–1970
Allentown, PA	NE	635,481	200,204	6.9	9.0
Amarillo, TX	S	173,699	149,230	20.3	−3.4
Atlanta, GA	S	2,029,710	425,022	27.2	36.5
Bangor, ME	NE	83,919	31,643	5.0	−2.3
Birmingham, AL	S	847,487	284,413	10.5	2.8
Boston, MA	NE	2,763,357	562,994	−4.7	7.9
Chicago, IL	NC	7,103,624	3,005,072	1.8	12.1
Flint, MI	NC	521,589	159,611	2.5	18.9
Indianapolis, IN	NC	1,166,575	700,807	5.0	17.7
Lexington, KY	S	317,629	204,165	19.1	25.8
New Bedford, MA	NE	169,425	98,478	5.0	7.9
New Haven, CT	NE	417,592	179,293	1.5	14.4
New Orleans, LA	S	1,187,073	557,515	13.4	15.4
Newark, NJ	NE	1,965,969	329,248	−4.4	12.2
St. Louis, MO	NC	2,356,460	453,085	−2.3	12.4
Salt Lake City, UT	W	936,255	227,440	32.7	22.4
San Antonio, TX	S	1,071,954	785,880	20.7	20.7
San Diego, CA	W	1,861,846	875,538	37.1	31.4
Seattle, WA	W	1,607,469	548,259	12.8	28.7
Sheboygan, WI	NC	100,935	48,085	4.4	11.8
Stockton, CA	W	347,342	149,779	19.3	16.4
21 SMSAs		27,665,390	9,975,761	NA	NA
All SMSAs		169,430,623	67,949,383	10.2	17.0
U.S. Total		226,545,805	67,035,302	11.4	13.4

*These are the names by which we will abide throughout the text. A few SMSAs have additional central cities, consolidated counties, or cross into other states. Their full names are: Allentown-Bethlehem–Easton, PA-NJ; Lexington–Fayette, KY; New Haven–West Haven, CT; St. Louis, MO-IL; and Salt Lake City–Ogden, UT.

†May include more than one central city if designated; see footnote above.

older central cities in the Northeast registering substandard absolute declines in population. Disparities in income level are evident between SMSAs as well as within. Median SMSA income ranges from a low of $14,042 in Bangor to $20,810 in Flint. Overall, our twenty-one metropolitan areas contain about one-sixth of the U.S. metropolitan population, and their aggregate growth rate for the 1970s was 7.2 percent, compared to the U.S. metropolitan average of 10 percent.

TABLE 1.1 *(continued)*

Central City Population Change 1970–1980	Central City Percent of SMSA Population 1980	Median Household Income 1980	SMSA Percent Black 1980	SMSA Percent Spanish Origin 1980	Number of Census Tracts	Mean Tract Population
−5.6	32	$18,333	1.4	2.4	155	4,100
17.5	86	16,979	4.9	8.6	63	2,757
−14.1	21	18,355	24.6	1.2	352	5,766
−4.6	38	14,042	.3	.3	27	3,108
−5.5	34	15,586	28.3	.7	204	4,154
−12.2	20	18,694	5.8	2.4	584	4,732
−10.8	42	20,726	20.1	8.2	1516	4,686
−17.4	31	20,810	15.1	1.6	125	4,173
−4.9	60	18,674	13.5	.8	269	4,337
88.8	64	15,688	10.0	.7	80	3,970
−3.2	58	13,965	1.8	3.1	46	3,683
−5.9	43	18,164	12.0	3.2	94	4,442
−6.1	47	15,883	32.6	4.1	327	3,630
−13.8	17	20,759	21.3	6.7	466	4,219
−27.2	19	18,510	17.3	.9	438	5,380
−7.3	24	18,641	.9	5.0	189	4,954
20.1	73	15,156	6.8	44.9	198	5,414
25.5	47	17,106	5.6	14.8	384	4,849
−6.2	34	20,726	3.6	2.0	367	4,380
−.8	48	18,719	.3	1.0	24	4,206
36.2	43	16,071	5.5	19.2	86	4,039
NA	36	NA	15.0	6.7	5,995	4,615
.1	40	17,880	12.7	7.6	40,319	4,202
3.0	30	16,841	11.7	6.4	43,222	5,241

2

A LOOK AT NEIGHBORHOODS IN 1980

OUR PRINCIPAL objective in this chapter is factual description of where metropolitan areas and their neighborhoods stand as of 1980. This chapter concentrates on examining the neighborhood statistics directly. It should help the reader get an overall sense of the kind of information the U.S. census provides for small areas and of the range of characteristics that exists for neighborhoods.

We will proceed by first comparing the distribution of characteristics across neighborhoods to that for the population for the nation as a whole. This will provide a sense of the way in which the nation's persons and families aggregate themselves into neighborhoods. A second component of our analysis will involve looking at the distribution of some of these characteristics within each of the metropolitan areas. This allows us to view the general sorting out process we spoke of in Chapter 1 on two levels: first, from nation to metropolis, and then from metropolis to neighborhood.

The work of this chapter helps set the stage for the subsequent analyses. Most of our later work uses the neighborhoods themselves as the units of analysis in statistical studies. This chapter will show what is in fact implied by such an approach.

Urban sociology and ecology suggest things to look for. The distribution of characteristics within the city (SMSA) is of first concern. What is the average of concentration of this attribute within the city, and what is its range or spread? How do these statistics compare to the nation across cities? Such questions begin to bear on several aspects of policy and information needed for decision making. Several examples may help.

The new waves of immigration to the United States might be expected to reveal themselves in the urban pattern, and we can ask: What is the average concentration of a particular racial or ancestry group in the city's neighborhoods? Alternatively, concern may be raised over the geographic incidence of poverty and the fraction of city neighborhoods that fall above or below some threshold, and how these figures compare with other cities.

One line of ecological reasoning holds that as city (SMSA) size increases, the degree of social differentiation should also increase. Neighborhoods in larger SMSAs should then be more specialized. Stated another way, in smaller cities we may expect each census tract to approximate the city distribution, while in large cities we expect more homogeneity within neighborhoods, at least with respect to fixed-size parcels, such as tracts of 4,000 persons. We can look for this in the descriptive statistics. If such a process takes place, we would expect the dispersion in the distribution of tract values to increase with city size.[1]

Another line of reasoning suggests quite the opposite—that we should expect neighborhoods in large cities to be quite diverse in their social and physical composition.[2]

---

[1]The statistical argument is a bit more complex. Given two cities with equal individual level distributions of persons with respect to a characteristic, let city A be much larger than city B, but census tracts are of the same size in each. Let each city also have complete differentiation among census tracts (e.g., each census tract contains only one segment of the total distribution and overlaps with no other—a circumstance of complete segregation.

Then in both cities we have internal homogeneity. Using the basic decomposition of analysis of variance, we can write:

$$SS_T = \sum_i \sum_i (x_{ij} - \bar{x})^2$$
$$= \sum_i \sum_j (x_{ij} - \bar{x}_i)^2 + J \sum_i (\bar{x}_i - \bar{x})^2$$
$$= SS_{WI} \qquad + \qquad SS_{BT}$$

(within-tract sum of squares)   (between-tract sum of squares)

where i indexes tracts, and j, persons within tracts up to J persons in each. Since we have chosen boundaries such that SS_{WI} is minimized, and since more within-tract homogeneity is possible in the big city, then its SS_{BT} will be the greater. There are, of course, other possibilities, which would lead to different results. There may be no or relatively little differentiation into tracts in either city, or they may have quite different initial distributions.

[2]Jane Jacobs, *The Death and Life of Great American Cities* (New York: Random House, 1961), pp. 143–238.

Our method is very simple. We examine *univariate* distributions for selected variables. The tracts themselves are the units of observation. (For example, we examine the distribution of neighborhood education, where for each neighborhood the value is the average educational attainment of the adult population.) For some characteristics we draw a histogram of the distribution of *all* the census tracts in the twenty-one SMSAs; where possible we superimpose a histogram of the U.S. population. For distributions within metropolitan areas, tables present the 25th, 50th, and 75th percentiles as well as mean and standard deviation. The median marks the point at which half the city's census tracts lie above and half below; it is an alternative to the mean as measure of central tendency. The interquartile range (IQR, the difference between the 75th and 25th percentiles) is a measure of spread or dispersion; by definition half the tracts in the city fall within that range, while under a normal curve two-thirds of the observations fall within one standard deviation of the mean. Using all of these statistics together, we can get a check on the shape of the distribution. There is a tricky aspect to working with these statistics: the tract values represent averages of averages.

Univariate Results:
Typical and Not-So-Typical Neighborhoods

As we travel through a metropolitan area and view its neighborhoods, we might be inclined to describe one or another neighborhood as typical or atypical. A typical neighborhood should be somewhere near the statistical average for the metropolitan area or the nation, while an atypical neighborhood should be more likely at an extreme. The statistics we present in this chapter give a numerical view of the notion of typical and atypical neighborhoods. Social science analysis has shown that socioeconomic status, life cycle stage, and ethnicity do much to explain the social differentiation process in major metropolitan areas.[3] The discussion below concentrates on variables taken to represent those three dimensions of urban social organization. We also include certain housing, density, and residential mobility characteristics linked to residential differentiation. Our choice of the specific variables was guided by our replication of these ecological analyses.

---

[3]We will use the convention of treating race, Spanish origin, and ancestry information in the census as indicators of a general characteristic, ethnicity.

26

Socioeconomic Status

Time and again it has been argued that socioeconomic status is the principal differentiator in the metropolis. Poor neighborhoods with residents who work in lower status occupations and have lower levels of education are found to be separated from the high status neighborhoods in the urban mosaic. Educational attainment and occupation are good overall indicators of a neighborhood's status. The level of income, correlated with these two characteristics, is the most direct indicator of a household's ability to purchase goods and services. In that it is correlated with education and occupation, it also provides some indication of ability to "purchase" status, or at least purchase a residence in what is regarded as a high status neighborhood. So then, what are typical levels of income in the neighborhoods of metropolitan areas, and what is the range?

Figure 2.1 presents a histogram for the distribution of income in the neighborhoods of this study and for households of the United States as a whole. The graph shows that about 13 percent of U.S. households had incomes below $5,000 in 1979 (reported for the 1980 census). Another 5 percent were at the upper end of the income distribution, having made over $50,000. Nearly half of households fell in the $10,000–$25,000 range.

That is the picture for households themselves; the picture for neighborhoods is a bit different, since we measure "neighborhood income" by an average measure of the incomes of the households within it. For the neighborhood average we use the median household income; half the neighborhood's households made less than this amount, half made more.[4] Not surprisingly, then, the histogram for the distribution of neighborhood has more observations (tracts) falling toward the middle of the U.S. distribution. This is the "average of averages" effect we mentioned above.

A "typical" neighborhood in one of the twenty-one metropolitan areas under study here would have an average household income in the range of $15,000 to $20,000. Many households within that neighborhood would still have incomes above and below that value. Few neighborhoods have average values as extreme as the national distribution of households. For a neighborhood to be in the $50,000+ category, over half of its households would have to make at least $50,000. In fact, only a negligible fraction of neighborhoods are this uniformly well-to-do.

---

[4]This median is the measure of central tendency (an average) for the distribution of income *within* the neighborhood.

FIGURE 2.1
Household Income: 1980

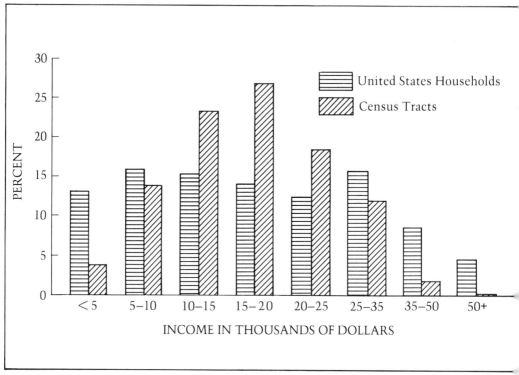

Similarly, at the low end of the spectrum, while 13 percent of U.S. households fall below the $5,000 mark, only about 4 percent of neighborhoods do.

In most of the work that follows we will be dealing with neighborhood averages of one sort or another for the social characteristics. It is worth remembering that these are averages of a distribution of values within the neighborhood. It is the neighborhood values, of course, that are of primary interest to us, since we are focusing on them as the sites for differentiation in the settlement system and communities in their own right.

Table 2.1 presents the distribution of neighborhood *median household income* from the neighborhoods within each metropolitan area of the study. This table allows us to compare the income level in the aver-

TABLE 2.1
Median Household Income: 1979

Metropolitan Area	Minimum	Lower Quartile	Median	Upper Quartile	Maximum	Interquartile Range	Mean	S.D.	Number of Cases
Allentown	3,815	14,337	17,422	20,157	31,898	5,820	17,192	5,063	155
Amarillo	5,773	10,421	15,918	18,795	31,948	8,374	15,884	6,048	63
Atlanta	2,453	10,732	15,599	20,685	42,170	9,954	16,071	7,515	352
Bangor	3,407	9,062	13,202	14,494	17,527	5,432	12,241	3,765	28
Birmingham	3,289	9,918	13,044	17,868	42,761	7,951	14,061	6,632	202
Boston	2,500	11,958	16,835	21,903	47,950	9,944	17,551	7,475	580
Chicago	2,168	12,406	17,559	22,875	56,721	10,469	17,949	8,199	1,485
Flint	5,119	14,531	18,946	23,118	33,575	8,588	18,618	5,713	124
Indianapolis	3,602	13,133	17,518	21,173	42,887	8,041	17,508	6,438	269
Lexington	2,500	11,463	14,586	17,548	33,569	6,086	14,708	5,240	79
New Bedford	4,371	9,333	11,759	15,732	19,772	6,399	12,279	4,095	44
New Haven	5,098	12,478	17,133	21,618	36,038	9,140	17,495	6,740	93
New Orleans	2,399	8,907	13,936	18,984	38,772	10,078	14,465	6,951	319
Newark	2,500	12,631	18,734	26,025	53,309	13,394	19,726	9,179	462
St. Louis	1,250	11,224	16,469	20,356	51,542	9,132	16,515	7,158	435
Salt Lake City	3,566	13,156	17,722	20,443	41,711	7,287	17,427	6,419	189
San Antonio	3,135	9,347	12,528	16,985	33,059	7,638	13,678	6,045	197
San Diego	2,500	11,567	15,889	20,621	46,330	9,055	16,890	7,183	379
Seattle	2,500	15,523	19,517	23,401	41,410	7,878	19,435	6,427	353
Sheboygan	8,578	15,398	18,510	19,273	22,971	3,875	17,701	3,657	24
Stockton	3,253	10,369	14,653	18,403	26,182	8,034	14,877	5,319	85

NOTES:

"Minimum" indicates the lowest census tract value in the metropolitan area.

"Lower quartile" indicates the value for which 25 percent of census tracts are lower and 75 percent of census tracts are higher.

"Median" indicates the value for which 50 percent of census tracts are lower and 50 percent higher; the text refers to this value as the typical neighborhood.

"Upper quartile" indicates the value for which 75 percent of census tracts are lower and 25 percent of census tracts are higher.

"Maximum" indicates the highest census tract value in the metropolitan area.

"Interquartile range" is the difference between the upper quartile and the lower quartile. It is a measure of spread or dispersion in the distribution.

"Number of cases" is the number of census tracts in the SMSA on which this tabulation is based.

Tabulations are not weighted for census tract size, and occasional apparent anomalies may result.

age neighborhood across metropolises as well as the distribution within the SMSA itself. There is great variation across SMSAs in this average, reflecting wages, cost of living, and even differential household composition. The values range from about $13,000 for Birmingham to over $19,000 per year in Seattle. In general, it can be seen that the larger northern metropolitan areas have higher levels of household income, although observers are quick to point out that cost of living is also much higher, perhaps offsetting much of the apparent advantage. The interquartile range provides some hint of the extremes of well-being that exist within a metropolitan area. The widest range of neighborhood income levels is found in Newark, about $13,000. What is particularly striking about Newark is that the value of the upper quartile is $26,000; that is, one-fourth of all neighborhoods in the Newark SMSA have levels of income above this. This is the highest value of any SMSA. Taken together, there is strong indication of extremes of wealth and poverty among the neighborhoods of the Newark region. Undoubtedly some of this is due to the linkage of the Newark SMSA to the New York–Northern New Jersey economic region. Contrast this with the picture of the distribution for Sheboygan, where less than $4,000 separates the top fourth of neighborhoods (tracts) from the bottom fourth.

What are the extremes in neighborhood income? In this table we also present the minimum and maximum values of household income (neighborhood averages) as reported by the residents of the census tracts for the SMSAs. In most metropolitan areas the poorest tract falls under $5,000, with some well below that. In almost every city the top neighborhood has a median household income of over $50,000, meaning that in this tract half the households made more than $50,000 in 1979. Chicago leads the list with one neighborhood at $56,000. Large metropolitan areas should be expected to have more extreme values because they have more census tracts and because of the process of differentiation we discussed above.

The interquartile range describes how much distance (in terms of dollars of average income) separates the top 25 percent of neighborhoods from the poorest 25 percent of neighborhoods in each metropolitan area. The largest SMSAs—Chicago, Newark, New Orleans, Boston, and Atlanta—show the greatest disparity in neighborhood incomes due to greater overall differentiation.

While income indicates the purchasing power that a household or individual has, occupation may provide a more generally recognized indicator of a person's status in society. Residential mobility helps maintain the mosaic as households search for a neighborhood of the appropriate status composition. Decennial census tabulations make available broad occupational classifications that we can use to infer the socioeconomic status of neighborhoods. The larger the fraction of workers employed in higher status occupations, the higher the neighborhood's status is suggested to be.[5]

Table 2.2 presents the distribution for all workers (of both sexes) classified by the census in professional and managerial occupations. Many of these are upper white collar workers, the top of the status hierarchy among the broad occupational categories of the census classification available for tracts. Again, substantial differences between cities as well as within are evident. What is perhaps most striking about the numbers in this table is how they point to changes in the economy over the past few decades. Services have grown at the expense of manufacturing, employing about 29 percent and 22 percent of U.S. workers nationally, respectively. This industrial shift has been accompanied by an occupational shift, away from blue collar toward white collar, to the point where these white collar workers now make up about 20 percent of the typical neighborhood's labor force in our study.

The metropolitan economic base is reflected in the occupational composition of its neighborhoods. In Birmingham and Flint, two cities with concentrations of traditional heavy industry, the typical neighborhood (column 3) has only about 15 percent of its workers in the white collar category, and in one-quarter of all neighborhoods (column 2) fewer than one worker in nine holds a white collar job. At the other extreme, concentrations of urban (and suburban) professionals, so often the focus of attention in recent years, can be detected as well. In Boston, for instance, they are particularly in evidence; the typical neighborhood contains over 25 percent of the work force (residing within the neighborhood) in the professional-managerial grouping (column 3); some 144 of the metropolitan area's 578 neighborhoods have over one-third in the category (column 4). In several metropolitan areas there are neighborhoods where the large majority of workers are in the professional-managerial classification (column 5).

Occupational status, like income, exhibits a large degree of sorting out in the SMSAs (column 6). Since job status so readily and often translates into income, these results parallel the case of income. The range is again greatest in Newark. Chicago, despite its prominent skyline and being home to many national financial institutions, is middle-range on this variable; testimony to the breadth of its metropolitan economic base; in fact, one-fourth of its neighborhoods have fewer than 11 percent managerial and professional workers, one of the smallest percentages. In Indianapolis the spread of about 15 percentage points

[5]In our own multivariate analysis of differentiation, reported in Chapter 3, we found that occupational status was the most consistent indicator of socioeconomic status differentiation in the SMSAs of our study.

TABLE 2.2

Percent of Workers in Professional and Managerial Occupations

Metropolitan Area	Minimum	Lower Quartile	Median	Upper Quartile	Maximum	Interquartile Range	Mean	S.D.	Number of Cases
Allentown	0.7	12.1	16.3	22.7	47.9	10.6	18.5	8.8	155
Amarillo	3.8	8.8	14.7	26.0	44.6	17.1	17.9	10.6	63
Atlanta	0.0	12.6	19.0	29.3	56.7	16.7	22.1	12.4	352
Bangor	11.9	19.0	23.4	26.8	42.9	7.9	23.9	6.5	28
Birmingham	0.0	10.7	15.4	22.1	59.5	11.5	18.9	11.9	202
Boston	0.0	17.7	25.6	36.7	100.0	19.0	28.2	13.9	578
Chicago	0.0	11.0	17.6	28.3	76.7	17.3	21.0	13.3	1,483
Flint	3.9	10.5	14.5	21.4	42.7	10.9	16.3	8.0	124
Indianapolis	2.3	11.7	18.3	26.4	60.1	14.6	20.7	11.9	269
Lexington	7.1	15.4	22.2	30.8	51.9	15.4	23.6	11.0	78
New Bedford	4.1	7.9	15.1	19.9	42.6	12.0	16.1	8.7	44
New Haven	6.9	15.8	24.3	33.7	53.1	17.9	26.4	12.2	93
New Orleans	0.0	12.9	21.2	30.5	58.7	17.5	22.6	12.0	319
Newark	1.7	13.6	23.2	35.8	62.3	22.2	25.1	13.8	462
St. Louis	0.0	13.2	18.0	26.9	58.1	13.7	21.3	11.5	434
Salt Lake City	0.0	16.6	21.2	31.5	52.5	15.0	23.9	10.6	189
San Antonio	0.0	9.6	15.9	28.0	54.6	18.4	19.6	12.6	197
San Diego	2.9	16.9	23.7	31.2	100.0	14.3	25.4	11.8	376
Seattle	0.0	19.1	24.3	31.8	58.1	12.7	25.8	9.8	352
Sheboygan	7.4	12.0	16.1	19.5	34.3	7.5	16.6	6.3	24
Stockton	0.0	9.5	15.6	20.2	100.0	10.6	17.0	12.6	85

NOTE: See Table 2.1, NOTES.

32

between the two quartiles is more like the other SMSAs. The smaller metropolises tend to have a more limited range, but the spread is also small for Birmingham, St. Louis, and Seattle, suggesting that the industrial concentration of these areas is more narrow as well. In the first two metropolitan areas the limited range is due to the relative absence of upper white collar workers, while for Seattle it is due to their relative abundance.

The income distribution tells only part of the story of relative economic position. For this reason, the poverty line criterion also takes into account the number of mouths to be fed and the cost of living. During the tabulation of the 1980 census, a statistical assessment was made whether each family (and hence all of its members) fell below the poverty line. Not only the extent of poverty but also its concentration has attracted attention. Policy analysts are concerned about the effects of growing up in neighborhoods where most of one's peers are severely disadvantaged.

Tables 2.3 and 2.4 shed some direct light on how extensive and how concentrated poverty is. In the typical neighborhood (Table 2.3, column 3) about one family in twelve lives below the poverty line, but this figure varies greatly both within and between metropolitan areas. As one would expect, there are many neighborhoods in which the fraction of families in poverty is at or near zero, but there are numerous instances where the incidence is much greater. In New Orleans and San Antonio the upper quartile figure indicates that in the poorest 25 percent of neighborhoods poverty hits one out of every four families. And in several of the largest metropolitan areas there is at least one neighborhood in which the vast majority (even 100 percent) of families lives in poverty. In the Newark SMSA, of the approximately 212,000 persons classified as poor, over 43,000 live in the poorest twenty-eight neighborhoods, out of a total of 463.

The picture is even more striking when we shift focus to the circumstance of children living in female-headed households at the time of the census. Table 2.4 counts the fraction of all children residing in female-headed households who fall under the poverty line. Between one-quarter and one-half of all children in such living arrangements live at a level below the established poverty threshold in a typical neighborhood. In almost every city there is at least one neighborhood in which all of the children in female-headed households are poor. While this statistic does not tell us how many of the tract's population are poor in such cases, it is clear that there are pockets of poverty in almost every American metropolis, and that women with children and no spouse are likely to reside within them.

TABLE 2.3
Percent of Families in Poverty

Metropolitan Area	Minimum	Lower Quartile	Median	Upper Quartile	Maximum	Interquartile Range	Mean	S.D.	Number of Cases
Allentown	0.0	2.7	4.1	6.6	32.9	3.9	5.9	5.8	155
Amarillo	0.0	2.8	5.7	11.2	33.8	8.4	8.2	7.6	63
Atlanta	0.0	4.1	8.4	15.9	79.1	11.9	13.6	15.3	352
Bangor	0.0	4.1	7.3	11.6	22.0	7.5	8.0	5.6	28
Birmingham	0.5	5.4	10.7	18.1	65.4	12.7	14.5	13.1	202
Boston	0.0	3.0	5.4	11.9	57.0	8.9	9.2	9.7	576
Chicago	0.0	2.4	5.8	18.1	100.0	15.6	12.6	14.9	1,478
Flint	0.0	4.5	6.9	14.6	42.6	10.2	11.1	9.8	124
Indianapolis	0.0	2.5	5.4	10.6	43.9	8.1	8.4	8.8	269
Lexington	0.8	4.4	10.2	14.7	57.2	10.3	11.5	9.4	78
New Bedford	1.8	5.8	9.7	15.2	30.1	9.4	12.1	7.7	44
New Haven	0.0	2.5	4.6	9.2	100.0	6.7	9.6	14.0	93
New Orleans	0.0	5.1	10.5	24.3	81.5	19.1	16.2	15.3	319
Newark	0.0	1.9	4.4	14.4	67.8	12.6	11.0	13.8	461
St. Louis	0.0	2.6	5.3	12.2	100.0	9.7	10.2	12.6	434
Salt Lake City	0.0	3.6	5.8	9.6	100.0	5.9	8.6	10.7	189
San Antonio	0.0	5.7	12.6	24.8	69.6	19.1	16.1	12.6	197
San Diego	0.0	3.9	6.6	11.7	39.3	7.8	8.8	6.9	374
Seattle	0.0	2.7	4.2	7.0	35.2	4.3	5.9	5.6	351
Sheboygan	0.8	3.0	3.8	4.8	10.3	1.8	4.0	1.9	24
Stockton	0.0	5.8	8.6	15.8	46.5	10.0	12.3	9.5	85

NOTE: See Table 2.1, NOTES.

TABLE 2.4
Percent of Children in Female-Headed Households in Poverty

Metropolitan Area	Minimum	Lower Quartile	Median	Upper Quartile	Maximum	Interquartile Range	Mean	S.D.	Number of Cases
Allentown	0.0	15.4	29.1	44.4	100.0	29.0	31.3	21.5	153
Amarillo	0.0	6.0	25.0	40.3	100.0	34.3	29.1	27.0	61
Atlanta	0.0	14.6	27.6	46.9	100.0	32.3	32.6	22.8	348
Bangor	0.0	28.8	34.8	44.8	62.4	16.0	36.1	15.3	25
Birmingham	0.0	21.5	39.8	55.2	100.0	33.7	38.9	21.6	199
Boston	0.0	18.1	31.3	49.1	100.0	31.0	33.7	21.4	567
Chicago	0.0	14.6	28.7	51.9	100.0	37.2	33.6	24.6	1,454
Flint	0.0	21.8	33.1	51.6	87.5	29.9	36.5	19.0	123
Indianapolis	0.0	11.8	27.0	40.6	100.0	28.8	28.5	20.6	268
Lexington	0.0	20.4	36.6	51.8	100.0	31.4	37.6	23.5	76
New Bedford	10.4	35.5	50.8	61.0	80.7	25.5	49.4	17.6	44
New Haven	0.0	13.3	28.5	47.9	100.0	34.6	31.7	22.6	93
New Orleans	0.0	20.0	40.4	57.6	100.0	37.6	39.9	24.4	316
Newark	0.0	13.4	29.4	48.3	100.0	34.9	32.1	23.9	457
St. Louis	0.0	14.7	29.9	46.5	100.0	31.8	31.4	20.4	431
Salt Lake City	0.0	22.0	30.9	43.7	100.0	21.7	33.4	20.8	184
San Antonio	0.0	24.1	44.8	62.3	100.0	38.2	43.2	23.3	190
San Diego	0.0	18.2	30.5	44.5	100.0	26.3	32.4	19.9	369
Seattle	0.0	12.4	22.8	33.8	100.0	21.4	24.7	17.1	346
Sheboygan	0.0	9.3	22.9	31.1	42.9	21.8	21.2	14.4	22
Stockton	0.0	25.2	38.8	53.7	100.0	28.5	41.8	21.7	83

NOTE: See Table 2.1, NOTES.

Family Status

Life cycle or family status characteristics form the second cluster of variables linked to social differentiation in urban areas. Changes in the age composition and household composition of the American population have received a great deal of recent attention. Between 1970 and 1980 the median age of the population increased by two years, as the birthrate remained low and the baby boom cohorts aged. Moreover, the size of the elderly population has been of some concern. In 1980, 11 percent of the U.S. population (2.5 million people) were over 65 years of age. At the same time, a variety of factors has pushed down the average size of a household in the United States to a point where it was 2.75 in 1980, down from 3.17 in 1970 and 3.67 in 1940. One hears concerns raised about the concentration of single-parent and nonstandard family types in certain areas of cities. To the extent that these family structures are perceived as social problems and are self-perpetuating, concern extends into areas of policy. A related issue is the concentration of such populations within particular neighborhoods. A few census characteristics can give us some measure of the spatial distribution of the life cycle and family type.

In Figure 2.2 we have graphed the actual household size distribution for the United States in 1980 and the distribution of the neighborhood averages. Since actual household sizes in the population can take on only discrete values (1, 2, 3, 4, 5, 6 +), we have grouped the neighborhood averages around these points. For the nation as a whole, over one out of every five households was occupied by a person living alone in 1980. About another third of households were occupied by two persons, most often a married couple. Households of three and four persons account for about another third of all. There is a noticeable drop in the number of households of over four persons. For census tracts, there is a very concentrated distribution around the national norm of two persons. (As with income, the census tract distribution is more peaked than the national distribution.) The number of neighborhoods with concentrations of large households (over four persons) is negligible.

The twenty-one metropolitan areas show very little apparent difference in average household size (Table 2.5). Variation in neighborhood household size may arise in a variety of ways, but usually the most influential factor is the fertility rate (or proportion of children) in the neighborhood. To the extent that there is significant clustering of both the higher fertility population and those living alone, the distribution of average household size will reflect it. For almost all SMSAs the median or typical neighborhood has just under three persons per household. In the Salt Lake City SMSA, where fertility is high, 25 percent of neighbor-

FIGURE 2.2
Persons in Household: 1980

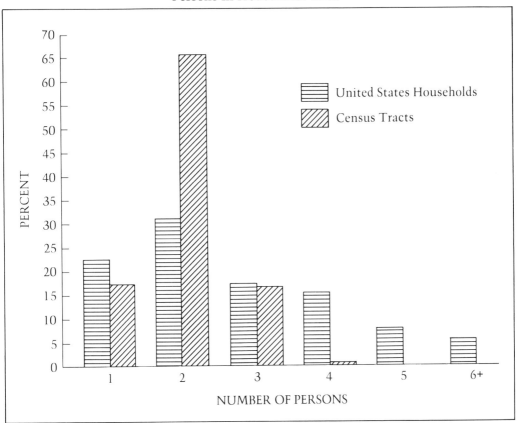

hoods have values over 3.7. The range of internal urban differentiation in most metropolitan areas is also modest, about one-half person between the 75th and 25th percentiles. The widest range of variation appears in Salt Lake City, but in Chicago, San Antonio, and San Diego the variation (here better indicated by the standard deviation than the IQR) is also substantial. In SMSAs at the other end of the spectrum, local homogeneity with respect to household aggregation and fertility is observed, such as in New Bedford.

Table 2.6 describes the distribution of the elderly population. It shows a modest amount of internal urban variation and also some substantial regional intermetropolitan variation, not always in the direction one might expect at first. The difference between the upper quartile of neighborhoods (most elderly) and the lowest quartile (fewest

TABLE 2.5
Mean Household Size

Metropolitan Area	Minimum	Lower Quartile	Median	Upper Quartile	Maximum	Interquartile Range	Mean	S.D.	Number of Cases
Allentown	1.6	2.5	2.8	2.9	3.3	0.4	2.7	0.3	155
Amarillo	1.6	2.3	2.7	3.0	3.7	0.7	2.7	0.5	63
Atlanta	1.3	2.4	2.9	3.1	4.1	0.7	2.8	0.5	352
Bangor	1.4	2.4	2.7	3.0	3.2	0.6	2.6	0.5	28
Birmingham	1.5	2.6	2.8	3.0	3.5	0.5	2.8	0.4	202
Boston	1.4	2.4	2.7	3.0	4.1*	0.6	2.7	0.5	579
Chicago	1.0	2.5	2.8	3.2	5.0	0.7	2.9	0.6	1,482
Flint	1.3	2.6	2.9	3.2	3.6	0.6	2.9	0.4	124
Indianapolis	1.3	2.5	2.8	3.0	3.9	0.6	2.8	0.4	269
Lexington	1.8	2.5	2.8	3.0	3.3	0.5	2.7	0.4	78
New Bedford	1.4	2.5	2.6	2.8	3.2	0.3	2.7	0.3	44
New Haven	1.6	2.5	2.7	3.0	3.4	0.5	2.7	0.4	93
New Orleans	1.1	2.4	2.8	3.1	4.8	0.7	2.7	0.5	318
Newark	1.4	2.6	2.9	3.1	3.9	0.5	2.9	0.4	462
St. Louis	1.2	2.5	2.8	3.0	4.1	0.6	2.8	0.4	434
Salt Lake City	1.1	2.6	3.1	3.7	4.7	1.1	3.1	0.7	189
San Antonio	1.4	2.7	3.0	3.4	4.6	0.7	3.0	0.6	197
San Diego	1.0	2.2	2.7	3.1	4.6	0.8	2.7	0.6	379
Seattle	1.1	2.3	2.6	2.9	3.9	0.7	2.6	0.5	353
Sheboygan	1.7	2.6	2.9	3.1	3.4	0.6	2.8	0.4	24
Stockton	1.6	2.4	2.8	3.0	4.0	0.6	2.7	0.4	85

NOTE: See Table 2.1, NOTES.
*There is one census tract in Boston in which the only occupied housing unit has seven persons. The remainder of the population is not in households.

TABLE 2.6
Percent Elderly (65 and older)

Metropolitan Area	Minimum	Lower Quartile	Median	Upper Quartile	Maximum	Interquartile Range	Mean	S.D.	Number of Cases
Allentown	1.2	9.3	11.8	15.9	44.1	6.7	13.1	5.9	155
Amarillo	1.0	5.7	10.2	13.8	24.7	8.0	10.5	6.0	63
Atlanta	0.8	4.8	7.8	11.6	34.4	6.8	9.1	5.7	352
Bangor	2.1	7.7	10.2	13.3	29.7	5.6	10.9	5.0	28
Birmingham	1.6	9.2	11.6	15.8	26.9	6.6	12.6	5.1	202
Boston	0.1	9.0	12.5	15.6	66.7	6.6	12.7	5.9	580
Chicago	0.0	6.0	9.8	14.3	58.4	8.3	10.8	6.1	1,486
Flint	2.9	5.4	7.5	11.4	24.5	6.0	8.8	4.3	124
Indianapolis	0.0	6.4	9.4	13.5	35.1	7.1	10.4	5.7	269
Lexington	0.6	6.5	9.4	12.2	24.5	5.6	9.5	4.7	79
New Bedford	6.2	12.5	15.3	17.7	49.5	5.2	15.7	6.4	44
New Haven	1.8	8.3	12.8	16.2	25.9	8.0	12.8	5.1	93
New Orleans	1.0	6.2	10.6	14.4	43.3	8.2	10.9	6.3	318
Newark	2.5	7.1	10.5	13.9	39.5	6.7	11.2	5.3	462
St. Louis	0.2	8.0	11.7	15.9	49.7	7.9	12.8	6.7	435
Salt Lake City	0.2	3.7	6.6	14.0	26.7	10.3	8.9	6.4	189
San Antonio	0.0	5.6	9.3	14.0	55.8	8.4	10.3	6.8	197
San Diego	0.0	5.4	9.8	15.5	79.7	10.0	11.5	8.8	379
Seattle	0.0	5.5	9.3	14.4	47.1	8.9	10.8	7.1	353
Sheboygan	7.4	9.6	11.8	15.2	30.9	5.6	13.2	5.4	24
Stockton	2.2	7.8	10.7	14.5	27.7	6.7	11.8	5.5	85

NOTE: See Table 2.1, NOTES.

elderly) hovers between 6 and 8 percent in most areas, a modest level of differentiation. If we look at the median census tract, about 10 percent of the population is over 65 years of age, a figure comparable to that for the nation, but when we examine the distribution a little more closely, some interesting features emerge. The metropolitan areas whose typical neighborhoods have the highest concentration of elderly (column 3) are not the metropolitan areas of the so-called Sunbelt but rather older industrial cities, many of which are located in the North (New Bedford, Allentown, and Boston are examples). The median census tracts in the faster-growing southern and western SMSAs (for example, San Diego, Atlanta) have smaller concentrations of elderly.

To be sure, the twenty-one metropolitan areas do not include the best known retirement cities, but a closer look at San Diego may provide some insight into how age groups are distributed within such areas. Overall, 10.3 percent of the San Diego metropolitan population is 65+ years of age. Although San Diego attracts retirees, this contrasts with some cities such as Miami (15.7 percent) and Tampa–St. Petersburg (21.4 percent). While a large fraction of census tracts have very few elderly residents—indeed, one-fourth have fewer than 5.4 percent—a small minority of census tracts is very heavily concentrated in older persons. In tabulations not shown, we found that in about 38 out of San Diego's 379 census tracts at least one out of every five residents was over 65. This is a higher concentration than in any of the other twenty SMSAs. There is even one census tract with nearly 80 percent of its residents over 65 years of age, according to the 1980 census. It is likely that such concentration exists in the retirement-oriented SMSAs; however, the elderly will be more pervasive throughout the metropolitan neighborhoods.

The final household type, which we examine in Table 2.7, is the percent of households we classified as nontraditional family households. A household that contains members who are related by family ties but is not headed by a married couple is included in this category. (Households can be divided into family and nonfamily; this latter category includes persons living alone as well as groups of unrelated individuals.) Most of the households counted in this category are single-parent families with young children present. The overwhelming majority in this group is headed by a female, so that while this classification is not congruent with female-headed families, it would show about the same distribution. The remainder tends to be extended kin households, including both multiple generations and across the same generation.

The concentration of nontraditional families is again most apparent in the larger metropolitan areas, with Chicago and New Orleans leading the list. In those two SMSAs, about one-seventh of households in the

TABLE 2.7
TABLE 2.7
Percent "Nontraditional Households"

Metropolitan Area	Minimum	Lower Quartile	Median	Upper Quartile	Maximum	Interquartile Range	Mean	S.D.	Number of Cases
Allentown	4.4	8.1	10.1	13.2	30.8	5.1	11.2	4.5	155
Amarillo	3.5	7.8	9.8	13.2	29.6	5.4	10.9	4.7	63
Atlanta	0.0	9.0	12.5	22.8	66.1	13.8	17.3	12.0	352
Bangor	0.0	9.8	11.0	13.2	27.9	3.4	11.7	5.4	28
Birmingham	5.4	9.3	12.3	21.4	44.8	12.0	15.9	9.1	202
Boston	0.0	10.7	13.4	17.7	64.2	6.9	15.7	8.7	579
Chicago	0.0	9.8	14.4	24.2	82.0	14.3	18.7	12.7	1,482
Flint	3.8	10.0	13.0	19.6	43.2	9.6	17.0	9.9	124
Indianapolis	1.8	7.8	11.5	18.1	44.2	10.3	13.9	8.2	269
Lexington	5.8	7.9	10.9	14.1	51.3	6.2	12.4	6.7	78
New Bedford	5.9	10.9	13.7	19.3	29.3	8.4	15.3	5.7	44
New Haven	5.0	9.6	11.7	15.6	62.5	6.0	15.1	10.0	93
New Orleans	2.2	11.0	14.5	25.0	76.6	14.1	18.6	11.6	318
Newark	0.0	9.7	13.5	23.3	61.0	13.7	18.1	11.8	462
St. Louis	4.1	8.9	11.5	17.6	53.2	8.6	15.6	10.4	434
Salt Lake City	2.6	7.8	10.0	12.1	36.8	4.4	10.3	3.9	189
San Antonio	0.8	9.6	14.0	18.2	44.2	8.6	14.7	7.3	197
San Diego	0.0	9.4	12.2	15.2	36.2	5.8	12.8	5.3	379
Seattle	0.0	8.7	10.5	12.5	42.9	3.8	11.1	4.5	353
Sheboygan	4.2	6.2	7.5	8.6	13.4	2.4	7.7	2.4	24
Stockton	0.0	9.3	12.4	16.4	41.7	7.1	13.9	6.5	85

NOTE: See Table 2.1, NOTES.

typical neighborhood are in this family type. In these large metropolitan areas we can see a handful of census tracts with very high concentrations of single-parent and extended-kin households. In Newark, 10 percent, or about forty-five of the neighborhoods, have at least 38 percent in nontraditional family households (not shown), with the maximum equal to 61 percent. Using some general rules of thumb for size, these forty-five neighborhoods contain on the order of 100,000 households, about 40,000 of which are in this other-family classification. By any criterion, this represents a substantial concentration of nonnuclear families within a small part of the metropolitan area. Taking the twenty-one metropolitan areas together, we find that 10 percent of all neighborhoods have concentrations of this configuration that approach one-third of all households in the tract. The larger SMSAs usually have the most extreme maximum values, with more than a majority of households in this type.

The dispersion of the neighborhood concentration of nontraditional families (indicated by both the interquartile range and the standard deviation) is especially noteworthy. In some cities, including Amarillo, Boston, Salt Lake City, and Seattle, there is relatively little difference in the concentration of such families from neighborhood to neighborhood, but in several metropolises the range is particularly broad. Atlanta, Chicago, New Orleans, and Newark are in this group. These metropolitan areas have substantial black populations, in which single parenthood has a higher incidence compared to the white population. Undoubtedly, racial residential segregation contributes to this dispersion in these metropolitan areas, but in any case some portions of their territory contain neighborhoods where nontraditional families are uncommon and other portions where they are fairly frequent.

Extrapolating a bit from our results, we find that in the average American neighborhood about one-fifth of all households consist of persons living alone, and an additional one-tenth are family households without a married couple. Despite the fact that the degree of congregation on the average is modest, we have ample evidence that there are, in almost every SMSA, selected neighborhoods that are highly specialized, in the sense that they contain an atypical concentration of one household type within them. Some neighborhoods feature nuclear families and child-rearing, while other sections have many, even predominantly, single parents, and still others have very many persons who live alone. Over the past several years nuclear families (couple with own children) have shrunk as a fraction of all households. At the same time, there has been a very large growth in the fraction of the population that lives alone, particularly in the young adult and the elderly ages. Analyses of trends in household structure and formation have pointed to rising incomes, decreased rates of fertility, marital instability, and perhaps preferences for living alone as contributing to the shifting household composition in the country. We see these national fractions represented in the settlement system of neighborhoods.

We include labor force participation of women among the life cycle characteristics, if only because it is expected to be linked to childrearing and other characteristics of the life course. Labor force participation among females has become increasingly prevalent in recent decades. By 1980 the female labor force participation rate exceeded 50 percent, up from 43 percent in 1970, and 25 percent in 1940.[6] Of interest to us is whether this labor force activity is visible in the residential character of the city, and how that residential differentiation has changed over time.

In almost every SMSA the proportion of women in the labor force (tabulations not shown) hovers near 50 percent in the median census tract, approximating the national average. In most cities about half of all neighborhoods are found in the band enclosed by 5 or 8 percentage points to either side of the 50 percent mark. The fraction of neighborhoods with very high participation rates (over 75 percent) is small, but so is the fraction with rates under 25 percent. What is important here is that while we can still observe (in other tabulations above) considerable specialization of neighborhoods in the metropolis with regard to the age or life cycle structure, the presence of children in a neighborhood does not immediately signal the withdrawal of its adult women from the labor force. The national statistics tell us that a smaller but still significant fraction of women with children work. Although childrearing is a visible component of life cycle variation in the metropolis, the image of a traditional nuclear family neighborhood in which all husbands work and all wives remain home is outmoded.

Ethnic Composition

Perhaps more than any other characteristic, the label that attaches to an American neighborhood is its racial and ethnic composition. Indeed, the very first tabulations of the 1980 census for the purpose of political redistricting included these characteristics.[7] Ethnic homogeneity is seen as an integral part of community cohesiveness by some; at other times it is viewed as a manifestation of conscious discrimination on the part of the majority group against the minority. We will look at ethnic segregation extensively, but the figures we will calculate

[6]Donald J. Bogue, *The Population of the United States* (New York: Free Press, 1985), p. 487.
[7]The Public Law 191 tape file released in 1981.

43

for segregation can give no hint about the relative size of the various groups in the neighborhoods of the city, nor how ethnic group composition differs across SMSAs. (In fact, the segregation statistics are designed to remove this feature of the distribution.) So now we describe the distribution of the population by race and ancestry in the metropolitan areas.

Although in current parlance race-ethnicity is often treated as a single dimension, the census classification involves several questions, and is therefore multidimensional. We make use of three classifications, each of which derives from a different census question. With major tabulation categories given in parentheses, these are:

1. Race (white, black, Asian, American Indian, other race)
2. Spanish origin (Puerto Rican, Mexican, Cuban, other Spanish, and not of Spanish origin)
3. Ancestry (fifteen distinct single ancestry groups, plus other single ancestry and not specified).

Every individual is classified under all three questions by self-identification. Items 1 and 2 were asked of all members of the population; item 3 was collected from the long-form sample.[8] Also on the long form individuals were asked their place of birth, so that we can tabulate the foreign-born population, a characteristic we will treat in subsequent work. We will reserve the term "ethnicity" for referring to this complex of related dimensions upon which the population can be classified. Following the census definitions, our analyses will treat each component distinctly.

Figure 2.3 shows dramatically how blacks and other racial groups (whites constitute the bulk of the nonblack population) rarely share the same neighborhoods. (No national distribution can be usefully superimposed here, but 11.7 percent of the U.S. population was black in the 1980 census.) Even though these twenty-one metropolitan areas differ in overall racial composition, it is clear that very few neighborhoods are of mixed race. The figure is U-shaped, with one side of the U shorter than the other. The picture one draws here for the nearly 6,000 neighborhoods pooled together foreshadows the kind of picture we would be likely to draw in any individual metropolis.

Table 2.8 accounts more precisely for both the differential racial composition of metropolitan areas and the distribution of the black pop-

[8] Some groups commonly found in discussions of race-ethnicity (e.g., Anglo, Jew) are not explicitly accounted for in any classification. This typology also contains some changes from previous censuses. More extensive discussions of these matters are available in census documentation and other volumes in this series, whose subjects are the status of racial and ethnic groups.

FIGURE 2.3
Distribution of Blacks: 1980
Neighborhoods of 21 Metropolitan Areas

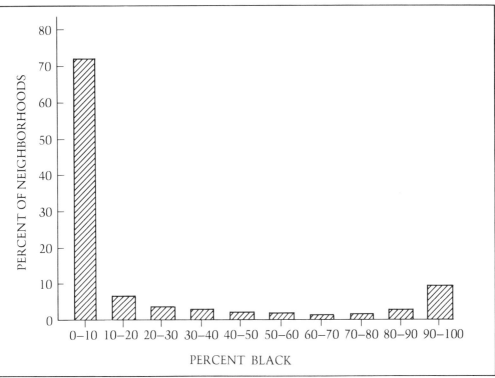

ulation within them and mirrors statistics for SMSA racial composition presented in Chapter 1. In almost every SMSA, there is a substantial fraction—usually over one-fourth—of neighborhoods that contain no blacks. In most metropolitan areas even the median neighborhood contains practically no blacks, despite the measurable fraction of the region's population that is black (Table 1.1). At the other extreme, we can see that, again almost universally, a small fraction of census tracts are nearly all black, and most major SMSAs have at least one tract, often several, that are virtually 100 percent black. The interquartile range gives further striking evidence of the disparity in racial composition for the census tract distribution. By construction the IQR bounds exactly half of the distribution, and so the larger the number, the wider a range is needed to capture half of the census tract values on racial composition. In metropolitan areas with substantial black proportions

TABLE 2.8
Percent Black

Metropolitan Area	Minimum	Lower Quartile	Median	Upper Quartile	Maximum	Interquartile Range	Mean	S.D.	Number of Cases
Allentown	0.0	0.1	0.5	1.6	25.6	1.5	1.8	3.5	155
Amarillo	0.0	0.4	1.0	2.7	97.8	2.3	6.6	17.7	63
Atlanta	0.0	2.0	8.1	56.5	99.8	54.5	29.9	36.9	352
Bangor	0.0	0.0	0.2	0.4	1.7	0.4	0.3	0.4	28
Birmingham	0.0	2.2	12.0	63.7	99.8	61.4	31.4	36.0	202
Boston	0.0	0.3	0.9	3.2	95.6	2.9	8.2	20.4	580
Chicago	0.0	0.2	1.7	38.1	100.0	37.9	25.4	38.9	1,486
Flint	0.0	0.1	1.0	13.4	95.9	13.3	18.3	32.1	124
Indianapolis	0.0	0.2	1.1	11.7	98.9	11.5	15.5	28.7	269
Lexington	0.0	1.6	3.7	8.8	74.9	7.2	9.8	16.4	79
New Bedford	0.0	0.3	0.7	2.6	13.5	2.3	2.2	3.2	44
New Haven	0.1	0.6	1.6	12.9	92.2	12.3	11.3	19.2	93
New Orleans	0.0	2.1	16.4	64.6	99.9	62.5	34.4	36.1	318
Newark	0.0	0.7	3.9	47.6	99.2	46.9	24.8	34.1	462
St. Louis	0.0	0.3	2.0	29.2	99.4	28.9	21.1	34.0	435
Salt Lake City	0.0	0.1	0.4	1.2	47.7	1.0	1.4	4.1	189
San Antonio	0.0	0.5	1.6	6.6	90.1	6.1	7.3	15.3	197
San Diego	0.0	0.7	1.6	4.5	79.6	3.8	5.1	10.4	379
Seattle	0.0	0.5	1.1	1.9	85.0	1.4	3.9	10.2	353
Sheboygan	0.0	0.0	0.1	0.1	7.8	0.1	0.4	1.6	24
Stockton	0.0	0.4	1.9	6.4	52.7	6.0	6.3	10.4	85

NOTE: See Table 2.1, NOTES.

the range is very wide; in other SMSAs the range is smaller, reflecting the fact that often almost all blacks live in a handful of census tracts. The segregation statistics we will present in Chapter 4 try to capture the unevenness of the entire distribution in one number.

The twenty-one metropolitan areas under study have about 7 percent of residents who are of Spanish origin, but Table 2.9 shows that there is a great deal of variation across the twenty-one areas. From the 50th percentile the concentration of Hispanic population in the southwestern United States is clearly evident. In San Antonio, which is more than 40 percent Spanish origin overall, the average neighborhood is 38 percent Spanish. Larger cities also tend to have measurable Spanish populations, and as in Boston, Newark, and Chicago, there are usually a few neighborhoods of heavy Spanish concentration.

The United States has always been a country of immigration, and these results from the 1980 census show again what a wide diversity of ethnic origins are present in American cities, and how, in addition, the demographic composition of neighborhoods helps to lend a particular character to metropolitan areas. For the first time in 1980, the census asked each person to identify his or her ancestry, giving us some new information about the heritage of the population and the persistence of ethnicity. The 1980 census tabulates ancestry at the level of the census tract for some fifteen groups, too many to explore individually in detail here. We can only give an overview, and show how some metropolitan areas are "specialized" with respect to particular ethnic groups.

Table 2.10 reports the median concentration for race and several ancestry groups across neighborhoods for each city presented in rank order by SMSA size, from smallest to largest. We use those persons who report only one ancestry and include the median columns from Tables 2.8 and 2.9 for comparative purposes. The table gives one a good idea of how differentially distributed the various groups are across the United States settlement system. English, German, Irish, French, Italian, and Polish (in that order) are the principal ancestry groups in the United States. The fraction of English, German, and Irish descent is nonnegligible in almost every SMSA. The concentration of the English ancestry population is evident in the cities of the South, as well as in Salt Lake City and Bangor. In midwestern SMSAs, the German ancestry population is especially evident. St. Louis is known for its neighborhoods of German heritage. In that metropolitan area, the typical neighborhood contains 15 percent of the population who claim German ancestry distinctly. The Irish and Italian populations are well represented along the Northeast seaboard. In the Boston SMSA, the median census tract is 13 percent Irish. The visibility of Italian-ancestry Americans is especially high in New Haven, where one out of six persons in the average neigh-

TABLE 2.9
Percent Spanish Origin

Metropolitan Area	Minimum	Lower Quartile	Median	Upper Quartile	Maximum	Interquartile Range	Mean	S.D.	Number of Cases
Allentown	0.0	0.4	0.8	2.1	36.3	1.7	2.8	5.8	155
Amarillo	1.3	3.1	5.8	8.9	70.9	5.8	9.5	12.4	63
Atlanta	0.0	0.7	1.0	1.3	13.2	0.7	1.2	1.1	352
Bangor	0.0	0.1	0.4	0.5	1.0	0.4	0.4	0.3	28
Birmingham	0.0	0.4	0.6	0.9	5.7	0.5	0.7	0.5	202
Boston	0.0	0.6	1.0	2.8	67.0	2.2	3.3	6.7	580
Chicago	0.0	1.2	2.6	9.6	90.3	8.4	10.8	18.3	1,486
Flint	0.4	0.9	1.4	2.2	9.2	1.3	1.8	1.5	124
Indianapolis	0.1	0.4	0.7	1.0	6.6	0.5	0.8	0.6	269
Lexington	0.0	0.4	0.6	0.9	2.4	0.4	0.7	0.4	79
New Bedford	0.5	1.3	2.4	4.6	16.3	3.3	3.6	3.3	44
New Haven	0.2	0.7	1.1	2.9	35.9	2.2	3.7	6.6	93
New Orleans	0.0	2.1	3.2	5.0	43.3	2.9	4.0	3.5	318
Newark	0.2	1.3	2.2	6.3	70.6	5.0	7.3	12.0	462
St. Louis	0.0	0.6	0.8	1.1	19.5	0.5	1.0	1.1	435
Salt Lake City	0.2	1.8	4.1	7.2	42.0	5.4	6.0	6.6	189
San Antonio	2.8	14.7	38.2	70.1	98.7	55.4	44.3	30.7	197
San Diego	0.3	6.4	9.9	18.2	92.5	11.8	15.4	15.3	379
Seattle	0.1	1.4	1.9	2.4	6.6	1.0	2.1	1.0	353
Sheboygan	0.2	0.4	0.7	1.4	3.2	1.0	1.1	1.0	24
Stockton	3.5	11.6	15.7	26.9	63.4	15.3	20.9	14.3	85

NOTE: See Table 2.1, NOTES.

borhood is of Italian ancestry. French and Polish are the remaining two of the six principal ancestry groups tabulated for geographic areas. The French population is strongly represented in New England (where many persons immigrated from French Canada), and in New Orleans. The concentration of Polish ancestry persons in the average Chicago census tract is greater than that for any other SMSA. We should point out that these tabulations apply to the entire metropolitan area, and that ethnic neighborhoods can be found in suburban locations as well as in the central city.

The remaining nine European ancestry groups occur much less often. Although the numbers are generally very small in Table 2.10, one can still find evidence of the specialization of certain ethnic groups in particular SMSAs. The Dutch are more visible in Sheboygan and Allentown than elsewhere. Salt Lake City and Seattle show a slight concentration of Scandinavians. Perhaps most striking in the table is that the small SMSA of New Bedford has such a concentration of persons of Portuguese ancestry that the average neighborhood is one-fourth Portuguese descent. The "other" category records all individuals who report a single ancestry other than one of the fifteen groups tabulated explicitly here. Since ancestry is tabulated for every person, the numbers in this column reflect the relative concentration of black and Hispanic populations in the SMSA as well as other European (and non-European) ancestry groups.

It is to the big cities of America that we attach the imagery of the "melting pot"; they are often described in the popular press and elsewhere as "cities of neighborhoods," where in turn the notion of neighborhood implies ethnic enclaves among other features. We can get a nice illustration of how a wider variety of ethnic neighborhoods (or clusters of ancestry groups) arise or become visible in larger metropolitan areas by examining Table 2.11, which presents the maximum ancestry concentration recorded for the tracts in the SMSA. In the table, metropolitan areas are also ranked from smallest to largest. While we know from the discussion above that cities and regions tend to "specialize" in certain groups, one aspect of the greater apparent diversity of the larger SMSAs is evident in this table. Since major metropolitan areas have more neighborhoods (tracts) in absolute numbers, there is more opportunity for a large concentration of various kinds of ancestry groups to arise.

Table 2.11 shows that this big city visibility holds. Every city has at least one or two groups with a high average concentration (for example, German in Sheboygan), but it is clear that the largest SMSAs tend to have more neighborhoods at the high end of the scale. Out of the fifteen single-ancestry groups (excluding "others"), Bangor has two with con-

TABLE 2.10

Median Neighborhood Racial and Single Ancestry

Metropolitan Area	Black	Spanish	English	French	German	Irish	Italian	Polish
Bangor	.2	.4	21.1	9.4	2.0	6.8	.8	.3
Sheboygan	.1	.7	2.1	.5	41.1	.9	.3	1.0
New Bedford	.7	2.4	7.0	6.8	.6	2.5	1.0	2.3
Amarillo	1.0	5.8	17.1	.8	5.9	5.2	.2	.2
Lexington	3.7	.6	24.0	.6	5.4	6.2	.4	.2
Stockton	1.9	15.7	7.4	.7	5.9	3.0	2.9	.2
New Haven	1.6	1.1	5.7	1.3	3.2	6.8	14.8	3.0
Flint	1.0	1.4	10.4	1.4	6.9	2.9	.5	1.6
Allentown	.5	.8	4.3	.3	23.9	2.8	3.4	1.8
Birmingham	12.0	.6	21.3	.4	2.3	5.5	.4	0.0
Salt Lake City	.4	4.1	24.9	.5	3.9	1.5	.7	.2
San Antonio	1.6	38.2	5.9	.4	6.5	2.4	.4	.6
Indianapolis	1.1	.7	14.1	.7	9.6	4.5	.5	.3
New Orleans	16.4	3.2	5.9	6.8	3.8	2.9	2.6	.1
Seattle	1.1	1.9	8.2	.9	6.6	3.1	1.1	.5
San Diego	1.6	9.9	9.4	1.1	6.3	3.6	2.0	.9
Newark	3.9	2.2	2.8	.3	4.4	4.8	8.8	2.7
Atlanta	8.1	1.0	20.4	.6	2.9	5.2	.3	.2
St. Louis	2.0	.8	6.5	.9	15.1	4.2	1.1	.8
Boston	.9	1.0	6.4	1.4	1.4	13.2	6.5	1.3
Chicago	1.7	2.6	2.1	.3	6.0	3.5	2.1	3.6

TABLE 2.10 *(continued)*

Metropolitan Area	Dutch	Greek	Hungarian	Norwegian	Portuguese	Russian	Scottish	Swedish	Ukrainian	Others
Bangor	.3	0.0	0.0	.2	0.0	.2	2.0	.7	0.0	3.9
Sheboygan	2.3	0.0	0.0	.5	0.0	.2	.1	.3	0.0	4.3
New Bedford	0.0	.2	0.0	0.0	26.6	0.0	.2	0.0	0.0	7.5
Amarillo	.4	0.0	0.0	0.0	0.0	0.0	.5	.1	0.0	9.1
Lexington	.3	0.0	0.0	0.0	0.0	0.0	.5	0.0	0.0	6.5
Stockton	.4	.1	0.0	.3	.9	0.0	.3	.6	0.0	21.8
New Haven	.1	.3	.5	.1	.2	.8	.5	.6	.3	6.6
Flint	.4	0.0	.6	.1	0.0	0.0	.5	.3	0.0	7.5
Allentown	1.6	.1	1.7	0.0	0.0	.3	.2	.1	.8	6.9
Birmingham	.3	0.0	0.0	0.0	0.0	0.0	.4	0.0	0.0	13.4
Salt Lake City	1.0	.3	0.0	.5	0.0	0.0	.8	1.2	0.0	9.6
San Antonio	.1	0.0	0.0	0.0	0.0	0.0	.2	0.0	0.0	44.4
Indianapolis	.5	0.0	0.0	0.0	0.0	0.0	.4	.1	0.0	4.9
New Orleans	0.0	0.0	0.0	0.0	0.0	0.0	.1	0.0	0.0	19.3
Seattle	.6	.1	.1	2.9	0.0	.2	.8	1.7	0.0	9.8
San Diego	.5	.1	.2	.6	.2	.3	.6	.7	0.0	16.8
Newark	.2	.2	.5	0.0	.1	.8	.4	.2	.3	13.1
Atlanta	.2	0.0	0.0	0.0	0.0	0.0	.4	.1	0.0	10.6
St. Louis	.2	0.0	.1	0.0	0.0	0.0	.2	.1	0.0	6.0
Boston	.1	.6	0.0	.1	.4	.8	.9	.5	0.0	7.1
Chicago	.1	.2	.2	.2	0.0	.1	.1	.6	.1	22.6

TABLE 2.11

Maximum Neighborhood Racial and Single Ancestry

Metropolitan Area	Black	Spanish	English	French	German	Irish	Italian	Polish
Bangor	1.7	1.0	45.4	27.5	4.0	15.3	3.0	2.0
Sheboygan	7.8	3.2	4.5	2.1	60.0	2.8	.8	1.8
New Bedford	13.5	16.3	22.2	21.5	2.1	8.8	4.5	7.5
Amarillo	97.8	70.9	30.6	3.9	13.4	13.9	2.0	4.0
Lexington	74.9	2.4	42.6	2.5	14.6	11.3	2.9	1.3
Stockton	52.7	63.4	20.0	1.9	28.2	7.4	16.4	2.0
New Haven	92.2	35.9	20.0	4.1	6.9	21.9	49.2	10.0
Flint	95.9	9.2	18.5	6.3	14.6	7.0	2.7	6.7
Allentown	25.6	36.3	17.7	1.6	48.5	8.9	25.4	8.3
Birmingham	99.8	5.7	50.5	3.4	15.4	14.7	7.8	3.1
Salt Lake City	47.7	42.0	39.3	3.0	12.4	7.0	3.8	2.1
San Antonio	90.1	98.7	19.3	4.3	43.4	8.2	3.7	18.6
Indianapolis	98.9	6.6	32.1	5.5	20.5	11.7	7.5	3.0
New Orleans	99.9	43.3	22.5	37.7	12.3	9.3	11.4	3.1
Seattle	85.0	6.6	17.1	8.9	16.0	15.4	5.9	3.5
San Diego	79.6	92.5	24.2	5.1	14.9	10.3	23.7	5.1
Newark	99.2	70.6	17.3	2.7	18.1	15.6	61.7	25.2
Atlanta	99.8	13.2	44.9	4.9	8.1	14.3	3.1	3.0
St. Louis	99.4	19.5	27.0	9.2	69.8	20.7	53.3	8.6
Boston	95.6	67.0	23.0	16.1	7.1	59.3	76.8	30.6
Chicago	100.0	90.3	22.6	4.4	29.1	39.2	43.1	67.1

TABLE 2.11 (continued)

Metropolitan Area	Dutch	Greek	Hungarian	Norwegian	Portuguese	Russian	Scottish	Swedish	Ukrainian	Others
Bangor	1.6	3.8	1.6	.7	1.1	3.4	4.5	2.3	.4	85.6
Sheboygan	50.7	.8	.4	2.1	.2	.8	.6	.9	.3	12.4
New Bedford	.7	2.6	.3	3.0	79.6	1.4	1.2	1.4	.3	55.9
Amarillo	2.2	.7	.4	1.3	1.0	1.0	3.7	1.3	.1	86.7
Lexington	2.3	1.5	.8	1.5	.3	.9	2.3	.9	.4	58.7
Stockton	21.1	2.3	.8	3.2	14.3	1.2	1.3	2.6	1.6	83.9
New Haven	1.1	3.4	3.4	.7	6.6	15.5	3.1	3.5	2.1	80.7
Flint	1.6	1.8	2.4	1.2	.2	2.5	3.5	1.6	1.9	86.8
Allentown	8.6	3.4	11.8	.8	9.9	3.1	1.4	.9	7.3	46.4
Birmingham	4.1	1.8	1.1	1.1	1.0	2.8	2.8	1.3	1.1	94.1
Salt Lake City	4.4	3.2	1.4	3.4	2.1	1.2	3.6	3.4	.6	64.1
San Antonio	1.8	1.2	.9	.8	.7	1.9	2.3	1.1	.4	94.6
Indianapolis	2.3	1.6	1.2	1.4	.3	4.0	2.0	2.6	1.5	91.1
New Orleans	3.9	1.9	1.7	1.8	1.1	4.6	1.8	1.4	2.1	91.8
Seattle	8.6	2.4	3.5	12.5	1.9	4.0	2.8	5.8	2.1	80.1
San Diego	2.5	2.2	2.3	3.5	25.6	9.1	3.6	3.0	2.3	100.0
Newark	3.4	11.5	7.9	6.6	62.9	14.1	3.0	2.0	1.5	93.5
Atlanta	2.5	2.9	1.0	1.5	1.7	5.7	2.7	1.7	8.7	95.3
St. Louis	3.4	3.1	3.4	1.0	1.2	14.6	4.6	1.6	2.5	94.1
Boston	1.8	13.8	2.7	3.2	42.9	21.0	5.8	5.0	1.4	90.7
Chicago	36.2	24.6	5.6	5.3	3.7	17.4	2.5	12.0	33.0	98.4

centrations over 25 percent, Sheboygan has two, and New Bedford one. Birmingham, Salt Lake, and San Antonio, in the middle-size category, also have two. In St. Louis and Boston, there are four and five neighborhoods, respectively, with concentrations of a single group over 25 percent. In Chicago nearly half of the ancestry groups have some neighborhood at the 25 percent level; another four have maximum values between 10 percent and 25 percent. If we were to take into account the additional fraction of a neighborhood's population that claims that ancestry group plus some other (as 31 percent of Americans do), the ethnic character of urban neighborhoods would be numerically even more apparent.

Thus, in almost every metropolitan area we find evidence from the census of one or two "ethnic" congregations, but in the largest SMSAs the pattern of congregation is more extensive: there are more neighborhoods with a wider variety of groups represented. This demographic visibility need not always translate into "street visibility": ethnic restaurants, language spoken, specialty shops, etc. For certain ancestry groups, especially the ones who arrived in some regions at an earlier time (for example, Irish, French), the concentration may be subtle or even invisible at the surface. Conversely, the presence of ethnic restaurants may not always be a sure guide to the extent of the uniqueness of the population composition of the surrounding community.

Cities in the South have less ethnic diversity for their size. Southern cities generally show very high concentrations of English ancestry persons, and few other groups.[9] The relatively high values in the "other" category are contributed by native-born American blacks of African ancestry. A similar story can be told for SMSAs of the Southwest with respect to the Hispanic population, who usually claim Mexican, Spanish, or South American ancestry.

Despite the common assumption of assimilation and the function of the metropolis in that process, we have in these demographic data some fairly clear evidence of the persistence of "ethnicity" in American culture. Many neighborhoods carry a very distinct ethnic imprint (as indicated by questions asked about race, Spanish origin, or ancestry). This persistence can be the result of the absence of assimilation (as would be indicated by ethnic intermarriage and residential dispersal), thus preserving a single ancestry, or from replenishment by more recent immigrants of the same ancestry group. The United States metropolitan areas no doubt serve as cauldrons of the mixing process, but that mixing is gradual, and despite some surface smoothness, much of the context retains its original flavor.

[9]Texas SMSAs, although in the South census region, form somewhat of an exception.

Density, Housing, and Mobility

Our final cluster of variables includes characteristics that do not fall neatly under the three primary headings of socioeconomic status, life cycle, and ethnicity, yet they are important and distinctly visible elements of the metropolitan topography. (Whether this physical differentiation is linked to social differentiation is another matter to be explored.) Residential mobility provides the agent of change in the settlement system, with resultant population increases or declines, swings in socioeconomic status, and turnover in ethnic composition.

In Figure 2.4 we have graphed the distribution of the population densities at which people live in the census tracts of this study. Like the other overview charts, the values here are influenced by the average SMSA density as well as by the distribution within metropolitan areas.

FIGURE 2.4

Population Density: 1980
Distribution in 21 Metropolitan Areas

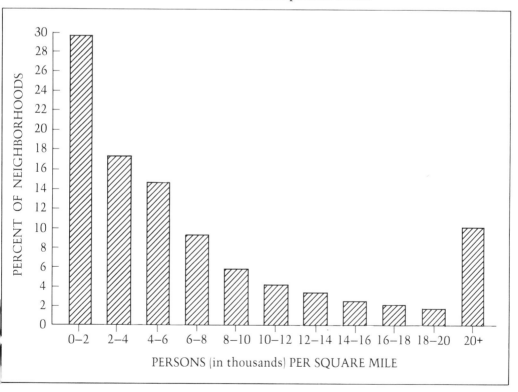

Nearly half of the neighborhoods in the study have under 4,000 persons per square mile, and there is a steady decline in the fraction of neighborhoods at higher densities. (We have grouped together the long right-hand "tail" of the density distribution.) Still, some 10 percent of neighborhoods are at densities of over 20,000 persons per square mile.

Part of what gives rise to the population density distribution is the type of housing construction within the neighborhood. The balance between single-family and multifamily dwellings lends a "character" to the residential community. Figure 2.5 plots the overall distribution of single-family dwellings in the twenty-one SMSAs. About one-quarter of all neighborhoods out of the nearly 6,000 contain single-family homes. Neighborhoods with an even mixture of single- and multifamily dwellings are relatively infrequent. Zoning ordinances would tend to reinforce any preference against neighborhoods of mixed density.

FIGURE 2.5

Single-Family Homes: 1980
Distribution in 21 Metropolitan Areas

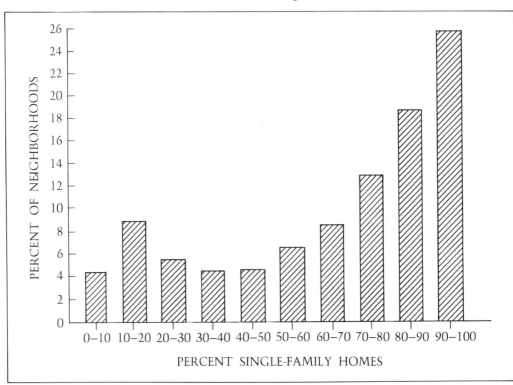

Table 2.12 further illustrates the specialization of spatial structure in terms of housing density, by focusing on the proportion of units in structures containing five or more units. In general, it is a good correlate with area housing density. In most cities, the typical tract has only a small fraction of high-density dwellings. Usually at least one-fourth of the neighborhoods have virtually no high-density structures. In the largest seven SMSAs (except St. Louis), the upper quartile has over 15 percent of dwellings in multiunit structures. Almost all metropolitan areas have a few neighborhoods that are heavily devoted to higher-density dwellings. With substantial portions of urban real estate devoted to apartment dwellings, the spread of the univariate distribution increases as well. Interestingly, the differentiation of neighborhoods by housing type is not so strongly matched by a specialization in family-household composition (above), even though most arguments about lifestyle and life cycle characteristics make links to housing type.

A common rule of thumb in population mobility is that about one-fifth of the population changes residence in every year, which lends credence to the designation of the United States as a highly mobile society. If this figure were to hold in a statistically independent way, after about three years half the population would have moved. We know that nationally, and especially in neighborhoods, there is great variation in the average length of time persons have spent in their home; these variations naturally give rise to the identification of certain neighborhoods as stable places and others as communities of high turnover. Such identities are in turn linked to perceptions of well-being, likelihood of crime, racial transition, and the like. Residential districts growing rapidly, or containing large college or military populations, are likely to have short average duration times, whereas neighborhoods of middle-aged homeowners are likely to have longer times. What in fact do American neighborhoods look like from this point of view?

In Table 2.13 we have calculated the average length of time that the householder (formerly termed household head) has lived in the dwelling unit.[10] In the typical American urban neighborhood (column 3), that value falls in the range of 3–5 years, corroborating the general perception of frequent mobility, but a bit longer than under statistical independence. Even in this average figure we can observe considerable diversity among metropolitan areas. In the cities of the Northeast, which are growing slowly if at all, the figure can average about twice that of the southern and western SMSAs. Since we observe people at

---

[10]Just like the household income case, we calculate for each tract the median length of stay, that is, half of householders are more recent than the value, half are longer-term residents. Again, Table 2.13 presents an average of averages.

TABLE 2.12

Percent High-Density Dwellings

Metropolitan Area	Minimum	Lower Quartile	Median	Upper Quartile	Maximum	Interquartile Range	Mean	S.D.	Number of Cases
Allentown	0.0	0.2	2.1	7.0	51.9	6.8	5.9	9.1	155
Amarillo	0.0	0.0	3.0	9.7	68.1	9.7	8.1	13.2	63
Atlanta	0.0	0.4	5.9	18.0	73.0	17.6	11.1	13.4	352
Bangor	0.0	1.4	3.0	7.7	85.7	6.3	10.2	20.4	28
Birmingham	0.0	0.1	1.1	4.8	51.8	4.8	4.8	8.9	202
Boston	0.0	1.5	6.7	16.6	88.4	15.1	12.9	16.9	579
Chicago	0.0	1.0	4.6	15.5	100.0	14.4	12.2	18.3	1,483
Flint	0.0	0.1	1.0	6.7	68.1	6.7	5.1	8.9	124
Indianapolis	0.0	0.2	1.7	6.3	74.8	6.2	5.4	9.8	269
Lexington	0.0	0.3	4.7	14.0	49.1	13.7	9.8	11.8	78
New Bedford	0.0	0.1	0.9	3.6	62.4	3.6	4.2	10.1	44
New Haven	0.0	0.9	4.5	12.5	54.6	11.6	9.5	12.5	93
New Orleans	0.0	0.2	3.1	11.4	74.7	11.2	8.1	13.0	318
Newark	0.0	0.9	6.8	21.1	88.2	20.3	14.4	18.4	462
St. Louis	0.0	0.4	1.7	5.6	86.6	5.2	5.4	10.8	434
Salt Lake City	0.0	0.2	2.3	10.1	90.0	9.9	8.4	14.6	189
San Antonio	0.0	0.3	2.6	13.4	68.1	13.1	9.0	13.2	197
San Diego	0.0	1.6	9.2	20.6	86.6	19.0	13.6	14.8	379
Seattle	0.0	1.3	7.8	17.5	90.7	16.2	13.3	17.5	353
Sheboygan	0.0	0.1	1.1	5.0	25.4	4.9	3.9	6.2	24
Stockton	0.0	0.9	2.7	12.1	74.9	11.2	8.9	13.5	85

TABLE 2.13
Length of Residence

Metropolitan Area	Minimum	Lower Quartile	Median	Upper Quartile	Maximum	Interquartile Range			Number of Cases
Allentown	1.6	3.8	6.0	8.1	17.4	4.2	6.3	3.0	155
Amarillo	0.4	2.0	2.6	3.8	8.9	1.8	3.0	1.9	63
Atlanta	0.4	1.9	2.6	3.8	13.9	1.9	3.0	1.8	352
Bangor	0.3	1.6	2.4	4.1	6.7	2.5	2.8	1.6	28
Birmingham	0.4	2.9	4.8	6.7	26.9	3.8	5.2	3.2	202
Boston	0.4	2.7	4.7	6.8	12.5	4.1	4.9	2.5	580
Chicago	0.4	2.3	3.3	5.8	19.8	3.5	4.3	2.7	1,485
Flint	0.4	2.7	3.6	5.3	11.1	2.6	4.1	2.0	124
Indianapolis	0.4	2.4	3.0	4.5	11.0	2.1	3.6	2.0	269
Lexington	0.4	1.7	2.7	3.5	8.1	1.8	2.8	1.5	79
New Bedford	1.8	3.4	5.3	7.1	11.9	3.6	5.6	2.6	44
New Haven	1.1	2.7	4.2	7.4	11.9	4.7	5.1	3.0	93
New Orleans	0.4	2.4	3.3	5.7	14.6	3.3	4.2	2.6	319
Newark	0.4	2.9	4.7	7.0	15.6	4.2	5.2	2.7	462
St. Louis	0.4	2.7	4.4	6.1	13.1	3.4	4.7	2.4	435
Salt Lake City	0.3	1.7	2.4	3.4	14.3	1.7	3.1	2.4	189
San Antonio	0.3	1.9	3.2	6.3	11.8	4.3	4.1	2.7	197
San Diego	0.4	1.3	1.9	2.6	10.4	1.3	2.2	1.7	379
Seattle	0.3	1.8	2.3	3.3	9.7	1.5	2.8	1.7	353
Sheboygan	2.4	4.0	5.2	5.8	7.4	1.8	5.0	1.5	24
Stockton	0.3	1.9	2.8	4.5	7.1	2.6	3.1	1.7	85

NOTE: See Table 2.1, NOTES.

59

their place of residence in 1980, we count all those who moved from the Northeast to, say, the Southwest, in their destination. Since the mean is greater than the median, length of residence has a skewed distribution. The upper tail of the distribution may be of some interest, since it identifies the most stable residential neighborhoods in each metropolitan area. In Allentown, New Bedford, New Haven, and Newark, areas that have experienced below average growth in the 1970s, one-fourth of neighborhoods have an average length of householder's residence of over seven years (column 4). In these northeastern cities, along with Birmingham—an older industrial exception in the South—the most stable neighborhood records an average resident's stay at between one and two decades.

Summary

Our objective in this chapter has been to provide a sense of the kinds of diversity that exist in neighborhoods of the settlement system and a feel for the social composition of neighborhoods. Our argument has been that the pattern of differentiation in neighborhoods will reflect social differentiation generally. The tabulations demonstrate the differences between metropolitan areas, as well as the differences within. Some characteristics, such as family size, exhibit only modest differentiation; others, such as poverty and housing type, are highly concentrated in certain geographic areas. Every city shows a degree of segregation and specialization with regard to ethnic groups. Overall we observe that, in accordance with theoretical expectations, a good deal more differentiation exists among the neighborhoods of the larger metropolitan areas than in the smaller ones. The task of the next two chapters is to investigate intrametropolitan differentiation more directly.

3

NEIGHBORHOOD SOCIAL DIMENSIONS

I N THIS chapter we look at the interrelationships among the many characteristics available for small areas in the decennial census. Motivation for this undertaking is twofold. On the one hand, we wish to speak to the desire among many users of census information for a "profile" of a region's neighborhoods. On the other hand, we inquire more generally about how social characteristics are intertwined in the sorting out process, and whether they point to independent underlying dimensions of urban differentiation. Our analysis draws from a substantial research tradition in social area analysis and factorial ecology. We begin by discussing the profiling concept and the factorial analysis methodology in more detail. After presenting the results of the factorial ecology for 1980, we discuss a model neighborhood profile.

Neighborhood and Community Profiles

Perhaps the most frequent use of census data is to look up basic statistics about the people who live in a community: family composition, ethnic background, income level, and the like. These statistics help the user understand the area, complementing what may be seen by eye or heard from residents. Such applications of census material often do not involve grand research designs but, rather, help improve planning and service delivery or provide the information to support a claim on the part of the residents. In many cases the resident or official seeking such information from the census material simply desires a statistical portrait of the community or neighborhood. Sometimes the desire for a statistical picture of communities takes on a more formal, organized aspect, and a compendium, or short statistical abstract, of smaller areas within the city or metropolitan area is produced.

Most community profiles are reference works, handbooks of basic social statistics for accepted geographical subareas. Profiles have several, often competing, objectives. They attempt to be at once concise and comprehensive. As a consequence, the compilers must make an effort to extract broadly useful items from the original sources, items that will be most widely comprehended with a minimum of redundancy. Many clients will be inexperienced with statistical data and look to the profile for an implicit decision about which characteristics are "best" to examine. Most profiles also seek to be objective. Rather than to advocate a particular interpretation of the data, the compilation of statistics is offered as an aid to the discussion of any policy issue for the neighborhood, city, or region.

G. M. Young of the U.S. Bureau of the Census has reviewed many such profiles and found little agreement on content or form.[1] His examples show that the range of information included in such compendia is quite broad. Census tabulations usually play a central role, although the balance of demographic, socioeconomic, and housing characteristics displayed varies considerably. Occasionally these data are supplemented with official statistics, such as birth and death rates, housing construction, crime rates, public parks, schools, etc. A verbal description of each neighborhood can be provided, with perhaps some historical data as well. In some cases, maps or graphics are used to facilitate presentation, particularly when comparisons are desirable. Young also distinguishes an intra-area versus inter-area focus in the profiles. The former concentrates on providing a picture of each particular place, while the latter makes comparisons across neighborhoods. Many examples of area profiling exist. The *Community Fact Book* for the city of Chicago is one of the oldest and best known and has served as a model for others.

Our contribution to the concerns for developing a profile is limited

---

[1]George M. Young, "Areas Profiling," Manuscript (Washington, D.C.: U.S. Bureau of the Census, 1979).

to aspects involving the representation of decennial census data.[2] The exact form of any profile—of metropolitan areas generally or within the city—will depend on the needs and desires of the community. We can still assist in the selection of data for inclusion. Our analysis to follow is directed at the issues of comprehensiveness, clarity, and conciseness, and is designed to help the practitioner select among available characteristics for inclusion in a profile. The analysis is of interest in its own right, for it tells us about how, in fact, characteristics do sort out into the mosaic of geographic areas we call neighborhoods.

Two methodological issues arise in profiling. The first is choosing an appropriate set of geographic units for the neighborhood profiles. New York City uses 59 community districts which average about 100,000 persons. Taylor et al., for instance, used neighborhood association boundaries (from various sources) to redelineate Baltimore; census data could be aggregated for these units from block statistics.[3] The 77 community areas within the city of Chicago, on the other hand, are constructed only by aggregating the city's several hundred census tracts.[4] Outside the city limits, community definitions rely on municipality boundaries. These boundaries were established in the 1920s and have remained stable since. The definition of community area could, in part, substitute for the definition of neighborhood. More recently, Bogue has experimented with another system to first define community areas out of census tract data and then test for the accuracy of the choices.[5] We use census tracts because of their desirable properties from the point of view of statistical geography and their availability for all SMSAs. There is no inherent reason that our analysis or even its conclusions could not be transferred to another system.

A second, more vexing, methodological issue concerns the choice of variables to be included. The utility of profiles is enhanced when a small number of comprehensible variables tells a great deal about the variety of characteristics within the neighborhoods. Existing practice

[2]Statistical information from noncensus sources, even though desirable, is not always collected in a way that is geographically comparable with the population and housing census data. Other social and attitudinal information about the population in each neighborhood may be of interest, but such information is usually difficult to collect in a reliable way for all the neighborhoods of the city or metropolitan area. The time and expense of collecting independent information make the census data tabulated for small areas all the more valuable.

[3]Ralph B. Taylor, Sidney J. Brower, and Whit Drain, *Toward a Neighborhood Based Data File: Baltimore* (Baltimore: Johns Hopkins Center for Metropolitan Planning and Research, 1979).

[4]Chicago Factbook Consortium, *Local Community Factbook: Chicago Metropolitan Area.* (Chicago: Chicago Review Press, 1984).

[5]Donald J. Bogue, *Procedure for Delimiting Ecological Community Areas*, draft manuscript, 1983.

varies widely. The Chicago fact book includes data on population, race and ethnicity, housing quality, labor force participation, and social status. In these cases and many others the decision about included variables was made a priori.

Another possibility exists. One can employ a statistical method designed to perform the sorting out task. One such method is factorial ecology. It has been used previously in this context, and we turn to it below. Goldsmith et al. have employed factor analysis in an effort to develop health area profiles.[6] Even some attention has been given to the methodological aspects of developing social indicators for small areas.[7] A continuing concern has been the combination of input variables and the interpretability of the output from such multivariate techniques.[8] Our approach tries to compromise, using these techniques as a first step and then working back to the original variables for the profile itself.

The Factorial Approach

One answer to the question, "What are the basic dimensions of urban differentiation?," is presented by the literature of social area analysis and, more specifically, factorial ecology.

Social area analysis is an analytical technique developed in the 1940s and 1950s for analyzing citywide differentiation, and is identified principally with the work of Shevky and Bell.[9] In most applications indexes of social status, family status, and ethnic segregation (terminology differs) are calculated for small urban areas, usually census tracts. Based on these scores neighborhoods could be classified into a three-dimensional typology.[10] There was an accompanying theory for social area analysis, although it seems to have developed after the initial index work was done.[11]

With the development of the statistical technique of factor analy-

[6]Howard Goldsmith, Ann S. Lee, and Beatrice Rosen, "Small Area Social Indicators", *National Institute of Mental Health, Mental Health Service System Reports Series BN#3* (Washington, D.C.: U.S. Government Printing Office, 1982).

[7]U.S. Bureau of the Census, *Social Indicators for Small Areas*, Census Tract Papers GE46. (Washington, D.C.: U.S. Government Printing Office, 1973).

[8]Herbert Bixhorn and Albert Mindlin, "Composite Social Indicators: Methodology and Results in Washington, D.C.," in U.S. Census Bureau, *Social Indicators*, pp. 3–17.

[9]See, for example, Ezref Shevky and Wendell Bell, *Social Area Analysis: Theory, Illustrative Application, and Computation Procedure* (Stanford, Cal.: Stanford University Press, 1955).

[10]Ezref Shevky and M. William, *The Social Areas of Los Angeles* (Los Angeles: University of California Press, 1949).

[11]R. J. Johnston, "Residential Area Characteristics," in George Theodorson, ed., *Urban Patterns* (University Park: Pennsylvania State University Press, 1982), pp. 297–315.

sis, social area analysis was replaced by "factorial ecology." Rather than create indexes, the several variables were subjected to the factor analysis procedure. The resulting factors, and the weights of the original variables on those factors, were then the subject of interpretation by the research for insight into residential differentiation.

Both of these techniques were criticized for being driven by data rather than theory, and for being aspatial. The social areas discovered statistically need not necessarily have any physical proximity.[12] Critical points notwithstanding, proponents of the factorial approach have accumulated a wide assortment of studies for a large number of cities in many cultural settings.

We employ the factorial ecology approach in this chapter because it can help determine the most compact set of variables to tell us about differentiation within the settlement system. Factorial ecology is a multivariate approach because it analyzes variation for a number of variables simultaneously. Given data on each observation (census tract in our case), the factor analysis routine determines which groups of variables cluster together and produces a set of independent "factors," which are weighted combinations of the original variables. These factors can serve as proxies for the component variables. For instance, areas with high incomes tend also to have high levels of education and more professional workers. This interrelationship may be captured by a single factor that weights the three variables. In this manner a large number of variables may be reduced to a modest number of factors which summarize the neighborhood variations in the region.

Previous analyses using factorial ecology have subjected anywhere from twelve to dozens of variables. These analyses can produce (depending on statistical conditions, combinations of variables submitted, et cetera) from one or two to several dominant factors. The researcher usually attempts to identify these with the general dimension(s). The factors are usually extracted in the order of their statistical importance, and usually the earlier factors are more easily labeled than the later ones.

A strong thread running through many of these analyses is the identification of three predominant dimensions in the pattern: socioeconomic status (SES), familism or life cycle stage (LC), and ethnic or racial segregation (ES). Such empirical regularities have led some to generalize about the existence of three fundamental underlying dimensions

---

[12]A more extensive exposition of the factorial analysis method, its applications, and some of the theoretical issues is contained in R. J. Johnston, "Residential Area Characteristice," and Bernard Hamm, "Social Area Analysis and Factorial Ecology," both in George Theodorson, ed., *Urban Patterns* (University Park: Pennsylvania State University Press, 1982).

of urban differentiation, which are causally independent and overlay one another on the urban mosaic.[13] We will return to these assertions in subsequent chapters, but for the present time we wish to determine for 1980 (1) which groups of variables cluster together; (2) what variables or characteristics explain the most about urban differentiation; and (3) what variable within the factors might be allowed to stand for the factor. The answers to these questions can help us draw up an informative and parsimonious profile of the urban area. It is in this regard that factor analysis can be of particular assistance.

We performed principal components analysis for the census tract data in our twenty-one cities.[14] The choice of variables in factorial ecology is central and problematic. After a considerable amount of preliminary work, we proceeded with a two-pronged strategy. We performed a small-scale (14-variable) factor analysis on every one of our twenty-one SMSAs. We then subjected our eight largest SMSAs to a 39-variable analysis to look for further confirmation of the basic hypotheses with a wider set of variables, and to explore for the finer details of variation.

The Basic Analysis

The 14-variable analysis included the 1980 companions of the twelve basic measures of SES, LC, and ES used in a well-known study,[15] and included in subsequent studies. Two more variables (Hispanic and Asian) were added to fill out the ES dimension, using some of the unique 1980 data and to reflect recent immigration patterns during the 1970s. The more extensive analysis was guided by an examination of some earlier benchmark studies and also by a comparative review.[16]

[13]Brian J. L. Berry and Frank E. Horton, *Geographic Perspectives on Urban Systems* (Englewood Cliffs, N.J.: Prentice-Hall, 1970).

[14]Principal components is not the same as classical factor analysis and, in fact, can be seen as a preliminary step in the extraction of the more complex factor analyses. H. H. Harmon, *Modern Factor Analysis* (Chicago: University of Chicago Press, 1967). Principal components rearranges the variables into a series of linear combinations (the factors) which predict the underlying characteristic. The loadings on each factor indicate the relative contribution of each variable to the factor. By construction the components or factors are orthogonal; that is, each factor is uncorrelated with every other. We actually performed several types of factor analysis, under different criteria, and for the most part they were consistent with the principal components approach. The principal components is the most straightforward and least controversial of the various techniques, and the one that assumes the least about the data. Another way of viewing factor analysis is as a technique for condensing the information contained in the correlation matrix of the variables.

[15]See B. J. L. Berry and Frank L. Horton, *Geographic Perspectives on Urban Systems*, p. 356, Table 10–16. Data are from Philip Rees, "The Factorial Ecology of Metropolitan Chicago," MA Thesis, University of Chicago, 1968.

[16]Philip H. Rees, *Residential Patterns in American Cities: 1960* (Chicago: Department of Geography, University of Chicago, 1979); and Bernard Hamm, "Social Area Analysis and Factorial Ecology," Theodorson, ed., *Urban Patterns*.

This work increases confidence that the results presented for the large cities are fundamentally sound and robust.

Figure 3.1 gives a synopsis of the 14-variable factorial results in the form of pie charts for four selected metropolitan areas. Figure 3.2 presents much more detailed information for each of the twenty-one SMSAs, including all of the variables that loaded on the factors. In all cases three or four factors were extracted, cumulatively explaining about three-quarters of the variation in the original variables across the data set.[17] In a typical city, then, three or four of these principal components—fundamental dimensions if they can be named—tell us almost as much about the distribution of social characteristics among neighborhoods in the metropolis as the fourteen original variables themselves did. There does not appear to be any relationship between the percent of variance explained and the size or region of the SMSA.

In the pie charts of Figure 3.1 we have given a label to the clutch of variables found together; they are listed in Figure 3.2 for each of four metropolitan areas. The size of the slice of pie indicates the relative importance of that factor or variable grouping. Prominent among these groupings are socioeconomic status, life cycle, and ethnicity. In most cities, some form of this three-part breakdown, central to conventional factorial and social area analysis, is evident.

Indianapolis (Figure 3.1C) best represents the conventional pattern. The first three factors are SES (including higher income, education, and white collar employment), ES (black), and LC (larger household size, presence of children, and absence of the elderly). A fourth factor, representing a small fraction of the explained variance, is devoted to the clustering of the Spanish origin population. In Indianapolis these four factors account for 81.7 percent of the variance, and 18.3 percent is marked in the pie chart as a remainder.

In Atlanta, SES, LC, and ES are all apparent, but the most prominent factor is one we have labeled "new development." The Atlanta SMSA grew quite rapidly during the 1970s, and this factor focuses in on neighborhoods with heavy concentrations of low-density, newer dwellings, and predominantly white and married-couple families of higher than average income.

Boston and Seattle SMSAs exhibit a "suburban" first factor, which emphasizes the presence of families with children, low-density housing (also newer in Seattle), and higher income. What is different about fast-growing Atlanta is that there we find distinct additional factors devoted

---

[17]Factor analysis can extract as many factors as there are variables entered initially. Stated another way, we can also make *N* linear combinations of the *N* original variables, which can exactly reproduce the value for each observation in the data set. We employed a cutoff criterion of 1.0 for the eigenvalues, and so do not report the smaller factors.

FIGURE 3.1

Distribution of Principal Components: 4 SMSAs

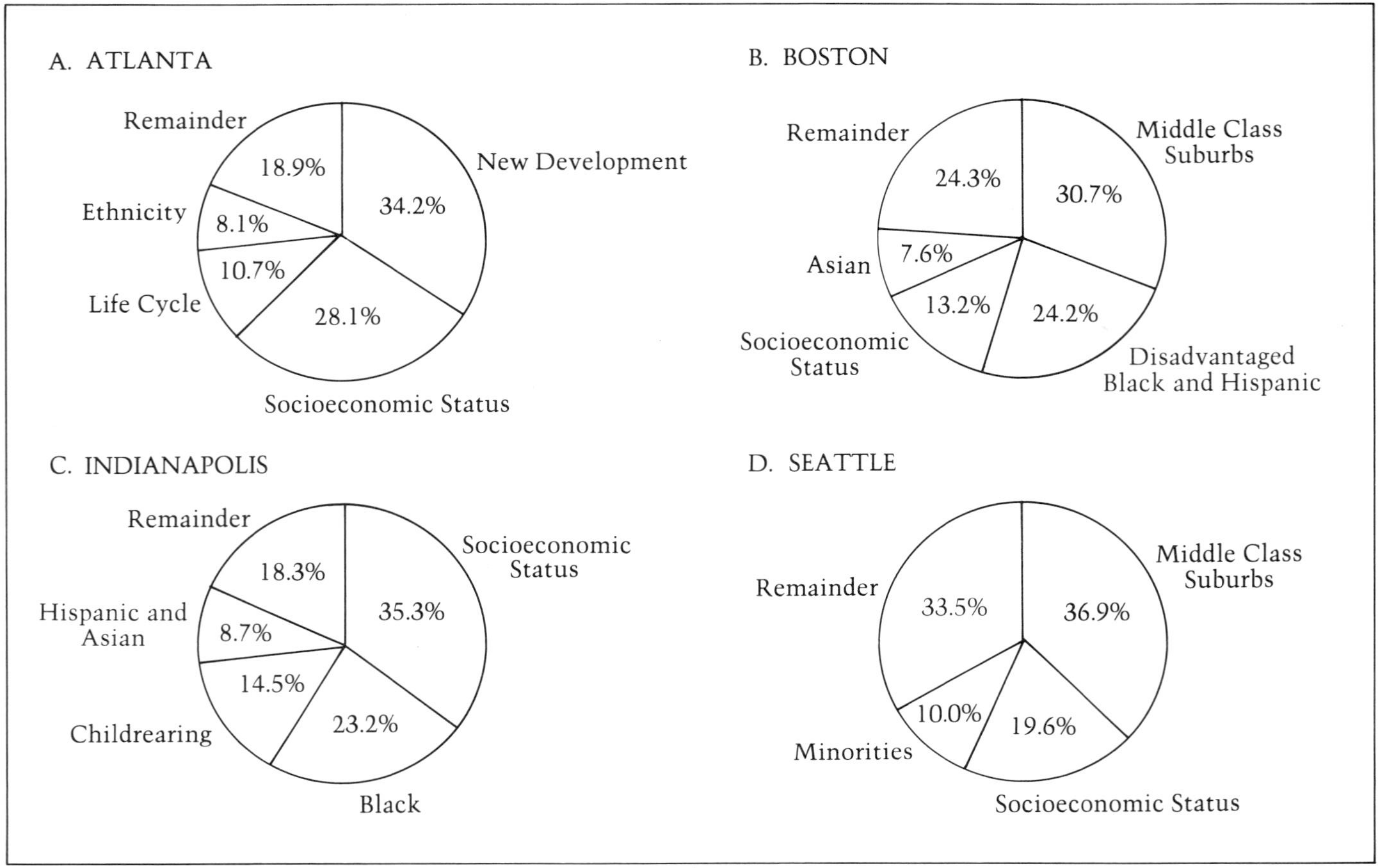

A. ATLANTA

New Development

Remainder 18.9%

34.2%

Ethnicity 8.1%

Life Cycle 10.7%

28.1%

Socioeconomic Status

B. BOSTON

Middle Class Suburbs

Remainder

30.7%

24.3%

Asian 7.6%

13.2%

24.2%

Disadvantaged Black and Hispanic

Socioeconomic Status

C. INDIANAPOLIS

Socioeconomic Status

Remainder 18.3%

35.3%

Hispanic and Asian 8.7%

14.5%

23.2%

Childrearing

Black

D. SEATTLE

Middle Class Suburbs

Remainder

36.9%

33.5%

10.0%

19.6%

Minorities

Socioeconomic Status

KEY TO FIGURES 3.2 AND 3.3

Life Cycle Indicators:
HHZ	Persons per household
KIDS	Percent population 0–15 years
ELDER	Percent population 65 + years
MCF	Percent married-couple family households
SPF	Percent of families headed by a single parent

Socioeconomic Status Indicators:
INC or MHINC	Median household income
WHCOL	Percent white collar workers
EDUC	Median educational attainment
CRAFT	Percent workers in craft occupations

Race and Ethnicity Indicators:
BLACK or BLK	Percent of population black
SPAN	Percent persons of Spanish origin
ASIAN	Percent Asian population

Housing and Density Indicators:
DEN	Population density persons per acre
NEWHSE	Percent of housing built since 1970

Additional Variables Used in Large SMSA Analysis: Figure 3.3
INCHI	Percent household with incomes over $35,000
INCLO	Percent households with income under $8,000
VAL	Median housing value
RENT	Median monthly contract rent
SERV	Percent service workers
LONE	Percent single-person households
GFR	Fertility ratio
CEB	Children ever born to women 35–44
AGE	Median population age
ANCSIN	Percent persons with single ancestry
FRENCH	Percent French ancestry
GERMAN	Percent German ancestry
IRISH	Percent Irish ancestry
ITALIAN	Percent Italian ancestry
POL	Percent Polish ancestry
SCAN	Percent Scandinavian ancestry
UNEMP	Percent population unemployed
LFF	Percent of females in the labor force
GRPQTR	Percent population in group quarters
MOVEIN	Median years since householder moved into unit
UNIT1	Percent housing units in 1-unit structures
UNIT10	Percent housing units in structures with 10 + units
OLDHSE	Percent housing units built before 1940
PLM	Percent housing units with plumbing deficiencies

* Secondary effect absolute value of coefficient ≥ .5
[ ] Primary effect absolute value of coefficient < .5
(−) variable loads negatively

Ch

Bo

St

A

N

S

I

FIGURE 3.2
Factorial Analysis of 14 Variables: 21 SMSAs

Scale: 0 5 10 15 20 25 30 35 40 45 50 55 60 65 70 75 80

Allentown — ·HHZ KIDS ELDER(−) MCF INC· | SPF SPAN BLK INC(−)DEN [NEWHSE−] | WHCOL ASIAN CRAFT(−) EDUC·

Amarillo — WHCOL EDUC CRAFT(−) SPAN(−) INC [NEWHSE] | HHZ ELDER(−) KIDS MCF | SPF BLK | POPDEN ASIAN

Atlanta — BLK(−) SINGPAR(−) MCF DEN(−) NEWHSE INC· CRAFT· | WHCOL EDUC INC CRAFT(−) | KIDS ELDER(−) HHZ | SPAN ASIAN

Bangor — HHZ MCF KIDS INC CRAFT ELDER(−)· | NEWHSE(−) SPAN WHCOL ELDER | BLACK SPF DEN ASIAN | EDUC WHCOL·

Birmingham — WHCOL EDUC INC CRAFT(−)· | SPF BLK DEN MCF(−) CRAFT(−) | HHZ KIDS ELDER(−) NEW HSE | ASIAN SPAN

Boston — HHZ MCF KIDS DEN(−) INC ELDER(−) | SPF BLK SPAN | WHCOL EDUC CRAFT(−) INC· | ASIAN NEWHSE

Chicago — MCF INC BLK(−) SPF(−) DEN(−) CRAFT [NEWHSE] | KIDS HHZ ELDER(−) SPF· | EDUC SPAN(−) WHCOL INC· | ASIAN

Flint — DEN(−) CRAFT SPF(−) MCF BLACK(−) NEWHSE INC· | HHZ KIDS ELDER(−) SPF· | EDUC WHCOL INC ASIAN SPAN(−)

Indianapolis — WHCOL EDUC CRAFT(−) INC ASIAN NEWHSE | BLK(−) SPF(−) MCF(+) DEN(−) CRAFT· INC· | HHZ KIDS ELDER(−) MCF· | SPAN ASIAN·

Lexington — WHCOL EDUC ASIAN CRAFT(−) INC | KIDS HHZ ELDER(−) NEWHSE MCF· DEN(−)· | SPF BLACK MCF(−) DEN [SPAN]

New Bedford — WHCOL EDUC DEN(−) INC NEWHSE [ASIAN] SPAN(−)· | ELDER(−) HHZ KIDS [CRAFT] MCF· | SPF BLACK MCF(−) SPAN INC(−)·

New Haven — SPF(−) BLACK(−) INC DEN(−) MCF SPAN(−) WHCOL EDUC· | HHZ ELDER(−) KIDS NEWHS MCF· | ASIAN CRAFT(−) EDUC WHCOL·

New Orleans — WHCOL EDUC INC BLACK(−) SPF(−) MCF· | HHZ KIDS ELDER(−) [NEWHSE] | CRAFT DEN(−) MCF SPF(−)· | ASIAN SPAN

Newark — MCF BLACK(−) SPF(−) INC DEN(−) WHCOL· | HHZ KIDS ELDER(−) | EDUC SPAN(−) CRAFT(−) WHCOL | NEWHSE ASIAN

St. Louis — BLACK(−) MCF SPF(−) CRAFT DEN(−) INC· | KIDS HHZ ELDER(−) [NEWHSE] | WHCOL ASIAN EDUC INC CRAFT(−)· | SPAN

Salt Lake — HHZ KIDS ELDER(−) MCF NEWHSE INC DEN(−) | EDUC WHCOL SPF(−) CRAFT(−) SPAN(−) INC· | ASIAN BLACK

San Antonio — ASIAN WHCOL CRAFT(−) EDUC SPAN(−)· INC· | DEN(−) SPAN(−) INC NEWHSE SPF(−) MCF· EDUC· | HHZ ELDER(−) KID(+) MCF | BLACK SPF·

San Diego — EDUC(−) WHCOL(−) SPAN CRAFT INC(−)· | KIDS ELDER(−) HHZ SPF ASIAN BLACK | MCF DEN(−) INC NEWHSE HHZ·

Seattle — HHZ KIDS MCF ELDER(−) INC DEN(−) NEWHSE | WHCOL EDUC CRAFT | BLACK SPF SPAN ASIAN

Sheboygan — KIDS ELDER(−) HHZ MCF INC SPAN(−) | SPF ASIAN DEN SPAN· | WHCOL EDUC CRAFT(−) [NEWHS(−)] | BLACK(−)

Stockton — EDUC WHCOL SPAN(−) INC NEWHSE BLK(−) | KIDS HHZ ELDER(−) SPF· | DEN SPF MCF(−) | CRAFT(−) ASIAN

FIGURE 3.3
Factorial Analysis of 39 Variables for Large SMSAs

Scale: 0 5 10 15 20 25 30 35 40 45 50 55 60 65 70 75 80 85 90

Row 1

INCHI HHINC VAL UNITI INCLO(−) RENT MCF EDUC WHCOL*
ODLHSE(−) UNEMP(−) PLM(−) SERV(−) POPDEN(−) LONEHH(−)*

| KIDS(−) HHZ(−) ELDER AGE LONE [GFR(−)] | ANCSIN POL CRAFT BLACK(−) ITAL SPF(−) | ENGL GERM SCAN FR [IRISH] BLACK(−)* | ASIAN [SPAN] | UNIT1 NEWHS [MOVE IN(−)] | LFF (−) | GRP QTR |

Row 2

EDUC WHCOL VAL RENT INCHI SERV(−)
HHINC ENG GERM INCLOW(−) UNEMP(−) SPF(−) [SCAN]

| LONE(−) HHZ MCF UNITI MOVEIN UNITID(−) KIDS POPDEN(−) [CEB] PLM(−) INCHI* HHINC* INCLO(−)* | AGE ELDER ANCSIN ITAL | FRENCH CRAFT BLACK(−) | GFR ASIA(−) | NEWHS OLD HSE(−) | IRISH SPAN (−) | GRP QTR LFF (−) | POL-ISH |

Row 3

VAL WHCOL INCHI RENT HHINC EDUC INCLO(−) UNEMP(−) SERV(−)
PLM(−) ASIAN OLDHSE(−) [GFR] [CEB] [SCAN] MCF*

| HHZ(−) LONE KIDS(−) ELDER AGE UNIT1(−) UNIT1 MCF(−) [GRPQTR] | ANCSIN GERMAN BLACK(−) SPF(−) CRAFT [ITAL] | ENGLISH FRENCH IRISH POPDEN(−) | MOVEIN (−) NEWHSE | SPAN POL-ISH | LFF (−) |

Row 4

VAL WHCOL INCHI RENT EDUC HHINC GERMAN POLISH CRAFT(−)
PLM(−) INLLO(−) ITAL [GFR(−)] [SCAN]

| ANCSIN BLACK(−) ENG IRISH SPF(−) SERVICE(−) UNEMP(−) FRENCH(+) [NEWHSE] GERMAN* CRAFT* INCLOWH* MCF* | LONE(−) HHZ(+) UNIT1 UNIT10(−) MCF KIDS[CEB] | AGE ELDER MOVEIN OLDHSE | LFF(−) POPDEN | SPAN ASIA | GRP QTR |

Row 5

HHINC VAL INCHI UNIT1 RENT WHCOL INCLO(−) ENGLISH MCF GERM [FR] UNEMP(−)
DEN(−) EDUC BLK(−) IRISH SPF(−) SERV SCAN LFM AGE

| HHZ(−) LONE AGE KIDS(−) ELDER UNIT10 | ITAL ANCSING ASIA | POL(−) CRAFT(−) | SPAN(−) MOVEIN (−) | LFF(−) CEB | OLD HSE (−) NEW HSE(−) | GRPQTR GFR(−) |

Row 6

MCF LONE(−) UNIT1 UNIT10(−) HHZ INCLO(−)
KID POPDEN(−) HHINC*

| ANCSING GERM SPAN(−) IRISH FRENCH ENGLISH SCAN BLACK(−) [SPF(−)] SERV(−) CEB(−) [POLISH] | VAL WHCOL INCHI (CRAFT) RENT HHINC MDEDUC(−) UNEMP | ELDER(+) LFF(−) AGE SCAN(−) | PLM GFR | NEW HSE(−) MOVEIN | ITA(−) OLD HSE(−) | GRP QTR (−) |

Row 7

LONE(−) MCF HHZ UNIT1 KIDS UNIT10(−) HHINC
INCLO(−) INCHI POPDEN(−) ELDER(−) SERV(−)
OLDHSE(−) SPAN(−)

| WHCOL EDUC VAL CRAFT(−) RENT UNEMP(−) CEB(−) GFR(−) | ANCSING GERM ENGLISH IRISH | LFF AGE | SPF BLK SCAN(−) | NEWHSE (−) MOVEIN | PLM GRP QTR [FR] | ITAL ASIA | POL-ISH |

Row 8

WHCOL VAL INCHI EDUC RENT HHINC INCLO(−) SERVICE(−) GERMAN
UNEMP(−) POLISH IRISH GFR(−) SCAN ANCSING* BLACK(−)* SPF(−)*

| FRENCH ANCSING CRAFT BLK(−) POPDEN(−) SPF(−) MCF ITAL | HHZ ELDER 65(−) KIDS LONE(−) AGE(−) OLDHSE(−) CEB NEWHSE MCF* | UNIT10 UNIT1 (−) | MOVEIN ENG | LFF (−) | GRPQTR PLM | SPAN ASIAN |

NOTE: Indicator variables are occasionally further shortened.

to SES *and* life cycle differentiation. In Seattle and Boston the life cycle differentiation is caught in this first factor.

How do we link the factors back to the neighborhoods? Returning to Indianapolis as our example, we find that we can rank all neighborhoods along a status dimension according to the SES factor. Several neighborhoods in the SMSA are far above average on income, education, and occupation; necessarily, other neighborhoods are low on all three. In Indianapolis the second dimension, racial composition of the neighborhood, generally indicates the segregation of blacks from whites. In the third dimension we discover that some neighborhoods, independently of status or race, are relatively familial in orientation, while in others families with children are absent. A final factor picks up the clustering of Asians and Hispanics.

The core of the SES factor is composed of occupational status, income, and educational attainment. For neighborhoods, average levels of household income, years of schooling, and proportion of residents employed in white collar jobs tend to go hand-in-hand. Neighborhoods scoring high on the SES factor would belong to the high status social area, even though they need not necessarily be in close physical proximity.

From Figure 3.2 we can observe many variations in the pattern across the SMSAs. These variations are important not only for the fact that they pick up idiosyncracies of the particular metropolitan region, but because enough exceptions begin to challenge common conceptions about the regularity of just three independent dimensions.

In several SMSAs this primary factor picks up a congerie of characteristics.[18] The "white middle class suburbs" factor (higher income, lower density, married-couple families, and lower proportions of blacks) also shows up here for Chicago, Flint, Newark, and St. Louis. In Chicago and St. Louis, this suburban factor is linked to the presence of craft workers as well; in Chicago and Flint it is linked to recently built housing. In these larger and older SMSAs the first factor is not simply status differentiation, but it does identify an important neighborhood type that is different in life cycle and ethnic composition as well as in race. In these large SMSAs we can usually identify an additional factor that identifies the status characteristics of occupation, education, and income.

The disadvantaged position with respect to status experienced by blacks can be observed by the negative loading of that variable on the first SES factor in several SMSAs. Such a finding suggests less a pure segregation effect than a strong intertwining of race (black) and status such that the two cannot be disentangled in the settlement system.

---

[18]As a rule, in factor analysis the first factor is often a "general factor" picking up loadings on a wider range of variables.

Life cycle differentiation is clearly evident in these results. Often the life cycle factor is homing in on middle class child-rearing communities, and we observe the "suburban" factor discussed above. In other cities, and occasionally in these, we observe a distinct life cycle factor, emphasizing household size and the age distribution (for example, Indianapolis, San Antonio), more akin to previous conventional factorial studies. When it does appear distinctly, the life cycle factor is usually second to emerge.

The factorial ecology literature usually identifies ethnic or racial status as the third dimension of differentiation. A distinct factor for the ethnic variables suggests that there is a component of ethnic clustering that is empirically independent and distinct from life cycle and socioeconomic status. In other words, it is within such a large, but segregated, ethnic group that we are most likely to observe a wide range of socioeconomic status and life cycle types across its distinct neighborhoods.

Our analysis included percent Asian and percent Spanish origin in addition to percent black. In almost every city we obtained a factor that can be labeled ethnic status, but the pattern of relationships is not always consistent with what one might predict from previous factorial ecology. Blacks are the largest minority group represented in most of these SMSAs. But the component on which the proportion black is the strongest usually contains several other socioeconomic variables as well, especially in the SMSAs with large black populations. Most commonly the single-parent family measure clusters with the proportion black, indicating that these two characteristics are found in the same neighborhoods. (Stated another way, the single-parent family types are not nearly so evident in nonblack neighborhoods and do not in most regions constitute a separately identifiable dimension of urban differentiation.) As we mentioned before, in several SMSAs the proportion black contributes (negatively) to the SES component. Only in a few metropolitan areas do we find a distinct factor that picks up the proportion black in urban neighborhoods (San Antonio, Sheboygan).

The position of Asians and Hispanics is particularly interesting. The ethnic status hypothesis holds that we should find distinct factors for Asian and Spanish origin populations, especially in the cities with large populations. In fact, we find a much more complex pattern. In most cities both of these groups are found on factors distinct from the black population.[19] A more common pattern is the coincidence of

---

[19]Exceptions to this are the clustering on the same factor of black with Spanish in Boston and New Bedford, of black with Asian in Salt Lake City, and of all three groups in Seattle.

Spanish and Asian percent on the same component, such as in Atlanta, Birmingham, Indianapolis, and New Orleans, cities with modest numbers of both groups. In the Texas and California SMSAs and in Chicago, where large Hispanic populations exist, the Spanish origin variable loads negatively on the SES factor. The Asian population, however, is the only ethnic-racial group to appear positively associated with SES. We cannot conclusively infer that it is the Asian population itself within these neighborhoods that has high SES, only that many higher SES neighborhoods also contain a larger than average fraction of the SMSA Asian population. Only in Chicago is there evidence of a distinct Asian factor upon which no other characteristic loads strongly, suggesting that there exists a number of neighborhoods that are distinguished by relatively large Asian populations, but varied life cycle and status composition.

The Large SMSAs

For the eight largest SMSAs in our group we also performed some more extensive analyses where the number of census tract observations would permit work with variables. Thirty-nine characteristics were analyzed by principal components for the tracts of Chicago, Boston, St. Louis, Atlanta, Newark, San Diego, Seattle, and New Orleans. These 39 variables included the 14 discussed above, as well as additional measures of each of the three generally recognized dimensions, ancestry detail, and a few measures of housing and physical characteristics. This extensive set allows more differentiation to be detected in the results, thus confirming, challenging, or extending the results we presented above. A summary of the results is contained in Figure 3.3, with SMSAs arranged largest to smallest.

In six of the eight SMSAs the SES factor was predominant, with measures of household income, value of home, rent, occupation, and education strongly apparent. As one might expect, we observe also in this factor that quality of housing (indicated by plumbing deficiency) and unemployment are associated with SES. Life cycle is the second distinct factor, with the variables identified in the 14-variable analysis present again. In San Diego and Seattle, the life cycle factor explains the most variance among neighborhood characteristics.[20] In addition to the cluster of characteristics previously identified with life cycle, this

[20]The presence of large military populations in both of these SMSAs may contribute to this finding.

analysis helps fill in some more blanks. Explicit measures of fertility behavior (children ever born and general fertility rate, or GFR) help demonstrate further that certain neighborhoods within the metropolis are distinct child-rearing (childbearing) communities. This differentiation is strong enough to appear statistically. In other cases we see evidence—albeit more modest—of communities composed of persons at the other end of the life cycle: elderly living alone and in higher-density housing.

Ethnic status factors are the most variegated across the several SMSAs. We have included the black, Spanish, and Asian measures, as above, as well as concentrations of the six principal ancestry groups identified by the Census Bureau tabulations: English, French, German, Irish, Italian, and Polish. A measure of the Scandinavian population (Swedish and Norwegian) is included, as is the fraction of the population reporting a single ancestry according to the six-group classification. The black, Asian, and Spanish patterns tend to be roughly similar to that identified for the groups before. We can also observe how some of the groups segregate from one another in this analysis, and what socioeconomic characteristics they (or more properly, their neighborhoods) tend to possess.

In Chicago, one factor draws heavily on single ancestry, Polish and Italian, but this factor also contains craft workers and indicates the absence of blacks. Another factor in Chicago finds the English, German, Scandinavian, and French. So we can observe in this one SMSA some evidence for racial and ethnic segregation as well as occupational and family type correlates. In Boston, the French population is associated with craft occupations, while the Irish and Polish emerge on distinct factors. In St. Louis the pattern emphasizes the German population, whereas in Newark it is the Italian population. By contrast, Atlanta and New Orleans exhibit much less ethnic diversity and differentiation of the groups, with English, Irish, and German clustering together with some measures of family type and status. The identity of the French-heritage population in New Orleans is visible in one component.

These results for the larger metropolises point to the relevance of a few variables in differentiation that are not particularly apparent in the more confined work presented before. Female participation in the labor force often is a distinct factor. Population density (outer suburbs) often loads strongly on a factor—usually family status—although it can appear agglomerated with other variables. The group quarters population, composed of individuals who do not reside in households, but in dormitories, barracks, elderly care facilities, etc., emerges distinctly in the large SMSAs. Finally there is some evidence of independence of mobility characteristics.

From Factorial Analysis to Neighborhood Profile

Taken together our analyses point to many of the same elements of urban differentiation that have been identified in previous research. The sorting out of the SMSA by socioeconomic status, life cycle, and race-ethnicity is clear. But there is more. On the one hand, SES is usually the primary differentiator—most variance explained—for metropolitan America. On the other hand, life cycle stage is the more clearly identified feature of the metropolitan landscape, associated with the most consistent set of variables. The clustering of race, Spanish origin, and ancestry is distinct enough in most metropolitan areas to produce independent factors in our principal components analysis; however, there is considerable variability across the SMSAs in the ways the clustering takes place, reflecting not only the ethnic composition of the region but also the differential SES and life cycle attributes of the various groups. The analysis of the larger samples has helped to point to the presence of other variables that contribute to the metropolitan differentiation—density, mobility, female labor force participation, group quarters—but which are not merely subsets of dimensions already identified.

We can "turn around" these multivariate analyses and use them to help define a profile of neighborhood in the American metropolis. In most instances the value of a particular variable on a given basic characteristic, taken to represent the factor, is more meaningful or comprehensible to a wider audience than the score on a factor.[21] Our approach takes these factorial results and uses them, allowing the most important set of variables to stand for the factor alone. To the extent that they are highly correlated with the factor—the magnitude of factor loading—they will give an adequate representation of the factor without much distortion. We have tried to choose variables that have appeared consistently in analyses across cities, and which are themselves understandable without resort to complex definitions.

A Model Profile

What are the most appropriate items to include in a handbook or profile? This question must ultimately be answered by the specific agency or person who compiles the information and knows the areas

---

[21]Scores on the various dimensions can be calculated for each observation, i.e., tract, and so it would be possible to calculate the SES score for each neighborhood in the city. An advantage of this strategy is that it would maintain the use of the factorial results.

and the needs of the users. We can, however, provide some assistance with regard to what sort of census data may make a good choice. Our multivariate analysis gave us a starting list of "nominees" for each of the categories of interest. From those nominees we have further selected variables that were among the strongest and most consistent predictors of a dimension, and are intuitively meaningful. The idea is to collect a basic set of census variables that taps different dimensions of urban differentiation, while remaining easy enough for the nondemographer to use without resort to reams of census documentation.

To that end the model profile of Table 3.1 was developed. The table contains a random sample of 30 census tracts from the 6,000 in our file.[22] As such it contains probably more variation than one would observe within any one of the twenty-one SMSAs (since within-SMSA variation is compounded with between-SMSA variation), but it lets all tracts within our file have a chance of being represented, and perhaps gives the most concrete picture of the kind of information with which this monograph deals. With the exception of density, the values listed in Table 3.1 are either those actually reported by the census tables or simple percentages or ratios calculated from the appropriate data items.[23] The profile emphasized population characteristics consistent with our orientation.

In the principal components analysis the proportion of workers in white collar occupations was the most consistent predictor of SES across metropolitan areas, followed by income measures, educational attainment, and a housing expenditure measure. What we are observing here, then, is the way in which achievement as measured by one marker (for example, education) translates into occupational status and subsequently income, consistent with most of the status attainment research in sociology. If the loading of the rent and value variables on the SES factor is any indication, we can see that income translates fairly directly into expenditures on housing and has the further advantage of being subject to less reporting bias than income, so that absolute numbers in a published table are less likely to be misleading.

Life cycle differentiation is represented in our profile by variables measuring mean household size, the fraction of the population over 65 years of age, and the proportion of married-couple families. We found in our factorial ecology analyses that household size itself was the strongest element in the life cycle variables: tracts with larger than average household size tend to be places of child-rearing; tracts with small household sizes very often tend to be places where the elderly reside, so that there is a correlation between these two variables.

[22]These were taken as a simple random sample without regard to SMSA.
[23]We supplemented the census data with information on the area of each census tract in order to calculate population density.

TABLE 5.1

Model Profile for a Random Sample of Neighborhoods

Neighborhood	White Collar Workers	Persons Per Household	Persons Aged Over 65	Married-Couple Families (% of households)	Black	Asian	Spanish Origin	Years Ago Head Moved In (Median)	Females in Labor Force	Population Density (per square mile)
1	20.2	2.5	7.9	48.5	1.6	2.1	25.4	2.2	40.1	165
2	32.3	2.6	11.6	58.4	1.6	0.6	17.2	4.5	42.9	2,309
3	48.7	2.2	15.3	47.0	5.9	0.9	1.2	1.8	51.4	2,717
4	50.4	2.4	12.9	50.7	3.1	2.4	1.4	3.5	49.3	2,227
5	64.3	3.3	3.3	84.8	0.2	0.3	1.0	2.5	57.7	453
6	45.9	2.4	13.5	47.5	19.4	0.2	0.5	2.3	42.0	4,274
7	69.4	1.6	14.4	23.0	11.9	0.9	1.0	0.5	61.4	3,641
8	67.8	2.8	4.9	63.0	1.2	0.3	0.7	2.3	59.0	3,436
9	36.4	2.9	11.2	35.2	35.0	2.7	34.3	4.3	32.5	10,782
10	51.7	2.7	9.1	28.2	93.8	0.2	3.1	5.8	46.6	14,716
11	54.5	2.3	15.7	39.3	0.4	2.7	14.5	2.5	55.3	15,892
12	48.7	2.6	12.2	58.3	0.0	0.2	5.0	2.9	60.3	7,254
13	75.1	3.2	10.5	75.4	0.0	0.7	0.8	8.8	52.0	6,862
14	79.7	2.7	17.8	57.8	0.4	1.6	1.1	6.2	51.0	5,347
15	57.1	2.3	10.4	36.1	9.4	1.2	18.7	2.1	59.0	2,471
16	52.6	2.4	12.8	56.6	10.6	3.0	8.4	2.2	57.3	3,708
17	60.8	2.7	11.8	65.0	0.1	0.2	0.8	5.4	50.4	3,263
18	83.9	2.6	15.5	68.4	12.8	1.1	0.8	2.8	49.8	2,700
19	83.1	2.0	2.7	38.8	6.0	0.7	0.6	0.4	80.5	1,860
20	47.6	1.9	19.2	16.1	79.1	0.5	0.7	2.1	58.2	13,564
21	37.6	3.1	8.8	76.9	0.0	0.0	0.2	4.3	44.7	51
22	82.5	2.2	8.3	56.1	1.7	1.5	0.4	2.0	58.3	4,114
23	58.5	1.6	23.4	20.0	17.1	1.7	8.5	1.2	44.9	18,313
24	56.3	2.5	11.9	39.1	50.8	2.6	4.3	2.8	60.8	18,228
25	73.5	2.6	3.9	64.8	2.2	1.5	1.7	1.9	66.8	880
26	58.3	3.1	8.1	83.0	1.6	0.0	0.1	4.8	55.2	130
27	65.2	2.5	7.5	55.8	1.1	4.1	7.4	3.1	59.7	4,410
28	45.4	2.9	10.0	64.8	11.2	7.9	18.9	0.9	46.5	2,475
29	53.9	3.3	6.4	78.6	1.1	3.8	1.3	2.7	53.4	1,668
30	42.6	2.7	13.7	73.1	0.8	4.7	9.4	3.8	48.1	138
MEAN	56.8	2.6	11.2	53.7	12.7	1.7	6.3	3.1	53.2	5,268
S.D.	15.7	0.4	4.7	18.7	23.1	1.7	8.7	1.8	9.2	5,512

No single characteristic suffices to represent ethnic composition. Rather, a profile must use several variables, usually guided by the overall metropolitan composition, as we saw in the descriptive analysis. Since the tracts of our hypothetical mini-city are sampled from all twenty-one metropolitan areas, we have included proportion black, Asian, and Spanish origin.

Finally, the model profile includes a few variables that did not cluster on the three commonly identified dimensions. Length of residence seems to capture an aspect of neighborhood population stability, one that is not merely attributable to age, race, or SES composition. Likewise our analyses occasionally pointed to a separate clustering for the proportion of the female population participating in the labor force. These often seemed to be sections of the city preponderant with single individuals, many of whom were working. We have included population density in the profile.

We now turn to describing some of the thirty neighborhoods in our model profile. While the metropolis is hypothetical, the data in each entry are those for an actual tract in our file, sampled at random from the 6,000. Neighborhoods are identified by sequential number in this profile only.

Neighborhood 1 contains a younger than average population with a large concentration of Spanish origin persons, the second most Hispanic tract in our sample. The neighborhood is far below average in socioeconomic status; in fact, it contains the lowest fraction of white collar workers in the city. Neighborhood 6 also has lower than average SES and typical life cycle indicators, but it contains many blacks and non-Hispanic whites. This neighborhood may be a stable interracial community or a neighborhood in transition, but one cannot tell from 1980 data alone. Neighborhood 10 is virtually all black. It is below average on socioeconomic status, and despite a very high population density the average household size is a bit above average for the sample. These characteristics, coupled with the very low fraction of married-couple family composition, suggest that we have come upon a disadvantaged inner city tract.

Contrast these with the case of Neighborhood 13, a clear example of a middle class, family-oriented community. Three-quarters of the households are married-couple families with 3.2 persons per household, the second highest among the 30 neighborhoods. Notice that still over half of the women in the working ages are in the labor force in this community. The neighborhood is residentially stable: the typical householder has lived there almost 9 years, and it is virtually all white and of above average occupational status.

We can also find evidence of residential communities that are definitely not devoted to child-rearing and family activity. They tend to be populated by young working singles and/or the elderly. Neighborhood 7, for example, has a very low average household size and a small fraction of married-couple families. This is one of three neighborhoods in which the average length of time living in the current residence is only one-half year! They may have experienced fairly rapid population turnover or be sites of very recent residential construction.

In Neighborhood 19, fully four-fifths of eligible women are in the labor force. The occupational status composition of the neighborhood is heavily white collar; there are very few elderly, average household size is small, and there are only modest numbers of nonwhites. The high level of residential mobility, as in the previous case, points most probably again to a community of young working persons. Neighborhood 23 shares the feature of not scoring high on the family variables; by contrast, it is composed of a large number of older persons. The neighborhood is of very high population density and records an average level of occupational status as well as a considerable diversity of racial and ethnic groups.

In Neighborhood 28, too, we observe below average SES, high family status, and a slightly younger population with relatively few working women. Neighborhood 28 also has large fractions of blacks, Asians, and Hispanics, and a high mobility rate. The suggestion here is that we are witnessing an area of second settlement undergoing racial and ethnic transition to several groups, but without firsthand knowledge of the neighborhood or information for other time points we cannot be sure.

The profile in Table 3.1 provides the opportunity to carry out an exercise in the identification of neighborhoods in the metropolis. One can use such information to classify the communities in the city. It should be clear that a small number of carefully selected census variables can tell a great deal about the character of a community. The census is not itself omniscient, however. It cannot provide a substitute for firsthand knowledge of a community and, of course, no single census provides much information about change. This profile should help the local administrator choose some of the most relevant variables for a similar analysis, and it should point out the value of supplementing that firsthand knowledge with the harder (and sometimes surprising) facts contained in the census.

Once again the descriptive statistics for this hypothetical city of 30 neighborhoods illustrate some of the extremes of socioeconomic and demographic variation in this monograph. The ethnic and racial composition variables show very high variation, as does population density. The variability of most of the life cycle characteristics is modest, and the SES measures fall in between. Such facts confirm in a micro-level way the kinds of pattern we observed for the entire file of census tracts in Chapter 2.

A Bivariate Check

The choice of letting key variables stand for entire factors was a compromise we made for the profile. How much of a gamble was it? How correlated are those characteristics? The bivariate (two-variable) simple correlations in Table 3.2 show the degree of interrelationships between key individual variables. The first three columns give the correlation of white collar, household size, and black, taken as key measures of status, life cycle, and ethnicity.

In most cities, the relationship between any two of these characteristics is modest. The overall relationship between white collar and household size is a negative one, while the relationship between proportion black and household size tends to be positive. The magnitude of the correlation between occupational status and proportion black exceeds .5 in six metropolitan areas. In Newark, for instance, racial composition is a good indicator of a neighborhood's socioeconomic status. We are observing in the two-variable case the folding over of race onto the socioeconomic status dimension that was also visible in the factor analysis results.

To give some indication of the correlation between two characteristics that measure the same factor in the principal components analysis, we show the correlation between tract white collar occupation and educational attainment in column 4 of Table 3.2. Here the correlation coefficients are usually over .80. As simple a test as Table 3.2 is, it encourages the use of selected key variables as indicators of underlying characteristics, without resort to some of the more complex and difficult-to-interpret techniques.

Summary

Our objective in this chapter has been to provide an analysis of which characteristics tend to cluster together in 1980, at least from a statistical viewpoint. The factorial ecology provides a kaleidoscopic view of some of the ways that the population is sorted out (voluntarily and involuntarily) into neighborhoods of the nation's metropolises. The common practice in ecological studies of identifying socioeconomic status, life cycle, and ethnic clusters (or dimensions) finds support in our results for 1980, with some exceptions. Race and ethnicity are fre-

TABLE 3.2

Intercorrelation of Key Variables: 21 SMSAs and Total File

SMSA	White Collar and Household Size	White Collar and Black	Black and Household Size	White Collar and Education
Allentown	.06	−.21	−.28	.68
Amarillo	−.17	−.40	.08	.84
Atlanta	−.29	−.57	.08	.90
Bangor	−.19	.07	−.32	.60
Birmingham	−.38	−.56	.19	.90
Boston	−.09	−.33	.07	.82
Chicago	−.39	−.33	.32	.83
Flint	−.35	−.53	.15	.72
Indianapolis	−.24	−.29	.08	.85
Lexington	−.42	−.38	.02	.82
New Bedford	−.01	−.57	.07	.84
New Haven	.17	.01	−.36	.87
New Orleans	−.12	−.51	−.11	.90
Newark	−.29	−.72	.18	.87
St. Louis	−.25	−.40	.29	.77
Salt Lake City	.00	−.42	−.02	.87
San Antonio	−.57	−.17	−.00	.88
San Diego	−.26	−.39	.22	.80
Seattle	.00	−.12	−.11	.84
Sheboygan	−.32	−.38	.21	.69
Stockton	−.24	−.32	.35	.80
POOLED FILE	−.21	−.37	.19	.81
MEAN (21 SMSAs)	−.06	−.36	.06	.81
S.D. (21 SMSAs)	.18	.19	.20	.08

quently found closely tied to status. A few other variables are not easily classified under any of the three rubrics. We also discover a middle class suburban cluster of neighborhood social characteristics distinct from the three standard dimensions in several of the larger older areas.

Many consumers of census data wish to develop a profile of their region and the smaller communities within it. We have tried to show what kinds of census data might be most effective in such an application, and how one might let a few key variables stand for many.

4

NEIGHBORHOOD DIVERSITY
AND SEGREGATION

W E CAN think of neighborhoods as the tiles that make up the mosaic of the settlement system. If we were to shade each tile of the mosaic according to the intensity of a social characteristic represented there, the unevenness of the shading would be an indicator of segregation. For example, we may use proportion of the adult population with college education as the indicator. If every neighborhood (census tract) were equal on this social status measure, then the map of the metropolitan area would be a single shade. If, on the other hand, some neighborhoods had high fractions of college graduates, while other neighborhoods had few, the map would show an uneven pattern. This unevenness or segregation (we use the terms interchangeably) is one face of residential differentiation. The common pejorative interpretation of segregation depends on context. We analyze segregation statistically, relying on an index to summarize the amount of unevenness in each metropolitan area.

Segregation has figured prominently in domestic urban policy for several decades now. Numerous programs, usually promoted and funded by the federal government, have been directed at the reduction of certain kinds of segregation in metropolitan areas. Most notable and controversial have been the efforts to desegregate public school systems and remove racial barriers from urban housing markets, but socioeconomic integration (through certain subsidized housing programs) has also figured as an objective.

Accurate and appropriate quantification of segregation is very important. It suffices not to say only that "big cities are very segregated" or that the "blacks are segregated from whites," but rather, this whole body of research has tried to provide a way of saying "how much" and to provide an interpretation of what a segregation index represents. We wish also to be able to make comparisons. "Are blacks more segregated than Hispanics?" "Are ethnic groups more segregated than social classes?" (A glance ahead to the figures accompanying this chapter will demonstrate our objective.) In Chapter 6 we ask whether levels of segregation have changed over the past few decades.

Does segregation increase with the size of the city? Some theories of urban differentiation mentioned in Chapter 2 would suggest that it should. Or are the older, industrial cities of the Northeast more segregated than the newer, faster-growing cities of the West? If a difference by type of city does exist, then national or state policies that explicitly or implicitly affect urban development by region or size class will perhaps also carry implications for the likelihood of altering segregation patterns.

Segregation and Diversity

A segregation statistic measures only unevenness. Spatial concentration carries with it a two-pronged interpretation. It may reveal processes of discrimination and prejudice. Its reduction may then become the object of policy. Yet segregation may represent (desirable or undesirable) processes of market forces and self-selection. Such geographic separation may even be incorporated into later planning. For example, delivery of services to special population groups (for example, the elderly) can perhaps be expedited if a large fraction of the eligible population is concentrated in a small area.

Concerns over the proper measurement of segregation and diversity—two sides of the same coin[1]—lead us directly into a series of methodological issues, which have resurfaced in recent years in the literature of several fields. The results presented in this chapter reflect

---

[1]While measures of segregation try to account for the degree of unevenness within the metropolis, measures of diversity try explicitly to quantify the degree of internal heterogeneity within the city's neighborhoods. In many applications one can be transformed into the other. See Michael J. White, "Segregation and Diversity Measures in Population Distribution," *Population Index* 52 (Summer 1986):198–221.

our work on the methodological issues. For the most part we will confine ourselves to simpler and more traditional indices. Direct measurement of segregation and diversity provides the best portal through which to view the results of the sorting process. We cannot, of course, watch community structure change continuously, but we can take a reading of the situation as of 1980.

The empirical work on segregation is extensive and the bulk of it has focused on the unevenness of the distribution of racial and ethnic groups in cities. Several classic studies have looked at racial segregation[2] or ethnic segregation[3] in a large number of cities. From this groundwork there have been several additions with more recent data[4] and also with historical data.[5] Some of the earlier studies established the intercity variation in the level of segregation. The greater segregation of blacks compared to foreign-stock white groups has been clearly demonstrated.[6] Results for the Spanish-speaking population are inconclusive and differ appreciably by region. Norman Kantrowitz shows Hispanics in New York City to be as segregated as blacks.[7] Douglas Massey, in a study of ten areas, most in the Southwest, found lower segregation for Hispanics than for blacks.[8]

Less frequently, segregation analysis has been extended to other population characteristics, even though in principle any well-defined population classification can be studied. Some work has been done on differentiation by occupation and industry.[9] The farther apart two groups are on the occupational status ladder, the more dissimilar is their distribution across census tracts. Other indicators of social status, such as rent level, income, or educational attainment, tend to show

[2]Karl E. Taeuber and Alma F. Taeuber, *Negroes in Cities* (Chicago: Aldine, 1965).

[3]Otis D. Duncan and Stanley Lieberson, "Ethnic Segregation and Assimilation," *American Journal of Sociology* 64 (1959):364–374.

[4]Annemette Sørenson, Karl E. Taeuber, and Leslie J. Hollingsworth, Jr., "Indexes of Racial Residential Segregation for 109 Cities in the United States: 1950 to 1970," *Sociological Focus* 8 (April 1975):125–142; and T. L. van Valey, W. C. Roof, and J. E. Wilcox, "Trends in Residential Segregation: 1960–1970," *American Journal of Sociology* 82 (January 1977): 826–844.

[5]Stephanie Greenberg, "Industrial Location and Ethnic Residential Patterns in an Industrializing City: Philadelphia, 1880," in Theodore Hershberg, ed., *Phildelphia* (New York: Oxford University Press, 1981).

[6]Stanley Lieberson, *A Piece of the Pie* (Berkeley: University of California Press, 1980).

[7]Norman Kantrowitz, *Ethnic and Racial Segregation in the New York Metropolis* (New York: Praeger, 1973).

[8]Douglas Massey, "Effects of Socioeconomic Factors on the Residential Segregation of Black and Spanish Americans in U.S. Urbanized Areas," *American Sociological Review* 44 (December 1979):1015–1022.

[9]Otis D. Duncan and Beverly Duncan, "Residential Distribution and Occupational Stratification," *American Journal of Sociology* 60 (1955):493–503.

similar patterns. Interest in the aging of the population has prompted some to look at segregation of the elderly.[10] Usually, these results show that age segregation, while certainly present and of importance for policy, is not as pervasive as race-ethnic or socioeconomic segregation.

Finally, comparisons can be made over time when the tabulations are quantified into the indices. Indeed, we now have for a large number of cities a time series of racial segregation measures from 1950–1970 calculated on the block basis.[11] The over-time analyses tend to show that levels of segregation are stable or decline modestly in most cities. Results by T. L. van Valey, W. C. Roof, and J. E. Wilcox[12] based on 1960–1970 tract data for 237 SMSAs confirm a decline but argue that it is very modest indeed, partly due to the addition of new SMSAs with lower scores. An interesting analysis of Philadelphia has reconstructed this information for some points in the nineteenth and twentieth centuries.[13] Taken together, much of this work of comparing groups and time challenges some assumed models of the spatial assimilation hypothesis, particularly as the interpretation that the experience of blacks is that of a "newer" immigrant group proceeding through the same series of steps. Also casting doubt on the assimilation hypothesis, Frances Kobrin and Calvin Goldscheider conclude that while the nature of ethnicity has changed over time, ethnic factors still continue to assert themselves in residential mobility as well as residential concentration.[14] Douglas Massey and Brendan Mullan, in a direct test of the spatial assimilation hypothesis, using tract data for several SMSAs, find that compared to that of Hispanics, black gains in socioeconomic status do not translate as well into physical distance from the ghetto.[15]

Such results, and further questions, produced by this line of research often bear directly on policy issues. Indeed, the great concern over discrimination in housing and employment demands accurate information about the degree of segregation, no matter what the causal mechanism offered or disputed. To evaluate a policy explicitly designed to reduce segregation by class, race, or other tract, we must be able to

[10]Donald O. Cowgill, "Residential Segregation by Age in American Metropolitan Areas," *Journal of Gerontology* 33 (1978):446–453; Joseph T. Tierney, "A Comparative Examination of the Residential Segregation of Persons 65–74 and Persons 75 + in 18 United States Metropolitan Areas for 1970 and 1980." *Journal of Gerontology* 42 (1987):101–106.

[11]Sørenson, Taeuber, and Hollingsworth, "Indexes of Racial Residential Segregation for 109 Cities in the United States: 1950 to 1970."

[12]van Valey, Roof, and Wilcox, "Trends in Residential Segregation: 1960–1970."

[13]Theodore Hershberg, ed., *Philadelphia* (New York: Oxford University Press, 1981).

[14]Frances Kobrin and Calvin Goldscheider, *The Ethnic Factor in Family Structure and Mobility* (Cambridge, Mass.: Ballinger, 1978), p. 226.

[15]Douglas S. Massey and Brendan P. Mullan, "Processes of Hispanic and Black Spatial Assimilation," *American Journal of Sociology* 89 (1984):836–873.

measure the state of the world before, during, and after any policy inter-vention. The recent waves of newer immigrants to America's cities re-vive again the issues of spatial and temporal assimilation. In this chapter we will be able to look directly at the degree of segregation for several ethnic groups as of 1980. We hope to determine which dimen-sions of the urban sociospatial structure are the most sorted out around the metropolis. Such results can then be viewed in tandem with the multivariate work (factorial ecology) contained within Chapter 3.

Segregation in 1980

What distinguishes our approach to segregation particularly is the simultaneous treatment of a broad range of socioeconomic and housing characteristics, in addition to race and ethnicity. Much of our data presentation will be restricted to the index of dissimilarity, in keeping with tradition in the literature. We group the characteristics according to the conventional dimensions of urban differentiation we explored in Chapter 3. For suitable variables we present tables measuring segrega-tion based on newer methods, looking across several classes of vari-ables. For each of the individual characteristics we show the correlation of the level of segregation with metropolitan area population size and growth rate.

The index of dissimilarity is the traditional favorite in the measure-ment of segregation specifically and sociospatial differentiation gen-erally. It is easy to calculate and interpret, and it has a long history of use in urban demographic studies, particularly after it emerged favor-ably from an early methodological review.[16] More recent publications have begun to question the supremacy of the dissimilarity index.

The index of dissimilarity is defined as

$$D = \frac{1}{2} \sum_{i=1}^{K} \left| \frac{P_{1i}}{P_1} - \frac{P_{2i}}{P_2} \right|$$

where P_{1i} equals the population of group 1 in the *ith* tract; $P_1=$ the pop-ulation of group 1 in the city; and the summation is taken over the K tracts in the city. The index of dissimilarity, D, describes the maximum vertical distance from the equality diagonal to the segregation curve and

---

[16]Otis D. Duncan and Beverly Duncan, "A Methodological Analysis of Segregation Indexes," *American Sociological Review* 20 (1955):210–217.

measures the proportion of the population of one group that would have to be redistributed to achieve an equal distribution among all neighborhoods.

The second measure we use derives from information theory and has been treated most extensively by Henri Theil.[17] The measure, which has several attractive properties, has received limited application in the urban sociological literature. The index is formulated as follows. For each neighborhood (tract), i, calculate the average entropy as:

$$H_i = \sum_{\ell=1}^{L} -P_{i\ell} \log P_{i\ell}$$

where ℓ indexes summation over groups present in the tract. For the SMSA or city, taken as a whole, we can also calculate the entropy:

$$H_c = \sum_{\ell=1}^{L} -P_\ell \log P_\ell$$

A measure of segregation is then the average reduction in entropy (increase in information) available from "knowing" the neighborhood information:

$$H = \frac{H_c - \left(\sum_{i=1}^{I} \frac{N_i}{N} H_i \right)}{H_c}$$

The index H takes on a value of 0 when there is no segregation, that is, when neighborhoods have the same composition as the city and add no explanatory power, to a value of 1 for complete segregation, or maximal neighborhood level information. This index also has a number of desirable properties, including the ability to measure segregation for characteristics with more than two categories.

We express both D and H in percentage terms in the tables. Thus, they vary from zero to 100.

Socioeconomic Status

The results of Chapter 3 underscored the important role that socioeconomic status plays in metropolitan differentation. Table 4.1 presents the incidence of segregation as measured by the index of dis-

[17]Henri Theil, *Statistical Decomposition Analysis* (Amsterdam: North-Holland, 1972).

TABLE 4.1

Dissimilarity for Socioeconomic Status and Labor Force Status: 21 SMSAs

Metropolitan Area	Education College+	Income $30,000+	Occupation Prof-Manage	Occupation Operative	Home Value $50,000+	Home Value < $25,000	Rent $200+	Rent < $40	Females in Labor Force	Unemployment
Allentown	28	25	22	22	46	47	46	40	10	16
Amarillo	36	36	28	25	62	60	51	44	11	26
Atlanta	38	34	25	29	55	56	61	63	16	24
Bangor	18	22	11	15	21	21	21	23	10	12
Birmingham	44	34	29	28	55	47	63	62	15	25
Boston	35	33	25	23	45	44	42	38	11	18
Chicago	38	31	27	27	58	63	54	54	14	28
Flint	30	24	23	18	48	47	38	34	9	19
Indianapolis	36	31	26	23	56	58	59	56	13	24
Lexington	33	29	23	25	43	58	48	50	15	23
New Bedford	32	27	24	27	44	25	56	36	8	14
New Haven	33	33	25	21	44	48	36	37	10	20
New Orleans	35	33	26	25	45	49	58	53	13	25
Newark	37	38	28	32	55	65	46	52	12	26
St. Louis	36	30	25	24	53	51	60	59	12	24
Salt Lake City	30	30	22	21	47	50	38	37	10	16
San Antonio	43	38	31	29	68	61	62	65	17	20
San Diego	30	34	21	21	45	50	41	46	14	16
Seattle	28	26	19	18	37	41	36	40	11	15
Sheboygan	17	15	15	10	27	27	22	18	6	17
Stockton	29	30	21	20	51	53	46	52	15	24
MEAN	32.6	30.1	23.6	23.1	47.8	48.5	46.8	45.7	12.0	20.5
S.D.	6.7	5.7	4.6	5.1	10.9	12.0	12.3	12.7	2.8	4.7
Correlation with:										
SMSA Pop. 1980	.38*	.27	.31	.36	.33	.41*	.27	.06	.28	.43*
SMSA Pop. Change 1970–1980	.06	.22	.00	.05	.15	.21	.11	.19	.45*	−.06

*Significant at α = .05.

similarity, *D*, for several socioeconomic status characteristics for each of the twenty-one metropolitan areas.[18] The index indicates that in most metropolitan areas about one-third of the college educated population of column 1 would have to move in order to be evenly distributed. The cities leading the list are Birmingham and San Antonio, where *D* is over 40 percent.

Status as measured by education is fairly closely approximated by that of income. Households reporting over $30,000 income constitute about 20 percent nationally. The average level of segregation for this group, column 2, is nearly 50 on *D*. SMSAs with large values for education tend also to have large values for income. In fact, the correlation of (median tract) education and income across the twenty-one SMSAs characteristics is .65. We tested for variation in the levels of segregation across regions (with an eta^2 statistic not shown) and with population size and growth rate (correlation coefficients). Even in our twenty-one SMSAs we observe an appreciable relationship between the levels of education and income segregation and SMSA size. The results are consistent with the claim that larger regions are more residentially differentiated than smaller areas. There are some regional differences as well, with the South being, on average, more segregated with regard to these status characteristics.

Columns 3 and 4 of Table 4.1 show occupational dissimilarity, with the top of the status hierarchy represented by professional and managerial occupations, and the other end of the spectrum represented by operatives. Each group is taken from all others. For example, the value of 34 for professional-managerial in Atlanta represents the degree of segregation from all other workers, the value of 25 for operatives measures their separation from all other occupational classifications. The level of segregation observed for professional-managerial workers very closely approximates that for college education in almost every SMSA. So here we are observing in the neighborhood pattern the link between higher education and higher status occupational attainment. Operative workers exhibit, on average, a little less unevenness than professionals and managers. From the correlation coefficients we see that larger cities tend to be more segregated.

How does this pattern of segregation by socioeconomic status hold up when we examine the segregation in more detail? Several earlier studies have found, not surprisingly, that workers at both ends of the spectrum were the most physically separate, mirroring in space the kind of social distance one observes in mobility across generations, or

[18]A cautionary note is in order regarding segregation statistics for continuous characteristics such as socioeconomic status. The choice of categories for the index of dissimilarity is arbitrary, and so can influence the computed value of the index.

across patterns of personal association. Due to changes in the coding of occupation for the 1980 census, we cannot carry out an exactly comparable analysis. We do, however, present Table 4.2, "Pairwise Occupational Dissimilarity," for six broad occupational groups. This is the value of D for each group compared to every other group, taken separately. The table contains values of D averaged over the twenty-one SMSAs. The most segregated occupational group is farm workers. This represents not only the physical separation of farms in the more rural territory of metropolitan areas, but also the concentration of farm workers (many of whom are migratory) into defined (poorer) neighborhoods in the more built-up sections of the metropolis. The two distinctly white collar groups (professional-managerial and support) exhibit very little segregation from one another. We also obtain a low value of D for the separation of two groups of blue collar workers (craft and operative), even though the former tend to have higher incomes. Segregation of white collar from blue collar workers is appreciable, particularly for those classed as professionals and managers. In order to make for a constant ratio between the professional-managerial group and operatives in every neighborhood, 36 percent of one group would have to change residence. Service workers, the gray collar portion of the labor force, fall in an intermediate range, and are not highly segregated from any of the other nonfarm groups except professionals.

For most households status attainment and income translate fairly directly (even proportionately) into housing purchases. Therefore we should anticipate that expenditure on housing, as indicated by rental level and value of home, should exhibit levels of segregation equivalent to that of other status measures. Nearly half the homes valued at over $50,000 or apartments renting for over $200 monthly would have to be "moved" in order for every neighborhood in a typical SMSA to have the same proportion. Results are parallel for the low end of the scale. This

TABLE 4.2

Pairwise Occupational Dissimilarity: 21 SMSAs

	Professional and Managerial	Support	Service	Farm	Craft	Operativ
Professional and Managerial	—	16	28	47	29	36
Support	—	—	18	44	18	25
Sevice	—	—	—	43	19	17
Farm	—	—	—	—	41	43
Craft	—	—	—	—	—	16
Operative	—	—	—	—	—	—

level of segregation is considerably higher than that for education and income and probably reflects in part the additional influence of family size and life cycle segregation on housing purchases.

In Table 4.1 we also look at segregation of two characteristics indicative of participation in the labor force. As of 1980, 44.7 percent of all women 16 years of age and over were participating in the labor force nationally, up from 30.5 percent in 1970. Values of D for female labor force participation range between about 10 and 15 for most cities, indicating that women who work are only very modestly segregated within metropolitan areas. The contention that there exist many neighborhoods devoted exclusively to traditional lifestyles (with women's time devoted to child-rearing and not wage labor) has little support from this segregation analysis. The unemployed, on the other hand, are segregated to a degree only slightly less than occupational groups, reflecting the differential incidence of job loss by socioeconomic status. In many cities, the incidence of unemployment is particularly concentrated. In Amarillo, Birmingham, Chicago, and Newark the level of segregation, D, reaches at least 25 percent.

Life Cycle

In Table 4.3 values of D for life cycle characteristics are presented. Despite the prominence of the life cycle in the factorial analysis of metropolitan structure, segregation levels for this group of characteristics are low. As expected, at the very bottom of the scale is segregation by sex, which has a value of only 3 or 4 for D in most cities; the influence of the military population on the demographic composition of San Diego is evident, where the only value of D over 4 occurs. Segregation of the population by age, particularly the separation of the elderly, has generated concern in some quarters. Segregation of children falls most often between 10 and 15 on D. Segregation of the elderly is somewhat higher. About one out of four persons living alone (many of whom are over 65) would have to change residence for segregation to disappear. Metropolitan areas in the South and West, which also show the greatest population growth during the 1970s, exhibit higher levels of segregation. The effect is particularly pronounced with respect to the elderly, where perhaps newly arrived migrants have taken up residence in distinct communities. Segregation of the elderly in the four SMSAs of the West is over 10 points higher than in the six SMSAs of the Northeast.

Nonfamily households (which include persons living alone as well as households with unrelated individuals) are slightly less segregated. The formerly married have on average a 19 percent level of segregation,

TABLE 4.3

Dissimilarity for Life Cycle and Household Status: 21 SMSAs

Metropolitan Area	Sex	Age <18	Age 65+	Household Type One Person	Nonfamily	Children in Single-Parent Households	Marital Status Sep-Wid-Div	Household Size 5+	Group Quarters
Allentown	3	10	18	19	17	25	15	14	76
Amarillo	3	14	28	26	25	23	23	24	74
Atlanta	4	13	26	30	29	37	21	21	72
Bangor	3	15	16	19	19	20	17	13	81
Birmingham	4	11	18	23	23	35	20	19	69
Boston	4	15	18	25	24	31	15	19	63
Chicago	4	16	26	27	20	40	19	23	69
Flint	3	9	21	20	17	33	19	16	73
Indianapolis	3	11	24	24	20	33	21	18	67
Lexington	4	14	22	22	25	28	18	17	73
New Bedford	3	8	14	17	13	28	15	11	57
New Haven	4	13	20	23	22	39	18	18	68
New Orleans	4	16	29	28	25	39	21	21	78
Newark	3	13	20	24	17	44	20	17	67
St. Louis	4	12	24	24	19	38	22	18	62
Salt Lake City	3	17	34	35	29	24	23	28	69
San Antonio	4	14	30	26	23	22	19	25	76
San Diego	6	19	30	30	24	22	19	30	76
Seattle	3	17	28	28	21	23	19	23	68
Sheboygan	3	7	13	19	17	21	17	15	58
Stockton	4	12	23	23	19	23	17	21	68
MEAN	3.6	13.1	22.9	24.3	21.4	29.9	19.0	19.6	69.8
S.D.	.7	3.0	5.7	4.3	4.1	7.5	2.4	4.8	6.2
Correlation with:									
SMSA Pop. 1980	.24	.38	.28	.37	.06	.46*	.09	.29	.10
SMSA Pop. Change 1970–1980	.35	.49	.67*	.62*	.66*	−.47*	.35	.72*	.45*

*Significant at α + .05.

and there is only a very small amount of variance across SMSAs for this characteristic. Amarillo and Salt Lake City show the highest levels of segregation. The usual SMSA size relationship does not hold here—for example, Boston is at the low end of the distribution—but significant regional differences in the degree of segregation exist, probably linked to the metropolitan age composition as explored above.

What is striking in this table is the degree of segregation of children who reside in single-parent families compared to other family types, averaging about 30 percent. The relationship between SMSA size and level of segregation $(R = .46)$ is one of the strongest we find among the socioeconomic characteristics, while the relationship between area growth rate and segregation works in the other direction. This means that in the large, demographically stagnant metropolitan areas, children are even more sorted out by household type; indeed, in the Newark SMSA 44 percent of children in single-parent homes would have to move for this type of segregation to disappear. Residence in a single-parent family is a much more common occurrence for black children than for others, and so metropolitan areas with large fractions of blacks also exhibit higher levels of segregation along this family dimension, reflecting racial segregation itself. Since childhood family type is so important in policy discussions, we return to the segregation of household type again below, examining its interrelation with poverty status and with race. Many single-parent families are poverty-stricken as well, and in a section below we explore this aspect in more detail.

We can think of the group quarters population as that which is purposefully segregated, by the group itself or by society. People living in group quarters include the military population in barracks, college students in dormitories, the prison population, and other institutionalized persons. This population classification shows the highest recorded value of D. This is not surprising, but these values of D near 70 give us a standard by which to compare other social and economic characteristics.

Ethnicity

Segregation by race and nationality in the metropolis attracts the most attention from scholars and policymakers. Values of the index of dissimilarity have been calculated repeatedly for cities and metropolitan areas since 1940. In Table 4.4 we can observe comparative levels of segregation for race, Spanish origin, and nativity, all of which were ascertained separately in the 1980 census. Racial segregation continues to divide the metropolis sharply. Segregation of the black population in the 21 SMSAs is no lower than 40 in Bangor (under 1 percent black citywide), and reaches 86 in the Chicago SMSA, which has traditionally

TABLE 4.4

Dissimilarity for Race, Spanish Origin, and Nativity: 21 SMSAs

Metropolitan Area	Race				Spanish Origin (5)	Race of Spanish* (6)	Foreign Born (7)
	Black (1)	American Indian (2)	Asian (3)	Other (4)			
Allentown	58	41	35	60	55	44	24
Amarillo	72	26	44	42	40	77	37
Atlanta	77	31	38	34	22	78	32
Bangor	40	52	37	28	21	98	17
Birmingham	72	37	44	38	20	74	38
Boston	76	38	47	60	52	47	26
Chicago	86	42	49	64	62	71	40
Flint	85	27	40	31	26	72	24
Indianapolis	79	33	36	32	22	74	30
Lexington	59	37	44	36	19	68	35
New Bedford	56	44	29	50	38	44	38
New Haven	68	38	38	58	53	43	18
New Orleans	70	39	53	34	27	68	35
Newark	79	43	31	60	59	46	28
St. Louis	82	29	38	29	20	81	31
Salt Lake City	54	32	23	37	33	57	25
San Antonio	59	24	39	32	56	57	25
San Diego	59	27	40	38	37	47	27
Seattle	66	27	37	25	16	58	22
Sheboygan	69	34	24	38	32	92	22
Stockton	56	18	37	34	33	53	27
MEAN	67.6	34.2	38.2	41.0	35.3	64.3	28.6
S.D.	11.9	8.0	7.5	12.3	15.1	16.3	6.7
Correlation with:							
SMSA Pop. 1980	.54†	.12	.39†	.40†	-.39†	-.04	.35
SMSA Pop. Change 1970–1980	-.41†	-.50†	-.07	-.40†	-.24	-.06	.10

*Black of Spanish origin versus nonblack of Spanish origin.
†Significant at α = .05.

recorded one of the highest levels of segregation in the nation. Taking the mean value as indicative of a typical value, over two-thirds of metropolitan blacks (or nonblacks) would have to change residence in order for the black–nonblack ratio to be equal in every neighborhood. The larger and slower growing metropolises exhibit significantly greater black segregation. Regional differences are statistically significant, too. In the five North Central SMSAs, D averages 80, whereas in the West it is under 60.

Three other racial groups, American Indians, Asians, and "others," are also examined. The remaining excluded group is that of whites. The Indian and Asian populations, which vary greatly across the nation, exhibit only about half the level of segregation of blacks. The level of Indian segregation is highest in Bangor, where the Native American population is substantial, and one census tract is coterminous with a reservation. Most SMSAs have a value of D for the Asian population of between 35 and 45. The cities of the West Coast, which have substantial Asian populations, do not have especially high levels of segregation; rather, the largest values of D are found in Chicago, New Orleans, and Boston. The "other races" population is difficult to characterize, and thus its value of D is correspondingly difficult to interpret. Its variation across SMSAs is large, suggesting that we are picking up inconsistencies of classification as well as the "true" level of segregation of individuals who did not fall into the white, black, Indian, or Asian categories. Since the census was self-enumerated, individuals could choose their racial identity as they wished, and many persons, particularly those of Spanish heritage, checked "other" on this census item. The Census Bureau has refrained from reclassifying many of these individuals.[19]

The 1980 census asked each person for his or her Spanish origin. Column 5 of Table 4.4 records the segregation of those who reported themselves as being of Spanish origin from those not of Spanish origin. Hispanics are much less segregated than blacks according to D, but there is fairly wide dispersion among the SMSAs. There seems to be little evidence that cities with large Hispanic populations show especially high or low levels of segregation. Column 6 reports the index of dissimilarity for racial segregation within the Hispanic population. That is, focusing only on those who identify themselves as Hispanics, we examine the distribution of those who classify themselves as black versus those who are nonblacks, a calculation made possible by a cross-tabulation of race and Spanish origin. Even within the population that

---

[19]To the extent that such individuals are randomly distributed within their own "true" racial group, such behavior would tend to depress the calculated value of D for "others" and the remaining four groups.

identifies itself as Hispanic, blacks are highly segregated from non-blacks. The value of D is nearly as large as that for the black population alone. There seems to be little identifiable pattern in the high and low values, although regional differences can be observed.[20] As the racial composition of the Spanish origin population varies (often by region of the country), the level of Hispanic segregation overall can be expected to vary accordingly.

A final calculation of Table 4.4 is that for nativity. We report the value of D for the foreign-born versus native-born populations, picking up in part the geographical selection of streams of immigration within these metropolitan areas. The foreign born are less segregated than any other group in the table. In Chicago, long known as a gateway city in the heartland, 40 percent of the foreign born would have to relocate to eliminate unevenness, but in eight SMSAs D is 25 or under.

A Single "Ethnicity"

Even though the vernacular notion of ethnicity holds that each person belongs to only one group, we have seen that the 1980 census uses several independent classifications, including race, Spanish origin, and ancestry.

In order to gather all of the population under a single wing of ethnicity, we have made some simple assumptions in order to assign each person to one ethnicity group only.[21] Table 4.5 contains the average values of pairwise segregation for the 21 metropolitan areas for this composite ethnicity variable. The variable has 13 categories and classifies every member of the census tract population into one. (Following this section we return to using the component variables separately).

Both black populations are highly segregated. Hispanic blacks ap-

[20]The differences we observe are consistent with the segregation of the Puerto Rican origin population (more likely to be found in the Northeast and to identify as black) from the Mexican origin population (more likely to be found in the West and to identify as white).

[21]To develop this variable we worked from race, Spanish origin, and ancestry. The Hispanic population was separated into its white and black components. The non-Hispanic white population was classified by ancestry into English, French, German, Irish, Italian, Polish, and other. This left the non-Hispanic black population as a distinct category, as also the Asian and American Indian populations. Those not otherwise classified were placed in the "remainder." The multiple ancestry population was distributed among the seven non-Hispanic white categories according to the relative distribution in the multiple ancestry classification. This created an undimensional "ethnicity" variable with 13 categories, which summed to 100 percent of the population. Overall the results in this table parallel those obtained in pairwise fashion for the three distinct variables that compose it.

TABLE 4.5
Composite Ethnic Segregation: 21 SMSA Average

	English	French	German	Irish	Italian	Polish	Other White (White)	Black (NH)	Asian	Indian	Spanish (W)	Spanish (B)	Remainder
English	—	16	14	12	26	28	19	70	40	41	37	78	46
French		—	16	15	25	27	22	70	39	40	35	78	45
German			—	13	24	26	19	70	38	41	36	79	45
Irish				—	23	26	17	69	38	39	34	78	44
Italian					—	29	29	71	39	46	39	79	47
Polish						—	30	72	41	47	41	80	49
Other White (NH)							—	71	42	41	36	80	47
Black (NH)								—	65	61	64	36	56
Asian									—	49	43	74	46
Indian										—	40	69	41
Spanish (W)											—	69	26
Spanish (B)												—	61
Remainder													—

NOTES: (NH) = non-Hispanic
(W) = white
(B) = black

97

pear to be doubly disadvantaged with regard to segregation. Values of D for this group approach 80, with most of the white groups several points higher than non-Hispanic blacks. Hispanic blacks are more likely to share a neighborhood with non-Hispanic blacks ($D = 36$) than they are with Hispanic whites ($D = 69$), which would suggest that race supersedes language in defining contemporary residential neighborhoods.

In contrast to blacks, the segregation of Indians and Asians is modest. The level of dissimilarity hovers around 40 for most comparisons. Interestingly, the table reveals no particular residential affinity or distance between these two racial groups and the several white ancestry and Hispanic groups.

Among the white ancestry groups themselves we find that the English, German, and Irish are at the low end of the scale, with the French slightly higher. These four are usually classified among the "old" immigrant groups, so we might expect them to be more spatially assimilated.[22] Americans of Italian and Polish ancestry show more segregation (D above 25) from each other group. Once we remove the overriding effect of race, white Hispanics exhibit a pattern of settlement consistent with the spatial assimilation hypothesis. These newest migrants to the American metropolis are less segregated than the racial groups, but several points more segregated than the six European ancestry groups.

Housing, Density, and Mobility

The conventional model of urban growth has the city expanding outward over time from the central business district. If such a model is applicable, we should observe considerable segregation of the housing stock by age, and also by structure density, as the peripheral neighborhoods become built up with low-density units. The impact of urban renewal and the more recent pattern of multi-unit construction in suburban locations might contradict this basic model. In Table 4.6 we can see that the conventional characterization is supported, at least in terms of patterns of segregation. The first measure of density looks at the unevenness in the distribution of all units that are at single addresses of 10 or more units. Reflecting both the age of neighborhoods and the effect of the prevailing rent density gradient, such housing types are fairly heavily clustered. In most cities about half of the units would need to be relocated to remove segregation.

Values of D of other levels of structure density are much lower.

[22]Lieberson's typology includes predominantly northwest European origins in the "old" group, with south central and eastern European origins in the "new" group. See Stanley Lieberson, *A Piece of the Pie*, p. 28.

TABLE 4.6

Dissimilarity for Housing, Density, and Mobility: 21 SMSAs

Metropolitan Area	Dwelling Unit Density 10+ Units at Address	Dwelling Unit Density 1 Unit at Address	House Built 1975–1980	Vacancy	Home Ownership	Movers 1975–1980	Moved Pre–1950
Allentown	53	38	41	23	31	15	25
Amarillo	54	38	52	26	32	21	50
Atlanta	50	44	47	24	43	20	43
Bangor	40	39	41	16	38	20	22
Birmingham	58	43	43	19	39	20	31
Boston	51	50	43	35	45	20	24
Chicago	56	56	60	28	47	23	41
Flint	58	40	46	22	34	14	27
Indianapolis	57	43	50	29	38	18	38
Lexington	50	38	47	21	28	22	41
New Bedford	63	57	51	26	46	14	17
New Haven	50	51	45	28	48	20	25
New Orleans	57	38	57	27	45	26	45
Newark	56	60	49	34	52	18	28
St. Louis	56	48	55	33	37	19	36
Salt Lake City	55	43	46	22	41	21	40
San Antonio	54	39	57	24	32	30	52
San Diego	45	40	42	27	43	24	50
Seattle	49	43	44	25	38	19	37
Sheboygan	47	27	26	20	27	10	14
Stockton	51	36	54	22	27	26	39
MEAN	52.8	43.3	47.4	25.3	38.6	20.0	34.5
S.D.	5.2	7.9	7.5	4.9	7.4	4.5	10.9
Correlation with:							
SMSA Pop. 1980	.13	.51*	.40*	.49*	.46*	.23	.24
SMSA Pop. Change 1970–1980	−.22	−.42*	.04	−.38*	−.23	.49*	.68*

*Significant at α = .05.

Single family homes and detached units, in the next column, have levels of D across the cities in the vicinity of 40 percent. Even though it seems as if we are measuring two sides of the same coin when we look at the unevenness of low-density and high-density dwellings, we see that there is a more consistent relationship between single family construction and city size and growth rate. Single family home construction is more segregated in the older industrial SMSAs, such as Boston, Chicago, New Bedford, New Haven, and Newark.

As the metropolis grows and ages, housing units are added and subtracted from the stock. How separated are the newly built units from the old? The value of D for recent (1975–1980) home construction averages just under 50 percent across the SMSAs here, comparable to the levels obtained for housing unit density. This is as we expect, since over the history of urban growth new housing tends to be built at lower density than housing already in existence. In Chicago, the metropolis that provided the laboratory for many of these ecological theories, we observe the greatest level of unevenness of the age of the housing stock. Similar patterns with regard to the SMSAs hold for unevenness in the neighborhood distribution of home ownership and housing vacancy (columns 4 and 5).

Does home ownership physically segregate owners from renters in the metropolis? Yes, but it is not as uneven as the physical characteristics of the housing stock. The dissimilarity hovers around 40 percent for most SMSAs. We can see from the additional statistics that neither the relationship with region nor growth rate is statistically significant. Unlike other variables we have examined, the fast-growing housing markets of the South and West have not resulted in appreciably more segregation by tenure. On the other hand, the older dense areas (Chicago, Boston, Newark, New Orleans) have many neighborhoods substantially given over to either rental or owned units.

Population mobility plays an important behind-the-scenes role in the processes of change in urban residential structure. Over the five-year period of 1975–1980, nearly half of all Americans changed residence. Such frequent turnover, combined with relatively free markets in housing and jobs, can quickly change the demographic complexion of the nation and of the neighborhoods within major urban areas.[23] Is the mobile population evenly distributed throughout the metropolis? Our results for the twenty-one SMSAs indicate that the mobile population is only modestly segregated. About one in five would have to change residence (again!) to achieve an even distribution, and this value

[23]Clark describes how families tend to move within the same SES zones. Although whites are willing to tolerate some blacks in their neighborhood, white mobility patterns still tend to be away from black concentrations. W. A. V. Clark, "Residential Mobility and Neighborhood Change," *Urban Geography* 1 (April–June 1980):95–117.

is fairly constant across SMSAs. Looking more closely at the numbers, though, one can discern how patterns of regional migration in the United States become manifest at the level of the neighborhood. Cities of the South and West (New Orleans, San Antonio, San Diego), which have been receiving many new residents and have comparatively active housing markets, show levels of segregation several points higher than the cities of the North. This contrasts particularly with the smaller, older, northern SMSAs, which have been experiencing net outmigration, such as Allentown and Flint. This leads us to infer that it is likely that the interregional migrants are living in newly built sections of the cities of the South and West and are hence segregated. Since we cannot measure outmigration for small areas in the census, it is impossible to tell if the movement out of some of these northern cities has been selective by neighborhood.

We can look at mobility in a second way, through a question on how recently the household moved into the present housing unit. The final column of Table 4.6 shows that the level of unevenness for the householders who have been in their homes for a very long time (since before 1950) is higher than that for the general mobility question. In fact, the value of D for the long-time residents approaches 50 percent in several SMSAs. Differences according to metropolitan growth rate are particularly pronounced. While the level of segregation for the mobile population is modest, segregation among those who have remained immobile (through personal choice or structural circumstances) is relatively high, and that is generally much higher in the so-called Sunbelt cities, where there are many new spatially distinct residential communities in which persons have recently arrived.

In sum, it is in the older metropolitan areas that we find evidence most consistent with a picture of the distinct separation of the housing stock into an old, dense core of apartment dwellings and a periphery of single family owned homes. While younger cities clearly show differentiation of the housing stock, it is not as sharp as in the older cities; however, their recent growth tends to manifest itself in more distinct patterns of neighborhoods composed alternatively of older and newer residents.

A Closer Look at Poverty and Family Type

Of special concern to many social scientists and policymakers is the interrelationship of race (ethnicity) and social class. A group of especially disadvantaged minority group members characterized by single parenthood, poverty, unemployment, and lack of opportunity seem to be concentrated in the central portions of large cities.

Table 4.7 begins to probe a bit deeper into the issue of the interrelation of race with poverty and family type. Based on family size and income, the Census Bureau classifies each family (and every person within it) as above or below the poverty threshold. These tabulations of poverty by race are available for census tracts and other geographic areas, so we can look at the interrelation of socioeconomic and racial segregation in metropolitan America. We examine, first, overall segregation by poverty and the poverty segregation within each major ethnic group. For example, within the black population we look at residential separation of those who live above the poverty line from those who live below it.

Tabulations of the index of dissimilarity, D, for segregation of families by poverty status yield a value of D similar to that for other socioeconomic characteristics: on average, about one out of every three poverty families would have to move to be evenly distributed throughout the SMSA. This might seem low to many observers. It is perhaps due to the residential proximity of the poor and those who live just above the poverty line. Consistent with a pattern we have observed for many variables, the largest cities have high values of D, with Newark and Chicago over 50 percent on family poverty. Tabulations of poverty segregation (column 2) produce a similar picture.[24] The distribution of D for the female-headed families is more compact.

Focusing on the tabulation for persons, we have broken down the classification of poverty status by race (white, black) and also for Spanish origin (independently of race) and calculated separate values of D for each.[25] That is, we treat each ethnic group as the universe and calculate

---

[24]We also examined the poverty-nonpoverty dissimilarity of families with female heads. Most values of D approximate those for all families, but the distribution across SMSAs was a bit more compact. We might have expected the statistic to decrease, since we know single parenthood is associated with poverty. The value did decline when controlled in the larger metropolises with substantial black populations. The results say, however, that the family poverty segregation cannot be attributed merely to female headship segregation.

[25]If the population of the respective racial or origin group in the tract fell between one and fifteen persons the respective tabulations were suppressed. Moreover, in our data file (STF3) individual pieces of "split tracts" (crossed by a higher level of geography) are subject to suppression, and thus when combined may underrepresent less frequent racial groups. A check showed that our figures for D account for 85 percent to 95 percent of residents in each racial classification. To the extent that such low frequency tracts or tracts split by many places have different ratios of poor to nonpoor, some inaccuracies could be introduced. For example, if blacks who live in predominantly white tracts are much less likely to be poor than average (a reasonable expectation), the calculated value of D would be biased downward. The argument holds conversely for poor whites. It seems unlikely, though, that the inclusion of all of these persons would greatly change the calculation statistic. Because of the split tract problem we look only at distributions within race rather than at racial segregation within other variables, since racial count is the criterion for suppression. The suppression problem was much worse for the Indian and Asian populations, and so we have excluded them from Table 4.7.

TABLE 4.7

Dissimilarity for Poverty Status by Race: 21 SMSAs

Metropolitan Area	Total Population		Poverty Dissimilarity for Persons, by Race or Spanish Group		
	Families	Persons	White	Black	Spanish
Allentown	31	29	28	40	52
Amarillo	35	33	29	21	35
Atlanta	40	39	27	32†	54
Bangor	25	27	27	NA	88
Birmingham	36	35	28	25	71
Boston	38	36	31	24	41†
Chicago	52	49	36	34†	33†
Flint	35	34	29	27	55
Indianapolis	38	37	33	32	65
Lexington	32	31	28	31	72
New Bedford	30	30	29	50	36
New Haven	45	44	36	23	39
New Orleans	43	42	27	28†	49
Newark	53	50	38	31†	45†
St. Louis	44	43	31	29†	68
Salt Lake City	26	27	25	65	40
San Antonio	39	38	39	34	26†
San Diego	31	27	24	31	28†
Seattle	28	27	25	29	52
Sheboygan	18	17	19	NA	58
Stockton	30	28	25	29	29
MEAN	35.7	34.4	29.2	32.4	49.3
S.D.	8.8	8.1	5.0	10.1	16.6
Correlation with:					
SMSA Pop. 1980	.59*	.56*	.38*	−.03	−.24
SMSA Pop. Change 1970–1980	−.34	−.38*	−.39*	.31	−.31

*Significant at $\alpha = .05$.
†SMSAs with the largest total populations of these ethnic groups.

the internal segregation of the poor from the nonpoor. Some informative comparisons arise in looking across the three final columns of Table 4.7. In almost every metropolitan area the level of poverty segregation for whites is less—often several points less—than for the total population, and the variance of the statistic across the SMSAs is reduced. The higher incidence of poverty among the nonwhite population combines with the racial segregation to increase the level of observed poverty segregation for the total population by several points. In the larger cities with substantial nonwhite populations (Atlanta, Chicago,

New Orleans, Newark) the value of D is lower by more than 10 points. On average, the level of poverty segregation for the black population separately is also reduced, but the variability across cities is increased slightly. Compared to the level of segregation for whites, D is lower among blacks in about half of the SMSAs for which it can be calculated. Several SMSAs with smaller fractions of blacks show very high levels of segregation on the poverty dimension. In the five metropolitan areas with the largest black populations, levels of black and white segregation are much more in line with one another.[26] Poverty segregation within the white population tends to be greater in the larger metropolises, but no such pattern can be discerned in the black population. These results accord generally with those of Reynolds Farley, who found that even after controlling for socioeconomic status, racial segregation remained appreciable in 1970.[27]

The level of poverty segregation for the Spanish origin population (final column) is intermediate. In the average city about half of the poor Hispanics would have to change residence in order for every census tract to have the same number of poor and nonpoor persons of Spanish origin. In the four SMSAs with the largest (absolute) Spanish origin population (in order: Chicago, San Antonio, San Diego, Newark, Boston) the level of Hispanic poverty segregation averages 34.6, more in line with that for whites and blacks.

We also know that the type of household differs by race. For instance, we saw in Chapter 2 that the percent single-parent family and percent black often were found together. The first four columns of Table 4.8 present the value of D for each of four basic household types for the total population.[28] Married-couple family households are the social norm, but they constitute only about 60 percent of all households nationally. In the twenty-one SMSAs, values of D for married-couple family households fall in the vicinity of 25 percent with relatively little dispersion across the SMSAs. The value for single-parent family households—which contain children and may be of either male or female head, but are predominantly the latter—is similar, although the

---

[26]For the few SMSAs with substantial Indian and Asian populations, poverty segregation is uniformly higher than for whites or blacks, often at a 30 point differential. Although smaller absolute numbers and problems with suppression make inferences fairly difficult, this is evidence that poor Asians and Indians live further apart from the nonpoor members of their own race than is the case for whites and blacks.

[27]Reynolds Farley, "Residential Segregation in Urbanized Areas of the United States," *Demography* 4 (1977):497–518.

[28]Other family households are defined as housing units that contain relatives but are not characterized by the presence of a married couple or a parent and child. For instance, adult mother and daughter or a family with a cousin present would fall into this grouping. Nonfamily households include persons living alone as well as groups of unrelated individuals sharing a dwelling unit.

TABLE 4.8
Dissimilarity for Household Type by Race: 21 SMSAs

Metropolitan Area	Total Population				Whites		Blacks		Spanish	
	Married Couple	Single Parent	Other Family	Nonfamily	Single Parent	Nonfamily	Single Parent	Nonfamily	Single Parent	Nonfamily
Allentown	21	22	17	20	20	21	44	35	47	35
Amarillo	27	18	21	29	16	28	17	30	39	47
Atlanta	35	31	24	34	19	37	23†	29†	68	47
Bangor	23	17	15	23	21	20	NA	NA	NA	NA
Birmingham	29	29	26	25	18	30	22	20	73	57
Boston	29	28	18	29	20	30	26	29	46†	49†
Chicago	30	38	23	29	20	30	25†	33†	31†	36†
Flint	25	28	22	21	17	23	22	20	55	56
Indianapolis	28	28	23	26	21	26	21	27	71	63
Lexington	26	27	20	26	22	27	26	27	81	66
New Bedford	21	28	12	18	27	19	33	49	43	40
New Haven	30	34	16	25	22	27	23	17	40	49
New Orleans	34	33	24	30	21	36	20†	24†	51	47
Newark	31	41	18	25	21	28	22†	24†	40†	31†
St. Louis	29	31	23	25	18	27	21†	25†	73	50
Salt Lake City	33	18	23	37	18	38	55	45	36	41
San Antonio	24	21	26	27	21	28	21	30	17†	27†
San Diego	29	22	17	33	20	33	28	39	24†	38†
Seattle	29	19	19	31	18	32	27	34	59	48
Sheboygan	21	19	17	20	18	20	NA	NA	73	65
Stockton	23	21	19	24	18	23	37	41	24	35
MEAN	27.4	26.3	20.2	26.6	19.7	27.7	26.9	30.4	49.5	46.3
S.D.	4.2	6.8	3.9	4.9	2.4	5.5	9.4	8.6	19.1	11.3
Correlation with:										
SMSA Pop. 1980	.45*	.54*	.29	.34	-.01	.36	-.14	-.00	-.18	-.29
SMSA Pop. Change 1970–1980	.21	-.49*	.24	.62*	-.27	.53*	.32	.44*	-.26	-.17

*Significant at α = .05.
†SMSAs with the largest total populations of these ethnic groups.

variation across cities is slightly larger. For these two household types there is a positive relationship between metropolitan area size and the level of segregation. In Chicago and Newark, segregation of single-parent families is about half again the average for the twenty-one SMSAs. Compared to married-couple families, households in the "other family" category are less segregated, and nonfamily households are more segregated. There is a modest degree of association of these two characteristics with SMSA size. Nonfamily segregation is strongly related to SMSA growth rate, and for a few SMSAs in the South and West it is the most segregated household type. The attraction of single migrants and the elderly to distinct neighborhoods within these regions is a likely contributing factor.

What happens when we control for race and Spanish origin? The final six columns of Table 4.8 give the segregation statistics of the single-parent and nonfamily household types, separately for whites, blacks, and the Spanish origin population. Compared to the total, the level of single-parent segregation among whites drops as much as 10 points, but values of D for nonfamily households increase more often than not, even if only slightly. Among blacks single-parent segregation is on average nearly the same as that for the total population, but there is slightly more variation across SMSAs. In the five metropolitan areas with the largest black populations, the average value of D is 22.2. That is 2.4 points higher than for the white population, but over 12 points lower than for the total population. Nonfamily household segregation is several points higher among the black population than in the total populace overall, but this does not hold for the five SMSAs with large black populations. Interestingly, the higher level of nonfamily segregation in the faster-growing metropolitan areas is maintained for both blacks and whites, presumably for the same reasons.

In contrast to both blacks and whites, levels of household type segregation among Hispanics are much higher than the general population, and the variance across cities is also very wide. Some of these very high values are contributed by cities with especially small fractions of Spanish origin populations, but even in those five SMSAs with the largest Spanish origin populations levels of D average 32 for single-parent households and 36 for nonfamily households, still several points higher than the corresponding white population.[29]

[29]Values of D for single-parent households are largest in Boston, Chicago, and Newark, where the Hispanic population is more likely to be of Puerto Rican origin and identify itself as black. Hispanics appear in columns 5 and 7 as well as 9. Unfortunately, we cannot control for race and Spanish origin simultaneously in the household type distribution. Therefore, we cannot readily separate the effects of internal racial composition from other factors (economic, cultural) influencing Hispanic family type spatial differentiation itself.

Taken together, the results in Table 4.8 demonstrate how ethnicity exerts an appreciable effect on the measured values of household type segregation. A good deal of the segregation observed for single-parent households is derived from racial segregation. In fact, levels of segregation by household type within the white and black populations are quite similar. Within the Hispanic population, on the other hand, these levels of household type segregation are higher on average and less consistent.

Using a More Comprehensive Measure of Segregation

One of the major disadvantages of the index of dissimilarity, D, in the analysis of segregation is the fact that it is effectively limited to dichotomies. If a characteristic of interest has more than two categories, one must, if using D, look at all pairs of categories to get a complete picture of the segregation in the system. For occupation and ethnicity we looked at averages of pairwise segregation, but in most of our tables we have examined each category against all others. Still, one might prefer a single number to summarize the degree of differentiation in that variable across all the categories.

In response to this polytomy problem and in response to some of the methodological concerns raised recently in the literature, we have performed a methodological analysis of index behavior.[30] Based on that work we introduced the second measure of unevenness or segregation. The entropy index, the H statistic, can take account of the distribution of variables with multiple categories, even those that are nominal in nature. When standardized it ranges from a minimum of zero (no segregation) to 100 (complete segregation), just like D. For dichotomies it ranks areas almost identically to D, although it produces lower absolute scores; that is, the two measures are nearly equivalent except for scale. H can be considered similar to an analysis of variance measure for a categorical variable.

In Table 4.9 we present the value of H for a selected group of census characteristics, including measures of ethnicity, life cycle, and status that we have examined previously with D. We now have the advantage of looking at only one statistic for each variable, no matter how many categories are contained within it. The level of racial segregation is very high by this measure, which now takes account simultaneously classification as white, black, Asian, Indian, and other. The same large

---

[30]Michael J. White, "Segregation and Diversity Measures."

TABLE 4.9
Entropy Statistic (H) for Selected Characteristics: 21 SMSAs

Metropolitan Area	Race	Spanish	Age	Household Type	Children's HH Type	Marital Status	Occupation	Income	Poverty Status	Housing Age
Allentown	19	24	2	5	6	3	4	5	8	18
Amarillo	30	17	3	7	6	4	6	9	9	27
Atlanta	53	4	3	11	14	5	6	11	15	20
Bangor	23	2	6	5	4	10	2	4	6	20
Birmingham	52	2	2	8	12	4	7	9	12	15
Boston	43	20	3	9	10	4	4	8	11	15
Chicago	58	35	3	11	16	4	6	10	20	27
Flint	55	5	1	6	10	3	4	5	10	16
Indianapolis	53	3	2	8	11	4	5	8	12	24
Lexington	30	2	4	8	9	6	6	8	10	24
New Bedford	18	9	1	5	7	2	4	5	7	18
New Haven	37	22	3	9	15	5	4	9	15	16
New Orleans	47	6	4	11	16	5	6	11	17	33
Newark	49	27	2	9	18	3	6	12	21	16
St. Louis	59	3	2	8	14	4	5	9	16	25
Salt Lake City	10	9	4	10	6	4	4	9	8	22
San Antonio	18	32	4	7	6	4	6	10	12	30
San Diego	19	14	6	9	5	5	5	9	6	21
Seattle	20	2	4	9	6	4	3	7	7	19
Sheboygan	11	6	1	4	5	2	3	2	3	9
Stockton	16	11	2	6	5	3	6	7	7	23
MEAN	34.3	12.1	3.0	7.8	9.5	4.2	4.9	8.1	11.1	20.9
S.D.	17.2	10.6	1.3	2.1	4.3	1.7	1.3	2.6	4.9	5.8
Correlation with:										
SMSA Pop. 1980	.50*	.48*	.15	.59*	.50*	.01	.21	.43*	.61*	.24
SMSA Pop. Change 1970–1980	−.45*	−.15	.51*	.23	−.44*	.12	.18	.20	−.33	.34

*Significant at $\alpha = .05$.

cities are at the top of the list. Western cities tend to be a little lower on this value, and SMSAs with large Hispanic populations seem to be a bit lower as well; this may be due to the fact that if a fraction of persons of Spanish origin check "other" for racial identification, the effect would be to reduce the measured amount of segregation. The Spanish origin population itself is much less segregated than the black population—this result agrees almost exactly with D—but there is very wide dispersion. Levels of Hispanic segregation are highest in San Antonio and Chicago.

When we turn our attention to the life cycle and family status variables (columns 4 to 6), we observe very little unevenness with this measure. Segregation by age (four categories) is almost nonexistent, as is segregation by marital status. In sharp contrast to the case for race, knowing the neighborhood in which a person resides would give almost no hint at all of his or her marital status or age. Our guess for household type would be correct only slightly more often. The family status (of children) shows a little higher degree of differentiation and a wider dispersion. This is very likely due to the differential distribution of single-parent families (usually with female heads) and the variation in concentration of this group within neighborhoods of the SMSAs.

It was the socioeconomic measures that stood out in the factorial analyses. In our presentation of SES segregation with the D statistic we looked only at the end segments of the distributions, such as professionals or operatives, those below the poverty line, or households with incomes above $30,000. In general, we would expect the greatest amount of segregation to exist for persons at the extremes of the distribution. Under the H statistic, which incorporates the segregation of the middle occupational and income categories as well as the extremes, the level of status segregation appears to be less pronounced. In fact, occupational segregation based on six categories (column 7) is at a level only slightly above that for marital status. Income (three categories) is more segregated than occupation, but no more than family type. No doubt this is attributable to the lower degree of segregation of persons of middle income and middle class occupational status from the other categories of the distribution.[31] Unevenness of the poverty population (another dichotomy) is more pronounced than that for income. The large SMSAs lead the list, and as we found above, some of the differentials across cit-

[31]Had we used more categories for income (or any other characteristic), the H statistic would most likely have been greater. We also analyzed spatial segregation using an imputed analysis of variance technique (see White, "Segregation and Diversity Measures"), which gave similar answers overall, although it could be more sensitive to those variables that possessed underlying continuous distributions. Census tabulations for tracts give fifteen categories for income.

ies are attributable to the higher concentration of poverty status within the segregated black population.

As a representative of the physical characteristics we have included the segregation measure for housing age (three categories). Despite the three categories—with middle-aged housing less segregated from either extreme value—the value of H for this characteristic is high, the highest in the table next to race. Larger and older SMSAs tend to be more differentiated, but the effect is not statistically significant.

Conclusion: The Ladder of Segregation

Is there a hierarchy to the way in which social characteristics are sorted out in metropolitan areas? If we establish a ladder that indicates no segregation at its lower rungs and complete segregation at its upper rungs, where would the range of characteristics under scrutiny here be placed?

Figure 4.1 depicts such a ladder for the ethnic groups under study. We plot the point representing the mean of the index of dissimilarity across the twenty-one metropolitan areas for the components of race, ancestry, Spanish origin, and nativity.[32] Summary statistics, of course, average out the intercity variation observed in the tables of this chapter.

A distinct gap of about 15 points separates the segregation of the white and black racial groups from the remainder. As we have observed before, the black population is the most segregated of any demographic characteristic. As blacks are higher than whites on the chart (see Table 4.5), blacks are more segregated from the remaining racial groups than are whites. Asians, Indians (Native American, Eskimos, and Aleuts), and other races occupy the middle rungs of this segregation ladder. Hispanics (versus non-Hispanics) occupy the same range. Almost all white ancestry segregation (white Hispanics, if shown would be appreciably less) falls at a level below this.[33] Of the six major ancestry groups

---

[32]The graph represents four independent classifications of the population, first by race (white, black, Asian, Indian, other races), second by ancestry (English, French, German, Irish, Italian, Polish), third by Spanish origin (Spanish), and a fourth representative of the race by Spanish origin tabulation (black of Spanish origin). These values of D are calculated for the reference group versus the sum of all other categories of the variable, and then superimposed. This contrasts with Table 4.5, where we collapsed race, Spanish origin, and ancestry into one variable.

[33]Ancestry is tabulated both as single ancestry, those individuals who claim only one country or culture of origin, versus mixed ancestry, where in addition to the group listed (first by the respondent) the individual records at least one additional ancestry group. Figure 4.1 makes use of single ancestry tabulations only. Corresponding values for multiple ancestry (which double-counts individuals) would show values about 10 points lower for English, Italian, and Polish, and about 12 points lower for Irish and German.

FIGURE 4.1

Mean Index of Dissimilarity for Race, Spanish Origin, and Ancestry:
21 SMSAs

70	
68	Black
66	
64	Black of Spanish Origin
62	
60	
58	
56	White
54	
52	
50	
48	
46	
44	
42	
	Other Races
40	
38	
36	
	Spanish
34	Indian Polish
32	
30	
	Foreign Born
28	French
26	
24	
22	German
	Irish
20	English

NOTE: Indexes are calculated independently within classification for:

race (white, black, Indian, Asian, other races)
spanish origin (Spanish)
race by Spanish origin cross-tabulation (black of Spanish origin)
ancestry (English, French, German, Irish, Italian, Polish)

we are able to identify for census tracts, Italians and Poles are the least intermingled with persons of other ancestries. For Americans of German, Irish, and English descent segregation is minimal. Overall about one-fifth of the persons claiming only these ancestries would need to move to establish an even distribution in our average metropolis. We expect more segregation among the Italians and Poles, since they arrived later than the others. The French, on the other hand, are relatively more segregated considering the usual inclusion among the older immigrant groups.

Only some of our results are consistent with the spatial assimilation hypothesis, whereby the most recent migrants to the American metropolis begin at the top of the (inverted) segregation ladder and work their way down over time. The "old" European stock groups are at this point now, the Lieberson "new" groups (here including Italian and Polish) are intermediate, with the "very new" Hispanics at the top. Race, however, upsets this paradigm. It is clear that racial segregation dominates the other classifications. Even the new arrivals (foreign born) show a level of segregation less than half that of the black population. Our results suggest that it would be premature to assume that spatial assimilation applies equivalently to all groups in the population.

A major objective of our analysis in this chapter has been a wide-angle view of patterns of spatial differentiation in the settlement system. We wish to bring under our lens other characteristics beyond those most commonly treated in segregation studies. Figure 4.2 attempts to summarize this broader point of view with respect to a number of characteristics, chosen to represent the major variables under discussion here. We have used the entropy statistic described earlier because it readily accommodates variables with multiple categories. For instance, our statistic for race measures in one number the combined segregation of whites, blacks, Asians, Indians, and others. We keep to our rough classification of the variables into four categories, and present the mean value calculated across the twenty-one metropolitan areas. Since neighborhood diversity and segregation are generally two sides of the same coin, metropolitan areas that are shown to be less segregated for a particular characteristic tend to have more diverse neighborhoods.

The most extreme segregation (and least neighborhood diversity) is found in housing. High-rise buildings and group quarters are the most separated in metropolitan neighborhoods. We are aware that tall buildings are sharply separated from single family homes, and the population in prisons, barracks, and dormitories is expectedly congregated in distinct neighborhoods. What is important about these two variables is that they give us a benchmark against which other characteristics can be measured. They indicate the maximum degree of segregation that we

FIGURE 4.2

Mean Entropy Statistic for Selected Characteristics: 21 SMSAs

	SES	Life Cycle	Ethnicity	Housing and Other
50				
49				
48				
47				
46				High-rise
45				
44				
43				
42				
41				
40				
39				Group Quarter
38				
37				
36				
35				
34			Race	
33				
32				
31				
30				
29				
28				
27				
26				
25				
24				
23				
22	Home Value			
21	Rent			Housing Age
20				Density
19				
18			Race of Spanish	
17				Ownership
16				
15				
14	Poverty-fem.head			
13				
12			Spanish	
11	Poverty-persons			
10				
9				
8	Education	Household Type		
7	Income			
6			Nativity	
5	Occupation			Mobility
4		Household Size	Ancestry-Single	
3		Marital Status		
2		Age		
1				
0		Sex	Ancestry-Multiple	

observe with our own eyes (building type) or which society purposefully acknowledges and plans (group quarters).

The remaining housing and mobility characteristics fall much lower on the scale. Housing age and dwelling unit density lead the remaining variables due to the physical permanence of the housing stock. The separation of owners from renters, often linked to housing type and density (inner city apartments versus suburban single-family homes), falls in behind. In contrast to the housing units themselves, the population within them can shift location quickly. Indeed, the mobile population itself is fairly evenly spread throughout the metropolis.

Seen against this backdrop the degree of racial segregation in these twenty-one SMSAs is especially dramatic. Indeed, about as much distance separates race from the maximum variable (high-rise) as separates race and the next characteristic below (home value). Separation of the races—especially whites from blacks—is a pervasive feature of the metropolitan landscape. The remaining entries in the ethnicity column recapitulate Figure 4.1. The white ethnic (ancestry) groups and even the foreign born are relatively unsegregated, while the Spanish origin population remains intermediate, and racial segregation within the Hispanic population is significant.

The roles of socioeconomic status and life cycle characteristics in residential differentiation have been stressed continuously. All life cycle characteristics rank low in spatial unevenness, particularly age (several categories), sex, marital status, and household size. Household type, which picks up the separation of single-parent families, nuclear families, and persons living alone, is still under 10 on this scale. Many neighborhoods, then, are fairly diverse with respect to life cycle.

Income, education, and occupation are basic elements of the status system, and they correspondingly have received a great deal of attention in the urban sociological literature. We find that the level of measured segregation for these three characteristics is relatively modest, although it does exceed most life cycle indicators. Our use of cruder categorical divisions for this statistic would tend to depress the calculation for income and education, but our other work with a statistic more sensitive to the categories suggests that the differences in levels of segregation are probably not a simple artifact of methodology. It remains true that the ends of the SES spectrum are clearly separated, but the middle class bulge tends to reduce measured segregation overall.

When we narrow our focus and use the poverty tabulation—which takes into account a calculated needs threshold and includes family size—the level of segregation jumps up several points on the charts. When we focus still further on the separation of poverty and nonpoverty households only among female-headed households, the average index rises another few points, exceeding now the observed level of Hispanic segregation.

Finally we examine rental level and home value, which have identical levels of segregation in Figure 4.2 when averaged over the 21 cities. On the one hand, rent and home value indicate the combined influence of SES and life cycle. On the other hand, value and rent may capture best the expression of social status in metropolitan areas, since housing accounts for so large a fraction of a family's total budget, and housing type and neighborhood location are visible manifestations of well-being. In this sense, they are excellent indirect indicators of status segregation, avoiding some of the problems in other SES measures: data quality, reporting bias, crudeness of categorization.[34] Using these two measures, we can observe a significant amount of SES segregation, more than any demographic characteristic except race. If one takes the more conventional tack of using education, income, and occupation, SES segregation appears lower.

Without question the levels of segregation we observe in several key characteristics—race, education, household type—are intertwined. To the extent possible we tried to disentangle them using two-way cross-tabulated data for neighborhoods. Our work shows that racial segregation is enough to raise overall poverty segregation and household type segregation by several points. Moreover, our analysis showed that among blacks and whites the level of household type and poverty segregation is less than that observed for other racial groups and the Spanish population.

We hypothesized in Chapter 2 that larger cities would be more differentiated than smaller SMSAs. To the degree that segregation is an indicator of differentiation, we indeed find this relationship to be the case. The correlation between SMSA population size and segregation statistic is positive for almost every variable we analyzed. It is statistically significant in several cases, including race, college education, poverty status, and several housing characteristics.[35] Our SES, life cycle, and household type indicators were noticeably less linked to city size than ethnicity, poverty, and physical characteristics.

Regional differences were often visible, and were apparently intertwined with the SMSA 1970–1980 growth rate. As a rule smaller

---

[34]One of the classic studies of residential differentiation which gave rise to the sector theory made use of rental levels. See Homer Hoyt, *The Structure and Growth of Residential Neighborhoods in American Cities* (Washington, D.C.: U.S. Government Printing Office, 1939).

[35]This requires a Pearson correlation coefficient of about .40. With 21 cases, SMSA size would statistically explain about 16 percent of the variation in levels of segregation across SMSAs.

metropolitan areas in the South and West posted greater growth rates for the decade. The manner in which region and rate of growth might influence segregation is open to discussion. On the one hand, growing areas are less "locked in" to historical patterns in population and housing distribution. On the other hand, their more mobile population can quickly segregate itself in new neighborhoods. In fact, we find evidence for both phenomena in the segregation data. Southern and western cities are more segregated by age and household type and less segregated by race, origin, and ancestry group. The higher rate of population growth and selective resettlement of younger and older migrants into neighborhoods of predominantly single-person dwellings could produce this result. Growth does not imply higher levels of segregation across the board, as the case of racial segregation illustrates. Although the relative influences of self-segregation and discrimination on racial segregation cannot be disentangled here, the fact that population growth at the SMSA level is negatively related to ethnic segregation should come as good news to many.

5

THE SPATIAL ORGANIZATION
OF THE METROPOLIS

I N THIS chapter we turn to direct analysis of the spatial patterns exhibited by metropolitan neighborhoods. To be sure, previous chapters
have examined some spatial phenomena, especially segregation. But
segregation and factorial ecology measures reflect only unevenness in
the distribution of social characteristics or their interrelations across
observations on neighborhoods, respectively. Neighborhoods could be
"shuffled" around the metropolis in any fashion, and the tabulations
would be identical. As a further step in the analysis of residential differentiation, we wish to take into account the proximity of neighborhoods to one another, searching for larger patterns in the distribution of
socioeconomic status, life cycle, ethnicity, and housing.

The analysis of systematic patterns of metropolitan development
has long been a subject of theory and research in the urban social sciences. In the next section we give a brief review of some of the competing models of urban residential structure. In the subsequent section we
introduce maps based on census tracts, which display some of the basic
characteristics for three metropolitan regions. Since distance from the
center of the city has traditionally been such a central organizing focus
of the metropolitan residential system, we then present tabulations of
distance quartiles or rings for selected characteristics. In the final, empirical section of this chapter we introduce our analysis of sociospatial
contours, a method that tries to combine statistical analysis and graphi-

cal representation for the social characteristics. Chapter 6 includes comparisons over time for these contours.

Models of Residential Structure

Residential structure is the term we use here to describe the way in which population and housing characteristics interact systematically with space. We have already shown in previous chapters that a large degree of differentiation of these characteristics exists for metropolitan areas, and that the degree of sorting (or segregation) can differ sharply by characteristic as well as by metropolitan area. We have yet to establish whether any of these manifestations of the social structure, so unevenly distributed, exhibit a systematic pattern in the metropolitan area, such as a series of concentric circles.

The literature boasts a number of models of urban residential structure. Authors of these models maintain that there is a systematic spatial pattern to metropolitan residential differentiation; some versions even claim that certain characteristics are paired with distinct patterns. Figure 5.1 describes these. A review of major developments in theory can help frame our subsequent discussion, although we necessarily omit some of the finer points of the arguments and the earlier empirical results.[1]

The most established model of the urban sociospatial structure posits that residential structure is oriented to the central business district (CBD), the commercial core of the city. Distance from the CBD, then, will say a great deal about the demographic composition of the population in neighborhoods, a model that has usually been represented by a series of concentric zones or rings (Figure 5.1A). In its original formulation by Ernest W. Burgess in 1925, there were five zones radiating from the center, generally increasing in socioeconomic status and decreasing in density and age of housing.[2] Ethnic groups tended to be clustered in the central zones in immigrant colonies and ghettoes. This model, derived from the pattern of the burgeoning industrial city of the early part of the twentieth century (especially Chicago), was soon well established in urban ecology, and undergirded much subsequent theory and

---

[1] More extensive overviews are contained in "Urban Spatial Structure," in Larry S. Bourne, ed., *Internal Structure of the City*, 2nd ed. (New York: Oxford University Press, 1982), pp. 28–46, and Brian J. L. Berry and John Kasarda, *Contemporary Urban Ecology* (New York: Macmillan, 1977).

[2] Ernest W. Burgess, "The Growth of the City," in R. E. Park and E. W. Burgess, eds., *The City* (Chicago: University of Chicago Press, 1967), pp. 47–62.

FIGURE 5.1
Schematic Models of Urban Structure

A. CONCENTRIC ZONE	ORIGINAL EXPOSITION	SYNTHESIS CONJECTURE

Burgess (1925)
Successive zones increase
  in socioeconomic status
  with exceptions for ethnicity

Life cycle
  varies in
  zones (radially)

B. SECTOR

Hoyt (1939)
Sectors alternate major
  socioeconomic status
  groups

Socioeconomic
  status varies
  by sector

C. MULTIPLE NUCLEI

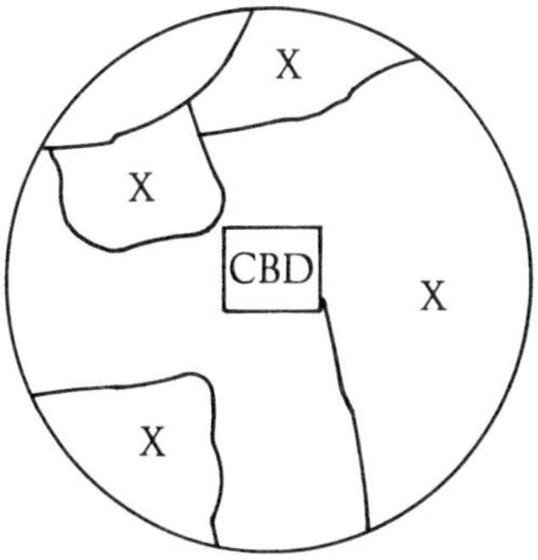

Harris and Ullman (1945)
Metropolis organized around
  competing centers, which
  form a nucleated pattern
Centers (X) are often alternative
  sites of economic activity

Ethnicity
  varies by
  nucleation

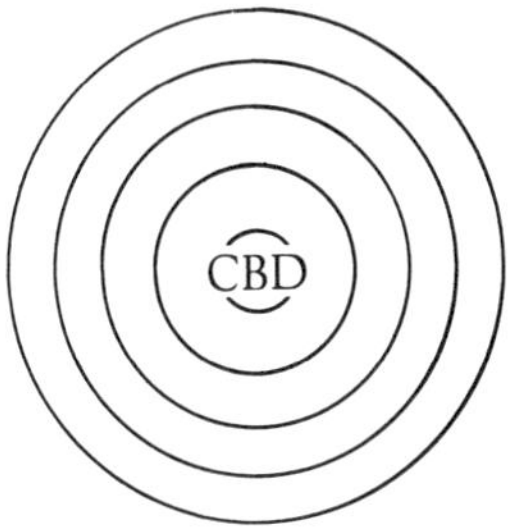

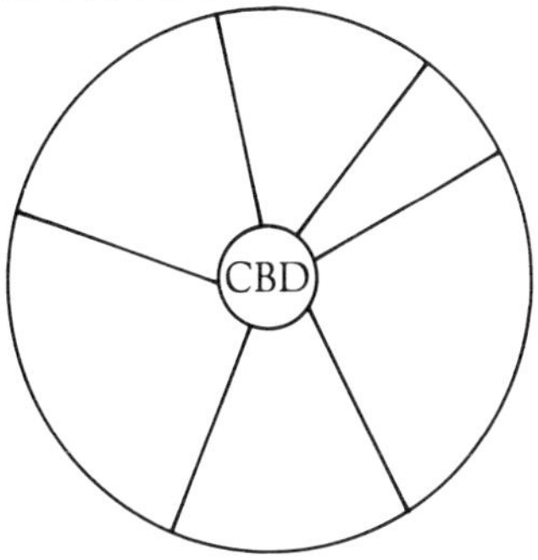

empirical research. Burgess was not unaware of the exceptions to the pattern found in Chicago and elsewhere, but the zonal configuration was seen as an appropriate summary at that time. The model provided a description of the growth of the city as well, with zones moving outward, and a process of housing and population succession proceeding within.

Models of urban residential structure developed by economists and regional scientists also tend to be premised on the orientation point of the CBD. Empirical analysis of density gradients confirmed the inverse relationship between distance from the CBD and population or housing density in census tracts or other land parcels.[3] Although such models are more mathematically formal and express the predictive power of distance in a continuous form, they bear a strong resemblance to the Burgess hypothesis. The zones of the latter can be seen as a discrete form of radial variation. Subsequent work along these lines has tried to show how the relationship between other population characteristics (most notably family income) and distance can be derived. A more contemporary treatment by Anthony Downs pictures the metropolis in terms of status rings, but overlain with a wedge (sector) of black occupancy, which replicates the majority ring distribution.[4]

Not all models see distance as the central organizing feature of the metropolitan area. A sectoral model (Figure 5.1B) generally attributed to Homer Hoyt posits that direction (azimuthal variation, with orientation to the CBD) rather than distance is the key predictor.[5] Following upon Hoyt's earlier empirical work on the distribution of rent paid for housing, the sector model describes the city as a set of pie-shaped wedges, radiating from the CBD, with each slice representing the residential neighborhood of a particular socioeconomic status group. As the city grows, it expands outward (just as in the zonal formulation) but the status levels of the wedges are maintained, each growing outward, as the residential need of the respective groups increases. Sector models are most consistent with a description of the metropolitan residential districts in terms of "the North Side," "the Western District," and the like where SES differences are implied.

[3]Richard Muth, *Cities and Housing* (Chicago: University of Chicago Press, 1969); Edwin S. Mills, *Studies in the Structure of the Urban Economy* (Baltimore: Johns Hopkins University Press, 1972); and Barry Edmonston, *Population Distribution in American Cities* (Lexington, Mass.: Lexington Books, 1975).

[4]Anthony Downs, *Neighborhoods and Urban Development* (Washington, D.C.: Brookings Institution, 1981), p. 91.

[5]Homer Hoyt, *The Structure and Growth of Residential Neighborhoods in American Cities* (Washington, D.C.: U.S. Government Printing Office, 1939).

A third model emphasizes yet another confirguration. The multiple nuclei model (Figure 5.1C) argues that metropolitan development cannot be explained solely or fundamentally in terms of orientation to the CBD.[6] Since a city has a topography and a history, other centers such as former towns, industrial sites, and immigrant clusters compete with the CBD as minor nodes, around which a suborganization develops. One thing is particularly important about the multiple nuclei idea. While it accepts that there is sorting out of the population in space, it maintains that this unevenness is not especially systematic with respect to the CBD, and a simple model oriented to the CBD could not capture the pattern(s). This issue speaks to the heart of the question before us: Just what sort of patterns exist in metropolitan areas, and how (if at all) can they be related to the center of the city?

These concepts have spawned a very large number of empirical studies of urban residential structure, most of which tend to find some evidence for the model under consideration. The distance relationship has undergone the most extensive analysis, both because it is the oldest and easiest to test, and because it has been of interest to both traditional ecologists and the gradient analysts. Studies have found that density, socioeconomic status, housing expenditures, ethnic concentration, household size, and other characteristics have been related to distance. Some of these variables have been found to exhibit sectoral variation as well, especially the status measures. Because of its hypothesis of asystematic spatial relations, the nucleation model seems to have been subjected to less concentrated study.

An ambitious attempt has been made by several individuals, most notably urban geographers, to provide a theoretical integration of the models.[7] The integrated model posits that socioeconomic status is distributed in a sectoral fashion, life cycle characteristics are distributed in a concentric manner, and race and ethnicity are nucleated. Brian J. L. Berry even goes so far as to state that the three models are "independent additive contributors to the socioeconomic structuring of city neighborhoods."[8] The formulation was developed as an attempt to synthesize the findings of factorial ecology, showing SES, life cycle, and ethnicity

[6]Chauncy D. Harris and Edward Ullman, "The Nature of Cities," *Annals of the American Academy of Political and Social Science* 142 (1945):7–17.

[7]Brian J. L. Berry, "Internal Structure of the City, in M. L. Boorne, ed. *Internal Structure of the City* (New York: Oxford University Press, 1971), pp. 97–103; R. A. Murdie, "Factorial Ecology of Metropolitan Toronto, 1959–61." Research Paper #116, Department of Geography, University of Chicago, 1969. See also Philip H. Rees, "Residential Patterns in American Cities," Research Paper #118, Department of Geography, University of Chicago, 1979, for a review and a slightly different formulation in the same tradition.

[8]Brian J. L. Berry, "Internal Structure of the City," p. 100.

as distinct factors, and the three available models of urban sociospatial structure.

Empirical analysis of the integrated model, or competitive tests of the several models have been limited. The mapping of factor scores has provided one set of interpretations, yet the link to the underlying spatial model is not always immediately obvious.[9] In 1961 Theodore R. Anderson and Janice A. Egeland attempted to test zonal versus sectoral orientation and concluded that "urbanization" varied principally in concentric (or radial) fashion, while prestige value (status) varied by sector.[10] A novel approach introduced by Roland Hawkes showed how distance and direction from the CBD could be incorporated into a single continuous model of spatial pattern for a variable.[11] Although Hawkes did not take up the issue of testing competing models explicitly, the distribution of educational attainment (SES) in his work appears to be strongly radial, with visible rings. I extended this line of work into an analysis called sociospatial contours, finding some evidence of all three patterns, but mostly orientation with respect to distance, and some evidence of nucleation for ethnicity.[12]

We are left with a circumstance in which we have a series of proposed models of residential structure, each with varying degrees of empirical support. The factorial ecology analysis and segregation analysis used here do not always imply the same kinds of differentiation. A series of questions then remain, on which we will try to shed some light in this chapter:

1. Is there in fact spatially systematic variation of the various population and housing characteristics collected in the 1980 census?

2. For which characteristics does space "explain" the most variation, and is this consistent with the relative degree of segregation manifested by that characteristic and the kind of place it held in the factorial ecology?

[9]See, for example, the mapped factor scores provided for Chicago in Brian J. L. Berry and Frank E. Horton, *Geographic Perspective on Urban Systems* (Englewood Cliffs, N.J.: Prentice-Hall, 1970), pp. 306–394.

[10]Their analysis used only a partial sample of census data from tracts for four cities and selected suburbs in 1950 and did not try to account for nucleation. Theodore R. Anderson and Janice A. Egeland, "Spatial Aspects of Social Area Analysis," *American Sociological Review* 26 (April 1961):215–225.

[11]Roland Hawkes, "The Spatial Patterning of Urban Population Characteristics," *American Journal of Sociology* 78:1216–1235.

[12]Michael J. White, *Urban Renewal and the Changing Residential Structure of the City* (Chicago: Community and Family Study Center, University of Chicago, 1980); White, "Sociospatial Contours for Ecological Analysis," in Donald J. Bogue and Michael J. White, eds., *Essays in Human Ecology II* (Chicago: Community and Family Study Center, 1984), pp. 90–108.

3. Are the spatial patterns we observe in census tract data consistent with the models of urban sociospatial structure? Are they more consistent with one model than another? Are they consistent with the conjecture of the integrated model?

The Mapping of Social Characteristics

A simple direct method for assessing the spatial patterns of social characteristics is to draw a map. Figures 5.2 through 5.10 do exactly that for three characteristics in three of our metropolitan areas. These maps, produced by the Donnelley Marketing Information Services for this book using their GraphicProfile procedure, depict the levels of each of the variables for census tracts. The maps outline the census tract boundaries, and are shaded to show the level of the variable—percent white collar workers, percent black, and household size—within each tract. The shadings define approximate quartiles of the values of the characteristics across the three metropolitan areas. Since each census tract represents about 4,000 persons, tracts with low population density will shade more area, while not necessarily representing more persons. We chose three modest-sized metropolitan areas for mapping: Flint, Stockton, and San Antonio. (For the San Antonio map the outer counties of the SMSA, Comal and Guadalupe, containing only 18 tracts, have been deleted from the map to preserve the scale of the central census tracts of Bexar County, which includes the city of San Antonio.) Since we have used the same cutoff points for every SMSA, the shadings of the map will also reflect the differing concentration of white collar workers, blacks, and household sizes across the SMSAs.

The distribution of white collar workers is a good indicator of socioeconomic status (Figures 5.2 to 5.4). In both Stockton and Flint the overall fraction of white collar workers is modest. From first appearances there is some sectoral distribution of status in these two maps, but notice also the relative absence of higher status residents in the central zones. Both of these cities show evidence of enclaves of smaller tracts with over half their residents in white collar occupations. In the Flint SMSA, the satellite city of Owosso also has its own higher status neighborhoods. In San Antonio the overall concentration of white collar workers is higher than in the other SMSAs, and the spatial distribution is a bit closer to the sectoral model. Much of the north side has neighborhoods of over 50 percent white collar workers. The central area is small in acreage but contains many tracts and a large percentage of the SMSA population; it also has a much lower concentration of white collar workers.

FIGURE 5.2
Percent White Collar Workers: 1980
San Antonio, Texas, SMSA by Census Tract

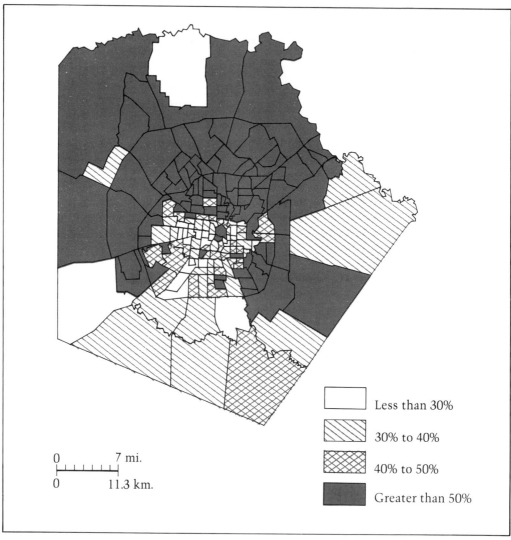

☐	Less than 30%
▨	30% to 40%
▧	40% to 50%
■	Greater than 50%

0   7 mi.

0   11.3 km.

SOURCE: *GraphicProfile,* Donnelley Marketing Information Services, 1984.

Household size is our indicator of life cycle variation. Mean household size has declined steadily within this century to a point where nationally in 1980 the average number of persons sharing a dwelling unit was 2.75, and about one-fourth of households were persons living alone. In the previous chapter, we found that segregation across neighborhoods

FIGURE 5.3
Percent White Collar Workers: 1980
Stockton, California, SMSA by Census Tract

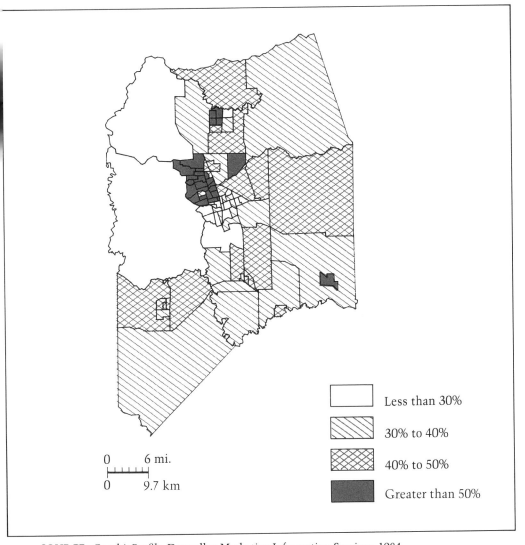

Less than 30%

30% to 40%

40% to 50%

Greater than 50%

0   6 mi.

0   9.7 km

SOURCE: *GraphicProfile,* Donnelley Marketing Information Services, 1984.

for household size was modest in comparison with some of the other socioeconomic characteristics being examined.

    Figures 5.5 to 5.7 indicate that there is some degree of spatial orga-
nization to average household size for neighborhoods. The central,
dense neighborhoods of the metropolitan regions tend more often to fall
in the bottom quartile; that is, they have relatively small household

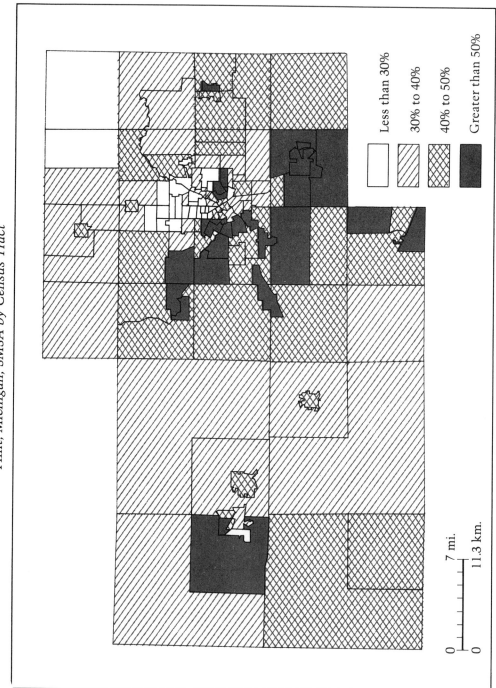

FIGURE 5.4
Percent White Collar Workers: 1980
Flint, Michigan, SMSA by Census Tract

Less than 30%
30% to 40%
40% to 50%
Greater than 50%

7 mi.
11.3 km.

SOURCE: GraphicProfile, Donnelley Marketing Information Services, 1984.

FIGURE 5.5
Average Household Size: 1980
San Antonio, Texas, SMSA by Census Tract

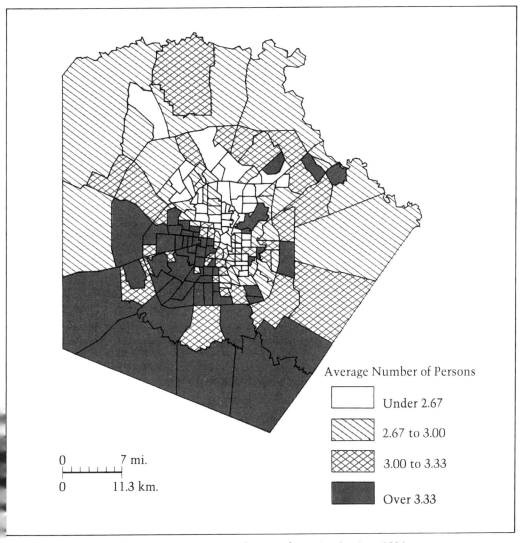

Average Number of Persons

	Under 2.67
	2.67 to 3.00
	3.00 to 3.33
	Over 3.33

0 ____ 7 mi.
0 ____ 11.3 km.

SOURCE: *GraphicProfile*, Donnelley Marketing Information Services, 1984.

sizes. It is the large peripheral or suburban tracts of the Flint and San Antonio regions that have household sizes of over 3.3 persons. Since much of the variation in household size is due to the presence of children, these tracts with darker shading are most likely to be neighborhoods devoted to child-rearing. Unshaded areas (under 2.67 persons)

FIGURE 5.6
Average Household Size: 1980
Stockton, California, SMSA by Census Tract

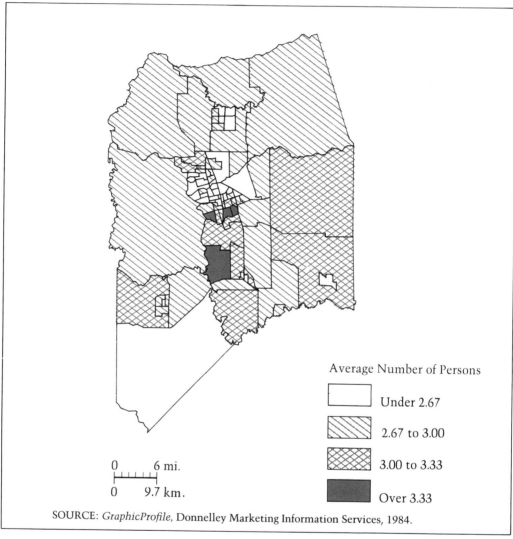

Average Number of Persons

Under 2.67

2.67 to 3.00

3.00 to 3.33

Over 3.33

0   6 mi.

0   9.7 km.

SOURCE: *GraphicProfile*, Donnelley Marketing Information Services, 1984.

contain higher fractions of the elderly, young singles, or childless couples. Household type manifests the most zonal variation, although again, exceptions can be observed, especially a few low-density enclaves scattered throughout the suburbs. These can be retirement communities, or suburbs of an older stage in the life cycle where children have left the nest.

FIGURE 5.7

*Average Household Size: 1980
Flint, Michigan, SMSA by Census Tract*

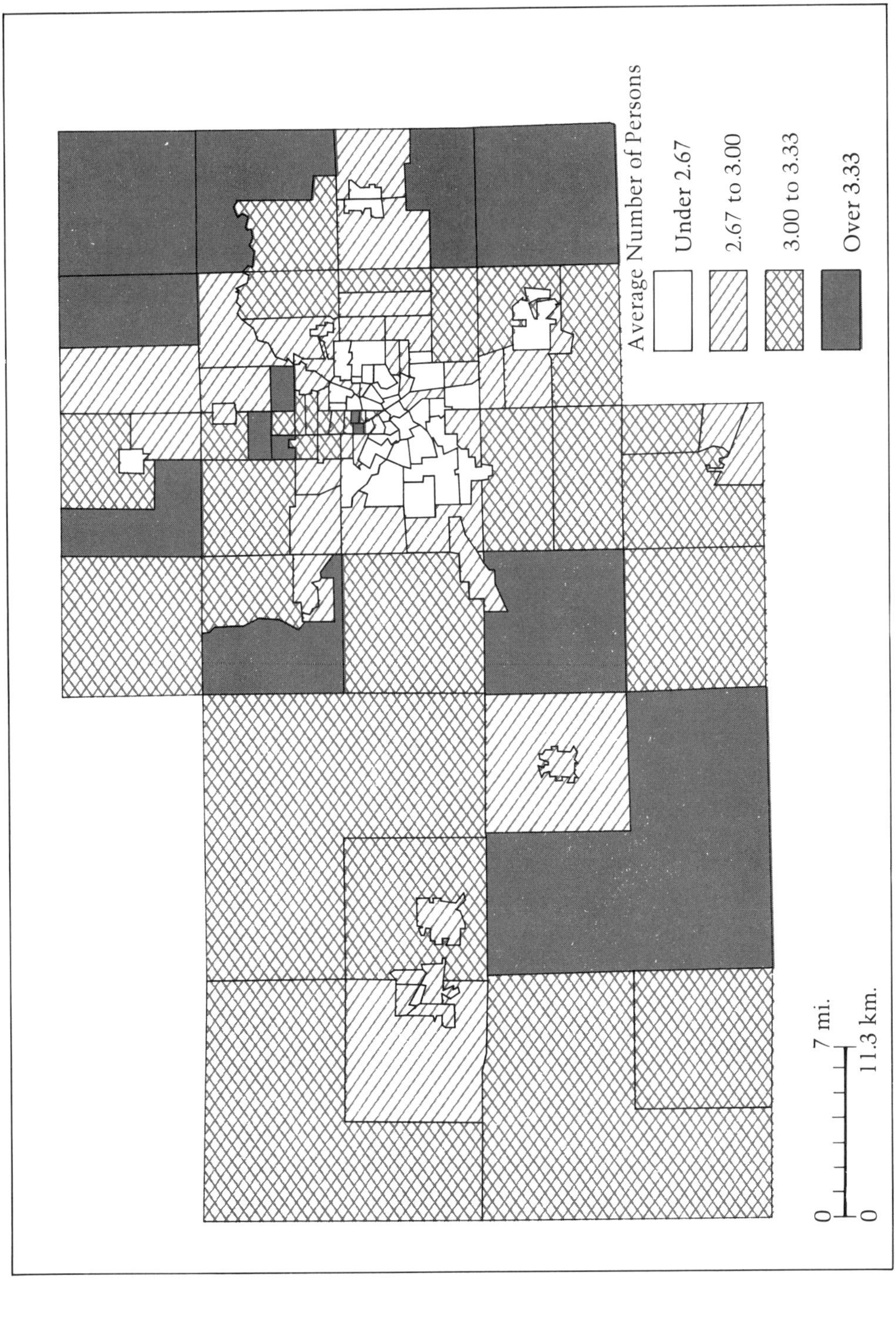

Average Number of Persons

Under 2.67

2.67 to 3.00

3.00 to 3.33

Over 3.33

0 — 7 mi.

0 — 11.3 km.

SOURCE: *GraphicProfile*, Donnelley Marketing Information Services, 1984.

FIGURE 5.8
Percent Black Population: 1980
San Antonio, Texas, SMSA by Census Tract

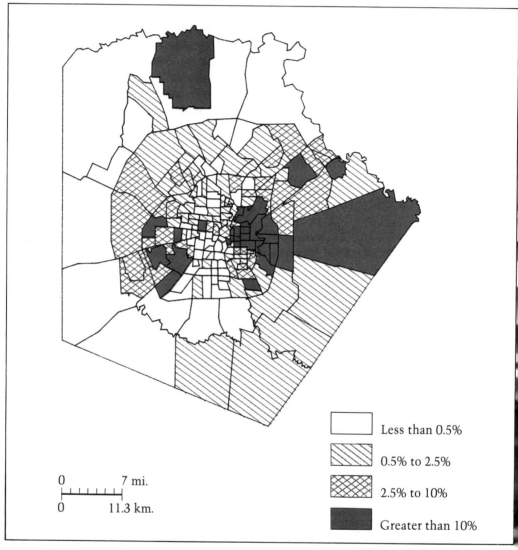

Less than 0.5%

0.5% to 2.5%

2.5% to 10%

Greater than 10%

0   7 mi.

0   11.3 km.

SOURCE: *GraphicProfile,* Donnelley Marketing Information Services, 1984.

Shaded maps can dramatically illustrate racial segregation, and Figures 5.8 to 5.10 show it here. In San Antonio the black population is concentrated, but in no single zone or sector. In Stockton most blacks are concentrated in the center of the city and in one peripheral neighborhood. These two SMSAs have relatively small black populations. In

FIGURE 5.9
Percent Black Population: 1980
Stockton, California, SMSA by Census Tract

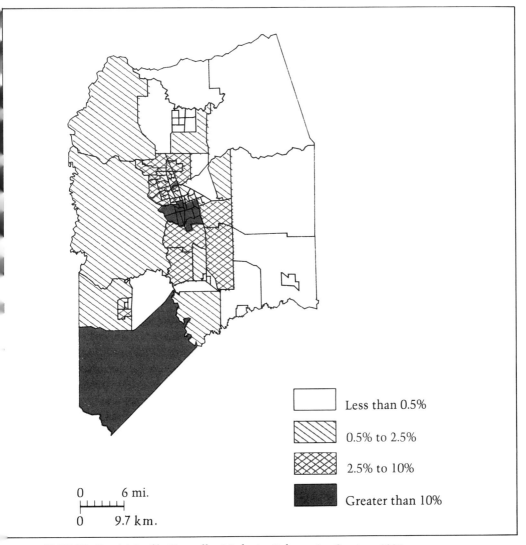

☐	Less than 0.5%
▨	0.5% to 2.5%
▩	2.5% to 10%
■	Greater than 10%

0   6 mi.

0   9.7 km.

SOURCE: *GraphicProfile*, Donnelley Marketing Information Services, 1984.

Flint, on the other hand, the overall black proportion in the SMSA is
15.1 percent and the index of dissimilarity is 85, one of the highest
in our twenty-one SMSAs. What is not shown all that well by the
map is the concentration of the black population even within the
heavily shaded area. Of these 34 tracts (out of 124 in the SMSA), which

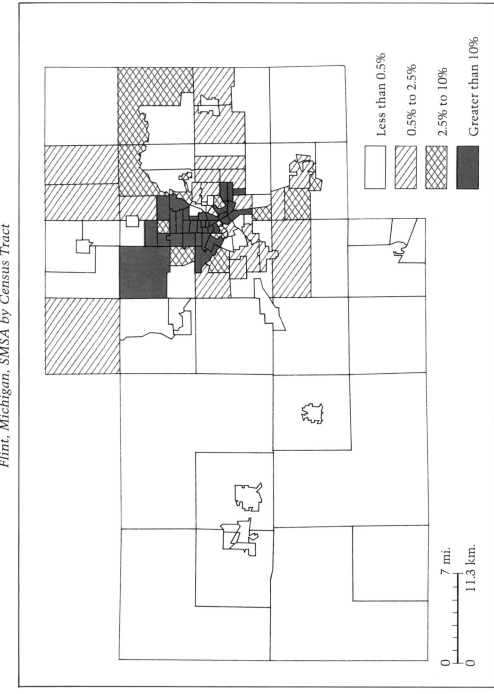

FIGURE 5.10
Percent Black Population: 1980
Flint, Michigan, SMSA by Census Tract

Less than 0.5%

0.5% to 2.5%

2.5% to 10%

Greater than 10%

7 mi.

11.3 km.

0

0

SOURCE: *GraphicProfile*, Donnelley Marketing Information Services, 1984.

are over 10 percent black, 17 have populations over three-fourths black, and they contain 63 percent of the black population in the Flint SMSA. Once beyond the boundary of the ghetto(es), however, the black population—a small minority of any neighborhood—is more geographically dispersed and less spatially systematic throughout the central country.

Looking across variables and within SMSAs now, can we observe an interrelationship between these characteristics in the maps? For San Antonio an inverse relationship between SES and household size is evident outside the inner city. To the north of the CBD we find more white collar workers and lower household size, while the pattern is reversed in the southern direction. In the central area itself, tracts are in the lower two quartiles of both variables. Any distinct relation with the distribution of the black population is hard to discern. In Stockton this status and household size flip-flop is also apparent, but there are neighborhoods (for example, directly east of downtown) where both household size and the fraction of white collar workers are relatively large. In Stockton the distribution of the black population is inversely related to the fraction of white collar workers.

The spatial patterns of Flint show less evidence of the inverse relationship between white collar and household size patterns. An overlay of the distribution of the black population still shows no appreciable correlation in the spatial distribution. This is roughly consistent with our statistical check of the correlation coefficients for these pairs of characteristics. In the Flint SMSA, white collar and household size (for neighborhoods) correlate at $-.35$; white collar and black at $-.53$; and household size and black at $.15$.

The Radial Distribution of Characteristics

To ask, "How much does socioeconomic and racial composition of a metropolis's neighborhoods change according to distance from the center of the city?," implies a direct test of the applicability of the zonal model of urban residential structure. Distinguishing among models (zonal, sectoral, multiple nuclei) is a bit more difficult. In this section we focus on distance because, by dint of previous research, distance from downtown appears to be of utmost importance in understanding a neighborhood's history and current composition.

Social characteristics may vary with respect to distance in either of two ways. First, the concentration of a characteristic (for example, race or income) may increase or decrease steadily (linearly) with each mile from downtown. This is consistent with the way gradient models propose that distance operates. Urban economists have often tested the fit of the logarithm of population density to distance from the center of the city. On the other hand, the relationship between distance and population characteristics may not be smooth at all but, rather, may proceed unevenly (rising and then falling again), or in discrete jumps. The stylized Burgess zones describe cities as if these changes were in fact discrete.

These two general orientations lead in turn to a pair of methods. In the first case, where we posit that the relationship is smooth and linear, we can measure the strength of this relationship with a regression of the characteristic for the neighborhood (for example, median family income for the tract) on distance from the CBD. A large positive or negative slope provides strong firsthand evidence for the smooth gradient hypothesis; values near zero would tend to indicate that there is no relationship between distance and residential structure, or that the relationship is not a linear one.

To examine the second possibility—that the relationship between distance and residential structure is uneven—we calculate the average value of the social characteristics for each "distance quartile" or ring within the metropolitan area. Out of all the census tracts in the SMSA we take the 25 percent closest to the CBD to be the innermost quartile (ring); the next 25 percent of the tracts become the second quartile; the next 25 percent form the third quartile; and the 25 percent of metropolitan census tracts furthest removed from the CBD constitute the outermost quartile. Dividing the metropolis into "true" Burgess-type zones is beyond the scope of our efforts here, even if such a classification could be agreed upon; however, this technique allows us to divide every metropolitan area into four concentric rings, each containing about the same number of neighborhoods. For each quartile we can calculate the mean value of the social characteristics of interest. Tables 5.1 to 5.4 contain these and two other statistics. The first is the ratio of the outermost to the innermost quartile, to see how things change as we move from the center to the periphery. The second is the value of eta^2; it describes how well quartile (ring) predicts residential differentiation. [13] Larger values of eta^2 are indicative of greater differences among the rings. As we work our way through the characteristics, we will implicitly be asking which ones are the most and least radially oriented, casting light on the validity of the various models.

[13]The value of eta^2 is from a standard analysis of variance of tract social composition explained by distance quartile. It is analoguous to the R^2 statistic from regression.

TABLE 5.1

*Radial Distribution of Population Density**

Metropolitan Area	Ring 1	Ring 2	Ring 3	Ring 4	Ratio	Eta
Allentown	7962	3829	2176	1699	.21†	.25‡
Amarillo	2679	3717	3028	1000	.37	.28
Atlanta	6202	2750	1470	242	.04	.26
Bangor	5531	750	383	790	.14	.69
Birmingham	4170	2956	1620	143	.03	.43
Boston	21937	13293	5278	2035	.09	.45
Chicago	22513	18700	7741	2865	.13	.40
Flint	6173	3952	1274	1067	.17	.44
Indianapolis	6234	3608	1880	840	.13	.48
Lexington	5390	3662	1060	224	.04	.59
New Bedford	12855	10702	8189	689	.05	.37
New Haven	9988	4498	1726	1361	.14	.60
New Orleans	15840	10828	6505	3412	.22	.37
Newark	24763	12144	4728	2305	.09	.55
St. Louis	7634	5624	2722	1099	.14	.40
Salt Lake City	5875	3849	2308	2477	.42	.26
San Antonio	6017	4737	2254	648	.11	.57
San Diego	7977	6054	4624	2260	.28	.29
Seattle	8401	4404	2680	1410	.17	.38
Sheboygan	4950	2849	112	93	.02	.70
Stockton	4452	3396	2998	1595	.36	.16
MEAN	9407	6014	3083	1345	.16	.42

*Persons per square mile.

†Ratio of Ring 4 to Ring 1.

‡Equals the value of eta^2 from an analysis of variance and, characteristic on ring.

Population Density, Status, Race, and Life Cycle

Population density is the one characteristic that has been most consistently linked to distance. Stemming from the earliest studies of Colin Clark,[14] through more recent, technically sophisticated analyses, researchers have found a strong empirical relationship between distance and density. Accumulated work on this subject has shown further that the density gradients themselves have declined, that is, flattened, appreciably throughout the twentieth century.

Table 5.1 reports the density in persons per square mile of census

[14]Colin Clark, "Urban Population Densities," *Journal of the Royal Statistical Society* 114 (1951):490–496.

TABLE 5.2

Radial Distribution of White Collar Workers (percent)

Metropolitan Area	Ring 1	Ring 2	Ring 3	Ring 4	Ratio	Eta
Allentown	45.6	50.3	42.5	40.1	.88*	.08†
Amarillo	33.4	47.4	54.5	52.2	1.56	.21
Atlanta	44.2	61.6	64.7	47.3	1.07	.23
Bangor	55.4	58.8	58.6	46.5	.84	.43
Birmingham	47.6	56.0	53.0	39.8	.84	.11
Boston	55.3	62.8	63.7	64.8	1.17	.07
Chicago	44.6	50.3	59.3	58.6	1.31	.13
Flint	38.7	37.9	45.6	40.9	1.06	.07
Indianapolis	38.0	58.6	66.4	47.7	1.25	.44
Lexington	50.5	68.3	56.0	37.6	.75	.45
New Bedford	38.0	33.4	36.7	52.5	1.38	.33
New Haven	48.5	55.1	64.9	59.5	1.23	.18
New Orleans	44.4	54.0	62.0	55.4	1.25	.14
Newark	39.5	57.4	66.2	63.9	1.62	.38
St. Louis	43.3	56.0	63.4	48.4	1.12	.25
Salt Lake City	57.3	58.8	56.2	49.5	.87	.06
San Antonio	41.4	49.4	61.0	52.2	1.26	.15
San Diego	54.4	59.2	60.7	55.8	1.03	.03
Seattle	60.7	62.4	60.9	49.2	.81	.18
Sheboygan	42.4	47.8	36.3	31.4	.74	.46
Stockton	39.3	44.1	50.7	40.6	1.03	.08
MEAN	45.8	53.8	56.3	49.2	1.10	.21

*Ratio of Ring 4 to Ring 1
†Equals the value of eta^2 from an analysis of variance, characteristic on ring.

tracts in the four rings. From ring to ring there is a sharp and consistent decline of density with distance. The larger SMSAs are, of course, denser in every ring, and there is large variety among the twenty-one SMSAs. In the average SMSA the outermost ring is only one-sixth as dense as the inner ring. The value of eta^2 averages over .4, and is particularly large in some smaller cities.

In Table 5.2, we find apparently inconsistent results for the relationship of distance to SES, again indicated by the fraction of neighborhood workers who hold white collar jobs. In nineteen of the twenty-one SMSAs the white collar percentage increases between the first and second ring, about 8 percentage points. Between the second and third quartiles the general trend is still upward (another 2.5 points), although now five cities are moving in the opposite direction. In moving from the third to the fourth rings, however, the dominant trend is a decrease in white collar workers. In only two SMSAs (Boston and New Bedford) is

TABLE 5.3

*Radial Distribution of Mean Household Size**

Metropolitan Area	Ring 1	Ring 2	Ring 3	Ring 4	Ratio	Eta
Allentown	2.5	2.7	2.8	2.8	1.13†	.23‡
Amarillo	2.4	2.7	2.7	2.9	1.18	.12
Atlanta	2.5	2.6	2.9	3.1	1.24	.23
Bangor	2.2	2.4	2.9	2.9	1.29	.41
Birmingham	2.5	2.7	2.9	2.9	1.20	.23
Boston	2.4	2.7	2.8	3.0	1.26	.20
Chicago	2.8	2.8	2.9	3.0	1.07	.03
Flint	2.6	2.8	3.1	3.1	1.19	.25
Indianapolis	2.7	2.6	2.8	3.0	1.08	.10
Lexington	2.5	2.6	3.0	2.9	1.20	.35
New Bedford	2.5	2.6	2.7	2.9	1.18	.32
New Haven	2.5	2.6	2.9	2.9	1.17	.22
New Orleans	2.4	2.7	2.7	3.1	1.28	.22
Newark	2.9	2.7	2.9	3.0	1.04	.09
St. Louis	2.6	2.6	2.8	3.0	1.12	.10
Salt Lake City	2.3	3.2	3.7	3.1	1.33	.48
San Antonio	2.9	3.1	3.1	3.0	1.05	.02
San Diego	2.3	2.7	2.9	2.7	1.16	.12
Seattle	2.1	2.5	2.8	2.8	1.33	.34
Sheboygan	2.4	2.8	3.1	3.1	1.29	.57
Stockton	2.5	2.8	2.9	2.8	1.11	.09
MEAN	2.5	2.7	2.9	3.0	1.19	.22

*Persons per household.

†Ratio of Ring 4 to Ring 1.

‡Equals the value of eta^2 from an analysis of variance, characteristic on ring.

there an increase between these last two rings.[15] The net effect as we move from the innermost to the outermost rings is quite mixed, as the ratio column indicates.

Even though the variation in occupational status is not described by a steady gradient from center to periphery, the sorting out by zones is still present, with an average eta^2 in the twenty-one SMSAs of 21 percent. Factories have leapfrogged over the middle residential rings—the old commuter suburbs—and have become established at the metropolitan outskirts. These peripheral areas then have a mix of high-status workers commuting into CBD offices or suburban office parks, blue and gray collar workers traveling to industrial parks and suburban commercial centers, and even farmers and farm employees in some SMSAs.

[15]New England SMSAs are relatively underbounded, because they are constructed from towns rather than counties. Metropolitan areas with larger outer counties will tend to pick up more peripheral industrial development.

TABLE 5.4

Radial Distribution of Black Population (percent)

Metropolitan Area	Ring 1	Ring 2	Ring 3	Ring 4	Ratio	Eta
Allentown	3.3	1.2	2.0	.7	.20*	.08†
Amarillo	19.1	4.8	1.5	1.0	.05	.18
Atlanta	66.3	35.8	7.7	9.9	.15	.42
Bangor	.5	.5	.2	.1	.25	.15
Birmingham	58.3	35.1	22.1	10.1	.17	.25
Boston	17.6	12.8	1.5	1.1	.06	.12
Chicago	38.3	36.3	20.8	6.8	.18	.11
Flint	39.8	25.8	8.2	.3	.01	.23
Indianapolis	41.4	15.2	5.1	.5	.01	.30
Lexington	20.0	6.4	7.1	5.0	.25	.14
New Bedford	6.1	1.4	.9	.8	.13	.46
New Haven	34.0	10.5	1.2	.8	.02	.48
New Orleans	64.1	43.2	15.0	16.2	.25	.33
Newark	60.9	23.0	9.1	5.9	.10	.41
St. Louis	52.5	24.1	5.6	3.2	.06	.33
Salt Lake City	1.7	.4	.4	3.2	1.84	.08
San Antonio	11.8	8.6	5.2	3.2	.27	.05
San Diego	9.8	6.6	2.1	1.9	.19	.10
Seattle	11.2	2.9	1.0	.7	.06	.17
Sheboygan	.2	.1	.2	1.3	6.91	.12
Stockton	11.9	10.3	2.0	1.3	.11	.21
MEAN	27.1	14.5	5.7	3.5	.54‡	.22

*Ratio of Ring 4 to Ring 1.
†Equals the value of eta² from an analysis of variance, characteristic on ring.
‡With Salt Lake City and Sheboygan eliminated the ratio equals .14.

This industrial location has not gone unnoticed in the past, but these tabulations demonstrate how strong the cumulative effect is on the ecology of socioeconomic differentiation.[16]

Table 5.3 presents the radial distribution of life cycle stage by household size. According to the synthesis hypothesis, and on theoretical grounds, we would expect the average household size of neighborhoods to increase with distance from center of the city,[17] and this does seem to be generally true. In almost every SMSA the mean household

[16]John D. Kasarda, "The Implications of Contemporary Redistribution Trends for National Urban Policy," *Social Science Quarterly* 61 (December 1980):373–400, and John F. Kain, "The Journey to Work as a Determinant of Residential Location," in John F. Kain, *Essays on Urban Spatial Structure* (Cambridge, Mass.: Ballinger, 1975 [1968]), pp. 29–52.
[17]Michael J. White, *Urban Renewal and the Changing Residential Structure of the City.*

size increases (or at least does not decrease) as one proceeds from inner to outer ring, yielding a net gain of about one-half person in the typical SMSA. Particularly striking is the range of spatial variation observed in Salt Lake City, increasing by 1.4 persons between the first and third distance quartiles (the highest value in the table), and decreasing again in the outer perimeter of the SMSA. In Newark and Indianapolis there is a decrease of mean household size between the first and second ring, reflecting the relatively large concentration of poor minority groups in the central zone. In Chicago and St. Louis a similar concentration is offset by high-density apartments with small households, and there is no change between Rings 1 and 2. On average the predictability of household size from ring is about 22 percent, about the same as the value obtained for race and white collar workers. In Chicago, curiously, the site of much of the empirical work that gave inspiration to the various theories, the explanatory power of the four rings is very small (3 percent), but in the Salt Lake City SMSA it is nearly 50 percent.

The results of Chapter 4 showed clearly how segregated the black population is from the remainder of the racial groups in metropolitan America. Table 5.4 examines how spatially systematic that unevenness is with respect to distance from city center. Studies comparing central city versus suburb have shown definitively that blacks are very centralized, although there have been increasing indicators of significant black suburbanization during the past two decades. Still, such comparisons are based on a simple dichotomy, and one that is based on a political boundary as well. When we shift the focus to the rings and the gradient, how centralized is the black population?

In most SMSAs we observe a significant drop in black concentration from the inner to the outer rings of the metropolitan area. (The wide variation in these numbers themselves is, of course, due to the large differences in racial composition.) The peripheral ring contains no more than one-fourth of the fraction of blacks in the inner ring in eighteen SMSAs. Racial composition is clearly demarcated among the rings in Atlanta, New Bedford, New Haven, and Newark, where eta^2 is over 40 percent.

Other Characteristics

We have performed such calculations for a number of additional characteristics, and summarize the results in Table 5.5. For each variable in the table we have calculated the value of the eta statistic (for quartile) averaged over the twenty-one metropolitan areas. Therefore, the number in the table represents, on average, how important distance

TABLE 5.5

Mean Radial ETA for Selected Characteristics

Ratio	Mean Radial Eta^2	
Housing Age	45.3*	Most Differentiated
Children in Single-Parent Families	43.7	Zonally
Low income	43.5	
Population Density	42.5	
Median Household Income	38.8	
Single Family Dwellings	36.7	
Owner-Occupied Dwellings	36.7	
Poverty Status	34.9	
Persons Living Alone	32.4	
High Income	30.4	
Mean Household Income	30.1	
Median Rent	27.8	
Recently Built Housing	27.4	
Home Value	25.9	
Elderly	22.9	
Household Size	22.5	
Black	22.5	
Foreign Born	21.8	
Support Workers	21.3	
Deficient Plumbing	21.3	
Education	20.2	
Journey to Work (time)	19.8	
Per Capita Income	19.7	
Spanish Origin	18.3	
Vacancy of Housing	18.2	
Operative Workers	17.3	
Children (0–17 years)	16.7	
Large Households (5 + persons)	15.8	
Managerial Workers	14.7	
Multifamily Units (10 +)	14.1	
Female Labor Force Participation	13.3	
Householder's Mobility	13.0	
Recent Movers	11.7	
Fertility (children ever born to women age 44–49)	8.4	Least Differentiated Zonally

*Equals the value of eta^2 from an analysis of variance, characteristic on ring.

from the center of the city is in understanding the variation of the characteristics. Entries in the table are sorted from top to bottom in order of their value on the eta statistic.

The table presents some very interesting results and a few surprises. The presence at the top of the chart of median housing age and population density is consistent with our notions of outward growth of the metropolitan region and with peripheral construction at lower net densities.[18] The finding that single family homes are radially ordered falls in step with the results. Certainly the traditional ecological models such as Burgess's predict such a relationship. In the typical metropolitan area, we can make a very good estimate of a neighborhood's housing age and density by knowing its location within one of the four rings, and any processes of urban renewal, gentrification, and the like have not proceeded far enough—even by 1980—to offset the primary orientation of these fundamental characteristics.

Measures of well-being fall in the 30 to 44 range on the eta statistic. This is a substantial amount of variance explained as well as an appreciable radial orientation. Our findings are consistent with those urban economic models that argue that the rent density function (with distance) and household consumption functions operate in such a way that higher-income households will choose peripheral locations. We find a steady increase in average income with distance from the center of the city. The poverty and low-income populations are more oriented to the radial structure (and more centrally compacted) than high-income households or average household income.[19] The second most radially oriented characteristic is the fraction of children in single-parent families. This statistic dramatically points to the severe inner city concentration of children in such families, heaped upon the already heavily segregated minority populations in many of these metropolitan areas.

In the central group of characteristics, those with scores of 20 to 30, we find SES still heavily represented. While overall housing age exhibits a strong radial orientation, the newest housing is less clearly defined in that way. In fact, the proportion of new housing declines noticeably between the first and second ring in Boston, Chicago, and Newark. Median value and median rent, which were two SES characteristics exhibiting a high degree of segregation, appear on the chart in this middle ring and are very close to one another again. Compared to these indicators of the consumption side of status, zonal differentiation produces a more modest level of eta^2 at about 20 percent in the cases of occupation and educational attainment. Although the proportion of managers and support workers correlates fairly highly across neighborhoods in most

[18]In several SMSAs (Allentown, Indianapolis, Lexington, Salt Lake City, and Stockton) the outermost ring has older housing than the third ring, most probably due to the fact that suburbanization has not yet fully overcome this quasi-hinterland.

[19]Conversely, we may not be able to explain the geographic location of the well-to-do as easily as the poor. In some cities, generally the larger, and older ones, values of eta^2 for income were in the range of 45–55, suggesting that the conventional model may not hold as well in the younger cities.

SMSAs, we find that the support workers are more radially oriented than the managers, at least in terms of variance explained.

The black and foreign-born populations, our two measures of ethnic status on this chart, appear at almost the same point. The black population, which we examined in Table 5.4 in detail, declines sharply from ring to ring in most cities. If the conventional ecological model is correct, the fraction of neighborhood residents of foreign birth should decline steadily with distance from the CBD, as succeeding generations would move outward through time, a pattern of spatial assimilation. Our tabulations (not shown) support the model, indicating a steady ring-to-ring decline, to the point at which the outer ring has about half the foreign-born population of the central ring.

The Hispanic population shows itself to be less radially oriented than blacks or the foreign born, although the fraction of Hispanics decreases with distance from the city center in most metropolitan areas. At the low ends of the chart we find fractions of children, large households, and measures of fertility, all characteristics that should, according to the integrated model, show a predominantly radial orientation. We found in Chapter 4 that there was very little segregation of these few life cycle characteristics. Since they are fairly evenly distributed across the neighborhoods of the metropolis (and therefore have very low levels of variation to begin with), zonal variation seems unlikely.[20]

In addition to simplicity, the ring analysis has the advantage of not constraining the change in neighborhood composition to be linear (and constant) with distance. Rather, it can be quite uneven. In most cases (characteristics and SMSAs) the increase or decrease is an even one, provided that differentiation exists at all. Our quartile analysis did point to the special position of the outermost ring. In particular, we find evidence of decreased social status in the periphery. This is symptomatic of the advancing wave of metropolitan growth cutting into the poor outskirts and the relocation of industry requiring lower skilled workers.

As a simple summary of Table 5.5 we can say that it shows that the physical characteristics of metropolitan neighborhoods (for example, density and the age of the housing stock) are the most differentiated by ring. This is followed by income and poverty measures. In the middle range group we find a large mixture of life cycle, ethnic status, and other socioeconomic indicators. At the low end of the scale appear measures of mobility, a few occupations, and several life cycle characteristics that revealed little segregation when examined in Chapter 4.

---

[20]For the case in which there is no variation at all in the distribution of characteristics, segregation would be zero and the radial eta would be undefined.

Metropolitan Contours

We turn now to a more complex and sophisticated method of measuring spatial organization throughout the metropolis. It is possible to incorporate distance and direction simultaneously into the prediction of the distribution of characteristics employing the tools of both regression and mapping. Throughout this analysis we will be interested in determining (1) how much of socioeconomic and housing composition in a neighborhood can be predicted or explained by spatial location; and (2) what shape that arrangement takes on and how it fits with basic models of urban structure. In Chapter 6 we will ask whether the degree of spatial organization has changed significantly over the decades.

We call the technique we employ "contour analysis" because we can think of the distribution of social characteristics about the metropolis as a kind of metropolitan topography. Instead of feet above sea level, "height" (the contour line) is given by the value of the characteristic at a particular spatial location. For example, just as we could draw a true topographical representation of the city—with hills, valleys, and so on—we can depict the distribution of income as a topographic surface. The hills are neighborhoods where the level of income is very high, valleys are neighborhoods where income is low. Income, then, can be envisioned in terms of a three-dimensional landscape. We can push this approach further, however, and gain even more insight than from a simple topographic representation. We can ask how much of this surface (the topography of income, say) is organized about the city center. In doing so, we can further investigate whether that organization is principally zonal (that is, radial), sectoral (azimuthal), or nucleated.

A few examples may help introduce this approach. Figure 5.11 is the metropolitan contour for the distribution of household income in Indianapolis. It is a very radially oriented characteristic, and consequently, its contours appear as concentric circles. By contrast, sectoral variation would appear in a metropolitan contour as a series of lobes, or flower petals. The distribution of laborers in Seattle (Figure 5.12) has some of this shape. It is, as we have mentioned, possible for neither description to fit. Nucleation may be the pattern, as the distribution of the foreign-born population in Lexington, Kentucky (Figure 5.13), indicates. The labeling of a particular pattern is partly a matter of subjective judgment, although we also have a statistical technique to provide some help.

Our strategy differs from mapping alone in that we first try to predict neighborhood social composition (for example, proportion black, median income), using distance and direction from the center of the city. We can make our prediction equation as simple or as complex as

FIGURE 5.11
Contour for Household Income: Indianapolis, Indiana

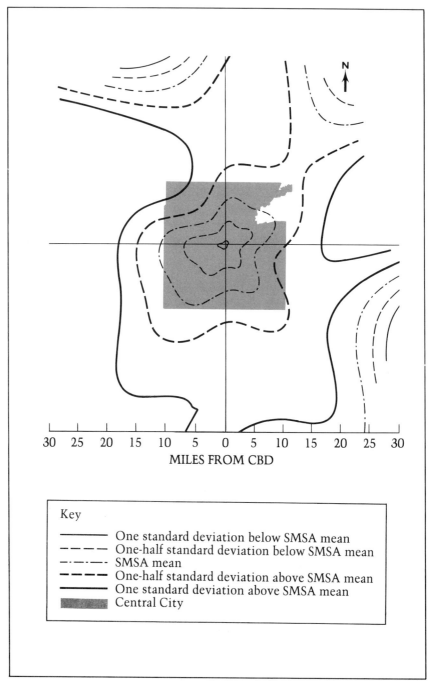

MILES FROM CBD

Key
——————— One standard deviation below SMSA mean
- - - - - One-half standard deviation below SMSA mean
-·—·—·- SMSA mean
▬ ▬ ▬ One-half standard deviation above SMSA mean
━━━━━ One standard deviation above SMSA mean
▨ Central City

FIGURE 5.12
Contour for Laborers: Seattle, Washington

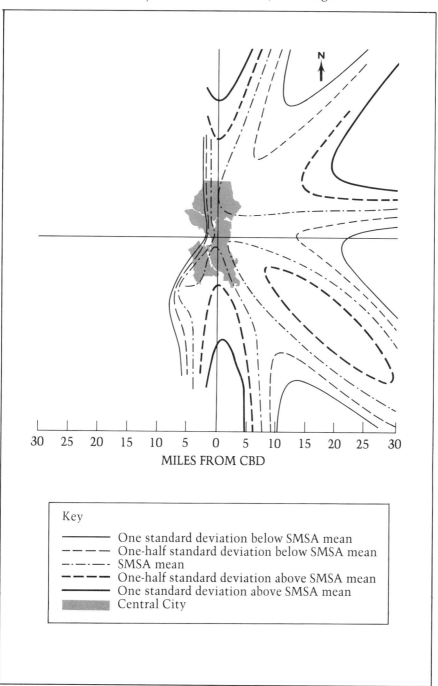

MILES FROM CBD

Key
——————— One standard deviation below SMSA mean
– – – – One-half standard deviation below SMSA mean
–·–·–·– SMSA mean
- - - - One-half standard deviation above SMSA mean
——————— One standard deviation above SMSA mean
▓▓▓▓ Central City

FIGURE 5.13

Contour for Foreign Born: Lexington, Kentucky

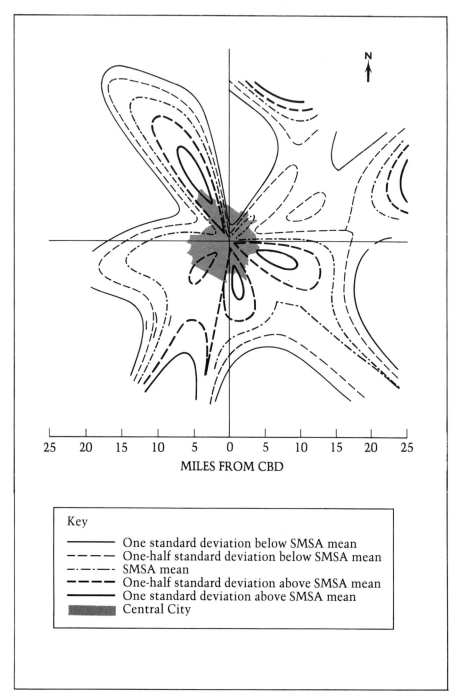

MILES FROM CBD

Key

———— One standard deviation below SMSA mean
– – – – One-half standard deviation below SMSA mean
–·–·– SMSA mean
– – – – One-half standard deviation above SMSA mean
———— One standard deviation above SMSA mean
▓▓▓▓ Central City

we wish; by including only a single term, a slope in distance, or by incorporating a large number of terms to produce very complex patterns of variation.[21] For example, income can at first increase and then decrease with distance. Sectoral patterns or even nucleation can be represented. Since we use regression analysis, at each step of the way we obtain a "goodness of fit" statistic, which describes how well spatial location is predicting the social composition of neighborhoods. Once we have estimated the statistical coefficients, we can turn the process on its head and use the statistical equation to produce a pictorial representation of the social topography of the metropolis. Each figure presents five contours: the mean of the characteristic, one-half standard deviation above and below the mean, and a full standing deviation above and below the mean, with respect to the distribution of tracts within SMSAs.

Contour Maps for Three Metropolitan Areas

We have produced these metropolitan contours for 19 SMSAs for 21 characteristics. The contours range from nearly perfect concentric rings, indicative of a pure zonal or distance gradient distribution, to completely unsystematic lines with little variance explained. We now look at selected contour maps for San Antonio, Stockton, and Flint, beginning with population density, the characteristic most intensely scru-

[21]Much of our discussion will be based on the analysis of these two models. Although we fit a number of intermediate cases, we felt that these two best summarized the relative simplicity versus complexity of the spatial distribution. In the simple, linear model we fit

$$f(r) = b_0 + b_1 r$$

where $f(r)$ is the value of the social characteristic, r is the tract's distance from city center, and b_0 and b_1 are coefficients to be estimated.

In the complex, contour model we fit a Fourier series to the distribution

$$f(r, \theta) = a + r \left[a_{10} + \sum_{m=1}^{6} a_{1m}\cos m\theta + b_{1m}\sin m\theta \right] + r^2 \left[a_{20} + \sum_{m=1}^{6} a_{2m}\cos m\theta + b_{2m}\sin m\theta \right]$$

where r = distance, 0 = direction, measured counterclockwise from a line due east of the CBD, and the remaining coefficients (26 plus a constant) are to be estimated. See Michael J. White, "Sociospatial Contours for Ecological Analysis," in Bogue and White, *Essays in Human Ecology II*, pp. 90–108. The sine and cosine terms capture the directional deviation.

For dependent variables that are proportions we have taken their logit, i.e., log $(p/(1 - p))$, so that all predicted values will be realizable. Previous tests showed that this gave reasonable results and is consistent with values predicted for the proportion itself.

tinized in gradient analysis and closely related to housing stock attributes. The standard progression of status (professional workers), life cycle (household size), and ethnicity (black population) follows.

Density.   Figure 5.14 describes our model for the distribution of population density in San Antonio.[22] The model fits well overall, with spatial location explaining 70 percent of the variation in neighborhood population density. The picture is somewhat star-shaped, a basic concentric zone model—density declines steadily with distance—reshaped by the major transportation corridors that produce the arms of the star in certain directions. In any single direction density still declines fairly steadily with distance. This is indicated on the map by the progression from the dark, solid contour line to the lighter broken line. The rate of decline varies by direction; for instance, toward the southeast the fall-off in density is relatively quick; in the northeast and north-northwest it is relatively slow. In the west and southwest the small lobes are due to a rise and fall in density with distance, evidence of slight nucleation.

In Stockton, California (Figure 5.15), we can explain about one-third of the variation in population density—which is substantial—yet it is certainly not the simple concentric zone picture that we have observed for other cities. The very center of the city has higher population density, but the density gradient is not at all consistent in the various directions. As a young SMSA, Stockton lacks the ecological substructure that we find in the larger, older cities.

Flint is an older urban area whose economy has been based on manufacturing. There is radial differentiation of the population density in the SMSA (Table 4.1; see also Table 5.6 below), but in our contour results the simple gradient model performs weakly and the detailed model is worse. Consequently, Figure 5.16 shows little pattern, and we can place less reliance on the picture drawn by the computer.

Status.   Our next contour map (Figure 5.17) for San Antonio takes up the distribution of the higher status occupational categories. Earlier we determined that San Antonio has a comparatively high percentage of white collar workers. We cannot predict the location of higher status workers as well as density.[23] The central area of the SMSA (extending

[22]In this case we have based our analysis on the whole SMSA rather than on Bexar County, as in the previous figures.

[23]The contour map actually plots the proportion of professional and managerial workers in the SMSA; the shaded map before plotted the proportion of white collar workers. The two percentages are fairly highly correlated in SMSAs; white collar workers include technical and support workers.

FIGURE 5.14
Contour for Population Density: San Antonio, Texas

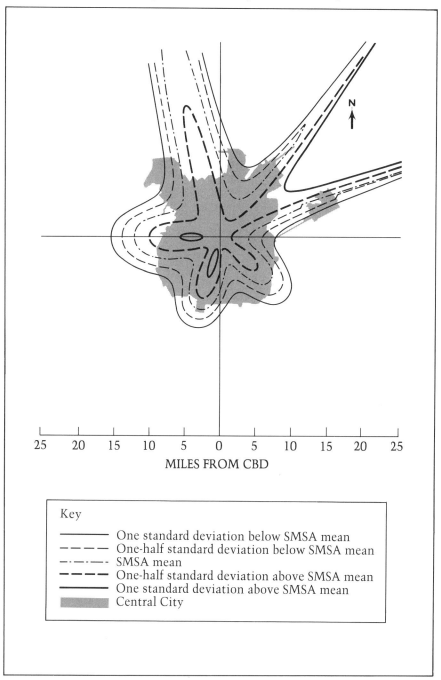

MILES FROM CBD

Key
——————— One standard deviation below SMSA mean
— — — — One-half standard deviation below SMSA mean
—·—·—·- SMSA mean
– – – – One-half standard deviation above SMSA mean
——————— One standard deviation above SMSA mean
▨ Central City

FIGURE 5.15
Contour for Population Density: Stockton, California

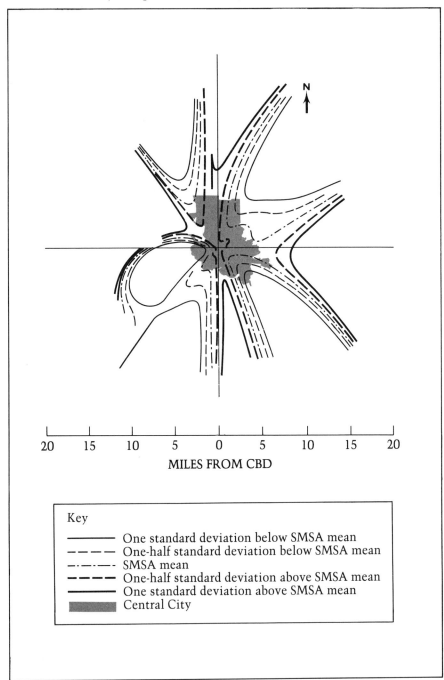

MILES FROM CBD

Key
——————— One standard deviation below SMSA mean
– – – – – One-half standard deviation below SMSA mean
–·—·—·– SMSA mean
– – – – One-half standard deviation above SMSA mean
——————— One standard deviation above SMSA mean
▓▓▓▓ Central City

FIGURE 5.16
Contour for Population Density: Flint, Michigan

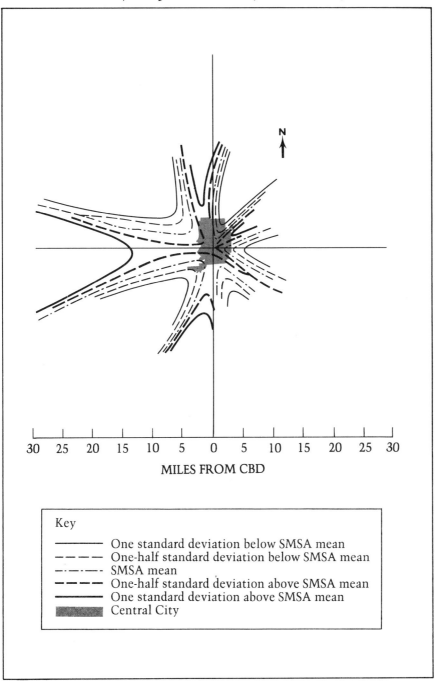

MILES FROM CBD

Key
———— One standard deviation below SMSA mean
– – – – One-half standard deviation below SMSA mean
–·–·– SMSA mean
– – – – One-half standard deviation above SMSA mean
———— One standard deviation above SMSA mean
▓▓▓ Central City

FIGURE 5.17
Professional Workers: San Antonio, Texas

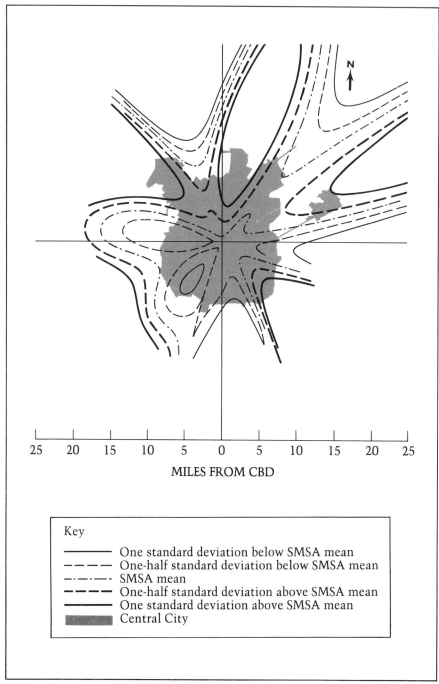

MILES FROM CBD

Key
——————— One standard deviation below SMSA mean
– – – – One-half standard deviation below SMSA mean
–·–·–·– SMSA mean
– – – – One-half standard deviation above SMSA mean
——————— One standard deviation above SMSA mean
▓▓▓ Central City

out to about five miles) has very low predicted concentration of managerial workers. Low status wedges appear in the northeast and northwest (lighter contour lines), and there are also nodes of low status workers in the southwest section. The overall picture is a mixture of the zone and sector model, with distance and direction helping to predict the location of professionals and managers.

In Stockton, the distribution of white collar workers by census tract on the shaded map showed little spatial organization, although there was certainly clustering. Our formal statistical analysis corroborates this. Although, as always, we can produce a predicted contour (Figure 5.18), the associated regression equation in distance and direction explains none of the variation in the location of managerial and professional workers. There is no support then for any model of spatial organization.

The professional population in Flint (Figure 5.19) also exhibits very little spatial pattern, and the prediction is poor. Consistent with the picture in the shaded map, to the west and to the southeast darker contours appear, indicating areas of higher SES concentration in an SMSA with fairly few white collar workers.

Life Cycle. The pattern for household size in San Antonio (Figure 5.20) is not so uniformly linked to distance. Overall, the associated statistical model explains about half of the variance in neighborhood household size. What does the pattern indicate? Household size varies by distance, but also by sector. The two north-side V-shaped patterns indicate that household size increases with distance, but these Vs are separated by a low-density, low household size sector. On the western and southern sides of the city we find two egg-shaped patterns; these indicate areas of comparatively high household density.

The contour map for Stockton (Figure 5.21) also fails to exhibit any simple pattern, but it does pick up the variations in the shaded map. On the whole, we do find that the more peripherally located neighborhoods tend to have the largest population per household, but that there are pockets of exceptions. It is these districts (as we shall see shortly) that contain some of the higher SES population. In Flint, household size presents a little clearer picture (Figure 5.22), and the statistical model can explain about 42 percent of its variation across neighborhoods. There is an increase in household size in almost every direction for about ten miles as one moves out from the center of the city, except in the heavily black northwest quadrant. The net effect is a modified concentric pattern, not unlike that for population density in San Antonio.

Race.   In San Antonio, the statistical model explains 43 percent of the variance in black proportion and there is some evidence of a sectoral pattern. The contour (Figure 5.23) mirrors the shaded map in showing the heavy concentrations of blacks in neighborhoods on the east side and their absence in the southeast section. Most of the areas of the city at a distance of a few miles are solidly white.[24]

Our segregation analysis determined an index of dissimilarity of 56 in Stockton for the black population. The pattern of Figure 5.24 shows this clear segregation, even though Hispanics constitute a numerically more significant minority group in Stockton. Both the contour and shaded maps indicate heavy concentrations of the black population at the center of the city—note the solid contours (and shading in Figure 5.9) surrounding downtown. Extensions of the black residential district—it cannot really be called a ghetto in the same sense as the word is used in some of the large cities—exist to the southeast and northeast of downtown. Most neighborhoods to the east and north are distinguished by the absence of black population. The far southern tract—which has been an exception to many patterns—also has a higher black concentration. The contour picks this up just like the shaded map. Overall, our model does well at explaining the distribution of the black population, with the spatial variable accounting for about half of the variance in race.

The lines are very clear in Flint's contour map (Figure 5.25), although they do not follow a simple zone-sector pattern. The inner section of the city is heavily black, as indicated by the dark contours; there is also a large concentration of black neighborhoods to the north of the CBD, and two clusters to the northeast and south of the CBD. The fall-off around these points is fairly sharp and distinct, that is, the contour lines are closely packed, providing two-dimensional evidence of residential segregation. The correspondence between Figure 5.10 and Figure 5.25 is apparent. The highly segregated racial pattern is, if anything, nuclear.

Some of the strengths and weaknesses of the contour procedure, as compared to the shaded maps of GraphicProfile, should be evident now. On the negative side the contours are more difficult to interpret, because of their underlying complexity. They can also be sensitive to aberrations in the metropolitan structure. A neighborhood that is seemingly out of place will still be incorporated into a least-squares fit over

---

[24]In San Antonio and Stockton, the principal minority group is the Hispanic population. Contour results for the Spanish origin population were obtained and are included in later tables.

FIGURE 5.18
Professional Workers: Stockton, California

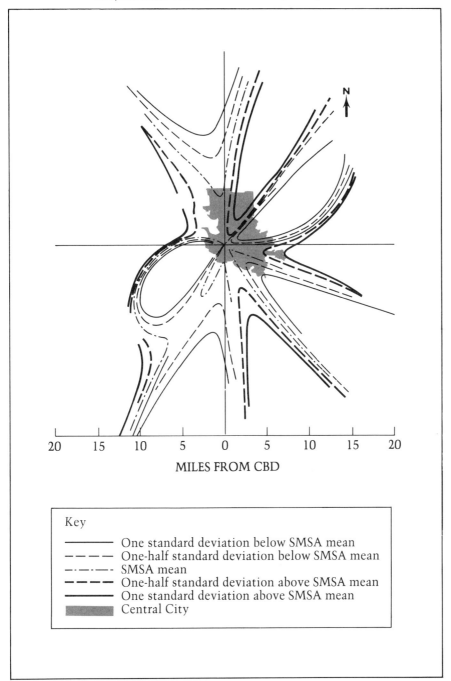

MILES FROM CBD

Key
——————— One standard deviation below SMSA mean
– – – – One-half standard deviation below SMSA mean
–·–·–·– SMSA mean
▬ ▬ ▬ ▬ One-half standard deviation above SMSA mean
▬▬▬▬▬ One standard deviation above SMSA mean
▧▧▧ Central City

FIGURE 5.19
Professional Workers: Flint, Michigan

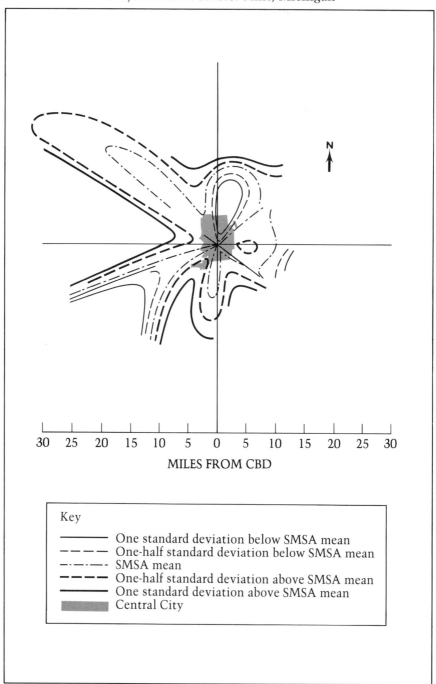

MILES FROM CBD

Key
——————— One standard deviation below SMSA mean
– – – – – One-half standard deviation below SMSA mean
–·–·–·– SMSA mean
– – – – One-half standard deviation above SMSA mean
——————— One standard deviation above SMSA mean
███ Central City

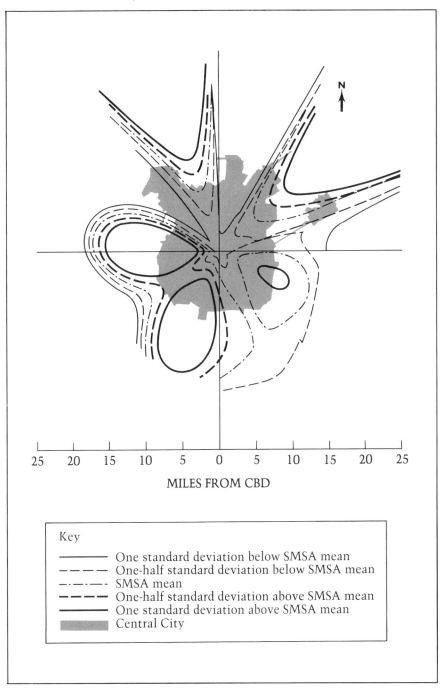

FIGURE 5.20
Contour of Household Size: San Antonio, Texas

MILES FROM CBD

Key
———————— One standard deviation below SMSA mean
– – – – One-half standard deviation below SMSA mean
–·–·–·– SMSA mean
▬ ▬ ▬ ▬ One-half standard deviation above SMSA mean
▬▬▬▬▬ One standard deviation above SMSA mean
 Central City

FIGURE 5.21
Contour for Household Size: Stockton, California

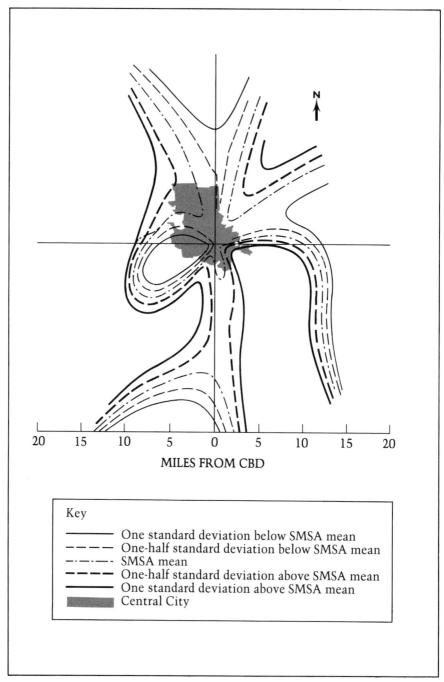

MILES FROM CBD

Key

——— One standard deviation below SMSA mean
- - - - One-half standard deviation below SMSA mean
-·-·-·- SMSA mean
 - - - One-half standard deviation above SMSA mean
▬▬▬ One standard deviation above SMSA mean
▨ Central City

FIGURE 5.22
Contour for Household Size: Flint, Michigan

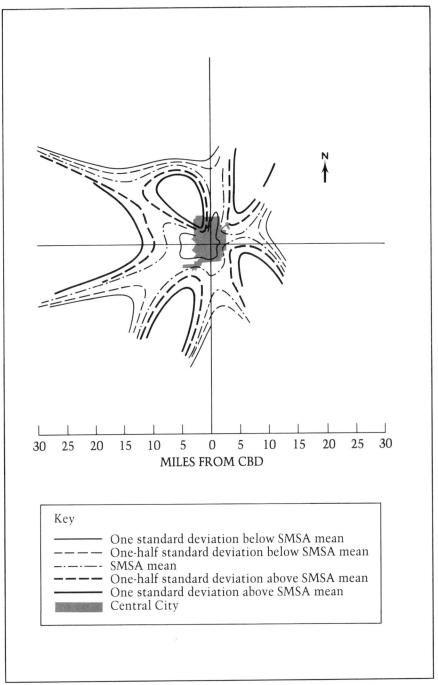

MILES FROM CBD

30 25 20 15 10 5 0 5 10 15 20 25 30

Key
——— One standard deviation below SMSA mean
— — — One-half standard deviation below SMSA mean
—·—·—· SMSA mean
— — — One-half standard deviation above SMSA mean
——— One standard deviation above SMSA mean
▓▓ Central City

FIGURE 5.23
Contour for Proportion Black Population: San Antonio, Texas

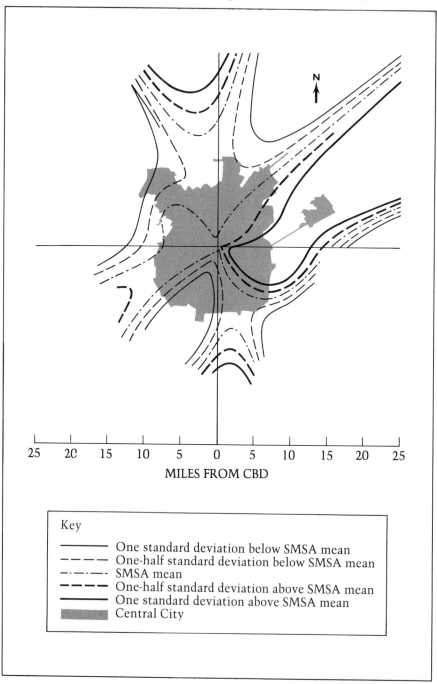

MILES FROM CBD

Key

——————— One standard deviation below SMSA mean
– – – – One-half standard deviation below SMSA mean
–·–·–·– SMSA mean
▪ ▪ ▪ ▪ One-half standard deviation above SMSA mean
━━━━━ One standard deviation above SMSA mean
▨ Central City

FIGURE 5.24
Contour for Proportion Black Population: Stockton, California

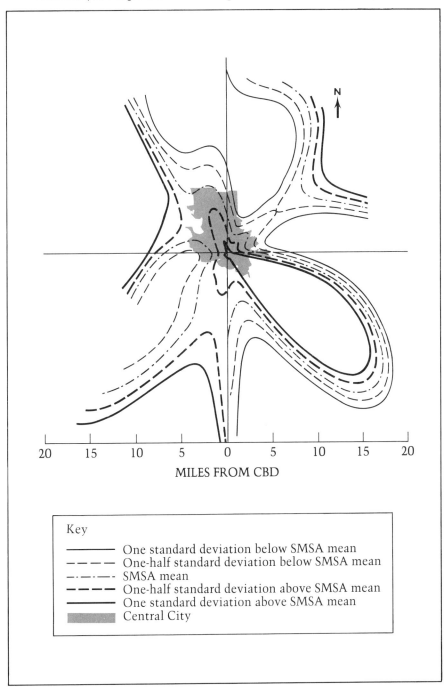

MILES FROM CBD

Key
——————— One standard deviation below SMSA mean
— — — — One-half standard deviation below SMSA mean
—·—·—·— SMSA mean
— — — — One-half standard deviation above SMSA mean
——————— One standard deviation above SMSA mean
▓▓▓▓ Central City

FIGURE 5.25
Contour for Proportion Black Population: Flint, Michigan

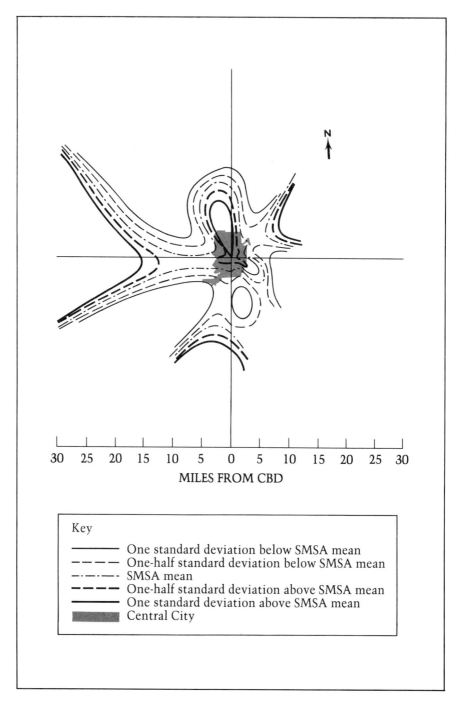

MILES FROM CBD

Key

——————— One standard deviation below SMSA mean
– – – – One-half standard deviation below SMSA mean
–·–·–· SMSA mean
– – – – One-half standard deviation above SMSA mean
——————— One standard deviation above SMSA mean
▮▮▮▮ Central City

all of the census tracts in the SMSA. On the other hand, the contour procedure allows us to get a statistical estimate of the accuracy of the picture, something not possible with the shaded map. To make the shaded map intelligible, we were forced to categorize the values of the characteristics and then shade by intervals. The contour, by contrast, can pick up all gradation in the intensity of the characteristic over space. Where the shaded map "colors in" an entire census tract, it tends to give visually disproportionate weight to the areally larger tracts, usually located at the periphery of the SMSA. The statistical procedure gives equal weight to all neighborhoods. In both maps, patterns in the crowded central core are more difficult to discern. Both techniques look only at one variable at a time, and necessarily make no correction for other characteristics of the population in the neighborhoods.

Statistical Results for Measuring the Contours

The maps give the best "feel" for the overall distribution of each characteristic in the metropolitan space, but statistical analysis can test whether a particular pattern is statistically significant in the formal sense. Equally important, the regression equation results provide an important tool to summarize the characteristics of community distribution in the metropolis. For each contour map we can calculate the percent of the variance explained by the regression equation, or R^2. This statistic ranges from 0 to 100 percent. The larger the value of the R^2 statistic, the better one can predict the composition of a neighborhood (for this characteristic) from spatial location alone. For a given variable, say, education, values near zero would indicate that the distribution of average educational attainment within a neighborhood does not depend on where within the SMSA it is located; conversely, a value closer to 100 percent (rare indeed) would point to an almost infallible prediction about a neighborhood's educational level merely from knowing its distance and direction from the CBD. The R^2 statistic is slightly sensitive to how many census tract observations there are in the metropolitan area. We calculate an adjusted R^2 statistic to control for this and thereby put all SMSAs on an equal footing for comparative analysis.

We are also very interested in how complicated a model (map) is needed to explain statistically the distribution of the characteristic. To help answer this we have used two regression equations that represent alternative statistical models. The first is an extremely simple model, which incorporates only distance from the CBD. We term this the "linear model." The second tests whether a more involved contour is required, and is called the "contour model." The first case is equivalent to describing the metropolitan topography in terms of a simple single peak with even slopes on all sides, akin to a volcano arising out of a flat plain. The more complicated contour is required if the metropolitan topography is more aptly depicted as a rugged mountain range. Sometimes metropolitan topography is not well explained by either model, for instance, when there is a random distribution of high and low points, peaks and valleys.

Population Density. Table 5.6 contains the statistical results for the nineteen SMSAs for population density.[25] The first two columns present the regression of density on distance only. In every city the slope is negative and statistically significant, indicating a decline in neighborhood population density with distance from the center of the city. The pattern of the flatter gradients in the larger cities found in earlier studies holds modestly.

Figure 5.26 graphs the 1980 population density for selected metropolitan areas. Each curve is the tracing of the predicted density for the neighborhoods at that distance. The highest peak of central density is reached in Boston at about 35 persons per acre predicted, and that city also shows a fairly sharp decline. Chicago, the other older northern city in the figure, has only a slightly lower central density and more flattened shape to its curve. Overall, Chicago is the denser of the two metropolises; the Chicago gradient crosses above Boston's at about two miles, and is still at substantial densities even twenty miles from the CBD. Allentown and Amarillo have fairly steep slants to their density gradient, but start from very low central densities, a typical pattern for smaller metropolitan areas. Perhaps San Diego provides a precursor of where metropolitan America is going. This SMSA, young but now the twentieth largest in the United States; is flat, that is, there is virtually no systematic differentiation in neighborhood population density by distance from the center of the city. Topography and the presence of the military undoubtedly contribute to this, but that is still only part of the story. Despite the seeming flatness of several of these curves, density remains one of the characteristics that is best explained by the simple linear model. In the average SMSA, distance alone can account for a bit over one-third of the variation in neighborhood population density.

[25]In keeping with previous studies, we fit the logarithm of density to distance. We did analyze the equation for raw (untransformed) population density, but found that the exponential version continues to give a better statistical fit. Another complication is that large expanses of nonresidential land use near the center of the city (CBD commercial uses, parks, abandonment, etc.) will contribute to lower population densities at the core. We have eliminated Bangor and Sheboygan from these tables because their small size makes it impossible to estimate the more complicated models.

TABLE 5.6

Sociospatial Contour Results for Density
(logarithm of persons per square mile in tract)

	Linear Model		Contour Model			
Metropolitan Area	B	adj. R^2	adj. R^2	F	Gain	N
Allentown	−.10	24.6	51.3	7.0*	4.2†	155‡
Amarillo	−.35	29.2	67.5	5.7	3.8	63
Atlanta	−.12	77.9	82.3	61.4	4.3	352
Birmingham	−.12	30.0	34.6	4.9	1.5	204
Boston	−.16	47.1	51.6	24.0	3.0	584
Chicago	−.08	21.0	24.0	18.7	3.3	1516
Flint	−.10	12.7	10.7	1.5	.9	125
Indianapolis	−.15	55.1	63.7	18.4	3.4	269
Lexington	−.24	62.3	71.8	8.4	2.0	80
New Bedford	−.39	46.0	73.2	5.5	2.8	46
New Haven	−.14	35.0	56.1	5.4	2.7	94
New Orleans	−.13	48.7	56.2	16.5	3.1	327
Newark	−.12	53.8	66.8	35.6	8.0	466
St. Louis	−.10	34.1	44.4	13.9	4.1	438
Salt Lake City	−.06	16.9	59.6	11.2	8.6	189
San Antonio	−.14	41.1	70.3	18.2	8.4	198
San Diego	−.06	14.5	32.2	7.7	4.8	384
Seattle	−.12	39.1	51.8	15.5	4.7	367
Stockton	−.14	10.4	34.2	2.6	2.1	84
MEAN	−.15	36.8	52.8			

*F value for the contour model, the associated degrees of freedom are (26, N − 27), where N is the number of tracts in the final column.

†F value for test of incremental explanatory power of additional variables in contour model, with associated degrees of freedom (25, N − 26), where N is the number of tracts.

‡Number of census tracts in the SMSA included in this analysis.

The adjusted R^2 statistic in the third column of Table 5.6 is the goodness-of-fit statistic that attaches to the contour maps discussed earlier. The higher the value of R^2, the surer we are of the shape of the contour and the larger fraction of all of the variation we are capturing. In almost every SMSA there is a net improvement, bringing the average variance explained to over 50 percent.[26] In a few, such as San Antonio

[26]Although the unadjusted R^2 statistic must increase with the addition of terms to the regression equation, the adjusted statistics need not improve. In fact, it may decline— see Flint—and even turn negative, indicating that the more elaborate equation really helps not at all. The additional terms are then statistically inefficient and not statistically significant.

FIGURE 5.26
Population Density Gradients: 1980
Selected SMSAs

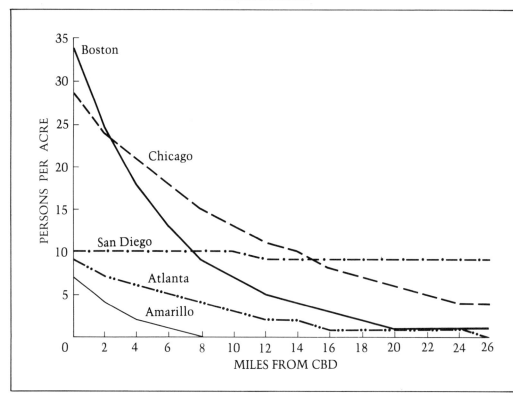

and Salt Lake City, the improvement is quite dramatic. Columns 4 and 5 contain two measures that provide a formal statistical test of the fit. They allow us to accept or reject the null hypothesis that the variations we observe in the data are really due to chance. The first value is an *F* test for the statistical significance of the contour model. The larger the value of this statistic, the more confident we can be about asserting that there is a relationship between spatial location and the neighborhood characteristic. The second statistic, the "gain," tests the degree of improvement in the contour model over the linear model; again, larger numbers give us more confidence in rejecting the null hypothesis and in asserting that there is a meaningful improvement in fit with the more elaborate regression equation.[27] In most cities we observe a statistically significant improvement in the ability to predict population density by resorting to the more complex model, but this improvement is relatively modest. In Flint, there is a simple linear relationship, but the other explanatory coefficients add nothing.

Socioeconomic Status. To represent SES, Table 5.7 describes the distribution of professional workers. As is evident from the first two columns, the linear model has almost no ability to explain the location of the professional and managerial work force; the slope coefficients are close to zero and the R^2 value is negligible in many cities. Performance is especially poor in the younger SMSAs. With the more complex model there is an improvement in most SMSAs and a marked increase in Indianapolis and San Antonio. The F test indicates that the contour model is significant in 14 out of the 19 SMSAs. Recalling the contour maps themselves, which correspond to the statistical results of columns 3 and 4, we have mounting evidence that the distribution of the population by occupation leans to the nucleated or clustered pattern.

Life Cycle. We have usually chosen average household size as an indicator of a neighborhood's life cycle stage, and statistical results for this characteristic are contained in Table 5.8. Again, in every metropolitan area the slope coefficient is positive, but the effect is slight. In the average city an increase of 50 miles away from the center of the city corresponds to a predicted increase of one person in average household size for the neighborhood. The linear model explains only about one-tenth of the variance in average household size. The contour model provides some gain, yet it is of little consequence statistically. The segregation index for household size (and many of the other life cycle characteristics) is low, and so, too, is its predictability by this method. To the extent that unevenness manifests a pattern, it tends to be modestly radial, but with many deviations, as in the contour map for Flint.

----

[27]While the goodness-of-fit parameters were adjusted to compensate for differential city size, these "F statistics" have not. SMSAs with more census tracts are likely to have larger F values, due to the fact that with more observations we can be more confident about making statistical claims. A sufficiently large F statistic allows us to reject the null hypothesis that no relationship (improvement) exists.

In the average size city of 300 census tracts, an F value of about 1.55 is sufficient to accept the hypothesis (at the 5 percent level) that there is a statistically significant relationship between spatial location and density; it is about 1.85 at the 1 percent level. For the smaller cities, a larger cutoff value would be required; the converse is true for the larger cities.

TABLE 5.7

Sociospatial Contour Results for Professional Workers
(logit of tract proportion in professional occupations)

Metropolitan Area	Linear Model		Contour Model		Gain	N
	B	adj. R^2	adj.R^2	F		
Allentown	.00	−.6	15.6	2.0*	2.1†	155‡
Amarillo	.09	8.6	72.3	7.0	6.5	63
Atlanta	.00	−6.3	25.1	5.3	6.6	352
Birmingham	.00	−.5	.4	1.0	1.0	204
Boston	.00	1.6	8.5	3.0	2.7	584
Chicago	.04	4.5	14.4	10.4	7.7	1516
Flint	.02	1.1	6.9	1.3	1.3	125
Indianapolis	.02	2.1	51.6	11.5	11.5	269
Lexington	−.01	−1.0	−17.8	.5	.5	80
New Bedford	.17	3.6	27.2	1.6	1.6	46
New Haven	.05	3.1	4.4	1.1	1.0	94
New Orleans	.01	−.2	5.7	1.7	1.7	327
Newark	.05	14.5	46.6	16.0	11.7	466
St. Louis	.01	.2	13.5	3.5	3.5	438
Salt Lake City	−.01	1.3	10.8	1.8	1.7	189
San Antonio	.02	.4	34.7	4.8	5.0	198
San Diego	.01	.1	13.5	3.2	3.2	384
Seattle	−.03	1.5	8.4	2.2	2.0	367
Stockton	.03	−.6	−5.8	.8	.8	84
MEAN	.02	1.8	17.7			

*F value for the contour model, the associated degrees of freedom are (26, N − 27), where N is the number of tracts in the final column.

†F value for test of incremental explanatory power of additional variables in contour model, with associated degrees of freedom (25, N − 26), where N is the number of tracts.

‡Number of census tracts in the SMSA included in this analysis.

Race.   Table 5.9 describes the spatial distribution of the black population. In all but one SMSA the slope coefficient is negative, perfectly consistent with the steady decrease in black concentration that we found in the quartile analysis earlier in this chapter. The largest values (in magnitude) for the slope are found in Flint, Indianapolis, New Haven, and Amarillo. In these places, and in older metropolitan areas generally, the black population is the most centrally constricted. Correspondingly, the value of the R^2 statistic is larger in these cities. On average we can explain about 14 percent of the variation in the location of the black population with the linear model, less than half the corresponding figure for density. The more elaborate "contour" model does improve the fit. In the average city we can explain nearly half of

TABLE 5.8

Sociospatial Contour Results for Household Size
(tract persons per household)

Metropolitan Area	Linear Model B	adj. R^2	Contour Model adj. R^2	F	Gain	N
Allentown	.01	7.3	18.1	2.2*	1.8†	155‡
Amarillo	.04	5.4	52.8	3.5	3.4	63
Atlanta	.02	19.9	36.4	8.4	4.5	352
Birmingham	.01	9.6	22.0	3.1	2.2	204
Boston	.03	19.9	37.9	14.1	7.5	584
Chicago	.01	2.1	15.7	11.4	10.4	1516
Flint	.02	7.9	41.6	4.2	3.7	125
Indianapolis	.01	6.0	8.1	1.8	1.2	269
Lexington	.03	21.2	12.5	1.4	.7	80
New Bedford	.05	31.6	6.1	1.1	.5	46
New Haven	.03	12.3	30.7	2.5	1.9	94
New Orleans	.02	9.2	28.1	5.7	4.3	327
Newark	.01	4.1	5.0	1.9	1.1	466
St. Louis	.01	8.3	15.1	3.8	2.3	438
Salt Lake City	.02	7.3	54.9	9.4	8.6	189
San Antonio	.00	−.5	55.4	10.0	10.5	198
San Diego	.01	1.7	30.5	7.2	7.1	384
Seattle	.02	18.4	38.7	9.5	5.6	367
Stockton	.01	2.9	14.0	1.5	1.4	84
MEAN	.02	10.2	27.6			

*F value for the contour model, the associated degrees of freedom are (26, N − 27), where N is the number of tracts in the final column.

†F value for test of incremental explanatory power of additional variables in contour model, with associated degrees of freedom (25, N − 26), where N is the number of tracts.

‡Number of census tracts in the SMSA.

the variance, although the statistical significance of the fit varies widely. The F value is the largest (and the results the most statistically significant) in those major metropolitan areas with substantial concentrations of blacks, such as Chicago, Atlanta, and Newark. In these same cities the gain (column 5) of the contour model over the linear model also has a high degree of statistical significance. Such a gain is consistent with a sectoral or a nucleated pattern.

The picture that seems to be emerging for race, then, is a more complex one than for density. In every city the black population is more centrally concentrated. In the larger metropolitan areas, which have both more neighborhoods and a larger number of predominantly black neighborhoods, the distribution is more complicated, but is systematic

TABLE 5.9

Sociospatial Contour Results for the Black Population: 1980
(logit of tract proportion black)

Metropolitan Area	Linear Model		Contour Model		Gain	N
	B	adj. R^2	adj. R^2	F		
Allentown	−.07	6.2	58.0	8.8*	8.3†	155‡
Amarillo	−.26	6.0	55.2	3.8	3.6	63
Atlanta	−.16	25.4	60.3	20.7	12.8	352
Birmingham	−.13	12.5	36.0	5.2	3.8	204
Boston	−.08	4.0	18.3	5.8	4.9	584
Chicago	−.10	4.9	40.6	39.3	36.0	1516
Flint	−.28	25.4	55.8	6.8	4.3	125
Indianapolis	−.28	34.0	56.6	13.9	6.3	269
Lexington	−.06	2.4	6.4	1.2	1.1	80
New Bedford	−.12	1.3	60.3	3.5	3.7	46
New Haven	−.24	28.9	52.3	4.7	2.7	94
New Orleans	−.09	4.2	44.7	10.7	10.1	327
Newark	−.19	23.3	45.5	15.3	8.2	466
St. Louis	−.15	13.5	44.5	13.9	10.4	438
Salt Lake City	.01	.1	35.9	4.9	5.0	189
San Antonio	−.02	0.0	43.0	6.5	6.7	198
San Diego	−.05	10.1	42.0	11.2	9.1	384
Seattle	−.11	35.1	46.5	12.7	4.0	367
Stockton	−.22	26.3	52.9	4.4	2.8	84
MEAN	−.14	13.9	45.0	10.2	7.6	

*F value for the contour model, the associated degrees of freedom are (26, N−27), where N is the number of tracts in the final column.

†F value for test of incremental explanatory power of additional variables in contour model, with associated degrees of freedom (25, N−26), where N is the number of tracts.

‡Number of census tracts in the SMSA.

enough to be picked up by the equation. In the smaller SMSAs, such as Allentown, the model explains a very large fraction of the variance in the black population distribution, partly because there are so few predominantly black neighborhoods for which to account. The extreme racial segregation that we observe in almost every American metropolis serves to reinforce this set of statistical results.

General Classification of Contour Maps. The analysis we have presented above has been repeated for every one of the variables under study in this monograph. Of particular concern throughout this chapter has been the kind of picture drawn by the characteristic, and whether this picture was consistent with the one of the chief models of urban ecological structure—zonal, sectoral, or nucleated—that we outlined at the outset. For each of 21 variables and for the nineteen SMSAs we classified the contour maps according to whether the variable seemed to exhibit a zonal, sectoral, or nucleated pattern, or whether it was a combination of patterns, or even something altogether different. This task involved the classification of about 400 maps by eye. Undoubtedly, the subjective judgments introduce error, but these classifications can be viewed as companions to the harsher quantitative judgments imposed by the formal statistical approach. Table 5.10 presents the percentage distribution for the predominant spatial pattern of each characteristic. [28]

The physical features of the metropolitan landscape clearly exhibit a zonal pattern. I classified 79 percent of the cities as having a population density distribution zonal in form. Age of the housing stock is uniformly zonal in its distribution, the only characteristic that so clearly exhibits a single pattern. While the inner city predominance of apartments and the suburban prevalence of single family homes still holds, the multifamily component of the housing stock is less geographically systematic than its age or overall density. We looked at two additional characteristics of the housing stock—vacancy and plumbing deficiency. Both vacancy rates and incidence of plumbing deficiency manifest predominantly zonal patterns. If age of the housing stock exerts an appreciable influence on its quality and desirability, we would expect a zonal pattern.

Socioeconomic status is usually linked to sectoral variation in the integrated model of Berry and others (see footnote 7) as well as in the original Hoyt model. No single pattern predominates for occupation in the nineteen SMSAs. For the highest status professional and managerial groups, the leading category (42 percent) for the map classifications was nucleated. This is consistent with the fairly substantial gain of the contour model over the linear model in the statistical tabulations of Table 5.7. The distribution of clerical workers is even more difficult to classify. Our labeling places the maps just about equally in each of the four categories (including "other"), casting doubt on whether there is any really identifiable pattern. The maps for laborers, while still difficult to discern, fell more often into the sectoral category than into any other. In any case, zonal patterns could not be discerned. Location of sites of blue collar employment along axial rail or road lines—yet further from downtown—could give rise to such a pattern.

Income and educational attainment, two other demographic measures of SES, are instructive by comparison. For education, the zonal

---

[28]For cities where the classification was clear the tabulation appears under respective entry; if nodes were evident the map was classified as nucleated. Where no predominant pattern could be discerned, the map was classified as "other."

TABLE 5.10

Predominant Pattern of Spatial Organization, by Characteristic

	Zonal	Sectoral	Nucleated	Other
HOUSING				
Population Density	79%	5%	— %	16%*
Housing Age	100	—	—	—
Multifamily Dwellings	58	16	21	5
SOCIOECONOMIC STATUS				
Professional	21	26	42	11
Clerical	26	21	26	26
Laborer	5	53	16	26
Educational Attainment	32	26	26	16
Income	79	11	11	—
Home Value	84	5	5	5
Median Rent	84	11	—	5
Home Ownership	79	—	21	—
ETHNIC				
Black	37	16	32	16
Spanish	26	32	37	5
Foreign Born	16	16	53	16
LIFE CYCLE				
Household Size	53	5	11	32
Young (Age<18)	42	32	16	11
Old (Age 65+)	42	32	11	16
OTHER				
Vacancy	37	21	21	21
Plumbing	47	32	11	11
Female Labor Force	21	21	11	47
Mobility	21	26	26	26

*Row totals may not sum to 100% due to rounding.

pattern holds a plurality. Income, usually seen to result from education and occupation, is very much distributed in a zonal fashion, to a degree that matches population density.[29] The housing questions on the census also give us considerable insight into socioeconomic status and its spatial distribution. Median rental level, median home value, and

[29]The actual characteristic graphed is household income, which is of course dependent in a very complex way on household composition as well as the prior educational and occupational attainments of its members.

rates of homeownership for neighborhoods are all very well described by the concentric zone model.

Although it is speculative, we can use these results to tell an interesting story about how the status attainment process translates into the metropolitan ecological distribution. Status attainment is generally conceptualized as a process in which education leads to a particular job in the occupational status hierarchy. Although occupation operates as the intervening variable in this process, we find that the spatial differentiation (using segregation and contour analyses) of occupation tends to be lower than education and especially lower than income. We suggest that people choose housing and neighborhoods on the basis of their status (real or desired), income, and journey to work, the last of which is controlled by the siting of employment. With the deconcentration of employment throughout the metropolis, employment nodes are scattered, although still specialized by industry. On the basis of this nodal aspect, reinforced by SES segregation itself, we find modest separation of the population on the basis of occupation. But the power of income outweighs occupation in differentiating people across neighborhoods. As the metropolitan area has deconcentrated in residence and employment, occupational differentiation has diffused, but status differences, as observed through the final product of income, remain visible.

Life cycle variation was measured in the contours by average household size, child population, and elderly population. Over half of the household size maps are classified here as zonal. Not surprisingly the classifications of the young and old population were very similar. So, even though our statistical models cannot explain much of the variation in age and household size across neighborhoods—partly because there is little variation (that is, segregation) to explain—there is an indication that life cycle differentiation does take on a more radial configuration.

Almost all of the ecological models maintain that the ethnic groups are the most likely to be nucleated in their spatial distribution. Even the Burgess concentric model allowed for clusters of ethnic communities around the city. The nucleated pattern occurs more often in these three characteristics than in the others, about one-third of the time for the Spanish and black groups, and about half the time for the foreign born. The centralization of blacks and Hispanics (evident in the ring analysis) is often observed in combination with some nonradial deviation. The foreign-stock population is the most nucleated of all the characteristics in the table. It includes a large number of distinct ethnic groups, who may occupy their own enclaves throughout the metropolitan area, rather than a grouping in spatially systematic fashion.

Rates of population mobility and labor force participation among women are two other characteristics we have been examining all along, although they are not easily linked to one of the three thematic categories. The statistical models only poorly predict the location of movers and working women. Moreover, the best fitting equation does not draw for us any particular kind of picture; the two characteristics are fairly evenly distributed across all four kinds of patterns.

Do these metropolitan areas themselves differ in the propensity with which their neighborhoods exhibit certain patterns? For instance, do large and older cities tend to be zonal, and the younger cities nucleated? Few theories exist about such differences. To check for any such relationships Table 5.11 presents the same information as Table 5.10 for the maps, but now tabulated by SMSA. Nothing emerges strongly enough to suggest a general hypothesis, but metropolitan areas do differ with respect to the likelihood of observing a particular kind of pattern. The most zonal are Chicago, Indianapolis, New Haven, Seattle, and Atlanta. The most nucleated patterns are found in Amarillo, Allentown, New Bedford, and (again) New Haven. Except for Flint, no city has a very strong representation of sectorally shaped contours.[30] The fourth category—indicating more the absence of pattern—is important in maps for Salt Lake City, Birmingham, and New Orleans.

There appears to be no clear relationship between pattern and size, age, region, or growth rate of city, our main classifications for this SMSA sample. Understandably, there is a bit of evidence for the distorting effects of local topography, tending in Allentown and Boston to produce more nucleated patterns than would otherwise be the case. At the outset we excluded large metropolitan areas with multiple independent CBDs, so that we could better observe the "intrinsic" ecological patterns. They would invariably exhibit more nucleation in such an analysis, almost by definition. Our results apply most simply and directly to the monocentric city, but it is evident that the organizing force exerted on neighborhood structure by the traditional CBD is weak in many American metropolises.

Simplicity Versus Complexity

How complex a statistical model do we need to describe adequately the spatial organization of a characteristic? The comparative performance of the simple linear model and the more complex contour regres-

---

[30]This Flint sector may be the "pull" on the contour exerted by the outer county of the SMSA and its own urban communities.

TABLE 5.11

Predominant Pattern of Spatial Organization, by SMSA

Metropolitan Area	Zonal	Sectoral	Nucleated	Other
Allentown	48%	5%	43%	5% *
Amarillo	29	0	62	10
Atlanta	57	5	19	19
Birmingham	38	10	19	33
Boston	38	14	24	24
Chicago	71	10	14	5
Flint	24	62	10	5
Indianapolis	71	0	5	24
Lexington	38	14	24	24
New Bedford	24	38	38	0
New Haven	62	10	29	0
New Orleans	48	14	10	29
Newark	33	43	0	24
St. Louis	52	10	29	10
Salt Lake City	52	10	0	38
San Antonio	48	43	0	10
San Diego	52	14	24	10
Seattle	62	29	0	10
Stockton	48	38	10	5

*Row totals may not sum to 100% due to rounding.

sion equation suggest an answer to this question. For 11 selected characteristics, Figure 5.27 contrasts these two models, averaged over the 19 cities we have been analyzing. The lower portion of the bar graph traces the adjusted R^2 statistic for the linear (distance only) equation, and the upper portion of the graph traces the corresponding statistic for the full contour regression equation. The higher the total bar, the better the overall degree of explanation; the greater the increase of the upper contour portion over the bottom (linear), the more one has to resort to the complicated model to describe metropolitan spatial patterns. From left to right the characteristics are ordered by increasing ratio of the upper to lower sections.

Population density and age of housing stand out as the two features of the metropolitan landscape linked most consistently to geographic position in all of the cities. Their pattern is predominantly concentric, in that the gain of the detailed contour model over the simple linear model is relatively modest. The socioeconomic status variables—here represented by neighborhood rental level, educational status, and professional and clerical workers—fall across a wide range. The prediction

FIGURE 5.27

Spatial Organization

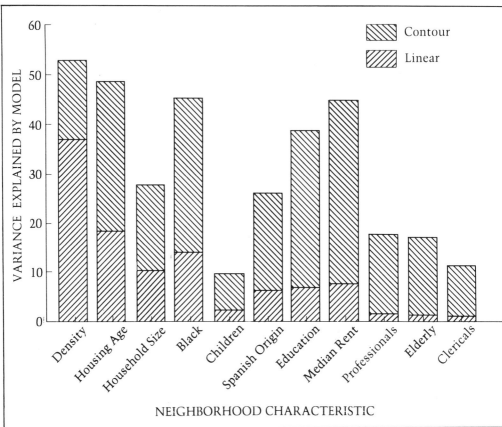

of the location of the two occupational groups is negligible with the simple linear model; all the variance explained comes from the more complicated terms in the regression equation, which raise the R^2 to between 10 and 20 percent, suggesting a more nucleated pattern, if any. Rent and educational status are better predicted by distance alone, but they also show a large gain in the contour model.

The life cycle characteristics are indicated by a neighborhood's household size and its age structure, and they are spread out across the chart. As indicated by the height of the graph, age structure is less spatially organized than social status or the physical character of the neighborhoods. To the extent that any pattern prevails, it appears in household size and is zonal.

Figure 5.27 provides proof of how concentrated blacks (and to a lesser extent Hispanics) are in the central portions of metropolitan areas. For blacks the size of the lower (linear model) bar graph is exceeded only by the two purely physical characteristics, density and housing age. Both of these ethnic groups show about the same relative improvement in the contour map over the linear model.

Table 5.10 and Figure 5.27 each try to get at spatial organization, but in slightly different ways. The table is a subjective classification of the pictures drawn by the contour coefficients and takes no account of variance explained. The figure, on the other hand, focuses directly on the explained variance (R^2) from that estimation procedure. For the most part the two summaries are in agreement. To the extent that no model explains the neighborhood composition well for the characteristic, there tends to be a more even distribution of the "pictures" across the various types. Without question, housing age and density are zonal under both criteria; household size and rental level tend to be, too. Zonal orientation goes a significant way toward explaining the pattern for black and Hispanic minorities. Beyond this, nucleation does contribute to the understanding of ethnic group residential location generally. At the other extreme are the proportion elderly and the two occupational measures. The contours showed them to be distributed across all types, with zonal patterns predominating for clericals and the elderly, and nucleation for professionals. Figure 5.27 presents little to dispute the conclusion from Table 5.10 that zonal variation predominates, with nucleation important for selected characteristics. Results are necessarily moot for those characteristics that display little spatial variation to begin with.

Conclusion: Urban Models and Spatial Organization

Besides treating residential differentiation as a window on American social structure generally, we are interested in how the various pieces of the metropolis fit together and function as a system. The industrial metropolis, which provided the foundation for so much urban theory, has now witnessed several decades of extensive change. Even the 1970s seem to have exerted special pressures on the old metropolises, a reflection of the changing technology of American production and transportation. Given the way in which time erodes the links between conceptual models and empirical reality, it is worth the return to a most fundamental question: Is there still a system to the metropolis? The total picture must include not only residential neighborhoods but also business and industry, schools, government, shopping, and recreational activity, as well as their interrelations.

The decennial census only gives us a view of the people and the places where they filled out their census forms on April 1, 1980. It tells a great deal about residential topography of the metropolis, and from it some inferences about the entire picture can be made. The present chapter goes one step further than the segregation analysis and asks whether there exists any spatially systematic pattern to the distribution of people and the housing stock. Our methods were several. We introduced analysis of distance quartiles (rings) and metropolitan contours in this chapter, to augment traditional approaches based on either depicting characteristics on census tract maps or calculating density gradients. Although abstract, the contour gave us the opportunity to incorporate spatial position in continuous terms, quantify the ability of location to explain statistically the variation in characteristics of neighborhoods, and represent numerous complicated patterns of population distribution by means of metropolitan contour maps. The maps and the statistics associated with them help tell the metropolitan story for 1980. Paralleling the philosophy behind our segregation analysis, we examined a wide variety of characteristics, searching for the spatial pattern in each one.

In the eyes of many urban theorists one of the most salient features of the metropolis is the way in which social characteristics are organized into spatial distributions, highly predictable according to some overarching model. The zonal, sectoral, and nucleation models attempt to distill metropolitan differentiation, placing the vast array of neighborhoods into an overall pattern. Several urban geographers[31] have offered a synthesis of these three forms of organization in an integrated model, building on the results of factorial ecology. They paired the zonal (ring) model with life cycle variation, the sectoral (wedge) model with SES variation, and the multiple nuclei model with ethnic status.

The present analysis concludes that there still is a system to the metropolitan topography. It supports the synthesis only to a limited degree. From our analysis here of a score of census characteristics for the neighborhoods of the SMSAs, we find the following relationships. Status variation is multifaceted. Occupation, income, educational attainment, and housing expenditures do not all trace the same contour on the metropolitan topography. To the extent that status (in the form of income and rent expenditures) can be put into the framework of one of these models, variation seems to be principally zonal. Occupation

---

[31]Berry, "Internal Structure of the City"; and R. A. Murdie, "Factorial Ecology of Metropolitan Toronto, 1959–61."

and education are much less consistent, leaning to more nucleated patterns in many metropolises. Rarely is status sectoral, as some models predict. This lack of fit between the results of participation in the labor market (income) and the origins of that participation (education and occupation) indicates the wide variation in economic returns to occupation in America, as well as complications introduced by family composition and the distribution of metropolitan jobs.

Life cycle differentiation is discernible, but it is not as strong as the features of race and status. To the extent that we can detect any spatial pattern, the orientation is zonal. Of this group, household size exhibits the strongest radial trend.

Even the earliest models allowed for nucleated congregation of the population on the basis of common culture or ancestry, often fueled by discrimination on the part of the majority. Our results are generally consistent with such a view. Many writers have pointed out that minorities are concentrated in central cities of SMSAs, but this distinction is based on the rough dichotomy of a political boundary. We have shown that there is a clear further concentration of minorities, particularly black and Hispanic Americans, into the innermost *rings* (quartiles) of the metropolis. The fact that our statistical contour model can also do a good job of predicting the location of minority neighborhoods is additional evidence of this clumping or segregation.

If we were to gaze at the metropolis from a distance and view its social topography, using the high-resolution telescope of the census, what would we see? Without question the metropolitan contour is quite variegated, with numerous peaks and valleys. The physical substructure of the housing stock and of population and housing density is really quite symmetrical and oriented to a single center. But built on top of that is a complex arrangement of social groups. From our vantage, we could certainly make out the fact that it is the higher-income and higher status groups that live further from the center of town, many across the imaginary boundary of the central city. We would have a great deal of trouble trying to tell one neighborhood from another on the basis of life cycle, although the careful viewer would observe family size increasing with distance from city center. One could identify the shadings of individual ethnic groups, although it might be very difficult to see any pattern in all of the colors.

Our statistical evidence is not yet overwhelming, but the case is building for the claim that the idea of a monocentric city, with the CBD exerting overarching determination on the metropolitan form, has given way to a more diversified form. Patterns of population distribution in the younger SMSAs for the several characteristics tend to be less well explained than for the larger, older regions. Such restructuring comes as no surprise to many observers, who would argue that the transformation has been going on for some time.

In the older metropolitan areas—the ones whose economies were most strictly devoted to smokestack industry—newer patterns are competing with, and may eventually obliterate, the old. Those metropolitan areas that came of age in more recent years display a landscape with less relief. To be sure, there are pockets of affluence and poverty, and ethnic segregation is apparent, but the old ecological models may hold least there. It remains to be seen whether young metropolises are pointing the way to the social topography of the future.

6

NEIGHBORHOOD CHANGE
IN THE DYNAMIC METROPOLIS

Metropolitan Transitions

I T HAS become a cliché to describe the modern metropolis as one "in
transition." Change is a permanent part of the metropolis. But what
kind of transition has gone on, and what will be the look of urban
America in the future? What do we mean when we say that the metropolis is undergoing change? The urban crisis has given way to the fiscal
crisis and these to the search for a new urban role within the transformation of the American economy.[1] It is clear that cities are different entities today than they were a half-century, or even a decade ago, but
have the changes wrought on the American settlement system in the
past few decades brought about a metamorphosis?

From the vantage point of the neighborhood, change implies a revision in the patterns of relationships that tie the local community into
the metropolis. Several of the agents of this change are readily
identified: technology is certainly one of the most potent forces. Transportation and communication in particular have altered the way in
which distance and time interact with production of commodities and
residential location decisions of households. Rail transport networks of

---

[1]See National Academy of Sciences, *Rethinking Urban Policy* (Washington, D.C.:
National Academy of Sciences, 1983), for a discussion of the last issue.

181

the early part of this century and the highway networks of the more re-cent decades have allowed the metropolis to spread out, its population now spilling out far beyond the limits of the formerly dominant central city. The technology of production has shifted the relative competitive-ness of central versus peripheral sites for manufacturing and some other forms of commercial activity, while in some areas there has been a con-tinued if somewhat unsteady growth in downtown office space. Retail trade, following the population, has also picked more suburban loca-tions.

Less apparent is the role played by changes in population and the social structure. In the last few decades households have become smaller; the population has aged as the baby boom generation has grown older and had fewer births, and as the survivorship of the elderly has increased. Family composition has moved away from the traditional nuclear form, even though that may be still the social norm. Many bar-riers to open housing for minorities have been lowered even as new minority groups have arrived on the shores and struggled to assimilate.

Government at all levels can be implicated in some of these changes. The federal government has been accused of fostering decen-tralization with its subsidy of home mortgage and interstate highway programs. On the other hand, it has been the job of various levels of government to administer and enforce housing codes, supervise new construction under a variety of "urban programs," and redistribute the income and wealth of the nation to the less well-to-do.

As the urban system itself undergoes change, there are often major repercussions for the small areas within cities. The dispersal of popula-tion implies a gain for some neighborhoods and a loss for others. Reloca-tion of jobs will place pressure on workers and their families to move, thereby shifting the distribution of occupations around the metropolis. This, in turn, may restructure the spatial pattern of status groups. Changing age composition will be seen not only in the age structure for individual neighborhoods but also in the way in which they begin (or cease) to specialize in particular groups. Perhaps most dramatically and visibly, the changing composition of the various ethnic groups in the city and its suburbs, combined with pressures for and against discrimi-nation, will affect the segregation maintained by the groups.

What kind of toll have all of these developments exacted on the metropolitan system, and how best do we measure it? We will concen-trate on three measurable changes: segregation change; realignment of spatial organization; and neighborhood evolution. In all three we limit ourselves to residential distribution, but even from population and housing data alone, we can infer a considerable amount about the underlying technological and economic forces shaping American cities. The remainder of the chapter turns specifically to these three areas.

First, we look at changes in segregation—the pattern of unevenness in the distribution of population groups across neighborhoods—and apply the techniques of Chapter 4 to the 1940, 1950, 1960, and 1970 censuses. This analysis is designed to tell us whether individual characteristics have become more or less segregated over time, and also whether the hierarchy of characteristics—the ladder of segregation—has itself shifted. Second, we return to the subject of Chapter 5 and describe changes in spatial organization of the metropolis. It is here that we can get an explicit measure of how much of the "pull" of the central business district (CBD) has been maintained. We can also use an over-time comparison of the validity of the ecological models introduced earlier. For this analysis we use data for a smaller number of metropolitan areas from 1970 and 1940.

For the earlier points in time we also use census tract data to measure segregation and develop the contours. Metropolitan areas are generally comparable from census to census. The major change is that entire counties are added (or deleted) from the metropolis, correspondingly adding to (or taking away from) the area of the region covered by neighborhoods.[2] Also, as a response to growth and decline in neighborhoods, census tracts are split or merged to try to keep near the 4,000 norm. Therefore, while it is true that some of the units of analysis have changed, this alteration is modest compared to the overall comparability of the metropolis taken as a population distribution system.

The third term, neighborhood evolution, is a new criterion, and we devote the bulk of our attention to it. By neighborhood evolution we mean the truly dynamic character of population and housing change in individual neighborhoods. Where the two prior analyses rest on comparative cross-sections, that is, successive snapshots of the city, here we delve into truly dynamic analysis and try to trace the course of population and housing change in individual neighborhoods. Tracking neighborhoods in this way requires matching up the same parcel of land at successive censuses. A number of thorny problems of definition and measurement arise, and we reserve these for later in this discussion. In contrast to the comparative snapshot approach, the dynamic analysis can begin to provide insight into the life course of individual neighborhoods.

[2]The Standard Metropolitan Statistical Area has been used from 1960 up through the present census, so there is a good deal of comparability over time. In 1950 and 1940 it was not yet the practice to establish census tracts for entire metropolitan areas, and so the neighborhoods that form the data base are somewhat underbounded compared to the more comprehensive SMSA data for the later decades. Despite this shortcoming, the census tracts for the early period include the central city and many of the built-up suburbs, thus covering the vast majority of the metropolitan population. Problems arise in the contours only when these omitted areas differ radically from what would be predicted for them by the model with the included data. It does not appear that this is a serious problem. A parallel argument holds for segregation.

Changing Segregation Patterns

In Chapter 4 we concluded with an analysis of the "ladder of segregation," the relative ranking of the various social characteristics in terms of the segregation indices. We have been able to calculate segregation indices for several of these characteristics back to the census of 1940. It is possible now to view nearly a half-century of the sorting-out process of neighborhoods in the metropolis. In keeping with practice in this monograph, several characteristics have been examined. Most of the census definitions are comparable over time, and we point out exceptions as they occur.[3]

Racial Segregation

The separation of blacks from whites has long been the principal focus of segregation analysis. A time series of racial segregation for major cities has effectively been accumulated, as the index of dissimilarity (D) has been recalculated at each decade.[4] Table 6.1 presents five decades of segregation indexes for the black population in the metropolitan areas. (Some areas did not exist as SMSAs at earlier points in time.) In 1940, when only eleven of the twenty-one SMSAs analyzed here were classified as metropolitan, the typical value of D was 75, meaning that three-quarters of the black (or nonblack) population would have to move in order to produce an even racial composition in every neighborhood. The magnitude of this statistic remained remarkably constant through 1970. There is some variation across the metropolitan areas, variation of the same sort observed in the 1980 analysis of Chapter 3. Chicago and Flint record the highest values of D in every one of these years.

In the 1970s a striking change occurred in segregation. The value of D declined in almost every city we examined, and the variation across

[3]Of course, even if definitions remain constant, the population can shift along the categories of a variable, especially those with underlying continuous distributions such as income and rent, and this redistribution may have an impact on the calculated segregation for any category within.

[4]Karl E. Taeuber and Alma F. Taeuber, *Negroes in Cities* (Chicago: Aldine Publishing Co., 1965); Annemette Sørensen, Karl E. Taeuber, and Leslie J. Hollingsworth, Jr., "Indexes of Racial Residential Segregation for 109 Cities in the United States: 1950 to 1970," *Sociological Focus* 8 (1975):125–142; and Thomas van Valey, Wade C. Roof, and J. E. Wilcox, "Trends in Residential Segregation 1960–1970," *American Journal of Sociology* 82 (1977):826–844. Sørenson, Taeuber, and Hollingsworth present updated 1970 data; van Valey, Roof, and Wilcox provide a census tract based analysis comparing 1960 and 1970 segregation in almost all U.S. metropolitan areas. The 1970 calculations in this book, made from raw data, correspond to those published by van Valey, Roof, and Wilcox.

TABLE 6.1

Racial Dissimilarity: 1940–1980

Metropolitan Area	Black versus All Other					1940–1980 Change	1970–1980 Change
	1940	1950	1960	1970	1980		
Allentown	NA	NA	73	66	58	NA	−8
Amarillo	NA	NA	NA	86	72	NA	−14
Atlanta	69	73	77	82	77	7	−5
Bangor	NA	NA	NA	NA	40	NA	NA
Birmingham	69	66	64	67	73	4	5
Boston	81	77	81	79	76	−6	−3
Chicago	94	90	91	91	86	−8	−5
Flint	88	90	86	86	85	−2	−1
Indianapolis	76	77	80	84	79	3	−5
Lexington	NA	NA	70	78	59	NA	−19
New Bedford	NA	NA	63	64	56	NA	−9
New Haven	71	64	65	67	68	−3	1
New Orleans	63	63	65	74	70	7	−4
Newark	65	NA	73	79	79	14	0
St. Louis	82	84	86	85	82	−1	−3
Salt Lake City	NA	NA	72	70	54	NA	−16
San Antonio	NA	NA	77	74	60	NA	−14
San Diego	NA	70	80	77	59	NA	−18
Seattle	71	74	84	77	66	−5	−11
Sheboygan	NA	NA	NA	NA	69	NA	NA
Stockton	NA	NA	74	74	56	NA	−17
MEAN	75.4	75.4	75.6	76.8	67.6	.9	−7.8
S.D.	9.8	9.6	8.2	7.7	11.9	6.7	7.2

cities increased as well. For nineteen SMSAs, segregation declined by an average of 8 points (about 10 percent) as measured by *D*. These findings for the index of dissimilarity were matched by similar findings for the other segregation statistics we have used.[5] The final column of Table

[5]There is one important exception, the "exposure index," which is an unstandardized measure of interaction between two population groups. Stanley Lieberson and Donna Carter, "Temporal Changes and Urban Differences in Residential Segregation," *American Journal of Sociology* 88 (1982):296–310, have argued on sociological grounds in favor of this asymmetrical index. This class of measures is, however, substantially influenced by citywide population composition. As a rule, cities with higher and/or growing black proportions would show higher black "isolation" index values. Moreover, such cities would show lower black-white interaction; that is, a smaller fraction of whites among people that the average black resident would encounter. Conversely, such cities would tend to show higher white-black interaction. This argument extends over time. In measuring unevenness we have consciously decided to remove the composition effect. Once standardized for composition the exposure indexes become nearly equivalent to the dissimilarity index. For a more complete discussion see Michael J. White, "Segregation and Diversity Measures in Population Distribution," *Population Index* 52 (Summer 1986):198–221.

6.1 shows that SMSAs in Texas and the West outpaced the remainder of the nation in segregation decline.

Some differences in the time trends across the cities are observed for the major SMSAs. Between 1940 and 1970 segregation steadily increased, up to 10 points, in the metropolitan areas of Atlanta, Indianapolis, New Orleans, and Newark. In San Diego and Seattle, the value of *D* peaked in 1960 before declining. These periods of increasing of the black population were times of growth for the SMSAs. In the large southern cities, it appears possible that the increase in *D* was due to the breakdown of social codes that allowed black and whites to live in physical proximity while maintaining strict social distance. But since some northern cities experienced increased segregation and some southern cities did not, the generality of this interpretation seems in doubt. A simpler explanation may be in the decline of domestic service (with coresidence among whites) for southern blacks.

Not only do these nineteen SMSAs show a decline in the value of *D* at the census tract level but other tabulations also point to widespread segregation decline in the 1970s.[6] Is it real or an artifact? Since racial classification in 1980 was handled differently from previous censuses, there is the possibility that the decrease may be due to changes in self-classification and processing in the Census Bureau rather than true declines in segregation. Table 6.2 addresses this question by looking more closely at 1970 and 1980 statistics for the index of dissimilarity.

In the first two columns of the table we repeat the value of the index of dissimilarity reported in Table 6.1. This value of *D* measures the segregation of the population reported as black against all other racial groups taken together. One of the possible sources of bias in the segregation statistics is the way the "other" population is treated in the two censuses. In 1970 many persons were reallocated to a white or black race if they left the question blank or used the "other" category, if there was other evidence about their race. In 1980 the policy was changed slightly, and many of the responses, particularly those in the "other" category, were left intact. This increased the relative proportion of "other" racial groups, and it affected the classification of the Hispanic population in particular. One way to control for the vagueness of the "other" category is to limit the analysis to black–white segregation, using the pairwise *D* statistics. Thus we look only at the differential neighborhood settlement of those classified as white and as black at each census. This would help correct for any deflation in segregation in

[6]See the 1980 statistics in Karl E. Taeuber, Franklin W. Monfort, Perry Massey, and Alma F. Taeuber, "The Trend in Metropolitan Racial Residential Segregation," paper presented to Population Association of America, May 1984.

TABLE 6.2
Racial Segregation Decline: Is It an Artifact?

Metropolitan Area	Black versus All Other 1970 (1)	Black versus All Other 1980 (2)	White versus Black 1970 (3)	White versus Black 1980 (4)	Non-Hispanic White versus Non-Hispanic Black, 1980 (5)	Black–Other Change 1970–1980 (6)*	White–Black Change 1970–1980 (7)†	Non-Hispanic White–Black Change 1970–1980 (8)‡
Allentown	66	58	66	58	59	−8	−7	−7
Amarillo	86	72	86	72	73	−14	−14	−13
Atlanta	82	77	82	77	77	−5	−5	−5
Bangor	NA	40	NA	40	41	NA	NA	NA
Birmingham	67	72	67	73	73	5	5	5
Boston	79	76	79	77	78	−3	−2	−2
Chicago	91	86	91	87	88	−5	−4	−3
Flint	86	85	86	85	86	−1	−1	−1
Indianapolis	84	79	84	79	79	−5	−5	−5
Lexington	78	59	78	59	59	−19	−19	−19
New Bedford	64	56	64	58	59	−9	−6	−5
New Haven	67	68	67	70	70	1	3	3
New Orleans	74	70	74	71	71	−4	−3	−3
Newark	79	79	79	80	82	0	1	3
St. Louis	85	82	85	82	82	−3	−3	−3
Salt Lake City	70	54	70	55	56	−16	−15	−14
San Antonio	74	59	74	60	61	−14	−14	−12
San Diego	77	59	78	62	64	−18	−16	−15
Seattle	77	66	78	67	68	−11	−11	−10
Sheboygan	NA	69	NA	69	71	NA	NA	NA
Stockton	74	56	75	62	64	−17	−14	−11
MEAN	76.8	67.6	77.1	68.7	69.6	−7.8	−6.8	−6.1
S.D.	7.7	11.9	7.7	11.6	11.3	7.2	6.9	6.7

*Column (2) minus column (1).
†Column (4) minus column (3).
‡Column (5) minus column (3).

1980 introduced by blacks and Hispanics checking off the "other race" category, as long as this propensity was not differentially distributed by neighborhood.

The pairwise dissimilarity, reported in columns 3 and 4 of Table 6.2, is the same or very slightly higher than the companion statistic for the same decade. As a consequence, the decline in pairwise segregation, reported in column 7 of the table, is only slightly less than that of the "versus all other" statistic. A second correction we made for 1980 tried to account explicitly for the distribution of the Spanish origin population, who could, according to Census Bureau definitions, be of any race. Here we look at non-Hispanic whites versus non-Hispanic blacks. The figures, reported in column 5, indicate that segregation is slightly higher than the first pairwise figure, but is of the same general level. This statistic shows a smaller decrease from the 1970 pairwise level, but certainly one that is not negligible. Again, almost every metropolitan area participated in the decline. We must conclude, then, that the decline in racial segregation in the 1970s is not an artifact; it is real, appreciable, and quite widespread.

Overall Segregation Trends

We have examined trends over time in segregation for a large number of characteristics. The general features of the change are reported in Table 6.3 for the 1940–1980 period and the 1970–1980 period. This table makes use of both the index of dissimilarity, which treats dichotomous categories only, and the entropy statistic, H, which was used in the summary chart of Chapter 4, an analogous measure of unevenness that can be used for variables with any number of categories. While changes in these tables are influenced both by the Census Bureau's coding and tabulation practices and by shifts in the distribution of the population across the categories over time, they still provide us with some idea about how the bases of metropolitan differentiation are changing, if at all. The table reports both absolute and relative changes.[7]

In the 1970s, a period for which we have information on nineteen metropolitan areas, we see (columns 4–6) few dramatic changes. Segregation change by socioeconomic status is mixed; overall segregation by

---

[7]The relative changes are calculated as the mean of the percent change for each SMSA. When values in the table for the absolute and relative change disagree, it is usually due to the diversity of experience in the individual SMSAs, and consequently the results are less indicative of any trend.

TABLE 6.3
Summary of Change in Segregation: 1940–1980

Characteristic	1940–1980 Change* Mean Absolute Change	1940–1980 Change* Mean % Change	1940–1980 Change* % SMSAs Decreasing	1970–1980 Change† Mean Absolute Change	1970–1980 Change† Mean % Change	1970–1980 Change† % SMSAs Decreasing
Home Value‡	.8	4.3	55	1.5	10.2	37
Rent	−4.4	15.8	82	.0	4.0	47
Education	−1.3	−9.1	73	−.2	1.2	63
Elementary§	−4.9	−13.4	82	.1	2.5	37
High School	−14.2	−47.9	100	−2.9	−12.9	79
College	−4.1	−9.7	73	−2.8	−7.6	95
Income	NA		NA	−.9	−5.0	74
Poverty Status	NA		NA	1.4	15.9	21
Persons Poor	NA		NA	1.6	5.6	21
Occupation	−2.9	−33.6	100	−1.2	−17.3	95
Professional	−3.1	−10.1	82	−2.0	−7.2	89
Clerical	−13.7	−55.6	100	−2.7	−19.0	100
Service	−7.9	−28.2	100	−2.6	−10.6	84
Craft	−1.0	−2.2	64	−.6	−2.0	58
Operatives	−3.6	−12.9	91	−1.0	−3.5	74
Age	1.0	121.1	9	.2	14.6	21
Children	.4	4.8	36	−.2	1.8	32
Elderly	6.6	68.2	9	−.8	−1.4	63
Fem. Labor Force	−.5	0.4	64	.6	50.1	5
In Labor Force	−2.2	−10.2	73	2.1	20.5	5
Household Size	1.0	63.2	18	−.4	−4.5	58
1 Person	2.9	28.2	18	−1.0	−3.1	58
5+ Persons	4.4	34.4	9	.1	3.4	37
Child's Family	NA		NA	−1.6	−12.6	84
Couple	NA		NA	−2.9	−7.8	84
Single Parent	NA		NA	−3.8	−10.2	84
Nonfamily	NA		NA	−2.8	−6.0	53
Marital Status	NA		NA	.2	31.6	32
Single	NA		NA	2.6	24.3	11
Married	NA		NA	2.8	18.7	16
Sep.-Wid.-Div.	NA		NA	−3.2	−13.1	89
Race	−3.2	−4.4	55	−11.6	−26.0	95
Black	.9	2.2	55	−7.8	−10.2	89
Spanish	NA		NA	−6.7	−34.3	79
Spanish	NA		NA	−12.7	−25.7	89
Nativity	1.5	64.1	27	.0	7.6	58
Foreign Born	6.0	35.2	9	−1.5	−1.9	63
Units in Structure	1.1	21.1	55	−3.6	−13.9	84
Single Family	5.5	22.0	36	−4.1	−8.4	84
Housing Age	NA		NA	−.1	2.0	47
Recent	NA		NA	2.2	6.8	32
Old	NA		NA	−.4	0.0	53
Mobility	NA		NA	1.1	34.9	21
Mover	NA		NA	2.3	14.0	16

*Based on 11 metropolitan areas.

†Based on 19 metropolitan areas.

‡Entropy statistic for all categories.

§Indented values are the index of dissimilarity.

education and home value is up. As increasing fractions of Americans moved into the high school and college educated categories, the segregation of these groups declined. Decline in occupational segregation occurs in every category and quite uniformly across SMSAs. Clerical and service workers record the sharpest declines over the decade. While some of this decline may be due to changes in the occupational classification system, the breadth of the trend suggests the continuing decentralization of employment sites. Income segregation has declined slightly.[8] More telling perhaps is the general rise in the separation of those below the poverty line from those above. In fifteen of the nineteen metropolitan areas the segregation of poor persons and poor families increased.

Life cycle segregation is very low in general; small absolute changes can produce larger relative changes. An example is age segregation. In relative terms it increased substantially over the decade, but the absolute change was modest. Segregation of the elderly declined slightly over the 1970s. Within the elderly group, however, the segregation of the 65–74 population declined, while the segregation of the 75 + group became more pronounced.[9] Household size, another major life cycle indicator, also declined overall, yet larger families, which are in some sense out of step with the times, found themselves more separated. Many of these households are poorer as well. In a decade characterized by increasing family disruption and decline in traditional nuclear family living arrangements, we find decreasing segregation of children's family arrangements.

General racial segregation declined by 26 percent over the 1970s (using *H*). Much of the decline can be attributed to changing black–white patterns, but some of it is also due to other groups and the increased self-identification as "other." Segregation of the Hispanic population is also down substantially, although, there again, the way in which the data were collected changed from census to census. Segregation of the foreign born shows little change.[10]

---

[8]Categorization of the continuous variables, income rental level, and home value is particularly arbitrary, making the use of *D* especially problematic. For this reason, and because we did observe some shift in the proportion in the high, medium, and low categories, we have excluded the values of *D* for these three variables and concentrated on *H*.

[9]Joseph Tierney, "A Comparative Examination of the Residential Segregation of Persons 65 + and Persons 75 + in 18 United States Metropolitan Areas for 1970 and 1980, " *Journal of Gerontology* 42(1987):101–106.

[10]We omit from the table ancestry segregation, due to a radical change in the way information was collected for 1980. Prior to 1980 the "ancestry" information would include only the first and second generation. Still, when we performed the analysis of change, the Irish and French ancestry population revealed the strongest declines, with the Polish and Italian the least, a fact consistent with their more recent arrival among the European stock groups.

Trends over the decade point to more mixture of single family housing units throughout the neighborhoods of the metropolitan areas. This is evidence of the increasing construction of multiple unit dwellings in the suburbs and less dense construction in central areas. There is little change in the separation of newly constructed housing from old. There is a noticeable increase in the separation of the mobile population.

For the 1940–1980 period we have information only for eleven metropolitan areas, and for fewer variables. Here the results presented in Table 6.3 point to decreasing segregation by education and occupation. There appears to be more life cycle segregation, although the absolute changes are quite modest. Compared to 1940, racial segregation in these eleven areas is down by a few points, but segregation of the foreign born is appreciably higher. At the earlier time point the foreign born were living more intermingled with native born than at present. Part of this transition is due to the greater diversity of ethnic origins among the foreign born of 1980. Segregation of women in the labor force has been modest (D for 1980 = 12), but it increased by over 20 percent overall between 1970 and 1980, and in almost every SMSA. The results (which run counter to the trends of the previous decades) are indicative of the development of distinct residential districts where working women prefer to reside, probably spurred by increased participation in the labor force, and less immediate entry into the family life cycle.

The picture we draw from Table 6.3 is one of the few dramatic changes in metropolitan segregation over the decades. On the one hand, we see a decline in segregation for several social characteristics, most notably race, occupation, housing expenditures, and children's family type. On the other hand, segregation of the poorest, least educated, and least mobile segments of the population has become more pronounced.

To gain a more complete sense of the time trend of residential segregation we focus on ten larger and older SMSAs for which we have complete data for each decade back to 1940.[11] Figure 6.1 charts the average segregation for this group for selected characteristics. Race has remained the dominant social characteristic separating neighborhoods during the forty-year period, but after increasing gradually in these cities, it made an appreciable turnabout in the 1970s. Housing type is also highly sorted out among neighborhoods. The post–World War II single family building boom in the suburbs is likely to have been the cause of the rapid rise in housing type segregation between 1940 and 1960. The construction of multifamily units in the suburbs since then has probably been responsible for the decline.

[11]They are Atlanta, Boston, Chicago, Flint, Indianapolis, New Haven, New Orleans, Newark, St. Louis, and Seattle.

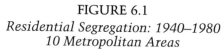

FIGURE 6.1
Residential Segregation: 1940–1980
10 Metropolitan Areas

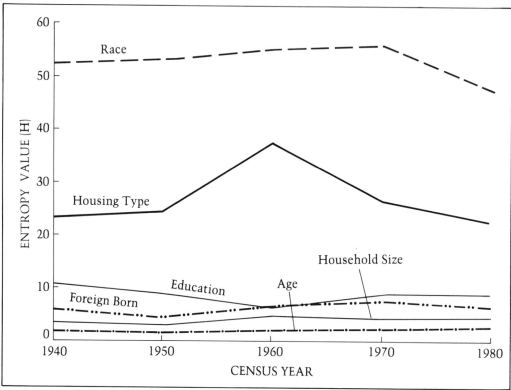

The other four characteristics show levels of segregation on the order of one-fifth that for race throughout the time period. Changes in age segregation and household size segregation are virtually imperceptible. In these ten SMSAs the segregation of the foreign born increased during the 1950s and 1960s, and has tailed off slightly since. Educational segregation declined and then increased slightly.

Changing Spatial Organization

The numerous social and technological pressures on the metropolis have undoubtedly been the stimulus to change in its spatial organization. No one questions the fact that metropolitan populations have dispersed over a wider space in the last few decades; however, it is less clear whether the way population distribution is organized in space has changed. From information on commuting and the location of employment and retail trade, we expect that the CBD has less pull on the metropolis's population than in the past. A further question is whether the types of spatial organization—ranging from zonal to nucleated—have shifted for individual characteristics over the time period. For example, has the distribution of the black population become more predictable or less?

We carried out essentially the same analysis of metropolitan contours at the 1970 and 1940 dates as we have described in Chapter 5 for the 1980 neighborhoods. We produced similar contour maps and associated statistics for eight of the larger cities that had sufficient data for the time period in question: Atlanta, Boston, Chicago, Flint, Indianapolis, New Orleans, St. Louis, and Seattle. Conspicuous by their absence from this list are some of the moderate-size, quickly growing areas of the Sunbelt; they did not have sufficient (if any) data to analyze for the earliest census. Therefore, our results will mostly tell a story about the evolution of some of America's larger and older metropolises.

We limit our work to the statistical analysis here; the contours generated by the analysis produce similar portraits, but the statistical results can give us a better assessment of change in predictability. We concentrate first on four variables representing different aspects of metropolitan social character, and then turn to a summary for a larger number which we have measured from decade to decade with contours for these eight cities.

Population Density

We have pointed to population density repeatedly as the characteristic linked most directly to the physical character of the metropolis. A large number of studies examine changes in density patterns over time. For example, Edwin Mills examined population and employment density gradients for a number of metropolitan areas during the period 1920 to 1963. In almost every case the slope of the gradient declined with time.[12] Such work has shown that larger cities have density gradients with higher central density (peaks) and flatter slopes, but that with time the peak has worn away and the slope has flattened.

Our own analysis repeats essentially the density gradient analysis, but we extend the model to incorporate directional (sectoral) deviation as well. The analysis for 1980 found that the original linear (zonal)

---

[12]Mills's work was based on analysis of central city–suburb data and not on census tracts. Edwin S. Mills, *Studies in the Structure of the Urban Economy* (Baltimore: Johns Hopkins University Press, 1972).

model alone explains the lion's share of the variance in population density. Table 6.4, Panel A, presents the statistics for the variance explained in density by the contour and its change over time. Column 1 repeats the information from the previous chapter, and again shows how well spatial location predicts density. In the most recent decade the results are mixed, but they point to a decreasing ability of spatial location to explain neighborhood density (column 3). In the 1940–1980 period the results are also mixed, with a slight net decline. The only SMSAs to show appreciable increases in spatial organization in the 1970s are Atlanta and New Orleans.[13] A clearer indication of what has been happening to population density in major American cities can be gleaned from Figure 6.2. Here we have graphed the density gradient from the linear equation for Chicago, the largest SMSA in our group.[14] Each of the three curves graphed traces the predicted value of population density with distance from the CBD for the respective decade. In 1940 we predict about 50 persons per acre (hypothetically) at the center of the city, and this declines sharply with distance. At five miles the density is already half that of the center, and by ten miles the figure nears ten persons per acre.

Between 1940 and 1970 the peak has declined and the slope flattened out, but the change between 1970 and 1980 is more striking and illustrates the substantial depopulation of central neighborhoods. In fact, the 1980 graph lies below the 1970 figure (implying fewer persons) at every distance out to 26 miles. For example, a neighborhood four miles from Chicago's CBD would be predicted to have one-third less population in 1980 compared to 1970. Even though the SMSA boundaries are identical for the 1970 and 1980 censuses, it is evident that by 1980 suburban development had extended to increasingly distant parts of the metropolitan region. This sort of flattening has taken place in almost every SMSA for the decades studied. Flat as it is for 1980, the Chicago curve is still much steeper than in many other metropolitan areas.

Basic Social Characteristics

Results in Chapter 5 indicated that in 1980 workers were highly nucleated. Column 1 of Table 6.4, Panel B, confirms this. Between 1940

[13]For the linear model about half the cities increased and half decreased in variance explained. The magnitude of the density gradient still declined in general. Taken together with the contour, these results indicate a continued leveling of the metropolitan population density, but one not always accompanied by disorganization.

[14]These statistics are not shown. Even though the explanatory power of the model increased for Chicago, the slope of the line decreased in magnitude. Density gradients have flattened for other SMSAs, too.

FIGURE 6.2

Chicago Population Density: 1940–1980

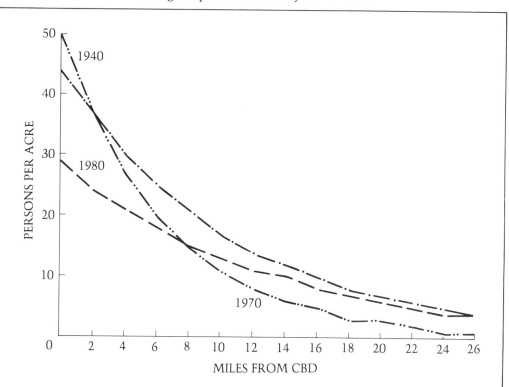

and 1980 there is a substantial decline in predictive ability in most of the cities, averaging out to over 20 percentage points. Inferring from columns 2 and 3, we can see that in every one of these eight SMSAs the contour model did a very good job at predicting the residential location of high status workers in 1940, with explained variance of four SMSAs over 40 percent. (Distance alone is still a weak predictor.) This substantial loss between 1940 and 1970 was partially offset in the 1970s with five of the eight cities gaining and three losing modestly. The fact that we can do a better job of predicting the higher status occupations in 1980 compared to 1970 may be due to an artifact, attributable simply to the revised occupational coding done by the Census Bureau for the 1980 census.[15] An alternative explanation is that some of the reshuffling of

---

[15]Acknowledging that the previous system was obsolete, the Census Bureau completely revised its classification, and therefore the contents of its occupational tabulation for the 1980 census. So our results may simply be picking up a different view of the labor force.

TABLE 6.4

Change in Spatial Organization: 1940, 1970, 1980

PANEL A: POPULATION DENSITY

	Contour Model		
	Expl. Variance 1980*	Change 1940–1980†	Change 1970–1980†
SMSA	(1)	(2)	(3)
Atlanta	82.3	64.9	5.9
Boston	51.6	14.4	−13.4
Chicago	24.0	13.8	−2.4
Flint	10.7	−83.1	−66.0
Indianapolis	63.7	−6.9	.4
New Orleans	56.2	−14.2	19.9
St. Louis	44.4	−29.9	−11.9
Seattle	51.8	−22.6	−18.6
MEAN	48.1	−7.9	−10.8

PANEL B: PROFESSIONAL WORKERS

	Contour Model		
	Exp. Variance 1980	Change 1940–1980	Change 1970–1980
SMSA	(1)	(2)	(3)
Atlanta	25.1	.2	13.0
Boston	8.5	−38.4	−1.3
Chicago	14.4	−4.1	−5.7
Flint	6.9	−39.1	14.7
Indianapolis	51.6	22.9	38.9
New Orleans	5.7	−39.1	4.3
St. Louis	13.5	−17.5	2.2
Seattle	8.4	−55.1	−3.6
MEAN	16.8	−21.3	7.8

*Explained variance is the adjusted R^2 statistic and may be negative.
†Difference in the adjusted R^2 from one period to the next.

the metropolitan labor force has taken place in directions that are decidedly more predictable. Establishment of SES enclaves, and particularly so-called gentrification in major metropolitan areas could influence the predictive ability of our equations. In any case, the relationship of occupational status to residence is not a simple one and, like the composition of the labor force itself, it is one that has been changing continuously.

To represent one aspect of the life cycle, Panel C of Table 6.4 looks at companion statistics for the proportion of the population under 15

TABLE 6.4 *(continued)*

PANEL C: CHILDREN

	Contour Model		
	Exp. Variance 1980	Change 1940–1980	Change 1970–1980
SMSA	(1)	(2)	(3)
Atlanta	11.4	4.8	6.3
Boston	7.7	−40.8	−14.3
Chicago	2.4	−.5	−16.4
Flint	−14.2	−86.8	−34.9
Indianapolis	3.7	−44.7	−.4
New Orleans	.3	−35.1	−3.6
St. Louis	−.1	−5.7	−10.1
Seattle	6.4	−68.9	−30.0
MEAN	2.2	−34.7	−12.9

PANEL D: BLACK POPULATION

	Contour Model		
	Exp. Variance 1980	Change 1940–1980	Change 1970–1980
SMSA	(1)	(2)	(3)
Atlanta	60.3	24.5	20.4
Boston	18.3	−33.2	.3
Chicago	40.6	1.7	−24.0
Flint	55.8	17.8	9.9
Indianapolis	56.6	33.7	19.6
New Orleans	44.7	21.6	22.8
St. Louis	44.5	7.2	13.4
Seattle	46.5	−23.0	3.2
MEAN	45.9	6.3	8.2

years of age. (Household size was not available at earlier decades.) We have already established that a neighborhood's life cycle characteristics are not as easily predicted by its spatial location. In the forty-year period as well as in the recent decade explanatory power declined in every SMSA but Atlanta. Declining fertility during the 1970s no doubt contributed to this loss of explanatory power.

The results also point to an underlying structural transformation. Suburbs (or at least the outer rings of the metropolis) have traditionally been viewed as the locus of child-rearing. Our results for the distance gradient in 1940 and even 1970 (not shown in table) indicate an increase in the predicted proportion of children with distance. While it still may be true that the suburbs are the preferred locus of child-rearing for the

American middle class, the decline in middle class fertility rates, coupled with the continued concentration of the poor and minority groups (with their higher fertility) in the central zones has so confused the spatial organization that it is no longer predictable by 1980.

The final characteristic we examine in Table 6.4 is race. The predictive power of the metropolitan contour increased in most SMSAs in the 1970s as well as in the longer term, to the point where in 1980 nearly half the variation in the distribution of the black population could be explained in the average SMSA. The increase over time would suggest greater spatial organization of the black population, surprising in the face of decidedly less segregation as measured by the index of dissimilarity. What accounts for the apparent disparity? The answer is partly statistical, due somewhat to the spreading out of the black population beyond traditional limits of the ghetto.[16] The fact that the linear model's slope has increased, though, suggests that the black population, for its desegregation, is still becoming more centrally concentrated.

An Overview

We have performed this kind of comparative analysis for several additional variables. Table 6.5 presents a summary of the comparison for the eight cities over time, under both the linear model (distance alone) and the contour model. What is striking in the table is the frequency of negative signs in columns 3–6, indicating a decline in the ability of the location to explain the distribution of neighborhood characteristics in both the 1970s and in the forty-year time span. In the most recent decade, 14 of the 18 characteristics (column 5) moved downward under the linear model. Simple radial orientation to the center of the city—the zonal model—has become less powerful. (Radial orientation has far from disappeared, as the values of column 1 and the findings of the previous chapter indicate). Under the contour model in that time span, 10 of those 18 characteristics became less predictable (column 6). The decline in orientation to the CBD has not been matched by an equally strong decline in more complex patterns. The 1940–1980 comparison is more consistent. Of the 16 characteristics we could examine at both points in time, 13 declined with respect to distance alone (column 3). With the exception of race, every characteristic showed declining spatial organization under the contour model.

It is a bit difficult to generalize from these results for eight larger

[16]Some of the increased predictive power may be associated with the larger fraction of blacks in the SMSAs at the later time points, and the larger number of non-zero tract values.

TABLE 6.5

Summary of Change in Spatial Organization: 1940, 1970, 1980:
8 Metropolitan Areas

| | Variance Explained 1980 | | Change 1940–1980 | | Change 1970–1980* | |
	Linear (1)	Contour (2)	Linear (3)	Contour (4)	Gradient (5)	Contour (6)
LIFE CYCLE						
Household Size	10.2	27.6	NA	NA	NA	NA
Children	2.4	9.6	− 6.6	− 34.7	− 3.0	− 13.0
Elderly Population	1.5	17.0	− 2.9	− 11.5	− 3.4	− 6.4
Females in Labor Force	0.4	5.6	− 24.7	− 42.3	− 1.6	1.1
STATUS						
Educational Attainment	7.0	38.3	− 0.0	− 2.0	− 1.5	− 1.7
Professionals	1.8	17.7	− 1.7	− 21.3	− 1.8	7.8
Clerical Workers	0.5	11.3	− 10.6	− 24.0	− 1.6	4.7
Laborers	0.9	10.7	− 4.1	− 26.9	0.2	− 4.7
Rent	7.7	44.6	− 4.8	− 5.7	− 3.8	4.1
Home Value	10.5	46.6	− 10.9	− 1.6	3.5	10.7
Household Income	13.0	48.4	NA	NA	8.0	22.6
Home Ownership	9.3	24.2	− 12.4	− 28.4	− 3.3	− 11.1
RACE						
Black	13.9	45.0	10.3	6.3	6.3	8.2
Spanish	6.4	25.9	NA	NA	NA	NA
Foreign	5.0	20.3	0.1	− 8.9	− 0.3	0.5
HOUSING DENSITY AND MOBILITY						
Population Density	36.8	52.8	6.4	− 8.0	− 4.3	− 10.8
Age of Housing	18.3	48.4	NA	NA	NA	NA
Housing Vacancy	1.6	12.1	− 6.5	− 21.9	− 1.0	− 5.2
Plumbing Deficiency	5.2	22.2	− 10.7	− 22.5	− 0.7	− 7.8
Multistory Housing	6.8	18.5	− 16.0	− 30.7	− 1.7	− 6.3
Residential Mobility	0.2	4.6	NA	NA	− 0.1	− 0.7

*Results for 8 larger metropolitan areas with data; see Table 6.4.

SMSAs. The summary statistics we present in Table 6.5 mask variation among the metropolitan areas in spatial organization. The physical extent of the metropolitan areas themselves changes over time. Nevertheless, the population has continued to disperse, and in more instances than not the predictability of a neighborhood's social composition and housing stock characteristics from its geographic position within the metropolis has decreased. Radial orientation of the neighborhoods to the CBD has continued to wane, while a few characteristics (mostly representing socioeconomic status) hint at greater nucleation.

Neighborhood Evolution

Just as we can track cities and regions over time, so too we can track individual neighborhoods. In fact, we do this all the time implicitly when we describe how a neighborhood has changed or is changing. Abandonment, gentrification, racial succession, housing construction, are all descriptions of processes that can be collectively gathered under the heading of neighborhood change. Arithmetically, adding up the changes in the individual neighborhoods will yield the aggregate change for the city or region, but of course this obscures the diversity of experiences that occur at the most local level. Indeed, we do not expect that every neighborhood will mirror the change—in population, housing quality, ethnic composition—that is occurring in the SMSA. Tracking individual neighborhoods is the most complete way to begin to draw that picture.

We already know what to expect in many cases. Most cities are flattening in terms of density; central areas are becoming more concentrated with minorities in many metropolises. But these are the broadbrush trends for the decade(s). The aggregate change can come about because a small fraction of the neighborhoods undergo great change, or because each neighborhood undergoes modest change. Our work to this point has been limited to extensive analysis of 1980 and comparative cross-sectional analysis. We have looked at the overall pattern—either segregation or spatial organization—at several points in time and made comparisons. These comparisons lead to inferences about the changes in individual neighborhoods, but we have not yet ascertained the decade-to-decade transformation of these small places.

An analysis of neighborhood evolution requires matching from one census to the next the individual parcels of land that constitute the neighborhoods. Only in this way can we directly measure the trajectory of change. The census tract—our statistical neighborhood—is the best suited for this task. The tract concept was initiated with the idea of temporal comparability. Thus, as much as is feasible the census tract boundaries remain the same from census to census. [17] We have matched

---

[17] The reality often falls short of the ideal, and Appendix A reviews in detail the establishment and maintenance of census tract boundaries. No matter how carefully the system is maintained, the task of establishing the census-to-census records for individual neighborhoods is substantial; conceptual issues and problems add to practical ones. To maintain their population sizes at about 4,000, census tracts are split or merged under circumstances of growth or depopulation, respectively. Sometimes the boundaries are changed to correspond to administrative boundaries or new physical features. Even where boundary changes do not occur the matching of tract data across censuses may be difficult.

1970 tracts with 1980 tracts, and this section presents some basic tabulations for 1970–1980 neighborhood change. In all of our tabulations the 1970 census tract data have been reallocated to 1980 census tract boundaries.

Models of Neighborhood Evolution

Neighborhood stage theory is an attempt to describe the natural evolution of the housing and population composition of neighborhoods. Its earliest exposition is found in the work of Edgar M. Hoover and Raymond Vernon's *Anatomy of a Metropolis* based on a study of the New York metropolitan area.[18] Hoover and Vernon describe neighborhood evolution in five stages. In the first stage the initial urbanization of undeveloped or farm land takes place, usually at the periphery of the city. In the second stage, transition, the neighborhood experiences continued population growth, construction in apartments begins, and effective density increases. The third stage, called downgrading, sees the older housing stock converted to higher residential densities, and population density continues to rise. Population decline begins in the fourth stage, called thinning. Hoover and Vernon predict a decline in household size, vacancy, and abandonment. In the fifth and final stage, which they term renewal, obsolete housing is replaced with multifamily housing, and the quality and effective use of space is improved. Often renewal takes place with the aid of the public sector.

Another twist on neighborhood stage theory is reported by Anthony Downs. Here the stages are labels for sections of what is really a continuum, and the "health" of the neighborhood becomes a focus of the paradigm. The five stages are: (1) healthy and viable; (2) incipient decline; (3) clearly declining; (4) accelerating decline, indicated for Downs by heavy deterioration; and (5) abandoned, unhealthy, and nonviable. In the third and fourth stages the neighborhood witnesses the transformation in tenure to renters, declines in relative SES, conversion to higher density, and pessimism about the future of the neighborhood in the real estate market. What distinguishes Downs's final formulation is the pos-

[18]Edgar M. Hoover and Raymond Vernon, *Anatomy of a Metropolis* (New York: Doubleday-Anchor, 1962). David L. Birch, "A Stage Theory of Urban Growth, 1981," *Journal of the American Institute of Planners* 37 (1971):78–87, describes a fairly similar pattern: (a) low density rural; (b) the first wave; (c) fully developed high quality; (d) packing; (e) thinning; and (f) recapture. While Hoover and Vernon focus almost exclusively on housing and density, Birch introduces explicit discussion of socioeconomic status composition of the neighborhoods at various stages.

sibility of two-way movement along the continuum, either in the direction of decline, or in the direction of revitalization.[19]

These stage theories have a parallel in the sociological literature on succession, which describes changing social composition and links neighborhood evolution to the models of the spatial structure of the metropolis. Chapter 5 discussed the competing models of metropolitan organization. In the zonal model the principal growth of the metropolis is outward, with the highest income groups at the leading edge of metropolitan development. As social groups move outward with socioeconomic betterment, they leave behind their older housing, which filters down to the next lower group on the ladder. A neighborhood declines in socioeconomic status as the process of invasion and succession brings to it repeated waves of new residents. This outlook is generally consistent with the stage model of Hoover and Vernon. Even the possibility of renewal is held out as the zone in transition experiences its predestined change, albeit to nonresidential uses, in the earliest Burgess formulation. In the original Burgess version there was no provision for a reversal of the evolutionary path, in contrast to the revitalization proposed by Downs and others.

The sectoral, nucleation, and synthetic models are more difficult to link to models of neighborhood evolution. In the sectoral model the city expands overall, but each status sector is maintained intact. Such a model allows little room for composition change within neighborhoods. Its prediction is mostly for stability of neighborhood status. The multiple nuclei model has even less to say about how neighborhoods change. Since it proposes competing nodes for metropolitan organization, we can extrapolate that over time there would be small-scale ripplelike effects much like those described for the zonal model. It is also difficult to surmise an exact dynamic prediction for the synthetic model. If the city grows radially, the complicated urban pattern, integrating zone, sector, and nodal forms, could replicate itself with a wider diameter.

---

[19]Anthony Downs, *Neighborhoods and Urban Development* (Washington, D.C.: Brookings Institution, 1981). Downs's model is close to one produced under contract for the Department of Housing and Urban Development. See James Mitchell, *The Dynamics of Neighborhood Change* (HUD, Office of Policy Development and Research, HUD.-PDR:108, 1985). Downs elaborates on ways in which this scheme can be used to help evaluate the way in which the public sector can intervene on behalf of neighborhoods. He develops a number of treatment strategies to be used in neighborhoods of different stages (pp. 153–172). These range from normal upkeep to preservation and redevelopment.

Research Paradigms

Despite the amount of writing on neighborhood change and transformation of the urban pattern, empirical analysis of neighborhood evolution has been limited, mostly due to the constraints on establishing comparable data files. Fairly common is the analysis of population totals, aggregate growth and decline in census tracts, and aggregates of these for community areas. The Chicago Community Area Fact Book is just one example of a publication that includes these over-time data. Many individual cities and planning agencies do look at the data for census tracts from one period to the next, using population, ethnic, and socioeconomic status information where possible.

The analytical use to which this kind of longitudinal data are most often put is the measurement of ethnic change: racial succession. On occasion a handful of neighborhoods are examined (with census tract data) for particular insights into the process of racial change.[20]

A more comprehensive succession paradigm involves classifying neighborhood racial transition into a variety of categories, depending on the relative and absolute population changes of the various neighborhoods.[21] This model has become the standard and has been used repeatedly. More recently a modified version has been extended to the Hispanic case in the work of Douglas Massey and Brendan P. Mullan and others.[22] Conventional succession analyses have generally included only measures of total population by ethnicity and a few socioeconomic characteristics. An alternative approach used a variety of characteristics in a previous decade to predict racial composition in the present.[23]

The succession model provides a good exercise in the ways in which neighborhood change can come about. Using status as the example, we can enumerate the ways a neighborhood's status composition can change. For a neighborhood to experience a decrease in status, the fraction of lower status residents must increase. Usually this would take place by higher status persons moving out, being replaced by lower

---

[20]Ozzie Edwards, "Family Composition as a Variable in Residential Succession," *American Journal of Sociology* 77 (1972):731–741, and Ronald M. Denowitz, "Racial Succession in New York City 1960–1970," *Social Forces* 59 (1980):440–455.

[21]Otis D. Duncan and Beverly Duncan, *The Negro Population of Chicago* (Chicago: Aldine Publishing Co., 1965); Taeuber and Taeuber, *Negroes in Cities*, p. 106, use the terms "established," "consolidation," "stable interracial," "displacement."

[22]Douglas Massey and Brendan P. Mullan, "Processes of Hispanic and Black Spatial Assimilation," *American Journal of Sociology* 89 (1984):836–873.

[23]John R. Logan and Linda Brewster Stearns, "Suburban Racial Segregation as a Nonecological Process," *Social Forces* 60 (1981):61–73, and Michael J. White, "Racial and Ethnic Succession in Four Cities," *Urban Affairs Quarterly* 20 (1984):165–183.

status persons in the process of neighborhood turnover. This is the mechanism most commonly assumed. But it is not the only mechanism that can be operating. The neighborhood may experience an absolute increase in both status groups, but the lower status group may grow more quickly, producing a net loss in status with appreciable turnover. Conversely, depopulating neighborhoods may witness varying rates of exit among the status groups.[24] For characteristics that are not fixed for individuals, persons in the neighborhood may shift categories, producing the observed change.

Gentrification and its companion issue, displacement, attracted a great deal of attention in the 1970s and early 1980s. Gentrification can be defined as residential upgrading or reverse filtering of a neighborhood, so that higher SES persons come to occupy a larger fraction of the housing units, and perhaps also constitute a growing share of the total neighborhood population. Most research has confirmed that gentrification exists to some degree in almost every major city of the United States but that its scope is limited, and its demographic impact is outweighed in almost all cities by long-standing trends of central area depopulation and declines in SES.[25] Much anecdotal evidence exists to indicate that gentrification is accompanied by the displacement of lower income persons. Displacement is particularly difficult to research, and although several studies have concluded that it is relatively infrequent, it may be impossible to recover an exact measurement of the kinds of persons forcibly moved out of their homes by the gentrification process.

Four Indianapolis Neighborhoods

The kinds of changes that are the subject of our tabulations in this section can be observed on the micro scale through four neighborhoods in Indianapolis. We can use the fortune of these neighborhoods as a window onto the wider changes in the nation's neighborhoods before we actually report those more extensive tabulations. We choose Indi-

---

[24]The assumed mechanism is equivalent to Taeuber and Taeuber's "succession" or "invasion." The final two examples correspond to consolidation in "growing" and "declining" areas, respectively.

[25]Shirley Laska and Daphne Spain, eds., *Back to the City: Issues in Neighborhood Renovation* (New York: Pergamon Press, 1980); Barret Lee and David C. Hodge, "Spatial Differentials in Residential Displacement," *Urban Studies* 21 (1984):219–232; and Howard Sumka, "Neighborhood Revitalization and Displacement: A Review of the Evidence," *Journal of the American Planning Association* 45 (1979):480–487.

anapolis because it is in many respects a typical metropolitan area. Its size is average among the group of twenty-one SMSAs. Its physical topography is more even than most cities, and so the social composition of neighborhoods is less likely to be influenced by features of the landscape. Indianapolis has experienced moderate growth in the 1970s, falling between the fortunes of the Sunbelt and the Snowbelt metropolises.

Table 6.6 reports the experience of four neighborhoods in the Indianapolis metropolitan area, chosen simply on the basis of their ecological position. In addition, the companion information for the city of Indianapolis and the SMSA is reported so that we can investigate the changing relative fortunes of the neighborhoods as well as absolute shifts in population, housing stock, and socioeconomic composition. The stories of these four neighborhoods, while they are specific cases, speak for the fortunes of many urban neighborhoods in America. The inner city neighborhood, about two miles from the CBD, is predominantly black and lower in status and income than average in 1970. The "mid-city" neighborhood is a tract located within the city limits but about five miles from downtown; it is predominantly white and average in educational attainment. It is below average in income but also in the incidence of poverty. We examine two suburban neighborhoods, one in a moderately growing area and far above average in the status measures in 1980. The second is in a rapidly growing area; in fact, tract 1105 for suburb 2 was split between 1970 and 1980, and we have recombined the information from these two tracts for the 1980 column.

During the 1970s the metropolitan area population grew 5 percent while the city itself lost about 6 percent. For the city of Indianapolis we can see that the 1970s brought a slight increase in the number of households, despite its population decline. The city was for the most part on a par with the metropolitan area in 1970 and in 1980, changing little over the decade. The most noteworthy differences are the greater proportions of blacks, female-headed households, and persons in poverty in the city. Population and socioeconomic trends in the individual neighborhoods diverged widely from those of the average for the metropolitan area and city.

The inner city neighborhood lost one-quarter of its population and over one-fifth of its households. While slightly below the metropolitan area level in 1970, the inner city neighborhood fell sharply in terms of relative income and education by 1980. The neighborhood was over 90 percent black in 1970 and during the decade the composition became increasingly consolidated. The position of the neighborhood also deteriorated with regard to poverty and number of female-headed families, to the point at which it had about three times the incidence of poverty and

TABLE 6.6
Indianapolis and a Few of Its Neighborhoods

	SMSA	City	Inner Tract 3509	Midcity Tract 3525	Suburb 1 Tract 2108	Suburb 2 Tract 1105*
TOTAL POPULATION						
1970	1109882	744624	4724	3920	5659	5976
1980	1166575	700807	3534	3500	6605	11769
Change (%)	5.11	−5.88	−25.19	−10.71	16.72	96.94
HOUSEHOLDS						
1970	353466	240979	1172	1640	1626	1707
1980	425757	264455	911	1636	2278	3796
Change (%)	20.45	9.74	−22.30	−0.28	40.06	122.35
				Ratio to SMSA		
EDUCATIONAL ATTAINMENT						
Ratio 1970†	12.20	0.99	0.93	0.98	1.02	1.00
Ratio 1980	69.30	1.00	0.63	0.86	1.17	1.16
Change in Ratio‡		0.01	−0.30	−0.12	0.15	0.16
INCOME						
Ratio 1970	$9,109	0.97	0.85	0.85	1.36	1.21
Ratio 1980	$18,674	0.93	0.64	0.81	1.25	1.48
Change in Ratio		−0.04	−0.21	−0.04	−0.11	0.27
FEMALE-HEADED FAMILIES						
Ratio 1970	10.0%	1.19	2.97	1.03	0.48	0.40
Ratio 1980	15.0%	1.27	3.12	1.09	0.65	0.40
Change in Ratio		0.08	0.15	0.07	0.16	−0.00
POVERTY STATUS—Families in Poverty						
Ratio 1970	8.8%	1.10	1.82	0.69	0.32	0.75
Ratio 1980	9.3%	1.24	2.85	0.73	0.42	0.18
Change in Ratio		0.14	1.03	0.04	0.10	−0.57
BLACK COMPOSITION						
Ratio 1970	12.4%	1.45	7.46	0.15	0.00	0.02
Ratio 1980	13.5%	1.62	7.21	0.08	0.02	0.03
Change in Ratio		0.17	−0.25	−0.07	0.02	0.01
CHILDBEARING: Children Ever Born per 100 Women 35–44						
Ratio 1970	3124	1.01	1.18	1.03	1.00	0.88
Ratio 1980	2704	1.02	1.63	0.48	0.96	0.94
Change in Ratio		0.01	0.45	−0.55	−0.04	0.06
HOUSEHOLD SIZE						
Ratio 1970	3.14	0.98	1.28	0.76	1.11	1.11
Ratio 1980	2.74	0.97	1.42	0.78	1.06	1.13
Change in Ratio		−0.01	0.14	0.02	−0.05	0.02

*Tract 1105 split in 1980 into 1105.01 and 1105.02
†Ratio indicates the city or neighborhood value divided by the SMSA value.
‡The absolute increase or decline in the neighborhood/SMSA ratio from 1970 to 1980.

female-headed families as the metropolitan average. On the life cycle measures the neighborhood continued to diverge from the metropolitan norm. By 1980 the fertility ratio of the neighborhood—children born in the last year per 1,000 women of childbearing age—was 60 percent higher than the SMSA and, correspondingly, the average household size was 40 percent higher.

The mid-city neighborhood started out in 1970 fairly close to the metropolitan average in 1970, but its socioeconomic position deteriorated slightly over the decade, in concert with many other neighborhoods in the city of Indianapolis. The neighborhood lost about 10 percent of its population but maintained the same number of households. Relative income fell slightly, as did educational attainment. Over the 1970s we observe a slight increase in female-headed families and poverty status, the former holding at the SMSA average and the latter below average. The neighborhood actually experienced a decrease in the black proportion. The sharpest change in the neighborhood was in the fertility ratio, which fell from a par with the SMSA to half the level of the SMSA.

Suburban neighborhood 1 experienced a 17 percent growth in population, but underlying this was a 40 percent increase in the number of households. It exhibits some mixed movement regarding trends in status and population composition. In 1970, incomes were over one-third higher than the SMSA average, but in 1980 they were one-quarter higher, so we see a slight deterioration in status of a relatively advantaged neighborhood. (The educational attainment statistics, on the other hand, move in the opposite direction.) The neighborhood continues to have a comparatively small fraction of its population residing in poverty and in female-headed families, although we see increases in the incidence of these two features over the decade. In terms of the life cycle characteristics of fertility and household size, the neighborhood is in step with the metropolitan average at both points in time. No blacks lived in this suburban neighborhood in 1970, and only a few resided there by 1980.

The final neighborhood, also in the suburbs, started out in 1970 with only slightly more population than the neighborhood we have just described, but by the end of the decade it had grown rapidly, almost doubling. It is here that we observe clear increases in relative status. By 1980, incomes in this neighborhood approached $30,000 annually, about 50 percent higher than the metropolitan average. The neighborhood was predominantly white with few female-headed families in 1970, and this changed little over the decade. The proportion of the population in poverty fell from 6.6 percent to 1.7 percent, in the opposite direction from the metropolitan trend. Over the decade fertility remained slightly lower than average, household size a little higher.

In summary, Table 6.6 draws for us a statistical portrait of neighborhood evolution set in the context of metropolitan change. The city declined slightly in comparison to its metropolitan suburbs in the measures of socioeconomic status, and in the increasing fraction of minorities. The inner-city neighborhood was predominantly black and slightly disadvantaged in 1970, but saw its position deteriorate markedly over the decade as many households, presumably those with more resources, pulled up stakes and moved into other neighborhoods. The mid-city tract is a clear example of an aging neighborhood in the residential heart of the central city. It is stable, but has lost most of its younger population (producing the dramatic decline in the fertility ratio), and has experienced some loss in status. It is the kind of neighborhood that is likely to continue to experience deterioration in SES over the next decade. It is ripe for turnover in racial and ethnic composition, as the present residents, after having raised their children here, begin to move out, making space available for newcomers. In the suburbs we observe one neighborhood that is stable in terms of population and social characteristics. The other neighborhood is undergoing a boom. New residents, most likely employed in the newly deconcentrated development of the vicinity, have moved into (necessarily) newly constructed housing. This new settlement overlays an older residential community, actually increasing its relative status as the newcomers begin to statistically outweigh the longer-term residents.

Five Thousand Neighborhoods: A Decade of Change

Stage theory is useful for framing the way in which we will look at neighborhood evolution statistically. Although we do not possess a complete life history (many decades) on each of these neighborhoods, we can see whether the empirical evidence for the 1970s is consistent with a particular point of view given by one of the models. We address two questions regarding neighborhood evolution. First, how stable are the characteristics over time? Second, how does the change in a neighborhood's status or stage accord with its location in the metropolitan pattern?

In working with comparisons over time we must be attentive to the issue of absolute versus relative comparisons, particularly with regard to population composition. Just as in the Indianapolis example, a neighborhood characteristic may increase in absolute terms while falling in relative terms, keeping pace with changes across most of the neighborhoods. When working with census data over time, a second difficulty arises. Categories of measurement may not remain exactly the same, so that absolute changes may reflect differences in measurement rather than underlying neighborhood dynamics.

For these reasons we have chosen to undertake most of our dynamic analysis in relative terms. We examine the changing relative positions of the tracts over time in the tables to follow. These tabulations have made use of the longitudinally matched census tracts of 1970–1980. Ideally we have data on the same parcel of land at both points in time.[26]

Neighborhood Stability

Table 6.7 presents a simple measure of neighborhood stability during the 1970s within the metropolis. For each SMSA we have calculated the rank order correlation coefficient for a variety of demographic and housing characteristics. If all the neighborhoods were in the same position in 1980 as they were in 1970, the value of the statistic is 1.0, and this would indicate perfect relative stability. Conversely, if there is no relationship between relative position at the two censuses, the coefficient would take on a value of zero.

For most characteristics we have examined there is a substantial amount of stability in the relative position of neighborhoods. Educational attainment is the most stable characteristic, and in most metropolitan areas the relative position occupied by a neighborhood in 1980 matches very closely its position in 1970. Particularly large values are found in Boston, Lexington, and New Haven, three cities with large university populations, which would tend to replenish selected neighborhoods with persons of the same educational level. The stability of the upper income population falls in very closely behind educational attainment, with most cities registering over 80 percent stability. At the other end of the income distribution, stability for poverty status aver-

---

[26]Our tabulations in this section are based on a sample of 4,985 tract observations from nineteen metropolitan areas. Bangor and Sheboygan are excluded because they were not SMSAs in 1970. These observations include (a) unchanged tracts; (b) tracts that were split between 1970 and 1980 and recombined for this analysis; (c) tracts that were merged due to depopulation in 1970 and 1980, for which 1970 data were recombined; and (d) tracts that could only be matched imperfectly. Because of the recombination and exclusion of tracts from counties added to SMSAs between 1970 and 1980, the sample is smaller. Of the nearly 5,000 tracts on which these tabulations are based, almost 95 percent were matched with consistent boundaries (see Appendix A). We have reexamined the tabulations with a number of different measures and some slightly different samples of census tracts (controlling for quality of match, etc.), and the results hold. Therefore, Tables 6.7 and 6.8 present the simplest and most inclusive of our results.

TABLE 6.7
Stability of Neighborhood Characteristics: 1970–1980*

SMSA	College Educated	High Income	Poverty Status	Black	Foreign Born	Children	Elderly	Recent Move-in	New Housing
Allentown	0.85	0.65	0.59	0.79	0.58	0.73	0.83	0.53	0.61
Amarillo	0.85	0.73	0.67	0.58	0.26	0.75	0.84	0.41	0.62
Atlanta	0.90	0.86	0.78	0.77	0.53	0.71	0.78	0.55	0.60
Birmingham	0.72	0.72	0.76	0.85	0.38	0.52	0.68	0.55	0.80
Boston	0.90	0.91	0.76	0.80	0.73	0.88	0.73	0.64	0.44
Chicago	0.86	0.86	0.78	0.83	0.77	0.75	0.65	0.60	0.51
Flint	0.77	0.81	0.71	0.82	0.30	0.71	0.76	0.60	0.69
Indianapolis	0.87	0.85	0.68	0.82	0.47	0.67	0.77	0.55	0.66
Lexington	0.92	0.89	0.87	0.77	0.25	0.79	0.79	0.67	0.70
New Bedford	0.87	0.76	0.75	0.86	0.67	0.79	0.81	0.51	0.42
New Haven	0.95	0.87	0.76	0.88	0.47	0.81	0.77	0.71	0.57
New Orleans	0.80	0.84	0.85	0.91	0.51	0.84	0.80	0.58	0.71
Newark	0.93	0.92	0.85	0.90	0.68	0.74	0.75	0.65	0.39
St. Louis	0.89	0.83	0.82	0.87	0.53	0.72	0.66	0.53	0.62
Salt Lake City	0.92	0.82	0.66	0.81	0.66	0.89	0.87	0.73	0.66
San Antonio	0.85	0.77	0.79	0.72	0.72	0.83	0.82	0.61	0.62
San Diego	0.82	0.82	0.61	0.74	0.58	0.84	0.85	0.65	0.60
Seattle	0.86	0.82	0.56	0.77	0.55	0.89	0.85	0.65	0.78
Stockton	0.80	0.69	0.65	0.89	0.58	0.74	0.69	0.48	0.50
MEAN	0.86	0.81	0.73	0.81	0.54	0.77	0.77	0.59	0.61

*Rank order correlation coefficient for SMSA between 1970 and 1980.

ages 0.73 in the 19 metropolitan areas. Interestingly, relative poverty is less consistent over time than relative affluence, although part of this is due to the fact that those in poverty constitute a smaller fraction of the population than the high-income group. Taken together, though, these results point to considerable stability in the distribution of resources and status about the metropolis.

Differences across SMSAs in the stability of status are visible in Table 6.7, although SMSA comparisons should be made with caution because stability is influenced by census tract boundary comparability. Newark in particular records very high levels of stability in all three characteristics, pointing at once to the lack of overall population dynamics in the metropolitan area during the 1970s and the relatively entrenched residential positions occupied by the income extremes.

The stability of the neighborhood black proportion is equivalent to what we observed for the high income population. Despite the reduction of segregation of the black population, neighborhoods in almost every metropolitan area are so separated between black and white that prediction from one decade to the next is very accurate. The faster-growing cities of the South and West have the lowest values. The same cities experienced the largest declines in segregation, suggesting that growth may not be accompanied by racial reconsolidation.[27] Measurement of the foreign-born population is consistent between 1970 and 1980, yet the lcvcl of stability is over 25 points below that found for blacks. This finding is consistent with the hypothesis that the foreign-born population is more mobile and that new immigrant settlements are not necessarily those occupied by the previous wave. If the ecological succession model applied completely, the value should be higher as old immigrant groups gave way to new groups in the same neighborhoods.

One might hypothesize that as a neighborhood aged, its residents would age in place, until the neighborhood turned over to a younger group, much like the case of the Indianapolis mid-city neighborhood. If such a pattern were to hold, we would anticipate far less stability in the correlation coefficient than the 0.77 value we observe for both children and the elderly. Stability over time for the life cycle, in fact, falls just under income and race. In the western SMSAs consistency of the residential distribution of the elderly is particularly apparent. This may be due to the fact that these regions do not lose as many of their elderly residents through migration as the northern SMSAs do.

---

[27]We made companion calculations for race group other than black or white, but the differences in the way the 1970 and 1980 censuses handled this category introduced a great deal of error into these values. Cities on the coasts with substantial Asian populations have levels of stability near to or slightly below that for blacks. In other SMSAs, the correlation is negligible.

Our final two characteristics of Table 6.7 are different; they are direct measures of neighborhood population and housing turnover; their stability indicates the persistence of change. If certain neighborhoods are characterized by transience and others by stability (in that residents never move), then values for the fraction of neighborhood residents who are recent arrivals should be about the same from decade to decade. In fact, the stability coefficient for this characteristic is below most race, status, and life cycle measures. The SMSAs where recency of residence is very highly correlated in neighborhoods over time include Lexington, New Haven, and Salt Lake City, three areas with very high values of the college-educated stability. As with age stability, these numbers are higher than suggested under a straightforward application of neighborhood life cycle theory.

Residents of housing built in the five years preceding the census are necessarily recent occupants, but this fact does not produce a correspondence between the figures in the final two columns of the table, even though the averages are nearly the same. There is a relationship between the stability of new housing construction and growth rate of the metropolitan area. In many of the growing SMSAs (New Orleans, Lexington, Seattle), the neighborhoods that receive new housing in one decade are likely to receive new housing in the next decade. By contrast, in the older metropolitan areas (Boston, Chicago, Newark) the over-time stability of housing age is quite low, indicating that newly constructed housing is more likely to be scattered over the metropolitan area.

Neighborhood Evolution by Ring

The second view we can take of neighborhood evolution is to break down the distribution of the types of changes according to the distance from the center of the city. We employ the scheme of previous chapters and break the metropolitan area up into four concentric rings.[28] If the stage theory of the neighborhood and conventional zonal theories of metropolitan ecological development are valid, we expect to see considerable variation in neighborhood dynamics by ring. Most neighborhoods

---

[28]Again, these rings have nothing to do with the central city–suburban boundary. Since they are the same zones that were used in the 1980 cross-sectional analysis, the merged data do not necessarily have the same number of tracts per ring. In general, the outer rings will have smaller numbers of census tracts due to recombination of split tracts there. For convenience we continue to call the innermost circular zone of the four a "ring."

of the innermost ring should be "thinning" and declining in socioeconomic status, although a few may show signs of renewal or recapture. The second ring should display similar trends, albeit not as extreme. No evidence of renewal should be visible. In the outer two rings
we should observe the bulk of population growth and increases in status
of the resident population. Although we know that most of these trends
tend to be generally true, analysis of neighborhood dynamics—the
change from decade to decade in individual neighborhoods—allows us
to determine the balance between those neighborhoods that are consistent with the trends and those that buck the trends.

Figure 6.3 presents an overview of population changes in metropolitan neighborhoods, including the mix of circumstances by ring. The
figure presents for the nearly 5,000 neighborhood observations in all 19
SMSAs the number in each ring gaining and losing absolute population,
and within each gain/loss category the average change. The vast majority of inner ring neighborhoods lost population. As one moves outward,
the fraction of neighborhoods gaining increases. This is consistent with
our expectations but it does not tell the whole story. While the average
loss in declining neighborhoods of each ring is about 600 persons, the
average increase in the gaining neighborhoods of rings 2 and 3 is over
2,500 persons, much more than the 700 for ring 1. So, as we compare
above and below the line, it becomes clear that there is a very real
diversity of neighborhood growth experience, even within broadly
defined zones, which aggregate calculations can miss. Table 6.8 reports
for the 1970s the percentage of neighborhoods (1970 boundaries) within
each ring gaining in the number of households, as well as the proportions of high income, black, and elderly residents, relative to the average neighborhood, much like our example for the case of the four Indianapolis neighborhoods. We chose these four characteristics because
they are indicators of overall growth (net of changing household size),
socioeconomic status, ethnicity, and life cycle, and because they were
comparable over time. Numbers close to 100 percent indicate that almost all neighborhoods within that ring gained relative to the average
(median) neighborhood, values close to zero point to near universal relative decline, and values in between indicate that neighborhood evolution was quite mixed. The fifth column of the table reports Cramer's *V*,
a measure of association for cross-tabulations. The larger the value of *V*
(which varies from 0 to 100), the more differentiated is neighborhood
evolution according to ring.[29]

[29]We also calculated an index of relative status change based, not on cross-tabulation
of gainers and losers but on numerical change in the relative position of the neighborhood.
For the most part, these results corroborated the cross-tabulations, although sometimes
they gave a more complete assessment of the magnitude of the differences by ring.

TABLE 6.8

Neighborhood Evolution by Ring: 1970–1980

SMSA	Variable	Neighborhoods Increasing Relative Position (%)				
		Ring 1	Ring 2	Ring 3	Ring 4	Cramer's V^*
Allentown	Households	41	48	52	60	0.14
	High Income	34	52	59	57	0.19
	Black	81	36	48	33	0.39
	Elderly	53	58	52	37	0.16
Amarillo	Households	0	33	69	100	0.75
	High Income	44	60	50	47	0.12
	Black	44	60	50	47	0.12
	Elderly	13	80	69	40	0.53
Atlanta	Households	15	61	87	92	0.59
	High Income	42	35	76	100	0.39
	Black	36	62	63	0	0.35
	Elderly	37	61	65	8	0.32
Birmingham	Households	18	33	59	86	0.53
	High Income	33	30	55	74	0.37
	Black	70	77	41	11	0.53
	Elderly	46	77	66	17	0.46
Boston	Households	34	35	57	79	0.36
	High Income	34	35	59	74	0.32
	Black	42	62	49	45	0.15
	Elderly	34	35	68	66	0.33
Chicago	Households	26	36	65	81	0.44
	High Income	40	26	64	74	0.37
	Black	46	44	47	66	0.17
	Elderly	36	42	71	51	0.27
Flint	Households	3	43	84	77	0.65
	High Income	32	43	72	58	0.30
	Black	48	75	56	19	0.40
	Elderly	29	64	72	39	0.36
Indianapolis	Households	13	33	92	78	0.63
	High Income	33	31	51	84	0.45
	Black	43	76	67	18	0.46
	Elderly	31	74	69	35	0.39
Lexington	Households	20	64	100	NA	0.62
	High Income	55	29	63	NA	0.28
	Black	40	64	50	NA	0.22
	Elderly	35	86	25	NA	0.51
New Bedford	Households	30	46	46	100	0.47
	High Income	10	64	55	71	0.47
	Black	30	46	64	57	0.26
	Elderly	20	55	55	86	0.43
New Haven	Households	4	50	75	100	0.64
	High Income	17	29	88	86	0.63
	Black	30	71	54	29	0.34
	Elderly	4	71	79	29	0.65

TABLE 6.8 *(continued)*

SMSA	Variable	Neighborhoods Increasing Relative Position (%)				
		Ring 1	Ring 2	Ring 3	Ring 4	Cramer's V^*
New Orleans	Households	20	25	84	89	0.63
	High Income	42	40	53	70	0.22
	Black	41	49	59	45	0.14
	Elderly	14	46	85	64	0.54
Newark	Households	33	40	59	85	0.36
	High Income	24	36	68	90	0.48
	Black	35	62	51	53	0.21
	Elderly	38	40	73	47	0.29
St. Louis	Households	8	42	77	85	0.61
	High Income	45	33	58	70	0.27
	Black	41	56	61	36	0.20
	Elderly	42	44	77	30	0.34
Salt Lake	Households	20	64	88	51	0.49
	High Income	30	70	88	32	0.46
	Black	63	36	42	51	0.21
	Elderly	28	79	42	57	0.39
San Antonio	Households	4	45	79	83	0.64
	High Income	43	40	44	75	0.26
	Black	25	57	74	42	0.38
	Elderly	41	77	63	11	0.48
San Diego	Households	10	35	80	88	0.65
	High Income	36	35	52	80	0.36
	Black	44	57	65	34	0.23
	Elderly	34	79	61	25	0.44
Seattle	Households	8	42	79	76	0.58
	High Income	36	31	66	68	0.34
	Black	39	61	61	31	0.27
	Elderly	21	74	76	24	0.53
Stockton	Households	5	35	81	83	0.67
	High Income	25	47	50	78	0.39
	Black	50	53	69	22	0.33
	Elderly	35	71	56	33	0.31
MEAN	Households	16	43	74	83	0.55
	High Income	35	40	61	72	0.35
	Black	45	58	56	35	0.28
	Elderly	31	64	64	39	0.41

*Cramer's *V* is a measure of association for a two-day table (range 0 to 1). Eta is a measure of the amount of variance attributable to ring location.

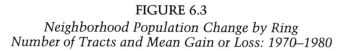

FIGURE 6.3

Neighborhood Population Change by Ring
Number of Tracts and Mean Gain or Loss: 1970–1980

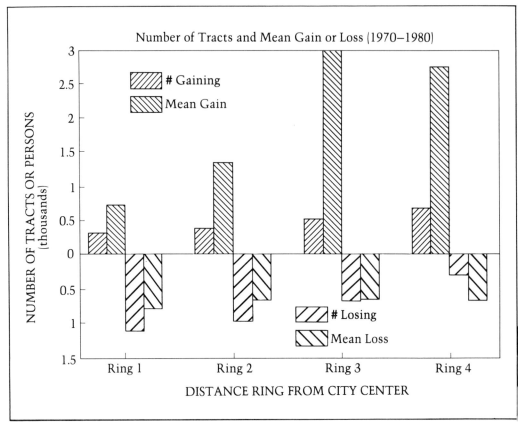

Household Change

The table shows quite dramatically how neighborhood change differs by ring, and how variable a neighborhood's fate can be within each ring. In the case of household change, in the typical SMSA the majority of inner ring neighborhoods lost households, in both relative and absolute terms. With each successive ring outward, the percentage of neighborhoods gaining in households more than the SMSA average usually increases. To return to Indianapolis as an example, about six out of seven inner ring neighborhoods saw slower than average household growth. In contrast, the vast majority of neighborhoods in the two outermost rings gained. (Related tabulations showed that while a typical Indianapolis inner ring neighborhood lost 137 households, the typical neighborhood in ring 3 added over 1,000 households and was likely to have split in the meantime.) In several of the older and larger cities the relative depopulation of the inner ring as compared to the outer ring is particularly evident. Overall metropolitan growth is likely to influence the number of absolute gainers and losers, too. The case of St. Louis is particularly striking. Over 90 percent of the neighborhoods in the inner ring experienced relative decline in number of households. (The average neighborhood lost 377 households.) In the smaller SMSA of Amarillo, three-quarters of the inner ring neighborhoods gained absolutely, but all of them grew more slowly than neighborhoods in the average metropolitan neighborhood. Of the four characteristics, household change is the most differentiated across ring, as indicated by the highest value of Cramer's *V*.

Status

According to models of the metropolis advanced by Burgess and by urban economists, the highest income households move outward with time, overtaking land once devoted to agricultural uses, and begin the housing filtration process. Neighborhoods at the periphery, then, should experience increases in relative status, as the high-income, metropolitan professional population inundates the resident rural population. In theory, any income improvement in inner city neighborhoods should be far outpaced by income gains in the more peripheral locations.

The results presented in Table 6.8 support the theory. In most metropolitan areas the fraction of neighborhoods gaining in relative status increases steadily by ring. Overall, the outermost ring has about twice as many neighborhoods increasing in status as in the inner ring. We do observe some exceptions to the steady progression, where the third ring gains more than the fourth ring, suggesting that these outer rings are the sites of decentralized industrial developments, more likely to have and attract lower-income workers.

Life Cycle

As an indicator of the life cycle composition of neighborhoods, we examine the change in the elderly population. Between 1970 and 1980 the fraction of the United States population that was elderly increased, and we can expect the typical neighborhood to increase as well. But the residential dynamics of the older population may be less clear. As we mentioned earlier, when neighborhoods age, persons may age in place, so that in older residential districts, say, the first two rings, we may observe increases in the relative concentrations of the elderly. Conversely, if child-rearing takes place predominantly in suburban locations, rings 3 and 4 will see a decline in the relative elderly concentration. There should be considerable variation by SMSA on this variable as the elderly migrate from one SMSA to another, the most mobile and affluent likely to move from the North to the South and West. In some SMSAs, the concentration of CBD employment may provide a stimulus to the location of younger working age persons in the central ring, thereby bringing down the relative age of the neighborhoods.

Our results support both of these contentions. The innermost ring shows the least growth in the elderly population. This is due to the growth of central employment for persons in the younger labor force ages, the central concentration of minority groups with higher fertility and younger age distributions, and, most probably, the lack of replacement of the resident elderly population by reason of mortality and migration to other portions of the SMSA or out of the region altogether. The greatest gains in the elderly fraction occur in rings 2 and 3. This is just as we found with the mid-city tract in Indianapolis. In the outermost ring, there were fewer such tracts because these are the areas of newer residential development in single-family homes, many of which are destined to become child-rearing communities. So even with this very crude measure of life cycle we can see evidence of life course evolution in neighborhoods.

Metropolitan areas differ appreciably regarding relative age change. In New Haven, for example, there is very little increase in relative age of the population in central neighborhoods, but aging of the residents in place is clearly evident in rings 2 and 3. In Atlanta, the "younging" of the outskirts is particularly evident. For the SMSAs in general, growth of the elderly population exhibits more differentiation across the rings than income or race, as indicated by values of Cramer's V. Household growth and housing unit construction are still more closely tied to geographic position. This is consistent with our findings that social characteristics, while clearly differentiated by position in the metropolis, are less regularly distributed than the housing infrastructure.

Race

We found in our analysis of segregation and spatial organization that the black population in American metropolitan areas was highly concentrated in selected neighborhoods—the ghettoes—and that this residential distribution followed a more nucleated form. It is difficult, then, to predict what will happen over time. The extreme segregation of the metropolis means that most neighborhoods are either all white or all black, and that the metropolitan "average" composition is unlikely to be found in a particular neighborhood. With the decline in segregation many predominantly white neighborhoods could experience large relative increases in their black proportion. However, racial succession and expansion would still proceed mostly from the traditional black residential area, and the ring-by-ring change would be inconsistent.

Table 6.8 confirms that there is less relation between ring and neighborhood racial dynamics; average Cramer's *V* is the lowest of the four. In most SMSAs, the inner ring is the area of heaviest black residential concentration (see Chapter 5), so that in a segregated residential system there is little opportunity for gain in relative position. On the other hand, some of these neighborhoods are experiencing construction of new housing, often under the aegis of a redevelopment authority. It is in the second and third rings that we observe the greatest number of neighborhoods gaining relative to the SMSA average. In the outermost ring the gain is also relatively small. Although many studies have now confirmed the extent of black suburbanization, we can see that it has not been so extensive as to penetrate the distant suburbs and exurbs. Only in Chicago, New Bedford, Newark, and Salt Lake City did a majority of outer-ring neighborhoods gain in relative terms. In Atlanta, all outer-ring neighborhoods declined in relative black concentration. In the Taeuber and Taeuber paradigm, such circumstances are referred to as "displacement." In our sample, displacement occurs more often in the South and in the SMSAs with substantial black populations historically located at the metropolitan outskirts.

Gentrification Evidence?

We have already alluded to the large amount of recent writing on inner city revival. Is there evidence of such revival among our 5,000 neighborhoods? To look directly for evidence of central district revival in these metropolitan areas we have tabulated the fraction of neighborhoods experiencing both an absolute increase in the number of households and a relative improvement in their status position as measured by income. This is not everyone's definition of gentrification, a rather vague and inconsistently defined notion to begin with; however, it does reflect increasing attractiveness of neighborhoods to new, higher-income residents. We cannot distinguish between rehabilitation of older residences (residential upgrading) and new construction. We also set the comparison in a metropolitan framework.

The results in Table 6.9 show little evidence of what would be termed gentrification. In most SMSAs only a handful of inner ring census tracts experienced both income and households gains.[30] Among the large, old SMSAs, Boston, Chicago, and Newark show more increases than the others. Some of the increase could be due to urban redevelopment strategies, while other portions could be due to changing population composition within the existing housing stock. Overall, though, gains in the inner rings of the metropolis are dwarfed by status and household increases in the outer rings.

Conclusion

Our results for metropolitan change do not point to a simple conclusion. There is plenty of change in metropolitan neighborhoods and in the way they fit together to construct the metropolitan mosaic. Among the socioeconomic characteristics, occupations seem to have become less segregated and oriented to the CBD, and perhaps more nucleated. Our results do show increasing segregation of the poor during the 1970s and suggest increased segregation by level of well-being. Life cycle characteristics became decidedly less predictable by our metropolitan contour; we did find some increases (modest in absolute terms) in segregation by age and marital status. Segregation by race and ethnicity declined appreciably. What may be most remarkable, however, is the way in which the "ladder of segregation" has remained virtually intact over the period we examine. Race and the physical characteristics of the housing stock continue to occupy the rungs of highest segregation, life cycle characteristics are at the bottom, and socioeconomic characteristics are in between.

Whereas the comparison of segregation statistics and the predictability of neighborhood composition give us a sequence of snapshot views of the metropolitan topography, it is the analysis of neighborhood-level information that lets us fill in the information about the underlying dynamics. The vast majority of inner city tracts

---

[30]Some observers will disagree about considering increase in households as part of this calculation. We included it because it is a simple indicator of the attractiveness of the neighborhood. An alternative is to focus only on income (status) changes in Table 6.8.

TABLE 6.9

Neighborhood Upgrading by Ring

Metropolitan Area	Percent Upgrading				Cramer's *V*
	Ring 1	Ring 2	Ring 3	Ring 4	
Allentown	16	29	46	40	.17
Amarillo	0	7	31	47	.47
Atlanta	4	22	72	92	.43
Birmingham	3	13	31	63	.36
Boston	14	10	34	62	.27
Chicago	9	10	43	65	.32
Flint	0	14	60	54	.41
Indianapolis	7	14	46	69	.43
Lexington	10	14	68	—	.50
New Bedford	10	36	27	71	.38
New Haven	0	17	63	86	.48
New Orleans	5	5	44	64	.39
Newark	9	13	44	80	.34
St. Louis	2	12	50	70	.41
Salt Lake City	7	49	83	24	.37
San Antonio	2	17	40	67	.41
San Diego	3	15	42	70	.41
Seattle	3	16	51	61	.38
Stockton	0	18	38	72	.46
MEAN	5.4	33.1	47.6	64.2	.389

are experiencing decline in relative status and are depopulating, while at the periphery of the metropolitan areas neighborhoods are gaining population rapidly and are actually increasing in relative status due to new settlement by metropolitan residents of higher incomes. The outer neighborhoods are becoming relatively younger and are devoted to child-rearing, while the neighborhoods of the middle two rings are aging. Inner and outer areas show the least gain in the proportion black. If the ethnic pattern is nucleated, we would not expect much of a systematic relationship of racial change to distance.

Are these results consistent with the combined ecological-stage theory for urban neighborhoods? In a general way they are. With information only at two points of time we cannot, of course, fully analyze the neighborhood life cycle and thereby evelute more critically the evolutionary model.

Finally, what comes through in these tabulations is the variety of neighborhood experience. Tabulations for many characteristics show a substantial minority of neighborhoods bucking the trend within their ring, lending support to Downs's contention that direction of movement along the stages is reversible. Our results also indicate, however, that the attention given to gentrification as a force in metropolitan change is out of proportion to its demographic and statistical impact.

7

EVOLVING METROPOLITAN
STRUCTURE

W E NOW turn to the issue of the structure of the nation's metropolitan areas. By structure we mean the way in which the
residential neighborhoods and major nonresidential activities
are organized in the metropolitan territory. A number of writers have
already described or conjectured about how trends during the 1970s
have changed the shape of the metropolis. In an attempt to fill out that
picture with detailed census information, we draw on our results regarding residential differentiation and spatial organization in the previous chapters, and add to it other information about changes in transportation and economic structure in the nation. In order to gain geographic
detail in the census, we must often sacrifice demographic detail for
small areas, but the results still provide pieces of the puzzle of metropolitan organization, and taken together, they can help us see the picture. At the same time we will make some suggestions for further
analysis that might shed more light on the issues and hypotheses we
raise.

Population Diffusion

The changes we observe in the metropolis and its neighborhoods
are intertwined with the redistribution of the nation's population

more generally. One of the most prominent features of the changes in population distribution during the 1970s was the nonmetropolitan "turnaround." During the decade, the population within constant metropolitan boundaries grew more slowly than the population outside of metropolitan areas. Moreover, the increase in the nation's urban population was the smallest since 1820.[1] This shift attracted a great deal of attention inside and outside of demographic and academic circles, because of the fundamental restructuring of the U.S. population settlement system that it symbolized. Careful research by a number of scholars has demonstrated that this turnaround was neither simply a statistical artifact nor a spilling over of the metropolitan population into still more peripheral "exurbs."[2] Furthermore, there occurred an increase in the fraction of metropolitan residents classified as "rural," from 12 percent to 15 percent, in the 1970s. Larry Long and Diana DeAre observe these trends to be "an indicator of growing diffuseness of the nation's metropolitan system: as it expanded into the countryside in the 1970s, the system itself was transformed in a manner different from the 1950s or 1960s."[3]

The changes of the 1970s, when viewed in tandem with the massive suburbanization of the 1950s and 1960s in major metropolitan areas, speak to an extensive rearrangement of population. This transformation has left its mark on the neighborhoods of the metropolis, affecting both their evolution and the overall pattern of orientation to the metropolitan cores. We call this pattern of spatial evolution population diffusion. Metropolitan population diffusion has three interrelated elements: the general dispersal or deconcentration of the population, the growing importance of nucleation over radial patterns, and a decline in spatial organization of residential territory.[4]

The nonmetropolitan turnaround marks the change at the regional level. Where a few decades ago the more rural (nonmetropolitan) areas of the country were devoted to agriculture and other extractive industries, sending migrants to the big cities for many years, they have now been receiving migrants and new economic activity. This activity is not farming, fishing, and mining but rather includes the post–World War II attraction of manufacturing and the more recent growth in office

[1]Larry Long and Diana DeAre, "Repopulating the Countryside: A 1980 Census Trend," *Science* 217 (1982):1111–1116.

[2]Calvin Beale, *The Revival of Population Growth in Nonmetropolitan America,* U.S. Department of Agriculture Economic Research Service Report #605 (1976).

[3]Larry Long and Diana DeAre, "Repopulating the Countryside," pp. 1114–1115.

[4]Our usage of population diffusion should be distinguished from that in the innovation-diffusion literature, in which a certain phenomenon (often an innovation) moves through space.

developments, research parks, and the like. The old rural–urban distinctions in types of economic activity are simply less valid for the 1980s than they were for the 1940s or 1950s, and the dominance of metropolitan centers over their rural hinterlands has declined. Without question, changes in transportation and communication technology and availability have encouraged, even spawned, this development. The exact nature of their role is not yet fully understood.

We accept the premise that social structure—stratification, race relations, life cycle—can be seen in the spatial patterns of the metropolis. Each neighborhood contains a particular cross-section of the metropolitan population, clustered together for reasons that can be traced to economic competition, life style preferences, or prejudice. One expects to find represented in the metropolis rich neighborhoods and poor neighborhoods, black and Italian neighborhoods, communities of young singles, the elderly, and nuclear families. The existence of such variegated communities speaks to the aspect of unevenness or segregation. Spatial organization, on the other hand, describes the way in which the various neighborhoods are related into a systematic whole, or alternatively the way in which the social composition of a neighborhood is predictable from its relative geographic location within the city and suburbs. In essence, the ecological models of Chapter 5 offer explicit hypotheses about spatial organization, accompanied by maps about how that organization takes shape. Spatial organization assumes that neighborhoods exhibit differences, but also that their location corresponds to systematic patterns.

The suburbanization that characterized the 1950s and 1960s challenged the overriding dominance of the central city (and city hall) in the metropolitan ecology. Many central cities, particularly those in the North, lost population in absolute terms, and lost dramatically relative to their suburbs. In the South and West, suburbanization occurred, too, although the more extensive initial boundaries and the greater facility for annexation (for example, in Texas and Oklahoma), often corralled the suburban population back within the central municipality. In 1940 for every two suburban residents there were three central city residents; by 1980 this ratio had been reversed.[5]

The central business district—the historical focus, even the metaphorical heart—of the metropolitan area no longer figures as prominently in the residential organization of the metropolis, nor is it as important for understanding the flow of persons, goods, and services

---

[5]Donald J. Bogue, *The Population of the United States* (New York: Free Press, 1985) pp. 129–135.

around the region. The circumferential highways, especially at their intersections with the major axial routes, have chipped away at the proverbial "State and Madison." To be sure, downtown is still the grandest center, and probably is the most important, but it no longer possesses the kind of organizing hegemony that it once did. Still, implicit in much of our thinking and planning about cities has been the idea that the conventional models still hold, needing only to be "stretched" outward to accommodate the spreading out of the population. To what extent is such a perception accurate?

Differentiation amid diffusion is a result of the structural transformation of American urban areas. Changes in the technology of transportation and communication in the last few decades have been so sweeping that access to the center is less critical. For the 1960s Brian J. L. Berry and Quentin Gillard documented the further extension of commuting fields into the periphery, the decline in core orientation, the rise in cross-commuting patterns, and the rise of a multinodal pattern.[6] While access to the center is less important, location itself is still meaningful, particularly in the residential environment. Who one's neighbors are is still an important choice—or constraint—for many in society.

The changing distribution of the metropolitan population is illustrated by the density contour of the city. Where once a sharp peak existed with a steep slope, time and technology have worn away at the gradient, leveling it in most cities. The relative growth of outer ring neighborhoods as compared to inner ring neighborhoods provides further evidence of dispersal. Americans have also moved from the older SMSAs to the younger, smaller SMSAs. The net result is that the average American lives at densities much lower than a generation ago. The flattening of density gradients is symptomatic of the deconcentration metropolitan areas have undergone. The post–World War II period has seen a decline in our ability to predict the composition of neighborhoods merely from how far they were from downtown, and in what direction, yet neighborhoods still remain very distinct in terms of their residential character. The general pattern—the segregation ladder—holds over time, and so does the absolute level of segregation for many individual characteristics, although during the 1970s racial segregation declined somewhat, while the segregation of the poorest in the population increased in most areas. The spreading out of the population, coupled with the decline in our ability to predict social and housing characteristics from geographic location, suggests intrametropolitan population diffusion. Distinct communities still exist. The dimensions of differentiation have shifted slightly, but orientation toward the

[6]Brian J. L. Berry and Quentin Gillard, *The Changing Shape of Metropolitan America* (Cambridge, Mass.: Ballinger, 1977), pp. 99–123.

center has waned. A more complete examination of the existence and extent of population diffusion would need to take on a direct analysis for a larger number of metropolitan areas than we analyzed here. We can say that our work for the 1940–1980 and 1970–1980 periods encourages the effort.

The Metropolitan System

Does the extent of population diffusion challenge the very notion of metropolis, a place traditionally defined by a high level of organization for the production of goods and services, one in which the division of labor in economic activity was translated into spatial differentiation of the workers and their families? Yes, but it does not erase that notion. If we abide by conventional definitions, American urbanization and metropolitanization slowed nearly to a standstill during the 1970s. [7]

What from one side can be seen as a ruralization of American society, an exercise of long-standing preferences for more spacious and amenable surroundings, can also be interpreted as a generalized urbanization of America. Living in places that are technically defined as rural and/or nonmetropolitan for many Americans may mean only a slight sacrifice in terms of access to economic and cultural resources of value to them. The metropolis has continued to expand throughout this century, first spilling over the boundaries of the central municipality into the suburbs and now leapfrogging out of the region altogether. It has become increasingly difficult to establish satisfactorily where the "city," the "suburbs," the "exurbs," and the "rural hinterland" begin and end. The statistical agencies of the federal government have revised their definitions repeatedly to keep abreast of population trends. Moreover, we have witnessed the shifting of population to the lower-order centers. The structure of these younger cities is generally less beholden to the traditional ecological models, which were based on the larger, industrial metropolis of the North.

Since the metropolis is part of the national economy, there are interrelations among the various urban agglomerations. This network forms the metropolitan system. The ties that connect it constitute the structure of the metropolitan system. Thus, we can speak of Chicago, or Denver, or Salt Lake City as actors in the metropolitan system. As the

---

[7]Since 1980 metropolitan growth has picked up somewhat, tipping the advantage away from nonmetropolitan areas. Still, the smaller metropolitan areas are growing more rapidly than larger metropolitan areas. Richard L. Forstall and Richard A. Engels, "Growth in Nonmetropolitan Areas Slows," U.S. Bureau of the Census, March 16, 1984.

system changes, responding to changes in the economy, we expect that the internal structure of each metropolis will begin to reflect that change.

It is not a simple task to encapsulate what the National Academy of Sciences has called "powerful and deeply rooted structural changes in the national and international economy."[8] A major component of the transformation is a shift away from traditional forms of production and distribution, away from so-called smokestack industries and toward finance, services, recreational industries. As silicon metaphorically replaces steel as the vanguard of American industry, cities themselves are transformed. Since industries vary substantially in their capital intensiveness, one's view of this changeover in the American economy differs by whether one counts contribution to GNP or workers in industry. The effect on the labor force has been substantial, and consequently we expect to see it in the residential distribution of the population.

Where once much of the economic activity was located in the major cities of the Eastern Seaboard and the Great Lakes, it has moved out of those cities to their suburbs, into new regions, and out of the old metropolitan system altogether. At mid-century Otis D. Duncan and others could describe the metropolitan system in terms of 56 metropolitan areas, interrelated in their economic activity. The core in the network was New York. Four additional areas, Chicago, Los Angeles, Philadelphia, and Detroit, were classified as national metropolises, all but one in the old northern industrial regions.[9] Although not exactly comparable in approach, Thierry J. Noyelle and Thomas M. Stanback have classified the 140 largest metropolitan areas as of 1980.[10] They identify 39 diversified service centers, with four—New York, Los Angeles, Chicago, San Francisco—of national significance. Another 44 metropolitan areas are specialized service centers, and the remainder are various types of subordinate centers, most of which are linked to production.

The fate of the cities of the *Metropolis and Region* heartland has been varied. Most central cities have continued to lose population to their suburbs, and several metropolitan areas have themselves lost population. Some SMSAs have succeeded in attracting new industry or in shifting to new kinds of economic functions, often developing into

---

[8]National Academy of Sciences, *Rethinking Urban Policy* (Washington, D.C.: National Academy Press, 1983), p. 1.

[9]Otis D. Duncan et al., *Metropolis and Region* (Baltimore: Johns Hopkins University Press, 1960), p. 271. As of 1950, 56 Standard Metropolitan Areas (the original term) had attained 300,000+ population. An additional 21 metropolitan areas were manufacturing centers, 21 served as regional centers, and 6 were special cases.

[10]Thierry J. Noyelle and Thomas M. Stanback, *The Economic Transformation of American Cities* (Totowa, N.J.: Rowman & Allenheld, 1983).

"command and control centers" in the terminology of the National Academy of Sciences. Between 1970 and 1978 New York and Chicago both added over 20 million square feet of office space, and San Francisco, Boston, Los Angeles, Houston, Philadelphia, Washington, and Denver each added over 8 million square feet of central business district space. The eight-year growth in all of these cities was 30 percent or more.[11] Seven other cities added at least 3 million square feet, with increases of 10 percent or more. This handful of cities, along with a few others, form the cluster of candidates for command and control centers. New York, Boston, Chicago, and San Francisco have been particularly successful in this regard. But the new economy has less need for as many specialized financial commercial centers as for resource-based manufacturing centers. Other northern cities (including a few in our group) have not been able to ride this new wave. Those left behind may indeed be in a deep trough.[12]

Meanwhile metropolises and nonmetropolitan areas of the South and West (as well as some nonmetropolitan areas of the North) have succeeded in bidding away various kinds of economic activity, as well as capitalizing on their own natural resources. Los Angeles first, then Houston, Dallas, San Antonio, Atlanta, and Lexington, have all seen their regions grow as a result of these structural changes. As individual places and economies grew, the United States added actors to its metropolitan system, expanding from 168 SMSAs in 1950 to 318 designated for the 1980 census.

This addition of places to the catalog of "metropolis" and the redistribution of population and economic activity around that network also implies that the designation "metropolitan" has changed meaning. One aspect of the change is purely a result of loosening the requirements for being metropolitan. As Calvin Beale has argued, many of the places currently classified as SMSAs fail to possess some of the attributes that some researchers would consider essential to metropolitan character.[13] Reflecting our interest in the settlement system generally we drew from all of the places designated by the 1980 census as metropolitan. We included smaller areas as well as larger ones, because people live in neigh-

[11]Brian J. L. Berry, "Islands of Renewal in Seas of Decay," in Paul Peterson, ed., *The New Urban Reality* (Washington, D.C.: Brookings Institution, 1985), pp. 69–96. Data collected by the Urban Land Institute and the Regional Plan Association of New York. The trend has apparently continued since 1980, but the suburbs are capturing a large fraction of new construction. "U.S. Cities Attracting More Offices, Less Housing," *New York Times*, October 21, 1986.
[12]The National Academy of Sciences report points to a "growing polarization" between headquarters cities and production centers.
[13]Calvin Beale, "Poughkeepsie's Complaint," *American Demographics* (1984):29–48.

borhoods within places of all scale. Nonmetropolitan areas are generally outside the census tract system. Translated into the analyses of this book, Beale's contention has some merit. The smallest SMSAs fail to exhibit some of the differentiation usually assumed to be indicative of metropolitan character.

The younger cities are not prisoners of the older infrastructure, and their newer form is even more indicative of the population diffusion. Since they are young, their history, too, is less confining. The ladder of segregation applies to the new cities as well as the old, but there are some noteworthy differences. In the faster growing cities of the South and the West, we found less racial and ethnic segregation; however, we found more age and household-type segregation. We have limited evidence that the keys to the sorting process may be shifting. These newer cities still have many of the same traits as their older cousins. If these metropolitan areas provide the leading edge of metropolitan development, they provide a portal on the urban future. As larger fractions of the population reside in them, their pattern becomes more the norm. The older metropolises of the industrial heartland are still major sites of population concentration, and many of them are beginning to "cope" with the economic restructuring. On the one hand, their history may retard the shift to a new order; on the other, it may provide assets for new kinds of growth and ecological reorganization.

Residential Differentiation: An Overview

If city and regions have changed so much, what about the neighborhood? Population diffusion has challenged or stretched the meaning of metropolis. What is the role of the neighborhood in this new, diffuse settlement system? At this point we can try to integrate some of the information of the past few chapters, incorporating evidence accumulated from other sources to answer that question.

Neighborhoods are the small geographically distinct communities into which people sort themselves. Although we may not be able to predict the social composition of a neighborhood from its geographic position as well as before, it is still true that distinct neighborhoods exist. Race, class, and housing type are the principal keys to the sorting process. Other factors that can be identified but are less differentiated include most of the measures of family and life cycle status, and some of the other components of ethnic identification.

At the outset, we discussed at length the problem of defining proper neighborhoods. A number of conceptual and practical issues are involved. Even the National Commission on Neighborhoods could not come up with a single, all-encompassing definition. Are there neighborhoods everywhere in the metropolitan area? We have argued that yes, indeed, neighborhoods cover the metropolitan territory. Even further, one can consider the neighborhood to be an element of the general settlement system. There are suburban neighborhoods as well as inner city neighborhoods, even as ethnic enclaves with active community life come to mind when the word "neighborhood" is used. The census cannot measure directly many of the intangibles so often considered important in defining the character of a neighborhood, but our analysis did show that demographically distinct neighborhoods can be found throughout the city and its suburbs.

Opinions differ on the appropriate size of the neighborhood, on whether neighborhood boundaries can overlap, and whether there are hierarchies of neighborhoods. Partly for statistical and tabulation convenience the Census Bureau uses tracts of similar size that are mutually exclusive and exhaustive with regard to the metropolitan territory. We have joined in this middle ground position. One implication of the research here is that metropolitan differentiation is multidimensional, and that boundaries drawn according to the levels of homogeneity of any one characteristic are bound to differ when compared to homogeneity along other characteristics. In almost every city there are competing neighborhood delimitations—the neighborhood statistics program is one such—and there may be hierarchies of neighborhoods, but the analytical utility of small-area urban information is enhanced if it comes in similarly sized discrete and distinct units. The census tract accomplished this, and may well be the best analytical unit for understanding the residential settlement system.

The concept of neighborhood need not be limited to big cities, but the nature of neighborhood does change with the size of the territory. Our results in Chapter 4 have shown that for a wide array of social characteristics, the larger the metropolis, the more differentiated its neighborhoods will be. Big city neighborhoods defined by population size (such as census tracts) will tend to be more internally homogeneous than those in smaller cities. On the other hand, the range of variation across the neighborhoods themselves is much larger for the larger cities. As Chapter 2 showed, the richest neighborhoods have much higher incomes, the ethnic neighborhoods are more concentrated, the apartment house tracts are more dense. The process of residential differentiation in the large metropolis brings about a different entity than in the small metropolis. The large SMSA's neighborhood is more likely to occupy a unique niche in the system.

Three Approaches

In Chapter 3 we repeated the factorial ecology analysis so often performed to get at metropolitan differentiation. We looked at segregation in Chapter 4 and spatial organization in Chapter 5. How do these three approaches help us piece together the puzzle?

Out of the factorial approach came the notion of social areas (contrasted with natural areas) of the city. These areas were identified by clusters of characteristics found along statistically independent dimensions. Socioeconomic status occupied a prominent, usually primary position in most cities. A second position was occupied by a life cycle cluster. However, in many instances we observed intertwining of these elements, sometimes with one another, and sometimes with race or ethnic status.[14] Despite the variety of approaches that can be taken with the factorial method and the many interpretations that can be laid on it, it is clear that a cluster of census characteristics linked to socioeconomic status forms of principal identifier in the internal residential system of the metropolis. In several SMSAs we found evidence of what might be called a "child-rearing suburb" factor, where the composition is dictinctly middle class, and married-couple families with children predominate. Ethnic status differentiation is certainly apparent in our analysis, but because of the close relationship of race to other characteristics, most notably income and family status, it less often emerged as a distinct factor.

Our segregation analysis probes the differentiation process in a different way. Instead of the multivariate grouping of traits taken by factorial ecology, segregation statistics examine each characteristic individually. While we lose the multivariate aspect of the factorial analysis, we also no longer suffer the problems of interpreting coefficients. The analysis of segregation, by almost any index we choose, shows sharp variation by characteristic in the amount of segregation displayed for the "typical SMSA." At the top of the ladder of segregation are the physical characteristics of the metropolis: high-density housing, group quarters, age of housing. Of all the demographic characteristics ethnicity stands out, with the segregation of black Americans exceeding Hispanics and other racial groups. Segregation of the white European ancestry groups is relatively low on the scale. Socioeconomic status, indicated by housing expenditures and poverty, is next in line, and corresponds to levels of segregation shown by housing age density and

---

[14]We repeated, but did not report, the factorial analysis of the 1970–1980 sample of comparable census tracts and a similar set of variables. For the most part the two decades were closely parallel and agree with the present discussion.

ownership rates. The education and occupation components of status are much more modestly segregated. We found that the various life cycle indicators showed the lowest overall levels of segregation in the system. Since mobility can produce a rapid shift in the composition of neighborhoods, it is no surprise that the physical characteristics of the metropolis show a good bit more segregation than the social characteristics.

Stated in other words, we find that blacks and whites very seldom share neighborhoods, although it is common for persons of various ancestry groups to live side by side. Although the metropolis is the source of images of poverty amidst plenty, we find that this certainly does not extend to the neighborhood level. The broad American middle class does tend to be so intermingled as to reduce the amount of status segregation. This is especially so for occupation and education as measured by the census, where we also find considerable overlap.

The factorial and segregation analyses concur on the importance of socioeconomic status, although it is highlighted more prominently in the former. Life cycle clusters emerge in the factorial ecology, but age, sex, and family type do not exhibit high levels of segregation. How can we account for this? It seems that the factorial analysis is picking up selected clusters of child-rearing (or child-absent) communities in the metropolitan areas. From companion loadings on the factors identified, these seem to be predominantly white middle class communities in the suburbs. Conversely, we observe certain communities in which persons at the upper end of the life cycle tend to reside: children are absent, many individuals live alone, etc. But these are selected identifiable communities; for the bulk of neighborhoods of the metropolitan area there is an appreciable intermingling of the various life cycle groups. Because racial segregation is pervasive and is correlated with other social characteristics, racial and ethnic composition often "folds over" onto other characteristics in the factorial analysis, so that proportion black appears on the SES or life cycle factor as well.

The contour analysis of Chapter 5 sought to analyze the spatial organization of the metropolis; that is, the orientation of the city about its center. If a given characteristic is highly differentiated in space, then we expect to find a relatively large segregation statistic. If, furthermore, that differentiation takes place in a spatially systematic fashion, then we expect to be able to predict readily the location of neighborhoods according to that characteristic. It is technically possible for the average neighborhood level of a characteristic to show a high degree of spatial organization, even though it has relatively low levels of segregation.

Our analysis of the metropolitan topography indicated that the characteristics linked most directly to the physical infrastructure of the metropolis clearly show the most spatial organization. Even in the diffuse 1980 metropolis, density and age of the housing stock fall off steadily as one moves from the center of the city toward its outer edges. While both race and SES exhibit nucleated patterns, the compacting of the black population in the center of the city is evident in our results. Occupation and age characteristics are not highly organized in metropolitan space, by contrast, and show almost no pattern with respect to the distance from the central business district. For occupation, though, there is some evidence of nucleation.

We are now in a position to step back to view the neighborhood in the metropolis from a more encompassing vantage point. Each of these three methods provides a different lens through which we have tried to view the metropolitan mosaic. There exists a hierarchy among the characteristics in the degree to which they are differentiated among metropolitan neighborhoods. These overarching characteristics and some of their underlying traits are represented in Table 7.1. To be sure, the four clusters each contribute to metropolitan differentiation, but they are not independent in a statistical sense, nor are they as physically distinct. Much of our thinking about the shape of the metropolis has been conditioned by the competition among the models of metropolitan structure offered at the outset of Chapter 5. It is to the issue of the form of the metropolis that we now turn.

The Emerging Form
of the Late Twentieth Century Metropolis

How do the models of urban residential structure introduced in Chapter 5 need to be revised? In this section we try to draw a revised map of the ecology of the metropolis, incorporating the analysis we have done in previous chapters.

The traditional models do not always sketch a consistent picture of the metropolis. The zonal model emphasizes socioeconomic status and race, and implicitly incorporates an assimilation dynamic. The sectoral model acknowledges zonal variation, but looks principally at status variation in sectors indicated by levels of rent paid. The nucleation model turns to placing more emphasis on the underlying physical structure and locations of employment, and assigns a relatively prominent role to race. These models are not antithetical to one another, and the work of Murdie, Berry, and others offered a synthesis. This synthesis paired the zonal, sectoral, and nucleation models with life cycle, status, and ethnic variation, respectively. These three characteristics were in-

TABLE 7.1

Hierarchy of Metropolitan Differentiation

Physical Infrastructure
  Density
  Housing Type
  Housing Age
Minority Status
  Black
  Hispanic
Socioeconomic Status
  Housing Expenditures
  Poverty
  Income and Education
  Occupation
Life Cycle and Age
  Household Size and Type
  Marital Status
  Age and Sex

terpreted to be underlying dimensions of urban differentiation, indicated by the interpretation given to the results of factor analysis with neighborhood or tract data.

This book has incorporated a variety of analytical approaches to the study of neighborhood differentiation, at the same time examining a wider variety of variables than has heretofore been the case. This gives us an opportunity to determine whether the results are cross-validating; that is, whether the picture we get of the metropolis using one approach is the same as that of another. In the previous section we showed how, indeed, many of the results of these approaches are consistent, although not in every respect.

The hierarchy of differentiation in Table 7.1 gives a starting point for building a model of residential differentiation. But how should the model be constructed? Should it follow one of the traditional models, the synthetic model, or some wholly new picture? Our repetition of the factorial analysis of Chapter 3 in combination with the metropolitan topography of Chapter 6 gives us pause about the applicability of the synthetic model of urban structure. Appealing as it is to ally each one of the three former idealized geographic schemes with an independent dimension of social differentiation, the evidence is not compelling for so elegant a match. Instead we observed above that elements of all three "dimensions"—"aspects" is a better word—can be seen throughout in the statistical results, but there was a considerable amount of overlap across the factors. Status and life cycle usually stood out most clearly (although sometimes even they were intertwined), but race often folded over onto status or life cycle. Second, the factorial analysis tends to pick out particularly strong clusters of social areas that may not be representative of variation along a single dimension.

The contours provided a way to quantify the pattern of spatial organization exhibited by a variable. The contours show that the principal form of the metropolitan topography is still zonal, although significant differences—or even the absence of pattern—exist for other variables. Physical characteristics were the most zonal, followed by income and housing expenditures. Race was visibly confined by radial distance but also exhibited some nucleation. The pattern for life cycle characteristics was varied, with household size finding a more zonal orientation (consistent with economic and ecological theory), and age showing nucleation to the extent that any differentiation at all could be found. Occupation, although presumably an element of SES, was found to be highly nucleated. Distinct sectoral patterns were difficult to detect.

Our analysis of neighborhood evolution demonstrated how outer rings gained in relative population and socioeconomic status, while middle rings aged and grew in minority concentration. Even though distance has declined as a factor in current locational decisions, it has played a major role historically, leaving its legacy in the transportation infrastructure and the housing stock. Therefore, in older cities particularly, we will still observe the relationship of distance to social composition, often working through age of the housing stock. Some degree of zonal orientation is thereby preserved.

If population diffusion has blurred the lines of the old metropolitan models, what then is the new shape of the metropolis, and how is it evolving toward the twenty-first century? We offer a revised model of metropolitan structure in Figure 7.1. This picture reflects our research on residential patterns in 1980, other current research, and the most salient features of the earlier models, which have left an impression, perhaps indelible, on the way we think about metropolitan organization. It also recognizes the most important of the nonresidential features of the metropolitan economy and landscape which cast their lot with metropolitan evolution. Being a product of this book, it also tries to reflect the variety of metropolitan experience, including the more modest-sized regions and the newer cities, where an increasing fraction of Americans live and work.

The Core

The central business district (CBD) still is the focus of the metropolis. The CBD supplies the metropolitan countenance. It is the most visi-

FIGURE 7.1

The Shape of the Late Twentieth Century Metropolis

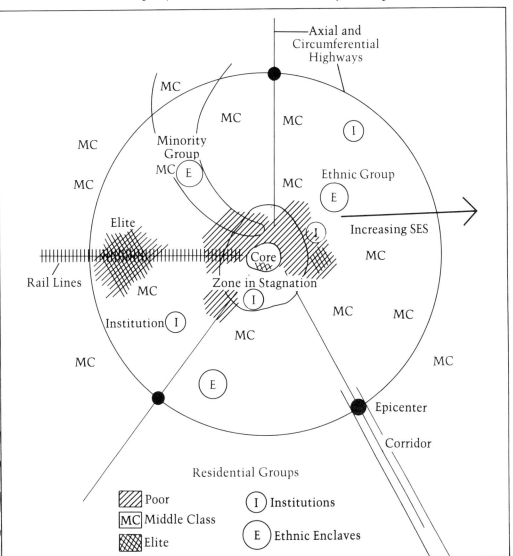

ble image of the region, appearing as the backdrop to national news reports from the locale, and visible to the traveler from an airplane, or
from ground level, driving or on foot. The work of Kevin Lynch and others has demonstrated the strength of downtown images in orienting the

residents of the region.[15] And the core is still the high activity node for a number of functions. Nevertheless, the functional specialization of the core has shifted significantly from what it was a generation ago. In the leading cities of the nation, the core is clearly the locus for the headquarters of the national and even multinational corporations. Skyscrapers are part of the legend of those organizations. New York remains preeminent in this regard, but Chicago, Houston, San Francisco, and many of the other major cities around the country have their corporate downtowns, devoted heavily to finance and management. Even Los Angeles, long mocked for being a congeries of suburbs in search of a city, has developed a clutch of skyscrapers in the traditional downtown area. Since it is so heavily nonresidential in character, the core goes unmeasured in much of our analysis with demographic data. We begin now to integrate the CBD into the overall picture, and paint into that picture the residential tiles that are part of the mosaic.

The corporate core ties the region into the expanding national and international system of cities and economies. The differential ability of cities to retain, attract, and develop the white collar core has had a substantial impact on their relative ranking within the national urban hierarchy. Thus the glass-and-steel skyscrapers of New York, Chicago, and Houston are testimony to their position within the national urban system.

But provocative and breathtaking as these images may be, they do not tell the whole story. The development of a corporate core is not limited to only the handful of financial centers in the nation. Moderate-sized cities show evidence of the core, often symbolized by a few skyscrapers which clearly dominate the horizon and are home to a local financial institution or the resident major national corporation. On the other hand, the core faces increasing competition from its suburbs and hinterland for the location of prestige office space. The relocation of corporate headquarters out of New York City is often in the direction of more campuslike settings at the periphery of the metropolis. Such trends are further evidence of the loosening of the reins of downtown.

The core is also the repository of the cultural artifacts and the historical roots of the city and region. Along with containing many of the region's major museums, it has become a bit of a museum piece itself. Usually, downtown was the site of first settlement. Downtown serves the function of greeting ground for the region's visitors. Hotels, convention centers, and related amenities are located there. San Antonio, one of the areas in this study, provides an excellent example of the success-

[15]Kevin Lynch, *Image of the City* (Cambridge, Mass.: MIT Press, 1960).

ful downtown transformation, with the Alamo, the Riverwalk, hotels, and convention center all within a short distance of one another.

This museum piece aspect of downtown development has become increasingly important. Several of the most successful urban rejuvenation schemes have taken advantage of the historical character of downtown or nearby areas, aided recently by tax credits for historic preservation. Buildings often once slated for demolition have been rehabilitated into areas of mixed use development, active in the evening as well as the daytime. Baltimore's Inner Harbor, Boston's Quincy Market, San Francisco's Waterfront and Ghiradelli Square, and Seattle's Pioneer Square feature examples of adaptive reuse of buildings and attest to the rediscovery of the urban waterfront in particular. These examples have attracted national attention, but many other cities have been able to cultivate such development, anywhere in scale from a single building to entire districts. These sections of the city possess a sort of mixed real and fantasy life character, becoming prime tourist spots as well as new (or traditional) parts of the local color. Moreover, they have become commercially viable.

The retail story of the core is mixed. Traditionally, the CBD has been the hub of commercial and shopping activity. In the largest metropolises, the major department stores set up shop on the "100 percent corner," often the most heavily traveled subway intersection. But with time, even the flagship stores have set out for the suburbs in search of their customers, and the 100 percent corner has moved to the intersection of the belt and radial highways. Once the major shopping area for the region's middle class, traditional downtown has declined in status if not in outright dollar volume. Many of the stores cater to a clientele of more moderate income than formerly, and the various attempts to revive the commercial core attest to this. Meanwhile, the downtown merchants who remain have tried various techniques to retain their customers, including advocating publicly supported parking structures and mall-like construction along the main street. This increased automobile access and facelift may have helped "stabilize" the commercial core.

Coincident with this decline of the major shopping area, many major cities have witnessed the development of "boutique zones." These small shops sell a variety of specialty merchandise, although the actual range in customer income and the price of wares may vary greatly. Often these shops are located in newly renovated historical sections. Some cities can boast the retention of major downtown stores which cater to an upper-income clientele. This is due in part to loyalty and in part to the concentration of higher income customers within the inner city, an aspect of the core to which we now turn.

Downtown was never a major residential district or a "neighborhood." To be sure, most big cities had their Gold Coast or Silk Stocking District in or near the CBD, as well as an area of transience and homelessness. Recent trends in the core of many major cities point to an increase in residential development in some of the innermost areas.[16] These arise out of planning for mixed use development (residential with commercial), and urban renewal's efforts to bring the middle class "back" to the city. The success of such projects hinges on the desire for downtown workers to save on commuting time to the office and entertainment opportunities.

This trend, while noteworthy, should not be overemphasized among the changes in overall metropolitan structure. We found evidence of high-density core residential sites, even increases in such sites over time. In a few metropolitan areas this central residential rebuilding was extensive enough to invert the traditional zonal pattern; that is, the innermost ring contained younger housing than the second ring. But in the average city these developments were not so strong as to deflect the metropolitan contour. Central residential development helps explain why occupation appears to be so unsystematic with respect to spatial location: we find clusters of workers located at a variety of nodes throughout the region, one of these points being in or near the downtown area. Many would argue that these Gold Coasts (and more modest versions of them) are stimulated by, and in turn stimulate, the other commercial rejuvenation of the core. While in some sense this does represent a return of the middle class to the city, this return is highly selective. Spatially it occurs within the central core. Demographically it is distinguished by the absence of children and the focus on persons of young working age. Occasionally, parts of downtown are developing into residential neighborhoods of substantial size.

The Zone in Stagnation

Ernest Burgess labeled the first ring of land surrounding the CBD the Zone in Transition, for he theorized that in the outward expansion of the city, this land would next be taken for downtown activity. Therefore it was a zone of marginal uses, dilapidated structures, and speculation. Economic activity here included warehousing and light and sometimes even heavy industry. The conjunction of Chicago's multitudinous rail lines gave a steely reality to this picture. The neighborhoods of this zone included the immigrant slums, the rooming house district, the bright lights, and the haunts of the criminal underworld.

[16]The residential portion of the core described here would comprise less than the inner quartile residential ring discussed in earlier chapters.

The expectation that the CBD would at some time encompass this zone turned out to be wrong. The CBD expanded upward rather than outward. This second zone today is quiet by comparison, and much of the land is vacant, or underutilized. One observes the few holdovers, such as produce or meat markets, or fledgling companies who have taken advantage of the inexpensive commercial space, but many of the industries have moved out to the suburbs.

The old slums have often been torn down by urban redevelopment projects, leaving vacant land frequently taken for institutional expansion (hospitals, universities). Downtown highway access, of course, is through this section. In some of the older cities residential recapture takes place in the old zone in transition. Loft apartments, for artists and other pioneers, are converted from partially or fully vacated warehouses or multistory commercial space. Occasionally some of the very oldest housing has been reconverted into residential use again. The younger cities, where the nineteenth and early twentieth century pattern is less prevalent, never had much of a zone in transition; instead of the old industrial and commercial zones, the downtowns tend to be surrounded by land that is vacant except for the inner loops and interchanges of the highway system. Kansas City and Dallas provide pictures of this sort.

We have still covered only a small fraction of the metropolitan territory. The remainder of the metropolis tends to be much more heavily devoted to residential use, and falls under the lens of our census microscope.

Pockets of Poverty and Minorities

Not far beyond the hubbub of commercial activity and the Gold Coast development reside some of the poorest residents of the metropolitan area. There is a serious constraint on the residential location of the poor. The notion of pockets of poverty goes beyond the expected class segregation. Our analysis points to the segregation of a small minority of very disadvantaged persons who are at the bottom of the metropolitan economic ladder, living in old, deteriorated housing and an environment of family disruption. Most often these neighborhoods are segregated with regard to ethnicity as well, home to the most disadvantaged of the minority population. It is within the pockets of poverty that the urban "underclass"—a poorly defined group, but one that is clearly out of the mainstream—is most likely to reside.

These pockets are most often located in the inner ring of the metropolitan area, frequently in the "zone in stagnation" within the old central city, but in major metropolitan areas poverty pockets can be found in the older peripheral suburbs as well. It is a mistake, though, to consider the existence of pockets of poverty to be an ecological condition of the older industrial cities only. We find evidence of poverty pockets in most metropolitan areas, although they are most readily detected in the more differentiated larger metropolises. Comparisons across larger geographic units, such as central cities and suburban rings, so common in policy analysis because of the importance of municipal boundaries and the relative ease with which such data are available, can obscure the generality of this phenomenon, particularly in regions with growing central cities. Their residential pattern may be out of line with the emerging twenty-first century metropolis. Residents of the pockets of poverty face serious risk of being cut off from the economic growth in peripheral portions of metropolitan territory save for the few that can capitalize on low-skill jobs becoming available in the corporate core of some cities. More important perhaps, the residents of such communities are more likely to lack the skills to compete in any economy, no matter how it manifests itself spatially. The existence of the pockets of poverty creates a serious challenge for public policy, and sharply divergent approaches have been suggested, an issue to which we return below.

Elite Enclaves

Upper income and high status groups maintain their social distance through physical distance. Our analysis shows that there is a substantial mixture of income and social class groups in metropolitan communities when we look across the entire spectrum, but when we focus on the rich and the poor, we can find that they are considerably separated from the middle class as well as from one another. About 6 percent of our neighborhoods have 1980 average household incomes over $30,000. In a typical metropolitan area, about half of all households with income over $30,000 would have to relocate in order to be evenly represented in every neighborhood.

In every city we observe enclaves of the most well-to-do of the metropolitan community. These households tend to reside in the outer bands of the suburban zone, but exceptions are found. Besides the Gold Coast discussed above, there are some high income neighborhoods that have enjoyed a historical existence, often located along mainline commuter rail links in the older industrial cities. As the city expanded the middle class has filled in around them.

Still, the newest homes on the spacious lots tend to be found on the suburban fringe. This centrifugal development is consistent with the traditional Burgess model of urban growth, but the picture is more complicated. This new urbanization often takes place in the midst of agricultural territory at such low density that the land is still classified initially as "rural." The relocation of research parks to the rural hinterland of many metropolitan areas is an example of the "cutting edge" of this sort of development: plenty of amenities, yet still within striking distance of the cultural and economic resources of the metropolitan core.

In the largest metropolitan areas the existence of elite enclaves is the most visible and the most striking. This is so for two reasons. First, in these major metropolitan areas, there is a large absolute number of very high income households. (Often the biggest metropolitan areas have a disproportionate concentration of high income households to begin with, because of their underlying employment structure.) This population constitutes a "critical mass," so that specialized services develop for it: clubs, restaurants, specialty stores. Second, the largest cities are more differentiated along almost every dimension, as we saw in Chapter 4, so that the census tract neighborhoods with the higher income groups are more easily spotted. We recalled from Chapter 2 that the distribution of neighborhoods along the various characteristics usually had the most extreme values in the biggest metropolitan areas. For instance, in the Chicago SMSA, the neighborhood with the top income had an average 1979 household income of over $56,000.

The Diffused Middle Class

The largest swatch of urban territory is occupied by the American middle class. Geographically, most of the middle class territory extends from the outer portions of the central city to the edge of the metropolitan area. As we have seen from our analyses of the metropolitan contour and of the residential rings, there is in most SMSAs a steady rise in income as one travels outward, and in many SMSAs a more modest rise in other status indicators. As one moves out through the middle class area, the neighborhoods become "newer" (at least in terms of housing stock), and considerably less dense. Our statistical analysis has shown that the social patterns do not change as consistently with distance as do the physical characteristics.

In the interior sections of the suburban middle class region, we are more likely to find older, settled neighborhoods. Often these are the sections where the children have left home, such as one neighborhood in the Indianapolis example. Here one is also likely to find the middle class pioneers (or invaders) of the metropolis's minority group population. These groups—especially blacks—are still segregated. There is now a substantial accumulation of evidence about the suburbanization of the black population, and limited evidence for other minorities. The higher status members of these groups now possess the resources to move outward to larger, newer homes and higher status neighborhoods, but this economic integration has only begun to partially offset prevailing patterns of racial segregation. In many metropolitan areas a highly visible ghetto extends from the concentrated central city poverty pockets into the suburbs. Our analysis suggests that these inner suburban areas are likely to serve as areas of second (or third) settlement for other members of the region's ethnic mixture. Although there is segregation among the various white ethnic groups, to the point that neighborhoods often express the identity of a particular group, the neighborhoods on the outer edge of the city and in the inner suburbs are more likely to contain a diversity of ancestry groups.

Traveling still farther outward we begin to encounter some of the archetypal American suburbs; their exact location depends much on the age of the city, and annexation success may determine whether they are located within the central city boundaries. Here we find the child-rearing communities that emerged often in many of the factorial studies, areas characterized by single-family homes, married-couple families, and of course the presence of school-age children. Although it has been popular to describe all of the suburban territory in these terms, suburban communities are really quite diverse. We can find scattered throughout the outer city and the suburbs communities containing single parents, the elderly, and a variety of ancestry groups. An increase in multifamily construction (garden apartments) in the suburbs has provided housing opportunities for the less stereotypical suburbanite. Many skilled blue collar workers reside in the suburbs. Not only can many of these families afford homes, but also sites of employment have so decentralized that they now live nearer their workplaces by living in suburban communities. Indeed, there are a number of working class suburbs, to use Bennet Berger's phrase, scattered throughout the metropolitan areas.[17] Since blue collar workers have lower occupational prestige by definition, whether they should be included in the middle class or considered separately is partly a matter of interpretation. Skilled blue collar workers earn more than many lower level service and office workers. Inner city working class neighborhoods still exist, and although clearly and evocatively described by such writers as William Kornblum, they are now less distinct in the statistical analysis.[18] These

[17]Bennet Berger, *Working Class Suburb* (Berkeley: University of California Press, 1971[1960]).
[18]William Kornblum, *Blue Collar Community* (Chicago: University of Chicago Press, 1974).

neighborhoods, tied as they have been to smokestack industries, have been heavily hit by the economic transformation away from manufacturing employment in metropolitan areas.

These suburban communities, while distinct from one another, establish no simple geographic pattern. Rather, nucleation is the appropriate term to describe the clustering of many demographic groups. The existence of historical settlements also tends to promote nucleation of the neighborhood pattern in the suburbs. As the metropolitan territory has been extended, increasing numbers of such settlements have been encountered. They offer older housing and often have their own ethnic and racial neighborhoods. Depending on how one views these satellite communities, either they throw a slight distortion into what one may view as a consistent overall pattern or they may be basic elements of a fundamentally different underlying pattern of the twenty-first century metropolis.

Institutional Anchors and Public Sector Controls

Hospitals, universities, and other institutions, often private but with a very visible public countenance, help shape the neighborhood pattern. Such institutions are large and generally have resources tied to a particular location. They therefore have a substantial stake in their immediate neighborhood, and can act as an anchor. Their sheer size and power make them fundamentally different from the individual neighborhood resident. Whereas the resident is almost always powerless to change the character of the neighborhood (save by banding together with other residents), the institution can marshal its resources and act to influence apparent trends in neighborhood evolution.

Pressure can be placed on City Hall to direct police protection, public services, and housing rehabilitation subsidies to the neighborhood. The institution sometimes possesses the resources to purchase parcels of land for construction of employee housing or nonresidential facilities. Such actions can defend turf and serve as an indirect control on neighborhood evolution. The urban renewal program even had a special provision for universities and hospitals—often trapped in the midst of deteriorating neighborhoods—enabling expansion and construction programs that served a public purpose. In several cities these quasi-public institutions have developed into nuclei for the metropolitan residential system.

A variety of policies has helped municipalities intervene and alter the composition of specific neighborhoods or change their evolutionary path. The most extensive of these can be traced to slum clearance and urban renewal programs.[19] Municipalities have always used conventional powers of eminent domain to take land for public use (highways, airports, other public facilities), often converting the type of land use in the process, and thereby influencing neighborhood development. The salient feature of these programs is that they helped pay for the local municipality (often through the action of an authority created by the state government expressly for the purpose) to condemn and clear land, making way for new construction. Many public housing projects were constructed in this way, in addition to moderate and upper income housing on urban renewal land. We will not recapitulate the exact mechanisms and details of the programs here,[20] but the point is that the locality—usually the central city, but other municipalities were often eligible as well—managed and controlled urban evolution. Such interventions have become a prominent feature of the metropolitan topography, and have their own impact on the prospects of neighborhood evolution. Public housing projects simply do not experience gentrification, and "failed" urban renewal programs have left a scattering of vacant lots in their wake.

While slum clearance and urban renewal involved the direct acquisition and disposition of land parcels by the public sector, a number of other programs involved a less intense intervention. Urban Development Action Grant and Community Development Block Grant funds in the 1970s represented additional efforts to target public policy geographically for subareas within the city.[21] These programs do not call for direct intervention into the residential structure, but to the extent that they are concentrated in certain neighborhoods they may have substantial spillover effects, some of which are the intended effects of the program.

A host of government structures and actions impinge indirectly on the shape of the metropolis and the evolution of neighborhoods within. Most frequently mentioned activities of the federal government are the home mortgage subsidies and the underwriting of interstate highways

---

[19]These actually involved a succession of programs that went through a number of metamorphoses, dating from the Housing Act of 1937 and continuing up into the 1970s.

[20]Henry Aaron, *Shelter and Subsidies* (Washington, D.C.: Brookings Institution, 1972), and James Q. Wilson, ed., *Urban Renewal: The Record and the Controversy* (Cambridge, Mass.: MIT Press, 1966).

[21]Urban Development Action Grants (since 1978) are given to economically distressed communities according to an entitlement formula. Public contribution is intended to be a catalyst (leverage) for private sector development. The Block Grant program dates to 1974 and provides outright grants to state and local governments for a wide variety of projects. U.S. Department of HUD, 1982 Annual Report (Washington, D.C.: U.S. Government Printing Office, 1982).

in metropolitan areas. Such activities have been alleged to accelerate the suburbanization of the middle class, weakening the tax base of central cities. While suburbanization proceeded apace throughout the post–World War II period, it is difficult to sort out definitively how much population restructuring was due to such policies.

At another level, the American tradition of home rule influences the metropolitan topography and changes in the residential structure. Most large central cities are ringed with independent municipalities, with control over taxation, public service expenditures, and zoning.[22] Such a system, Charles A. Tiebout and others have hypothesized, allows metropolitan households to "vote with their feet" and choose a combination of taxation and expenditure that best meets their needs.[23] The local public school system is most often singled out among these elements of the package of public services "purchased" with a home by new residents. Middle class families can escape the tax burden of central cities, where they must compete with other groups for resources, and can concentrate on local public expenditures of primary importance to them, such as schools.

Zoning is but another tool for managing or restricting neighborhood residential structure, although opinions differ on how powerful it is in the face of changes in the private market demand for land. Home rule communities can exclude or encourage certain groups with zoning ordinances. Manipulation of the tax rate and provision of public services can serve this aim, too. The local political economy can help to further differentiate the metropolitan social topography, although the character of neighborhoods in home rule communities is broadly consistent with prevailing ecological patterns.

Epicenters and Corridors

We cannot discuss the changing residential structure of the metropolis without reference to the transportation network and sites of employment. The changing distribution of housing units and of the people who reside in them owes a great deal to changes in the physical and economic infrastructure. During the twentieth century the American metropolis has moved from a walking city, to a streetcar and train city with its first trainline suburbs, to an automobile region. The technology

---

[22]This, of course, varies regionally within the United States, as does the ability of central municipalities to annex their surrounding territory.

[23]Charles A. Tiebout, "A Pure Theory of Local Public Expenditures," *Journal of Political Economy* 64 (1956):416–424.

of transportation, spurred on by population growth and traditional preferences of Americans for more space and small-town environs, undergirded the great spreading out of the modern metropolis.

A number of important trends in the location of economic activity have occurred since World War II. First to be noticed and studied was the suburbanization of manufacturing. Changes in the technology of production favored horizontal assembly over the former vertical pattern, encouraging producers to decentralize and take advantage of cheaper land prices at the urban fringe. The retail industry had to suburbanize rapidly, following a suburbanizing middle class. Similar economic pressures encouraged the wholesaling sector to decentralize, a trend documented by several economists.[24] Firms left behind in the old central industrial belt possessed fewer resources for suburbanization or still carried out activity that encouraged central location. The departure of many firms left some portions of the central core abandoned, but this move also freed up some space for smaller-scale industrial development and for the conversion of loft space to residential use in selected places. The picture for office and other commercial activity is more mixed. Many offices employing large numbers of white collar workers decentralized during the 1950s and 1960s, but this was a period of growth in downtown office space for the "leading cities" we spoke of earlier. The "Manhattans" of the United States grew, responding to intense competition for central real estate by the expanding financial and service sector activities, which desired central proximity.

One of the most prominent features of the emerging metropolis was the development of metropolitan epicenters, peripheral nodes that competed with the CBD for the location of industry and commerce. The intersections of axial and circumferential highways are the most frequent spawning points for epicenters, and they became the organizational foci of nearby territory. Urban analysts have noticed the emergence of such competing centers throughout the 1960s and 1970s.[25] Although the CBD in most SMSAs retained its role as the primary center, there has been a functional specialization among the various nodes. The CBD retained the corporate core and a number of other functions, while the epicenters tended to have manufacturing, wholesaling, and retail trade activity. Office space was a growing component, as population servicing offices—banks and medical professional parks—were

[24]See, for example, John F. Kain, "The Distribution and Movement of Jobs and Industry," in *Essays on Urban Spatial Structure* (Cambridge, Mass.: Ballinger, 1975 [1968]), pp. 79–114, and Edwin S. Mills, *Studies in the Structure of the Urban Economy* (Baltimore: Johns Hopkins University Press, 1972).

[25]Kasarda now speaks, for example, of the "polynucleated metropolis." John D. Kasarda, "The Implications of Contemporary Redistribution Trends for National Urban Policy," *Social Science Quarterly* 61 (1980):373–400.

joined by decentralized corporate headquarters and ancillary functions, often located in settings with environmental amenities.

Researchers often describe these developments as "new suburbs" and show how their development has differed from what came before in the 1920s and the post–World War II period.[26] Many of the municipalities in or near epicenters experienced continued growth during the 1970s. Examples of these metropolitan epicenters include Framingham, Massachusetts, in the Boston SMSA; Stamford, Connecticut, White Plains, New York, and Paramus, New Jersey, in the New York SMSA; and Schaumburg, Illinois, in the Chicago SMSA. The simple distinction between satellites and suburbs no longer suffices; rather, suburbs are participating in the new economic growth not merely as residential communities but also as potential sites for economic activity. There is concern that this competition may result in a new and more vexing stratification among suburbs, as some become winners and others losers in the grab for development that brings in tax revenue and demands few services.

Corridor development augments the decentralizing effect of the epicenters. The roads connecting older centers, or circumnavigating older centers, become sites of intense linear development. Corridors serve as the new main streets. In the most abstract form, they, together with the epicenter, form the structural grid underlying what appears to be a less focused employment and settlement pattern. The so-called Silicon Valley near San Francisco, the Johnson Freeway near Dallas, the Capital Beltway surrounding Washington, D.C., and Routes 128 and 495 in the Boston area provide examples for the current decade. Thus, not only do some of the region's highest status residents live at the outer edges of the SMSA and commute to downtown office towers, but others—their neighbors perhaps—commute to nearby research and office parks. In the suburban ring, two-thirds of residents commute to suburban jobs, and in many localities this diffusion has produced a decrease in commuting time consistent with a nucleation hypothesis rather than a sprawl hypothesis.[27] Support staff workers at such peripheral sites often find housing in the vicinity.[28] We have actually found slight increases in the diversity of occupations represented at greater distances.

[26]Leo F. Schnore, "Satellites and Suburbs," *Social Forces* 36 (1957):121–127; John R. Logan, "Industrialization and the Stratification of Cities in Suburban Regions," *American Journal of Sociology* 82 (1976):333–348.

[27]U.S. Summary D Table 291; Peter A. Morrison and Allan Abrahamse, "Is Population Decentralization Lengthening Commuting Distances?," December 1982, Rand Note N-1934-NICHD.

[28]Some of our tabulations (not shown) indicated that the journey to work (in time) was about the same (20 minutes) in each of the four rings. In the several larger SMSAs more distant rings actually exhibited shorter travel durations.

Conclusions

Shifts during the 1970s in the distribution of the population interregionally and within the metropolis have been generally toward places of lower density. Peripheral portions of metropolitan areas have continued to experience growth in population, new housing, employment, and relative increases in socioeconomic status. The changing location of transportation routes and sites of employment have produced peripheral epicenters and corridors of activity that compete with the traditional downtown central business district. The public sector, too, plays a role in shaping the metropolis by direct and indirect means. Seen against the backdrop of traditional models, these factors have exerted new pressures on the organization of the metropolitan population.

The metropolis of the late twentieth century appears to be experiencing diffusion. Its population has spread further, and new nuclei and corridors challenge the hegemony of downtown. The new nodes and their interconnections form a latticework that extends over the entire urban region. Yet, at the level of residential neighborhoods we may still identify the sorting out of the population along traditional lines.

8

NEIGHBORHOODS, METROPOLITAN CHANGE, AND PUBLIC POLICY

A S A NETWORK of sites for the production of goods and services, the system of metropolitan areas in the United States plays an important role in the economic well-being of the nation and the patterns of opportunity that prevail for its workers. Opinions differ on exactly how manipulable that role can or should be. Proponents of one argument hold that cities, and places generally, should be the object of policy. Arguments for an explicit national urban policy as voiced during the Carter administration fall into this category. But in recent years an increasing number of voices claim that the public sector should deal directly with people and not use "places" as intermediaries in the execution of policy. For instance, Paul Peterson writes, "Instead of developing remedies on behalf of urban areas, the federal government should concentrate its attention on policies that have no specifically urban component to them at all."[1] In this concluding chapter we discuss the interrelationship of the metropolitan system, residential neighborhoods, and opportunity. We will attempt to illuminate that discussion with some general inferences drawn from the research carried out here.

---

[1]Paul E. Peterson, ed., *The New Urban Reality* (Washington, D.C.: Brookings Institution, 1985), p. 25.

National Trends

The metropolis offers a mirror of American society. The reverberations of societal changes are felt in the residential areas of the metropolis, its neighborhoods. Major changes in the American social structure in the past few decades have had a differential impact on urban areas and neighborhoods within.

Family and Household Structure

Between 1950 and 1980 the average household size fell from 3.37 to 2.76.[2] A large fraction of the population—about one-fourth of all households—now lives alone. Shifting age structure, rising rates of marital disruptions, and lower or delayed fertility have brought the nuclear family down to a smaller fraction of all household groups. At the same time, women have entered the labor force increasingly: 51.6 percent of all women over 16 years of age were in the labor force in 1980[3] as were 60 percent of all women aged 16–64.[4] These developments shift the set of opportunities and constraints that help determine the way people make residential location decisions.

We often hypothesize that the family life cycle is one of the principal differentiators in the metropolitan fabric. How does this hold up when such a variety of alternative household forms and living arrangements exist? Despite the decline in nuclear family living, we can still detect the presence of distinct neighborhood types devoted to "middle class child-rearing" in several metropolitan areas, although this life cycle segregation is fairly modest. It is true that the elderly are segregated, as are single parents, and those living alone or in groups of unrelated individuals. Our analysis picks up regional differences in life cycle segregation, as well as how differential household composition relates to other characteristics, for example, female-headed households in the black population. The population dynamics of the 1970s have maintained the diversity of neighborhoods with respect to life cycle. If anything, we find that the elderly, persons living alone, and most family types became distributed slightly more evenly.

---

[2]U.S. Bureau of the Census, *Statistical Abstract of the United States* (Washington, D.C.: U.S. Government Printing Office, 1985), p. 40.

[3]Ibid., p. 390.

[4]Ibid.; U.S. Bureau of the Census, *Census of Population and Housing, 1980.* Part C, U.S. Summary, Table 103.

252

The Ethnic Transformation

In the two decades following World War II, large numbers of blacks moved out of the South and into the central areas, the ghettoes, of the northern industrial cities. This racial transformation of the American metropolis occupied much of the attention of policymakers and scholars during that period. Issues of housing segregation, economic opportunity, availability of public services, and political enfranchisement became salient. Comparisons were often made between the black migration from the South and the waves of European migration to these same cities at an earlier time in the century. In the 1970s the gathering wave of Hispanics and Asians to the United States added yet another layer to that picture. Before the detailed analysis of the 1980 census data, questions remained as to whether recent black suburbanization presaged decline in racial segregation in the metropolitan areas of the nation or whether it was just a further extension of the central ghetto beyond the corporate limits of the central city. It also remained to be seen how the full range of ethnic segregation manifested itself.

The 1980 segregation statistics still show substantial separation between the races in metropolitan areas. No segregation statistic can distinguish between residential preferences and prejudice, but if assimilation implies the complete mixture of ethnic groups in society, it is clear that there is a long road ahead. Nevertheless, we observed in 1980 the first genuine signs of progress. Racial segregation decreased between 1970 and 1980 in almost every one of the twenty-one metropolitan areas we studied. Our analysis showed that the separation of Asians and Hispanics from the "majority" white population was appreciably less than that for blacks.[5] Segregation within the majority white population was comparatively modest. We discuss some implications of these findings shortly.

The New Economy

The restructuring of the American economy has implications for the shape and social composition of American cities, several aspects of which we have already described here. So-called smokestack industry has declined, and the cities with large concentrations of such industries

---

[5]We could not separate our recent arrivals from long-time residents and higher-order generations.

have suffered, losing capital and population. On the other hand, "high technology" has become the current buzzword for economic development, with cities and states eager to attract their own "silicon valley" complexes locally. This industrial restructuring has affected urban America and the neighborhoods within the nation in two ways.

First, there has been a decided shift in the location of jobs, and the population balance among regions has begun to shift accordingly. As employment has continued to move from the Northeast industrial core metropolises, population has followed. Second, the new employers are less confined to the old locational decisions, constraints that gave birth to the industrial metropolis in the first place. Many sites for the new industry have been on the metropolitan periphery, or in nonmetropolitan areas, removed from the pool of the most disadvantaged. The transformation presents a challenge for public policy. Certainly the overall competitiveness and health of the economy is a desirable objective. But several key questions remain regarding the distributional aspects of economic restructuring. Such questions inevitably arise when economic transformations impinge on the regional distribution of employment opportunities. Who will participate in the new economy? Will there be people left behind? Is the concentration of the impoverished in some neighborhoods the fault of previous urban policy? The question for policy is whether those individuals will have the opportunity to relocate to the new sites of growth, or whether they are trapped. Is it better to try to bring employment opportunity to them?

A Melting Pot?

One of the most persistent images of the American city is that of the melting pot. The large American city has been viewed as a great cauldron mixing together people from varying cultures: ethnic groups, peasants, bureaucrats, the old and the young, singles and families. More specifically, the melting pot notion was applied to the admixture of a variety of racial and ethnic groups who migrated to the large industrial metropolises from overseas and from the American South or farmland. The presumption of the melting pot was that over time the various cultures would, of course, assimilate, disappearing into the American mainstream.

Such a notion has been challenged repeatedly. Nathan Glazer and Daniel Moynihan, in the widely cited *Beyond the Melting Pot*, showed how the various ethnic groups of New York City found individual niches in the urban economic, social, and political structure, niches that tended to maintain the distinctiveness of the groups.[6] The large body of research on ethnic composition has certainly documented that the "old" immigrant groups, which arrived in the latter part of the nineteenth century and the early part of the twentieth, have not disappeared completely into the mainstream.[7] Ethnic neighborhoods, voting blocs, and informal associations are still quite visible and important in American cities.

Spatial Assimilation

In the genre of urban sociology the melting pot notion found expression in the spatial assimilation model, advanced implicitly by Ernest Burgess and more explicitly by others.[8] The spatial assimilation model hypothesized that the newest arrivals to the metropolis were also at the bottom of the socioeconomic ladder. These lower SES ethnic and immigrant groups settled in the central sections of the city, in the areas of poorest housing quality and nearest to the central sites of employment. The theory suggested that with time the immigrant groups would begin to assimilate into American society, a process expected to work across generations. Socioeconomic assimilation was paralleled by a spatial assimilation process, in which the groups moved outward first to areas of "second immigrant settlement" and then onward into the middle class zones, as the process of blending made them indistinguishable from the mainstream.

Just as it challenges the melting pot hypothesis, the persistence of ethnicity challenges the spatial assimilation idea. With the 1980 census we could ascertain for the first time the ancestry of every American, whereas in previous censuses the third and higher-order generation were de facto assimilated.[9] Chapter 2 pointed out how distinct ethnic neighborhoods exist in all SMSAs, and Chapter 3 has shown in detail how segregation among the ancestry groups persists. A sharper criticism of the spatial assimilation hypothesis was advanced by Theodore Hershberg and colleagues. A detailed analysis of manuscript census informa-

[6]Nathan Glazer and Daniel P. Moynihan, *Beyond the Melting Pot.*
[7]Stanley Lieberson, *A Piece of the Pie* (Berkeley: University of California Press, 1980), provides a particularly extensive analysis.
[8]Ernest Burgess, "The Growth of the City," in R. E. Park and E. W. Burgess, eds., *The City* (Chicago: University of Chicago Press, 1967 [1925]); R. McKenzie, *On Human Ecology* (Chicago: University of Chicago Press, 1968), p. 31; and Paul F. Cressey, "Population Succession in Chicago," *American Journal of Sociology* 44 (1938):56–59.
[9]They were classified as native born of native-born parents and no ethnic origin was obtained.

tion for the city of Philadelphia in the nineteenth century as well as companion analyses for the twentieth century revealed an increasing segregation of ethnic groups in the city.[10] Neighborhoods were once defined by occupational composition, determined by proximity to sites of employment in the walking city; but industrial development was accompanied by increasing differentiation along the lines of ethnicity in Philadelphia's neighborhoods. The research we have conducted here can shed some light on the applicability of the myth of the melting pot to American socioeconomic structure. The United States continues to attract repeated waves of immigrant groups, many of whom still select large urban areas as sites of first settlement, and arrive poorer than the bulk of the resident population.

In our analysis of ancestry segregation with the 1980 census, the various groups show relatively modest degrees of segregation, generally between the levels observed for socioeconomic status and life cycle characteristics. We do observe some important differences—consistent across cities—among the various groups. The "older" ancestry groups, that is, the ones whose members reached the United States earlier, tend to show less segregation than those who arrived later. We observe less segregation for individuals of British, Irish, German, and French stock than for Italians and Poles. Such findings are consistent with those of earlier studies, which used slightly different tabulations from the earlier censuses.[11] Stanley Lieberson, for instance, argues that residential segregation can serve as an indicator of general shifts in the positions of the groups.[12] Because the census question regarding ancestry was new to 1980, it is impossible to make direct comparisons over time in the relative segregation of the various (predominantly white) ethnic groups that have been examined here. When we focus only on the foreign born (not separated by ethnic group), we find an increase in segregation from 1950 to 1970, and a slight decline to 1980. On the 1980 ladder of segregation the foreign born were only slightly more unevenly distributed than single ancestry groups. Evidence from the cross-sectional data of 1980 suggests spatial integration, but it is not so pervasive to support a simple melting pot theory. Some like to call the current picture more of a stewpot in which the various groups remain identifiable even after several generations.

These results have important implications for the spatial assimila-

---

[10]Theodore Hershberg, ed., *Philadelphia* (New York: Oxford University Press, 1981). The work of Lieberson, *Piece of the Pie*, corroborates several of these findings.

[11]Stanley Lieberson, *Ethnic Patterns in American Cities* (New York: Free Press, 1963).

[12]Looking over the period 1890–1930, Lieberson's "central conclusion" links the deterioration of blacks' socioeconomic position vis-à-vis European ethnics to their increasing isolation, versus a decreasing isolation for the Europeans. Stanley Lieberson, *A Piece of the Pie*, p. 291.

tion model. One would expect from that picture of the metropolis that the first generation of Americans would be very concentrated (maybe further subdivided by ethnicity) in the central areas of the city. While it is true that the new arrivals are more centrally located than subsequent generations, their spatial concentration is modest. Thus, the spatial assimilation model seems to hold less here. We can suggest—although we were not able to produce a direct test—that the new immigrants from the traditional locations are residing in the vicinity of the higher-order generations. The fact that these ancestry groups are not highly segregated would further lower the segregation indices.

Douglas Massey and Brendan Mullan have provided evidence of spatial assimilation, but there is no guarantee that settlement proceeds smoothly in a radial fashion outward from the city center.[13] A more likely picture is that immigrant ethnic clusters become established in a nucleated pattern around the metropolis. As assimilation progresses, succeeding generations move outward from the old nucleus predominantly in a direction away from the CBD (therefore consistent with concentric spatial assimilation) but also leapfrogging over other neighborhoods. Subsequent waves of immigrant groups establish nucleated residential patterns. They tend to be more centrally located because of the age of the housing stock, but they need not repeat the spatial pattern of predecessor groups. (We find, in fact, that proportion foreign born is only a moderately stable characteristic in the 1970s.) Thus, there is assimilation across the generations, and it has a spatial component, but especially in the current period it cannot be so tightly linked to the concentric model. The differential self-congregation, rates of assimilation, and discrimination, as well as the changing morphology of the metropolis, mitigate against it. As we concluded in Chapter 4, the pattern applies more to white groups, probably including Hispanics, than to blacks.

The Pervasiveness of Race

Our results show strikingly that no major socioeconomic characteristic in the American metropolis is as differentiated as race. Blacks in particular have resided in large numbers in many American metropolises for three or more decades now, and like the immigrants from across the ocean, they came to the northern industrial belt in search of economic opportunity. The obstacles they faced in achieving social and economic integration into the mainstream have been well documented,

---

[13]Douglas Massey and Brendan Mullan, "Processes of Hispanic and Black Spatial Assimilation," *American Journal of Sociology* 89 (1984):836–873.

and we have been able to observe the legacy in the neighborhood pattern. Reynolds Farley writes out a mixed scorecard on black progress since the 1960s, noting relative gains in educational attainment and earnings, but no improvement in unemployment and labor force participation.[14]

Racial segregation across urban neighborhoods remains very high, well above the segregation observed for other ethnic groups. It is the black population that is the most separated of all racial groups in metropolitan areas of every size and region. About two-thirds of blacks in our typical SMSA would have to move in order for each neighborhood to have the same racial composition.[15] Even within the Hispanic population blacks are very segregated from whites.

We do find evidence of assimilation of blacks and other minority groups. The black population is suburbanizing. There is also evidence of substantial recent decreases during the 1970s in the level of segregation. The civil rights movement and the Civil Rights Act of 1968, banning housing market discrimination, are likely contributors. Nevertheless, compared to white ancestry groups, and even to the other census-identified racial and Spanish groups, blacks lag behind. The presence of Asians, in sharp contrast to blacks and Hispanics, is positively associated with neighborhood SES in the factorial analysis for several cities.

One can always question the degree to which any observed differences in the neighborhood pattern are due to intervening factors (such as economic differences among the groups) or to preferences in residential location among all groups, yet the vast differences observed for a population that has resided in the metropolitan structure for such a long time constitute a fundamental challenge to the notion that the melting pot and spatial assimilation extend equally to all groups in American society. If the urban neighborhood pattern is seen to reflect the structure of economic opportunity in the nation's cities, there is evidence that the large gaps separating the races—gaps that have been so pervasive and persistent—have only begun to be closed. The causes of recent declines in black segregation and their link to assimilation deserve further research.

---

[14]Reynolds Farley, *Blacks and Whites: Narrowing the Gap?* (Cambridge, Mass.: Harvard University Press, 1984), pp. 193–201.

[15]The racial segregation of urban neighborhoods even confounds the tabulation of segregation for other characteristics. That is, social characteristics that have a greater incidence in the black population than in other groups manifest higher levels of residential segregation than might otherwise be the case. This phenomenon is particularly noticeable in the segregation of the female-headed household type. More detailed tabulations for population and housing characteristics exist, but a full exploitation of them was beyond the scope of this research. Such multiway tabulations might offer a clearer picture of residential differentiation.

Neighborhood Attachment and Identification

Neighborhood activists, community researchers, local news media, and, of course, residents often speak of the intangible qualities of neighborhoods, the sense of community that individuals feel for their local areas. These sentiments and ties often form the basis for heated arguments for or against change in the neighborhood, such as advocacy for an elderly citizens center, a park, or opposition to development projects perceived as imposed from "outside."

These intangibles are never directly the subject of the census. But can we use the present detailed analysis of census characteristics to tell us something about the bases of attachment to neighborhood in contemporary urban society? Our work in Chapter 3 should be of help. Race, class, and the physical attributes of the housing stock are the principal sources of neighborhood differentiation in the metropolis. Are they the fundamental elements of neighborhood attachment as well? It is likely that they operate partially and indirectly, setting the conditions upon which neighborhood sentiment can be founded. These are the elements that help define neighborhood "character" internally and externally. Neighborhood lobbying and organization often take place on the basis of qualities that seem to inhere in the physical setting itself, the boundaries drawn by the complex process of interaction among neighborhood residents, community leaders, and external actors.

The most vocal neighborhoods often appear to be those of moderate status, coupled with a distinct ethnic composition. This is consistent with our findings about metropolitan differentiation. Ethnicity in particular carries a two-edged sword. On the one hand, the religious, cultural, and other networks that are associated with a particular ethnic identity attach in part to the local community, and can be translated into general community sentiment (even for those of other ancestries or mixed ethnicity), and onward into political activism. The other side of the sword is more sinister. Ethnic purity and exclusion can be the explicit or implicit goal—the hidden agenda—of community organization. The long history of racial discrimination in housing, amply manifest in the statistics we have analyzed for successive censuses since 1940, is consistent with a claim that neighborhood attachment is based on exclusion. To be sure, many cities can now point to racially integrated, ethnically diverse communities, which have many of the intangible qualities of community attachment, and many community organizers and umbrella organizations do not encourage racial and ethnic antagonism. Nevertheless, the case of the racially integrated neighborhood is far from the norm. Diversity among white European stock ethnic groups and Hispanics is much more evident.

Although the degree of overall income segregation turned out to be less than originally anticipated, our analysis detected a very clear separation of the well-to-do from the poor. Households making over $30,000 per year are separated from those making less than $5,000 by about the same amount that separates blacks from whites. We find segregation between the ends of income distribution to be much more substantial than that across occupational or educational groups. Middle and upper class neighborhoods have their forms of community organization and attachment too. Often these take slightly different organizational forms and public postures, but these residents can become highly vocal—revealing their attachment to the neighborhood—if a project threatens their community.

Our work on social areas using the factorial methods of Chapter 3 pointed out a few additional clusters, most important of which were middle class child-rearing communities in larger metropolitan areas. Identification and sentiment may be associated with these neighborhoods, yet here it takes a different form. In many regions such child-rearing communities are separately incorporated municipalities. The political lines help preserve that identity as well as provide a source of internal political expression and a possible invisible wall against intrusion from the outside, at least in those communities that practice the politics of exclusion.[16]

The life cycle characteristics, as a rule, occupy lower rungs on the ladder of segregation, and are less differentiated in other views of the metropolis. Consequently, life cycle less often serves as the unifying thread and rallying point of neighborhood organization. Although life cycle concerns are always present, and all neighborhoods tend to show some degree of specialization, class and ethnicity are more easily discerned in the public countenance of neighborhoods.

The Policy Context

In this section we return to several issues that help shape the way we view neighborhoods and their role within American society. We refrain from making explicit policy recommendations; instead, we draw out from our research results and issues that bear on policy discussions.

___

[16]An analysis of the mechanisms of exclusion and its consequences is given in Michael N. Danielson, *The Politics of Exclusion* (New York: Columbia University Press, 1976).

People Versus Place

Policy has shifted in recent years with regard to the importance given to "place" in defining the domain of activity of the federal government, as well as state and local governments. President Carter in 1978 was able to announce the "first" truly comprehensive and urban policy, replacing a patchwork of individual programs designed to aid large cities, smaller towns, and the communities within them. No sooner was the 1978 policy written than the tide of opinion began to flow in the opposite direction. The McGill report on "Urban America in the Eighties" called for a diminution or end to the large-scale urban oriented geographically targeted policies of the 1960s and 1970s, stating that "the purpose and orientation of a 'national urban policy' should be reconsidered. There are no 'national urban problems,' only an endless variety of local ones."[17] The report concluded, "People-oriented national social policies that aim to aid people directly wherever they may live should be accorded priority over place-oriented national urban policies that attempt to aid people indirectly by aiding places directly."[18] A more detailed report by the National Academy of Sciences echoed this theme, and brought in a range of research to buttress the point. The National Academy argued that the United States was in the midst of an economic transformation and that the best strategy called for a rethinking of urban policy. It suggested that the public sector should aid the social adjustment to the economic transformation, rather than resisting it by shoring up old and outmoded forms of economic and geographic organization.

The 1982 *Urban Policy Report* (under President Reagan) emphasized the role of the private sector, and argued that the "key to healthy cities is a healthy economy."[19] In contrast, Anthony Downs, working from an extensive body of research on urban development, countered that private sector growth does not offer the solution to urban problems. He takes note of the double transformation of big American cities—shifts in economic structure and changes in demographic composition—and provides an optimistic outlook on his own critique of current policies.[20] This debate prompts us to ask in a wider way what light our research casts on the "urban-economic transformation" now

[17]President's Commission for a National Agenda for the Eighties, *Urban America in the Eighties* (Washington, D.C.: U.S. Government Printing Office, 1980), p. 99.

[18] Ibid., p. 102.

[19]U.S. Department of Housing and Urban Development, *President's National Urban Policy Report* (Washington, D.C.: U.S. Government Printing Office, 1982), p. 1.

[20]Anthony Downs, "The Future of Industrial Cities," in Peterson, ed., *The New Urban Reality*, pp. 281–294.

facing the nation, and whose script neighborhoods are likely to follow as that drama unfolds. In particular, we need to question the role of place in a settlement system that is undergoing population diffusion.

The most haunting problem in the call for the shift from places to people as we move forward with the economic transformation is "what about those left behind?" Not only will there be—as there are indeed now—persons left behind possessing few skills to compete in the transformed labor force, but there will also be people literally left behind, physically trapped in areas of deprivation, and in cities with (perhaps) declining ability or willingness to provide any sort of assistance. There are two cases where the intersection of social and geographic separation is particularly acute: racial segregation and pockets of poverty.

Repeatedly this work has documented the way in which ethnic segregation dominates the social landscape of metropolitan America. The segregation of blacks from other groups far outdistances the segregation experienced by any other racial or ancestry group we have been able to measure with census statistics. While census tabulations cannot discount the operation of self-congregation or the operation of some intervening factor, a *prima facie* case for racial discrimination in the residential market remains. Poverty status, imprecise a measure as it is, is also fairly tightly clustered within the nation's metropolitan areas, more clustered than other socioeconomic characteristics we examined.

The problems of poverty and racial discrimination are, it seems, inextricably bound up with "place" in the present metropolitan system. Despite the diffusion of the economy, infrastructure, and population, distinct pockets of the poor remain, and near total separation of blacks from whites persists. To the extent that this separation coincides with the existence of municipal boundaries, the segregation problem spills over into the issue of the political economy of metropolitan areas. A simple reliance on public sector initiatives and "people oriented" policies may not resolve this problem satisfactorily. Some degree of "place-specific" action by the public sector may be needed, either in the form of funds directed to particular places or in targeted assistance to those persons trapped within areas of disadvantage.

Conventional models of the metropolis claim that we can tell a great deal about the social composition of a neighborhood by its location within the metropolis, particularly with reference to the CBD, and that we can predict a neighborhood's evolution from its position as well. But if the population diffusion trend is genuine, and is likely to continue, then neighborhood composition and evolution may be freed from the bond of geographic position. The dynamic aspects of the theory—including the melting pot concept and its more formal exposition as the theory of spatial assimilation—have also been predicated upon the idea of a unified urban system that experienced the inexorable power of ecological evolution. There was in the formulation, no matter how mythical, a quality of inevitability of assimilation for successive waves of social (ethnic) groups and the trajectory of occupancy given over to individual neighborhoods. Present trends challenge this ecological inevitability. Obsolescence of the conventional model would lend more credence to the neighborhood-based policy interventions advocated by Downs and others.[21]

The early twentieth century model of the metropolis in which political, economic, and residential systems were coextensive has been largely replaced by a "vote with your feet" residential system where the choice of neighborhood of residence not only implies a certain composition of the housing stock and social composition of the neighbors but also participation in a differentiated political structure. As the social mosaic has become overlaid with the political web, the powers of home rule offer mechanisms for localities to exert even further control over their own neighborhoods' destinies. This prospect challenges further the conventional dynamic theories of spatial assimilation, which hold out the promise of future participation in the mainstream to all social groups.

No discussion of the metropolitan transformation can be complete without reference to the phenomenon of gentrification. The rehabilitation of older neighborhoods by new urban residents has received a great deal of attention in local and national media. It has been heralded as a harbinger of socioeconomic rejuvenation of older metropolises, and as a source of fiscal revitalization. A considerable amount of evidence has accumulated to date on gentrification—itself defined in a number of conflicting ways—but systematic metropolitan-level study is only very recent. Research shows that some degree of gentrification exists in almost every major city,[22] but in the bulk of cities it is extremely limited in geographic scope. Brian Berry describes the present circumstance as "islands of renewal in seas of decay."[23] Gentrification undoubtedly produces some displacement, but the extent and adverse effects of this may be less severe than feared.[24] On balance there is still a loss of persons

---

[21]Anthony Downs, *Neighborhoods and Urban Development* (Washington, D.C.: Brookings Institution, 1981).

[22]Michael H. Schill, "Neighborhood Reinvestment and Displacement," Princeton Urban & Regional Research Center, Princeton University, 1981.

[23]Brian J. L. Berry, "Islands of Renewal in Seas of Decay," in Peterson, ed., *New Urban Reality,* pp. 69–98.

[24]Howard Sumka, "Neighborhood Revitalization and Displacement: A Review of the Evidence," *Journal of the American Planning Association* 45 (1979):480–487.

and households from the central areas of the city, including loss of the middle class.[25]

Our own research showed that it was possible in the 21 SMSAs to detect gentrification at the census tract level, but most first and second ring neighborhoods continued to experience relative decline, both in population and in socioeconomic status. Some inner city areas received newly constructed housing, but definitions differ on whether this counts as gentrification. It is in the "leading" cities, with the growing corporate core, such as Chicago and Boston in our sample with large absolute and percentage growth in downtown office space, that the rehabilitation of older inner neighborhoods, with growth in relative income and number of households simultaneously, is most visible. These neighborhood results corroborate the conclusion of Brian Berry, who argues that the process of gentrification "is limited to urban centers of strategic national and regional importance in which the expansion of modern headquarters complexes and related producer services has led to significant new central business district growth."[26] In sum, gentrification is a very real phenomenon, and one that may be healthy. Compared to the attention given it, it is far outweighed by patterns of metropolitan expansion, the kind of forces that we saw operating on the Indianapolis neighborhoods of Chapter 6.

As economic activity itself decentralizes, certain suburban municipalities have become particularly successful (sometimes to their chagrin) in attracting industry and commerce.[27] Such places may become metropolitan epicenters. The new nodes in the metropolitan grid are built up within small self-contained jurisdictions. In a system that derives revenue for public services from property taxes, epicenter development can contribute to the unevenness of distribution of resources in the metropolis. Future research should look more carefully into the role epicenters and corridors play in the evolving metropolis.

Such a development raises the specter of a socially divided, politically balkanized metropolis, in which the poor are trapped in communities with no tax base and declining infrastructure, while others are sequestered in suburban enclaves, so that little promise of local income redistribution exists. The reality is more complex. Annexation, and the operation of the market itself, can serve to mitigate such trends, but

---

[25]Larry H. Long and Donald Dahman, "The City-Suburb Income Gap: Is It Being Narrowed by a Back-to-the-City Movement?" U.S. Bureau of the Census, Special Demographic Analysis, CDS-80-1 (March 1980).

[26]Brian J. L. Berry, "Islands of Renewal in Seas of Decay."

[27]A number of such suburbs have enacted growth control ordinances and taken up other strategies for balancing residential and commercial developments. See, for example, New York Times, "Fast Growing Suburbs Act to Limit Development," December 2, 1985; "After Years of Growth, White Plains Draws the Line," November 11, 1984.

this picture varies greatly by region of the country and for metropolises within. The political boundaries surrounding the older industrial cities tend to be fixed. In younger, fast-growing cities of the South and West opportunities to annex still exist, and they occur. The danger is still that in the new diffused system of population and economic activity, the poor and minorities may become further excluded from participation in the market and political arena.

Economic Mobility and Community Competition

Cities have always competed for economic growth and resources. Thus, Boston, Philadelphia, and Baltimore competed in the days of sea trade; and Chicago and St. Louis vied to become the rail nexus for the western expansion. At the present time cities use the tools of tax abatements, infrastructure construction, and marketing to attract desirable industry and thus population. A number of additional tools have been provided by legislation at the federal level. Urban renewal is the one such program that has gained the most notoriety, but urban development action grants, general revenue sharing, the proposed urban enterprise zone program, and a large number of housing programs have all been used in a more or less targeted fashion.

In our present context, this interregional struggle becomes manifest within the region in the form of "downtown versus the neighborhoods." The interests of low and moderate income groups (in the residential neighborhoods) are pitted against those interests favoring economic growth in the more attractive (downtown) industries, particularly those of the corporate core. Neighborhood residents and community leaders see themselves as being consciously left out of the decision-making process. The fact that in the cities of the old industrial belt, the outer limits of the municipality are almost permanently fixed further exacerbates the pressure and the conflict.

Under the traditional model of the metropolis the central location of the poor was not disadvantageous, because jobs were centrally located (relatively speaking) and inexpensive means of transportation were available throughout the central area. At present there is a sharp spatial mismatch between the areas of economic growth and the lower skilled labor pool. This mismatch is acknowledged by almost all who deal with urban policy. What to do about it is much less a matter of consensus. The McGill Commission and the National Academy argue that it is at once inefficient and foolhardy to subsidize the continued residential location of the disadvantaged population within cities and metropolitan areas that are declining in competitiveness. Some go on to say that it is downright inequitable. Proponents of this view argue for residential mobility as a solution to the problem: a people-to-jobs strategy.

On the other side are those who contend that the residents of these low and moderate income neighborhoods are the least able to move and that the public sector should attempt to bring economic activity to those places where there is a pool of unemployed and underemployed, or alternatively undertake action to keep industry in places where jobs are threatened. In addition, the residents of such neighborhoods sometimes contest that they do not wish to move, that they like their community, and that it should not be ripped apart. Often such arguments are phrased in terms of rights to jobs and community. Both of these groups fall into the jobs-to-people strategy.

In the United States there has always been a tug of war between economic development and its attendant demands for residential mobility and the striving for community. Mobility makes for an improved standard of living, and it allows individuals and families the opportunity to "choose" community for reason of social norms, perceptions of status for upward mobility, or otherwise. Over against that we have the maintenance of community, where stability and continuity help to maintain the pattern of social norms and feeling of belonging. The quest for community has its unseemly side, too, as it becomes an opportunity to discriminate against other groups in their own quest for social advancement.

Our research is consistent with the notion that some groups within society are indeed trapped spatially. For blacks, the poor, certain family types, and undoubtedly certain combinations of these, the evidence for segregation is clear. Their spatial separation can be a double-barreled disadvantage. Not only are they segregated within the metropolitan settlement system, and thus removed from proximity to jobs and networks about employment opportunities, but these highly segregated groups are, in many instances, concentrated within labor markets that are themselves providing fewer and fewer lower skilled entry level positions. Such neighborhoods in addition are burdened with other social problems, including crime and family disruption.

We have witnessed, over the period covered by this work, substantial swings on public policy with regard to the conception of "community" and the position of community within the policymaking agenda. As the economy evolves increasingly toward service sector employment, and an ever higher fraction of the labor force possesses a high level of educational achievement, alternative sources of social networks and communities evolve. Professionally based networks are only the most prominent and obvious examples of this. Improvements in transportation and communication technology further reduce the need for proximity as a means of "staying in touch" with kin, friends, and others in one's communities of reference. This trend, it would seem, points to the decreasing relevance of spatial relations and neighborhood in the lives of American urbanites.[28]

Yet, on the other hand, we have heard the call for neighborhood preservation. This may be a true measure of the importance of the immediate residential community in the lives of city-dwellers or it may reflect simply a resistance to the technological developments that enable an individual to maintain a sense of physical proximity. Those who fear being left behind and for whom locally based community is still of continuing importance may cry the loudest. The vitality of the neighborhood movement reflects in part a framework for resistance to perceived downtown power interests discussed earlier, for neighborhood can also drown out deeper interests in the maintenance of property values, and even the exclusion of undesirable social groups.

Despite the dramatic technological changes that have been wrought on the settlement system, the landscape continues to be a highly important sorting ground for social differentiation. Seen from one side, neighborhood can become an important way of maintaining or expressing social status in a mobile society. From the other side, neighborhood still carries with it some of the intangible qualities of community. In searching for a "good neighborhood" in the market for housing, many Americans are also selecting a community of limited liability, a metaphor offered by Morris Janowitz and expanded upon by others since.[29] Here the urban dweller not only chooses a house, a school system, an overall social composition, but also a pattern of interaction and life style. We should not be too eager to assume that technology will vitiate the local community. Rather the sorting out of the metropolis on the basis of social characteristics and the continuing call for community based services and public sector activity attest to the persistent (if limited) role of community in the daily lives of ordinary urban dwellers. What has changed is the way in which community plays a part in life, and the way in which we play a part in community. Increasingly community itself, along with neighborhood, is something consciously purchased through a market, a bundle of goods that comes with the residence.

[28]Melvin Webber argues this point at length in "The Urban Place and the Nonplace Urban Realm," in M. Webber et al., *Explorations into Urban Structure* (Philadelphia: University of Pennsylvania Press, 1964), pp. 79–153.

[29]Morris Janowitz, *The Community Press in an Urban Setting* (Chicago: University of Chicago Press, 1952); Gerald D. Suttles, *The Social Construction of Communities* (Chicago: University of Chicago Press, 1972).

Neighborhood and Metropolis

We can examine the neighborhood pattern with a variety of purposes in mind. For some, neighborhoods represent sites of community sentiment, and the composition of individual communities becomes of paramount interest. For others, the neighborhood pattern is the spatial illustration of the sources of social differentiation in the society. In our work we have gone from the individual case, the profile, to the general, the pattern of spatial organization, in an effort to understand how the neighborhoods fit into the metropolis in 1980. We have also consulted previous census data to look at how this relationship between neighborhood and metropolis changes over time. A few themes emerge from our work.

Foremost, the analysis of American neighborhoods reveals how finely grained social differentiation in urban space can be. The population sorts itself out, through the operation of the marketplace and public sector action, into small neighborhoods, which are by consequence more homogeneous. But this is far from the whole story. The sorting out process is much more extensive for some characteristics than for others. Race and certain housing types are particularly segregated. Socioeconomic status is moderately differentiated with a fair range of intermixture of the broad middle classes. The top 15 percent of households in the income distribution live apart from the bottom 15 percent about to the same degree that separates blacks from whites. Segregation on the basis of family and life cycle characteristics and on the basis of ancestry within the white population is, by comparison, quite modest, despite the attention that ethnic community cohesion and elderly residential location have commanded in the recent past.

Major metropolises are much more differentiated than smaller places, as one would predict by theory and based on similarly sized statistical neighborhood units. Understandably, then, neighborhood life in big cities and small cities is quite different. In the big metropolis, one's neighbor is more likely to be of the same ethnic group, live in the same kind of housing, and be of similar socioeconomic status than would be the case in a medium-sized or small-sized place. Growing metropolitan areas exhibit lower ethnic and housing type segregation but more life cycle segregation. Whether this indicates a shift in the keys to the sorting process remains to be seen. Almost paradoxically, the diversity of the major metropolis occurs in the extreme range of neighborhood types. As the resident of the big city travels outside the neighborhood of residence, the whole panoply of residential communities comes into view. Neighborhoods of extreme wealth and poverty are more likely to be found, as are neighborhoods devoted to particular life cycle groups, and of course the range of distinct ethnic communities is particularly evident.

In 1929 Harvey Zorbaugh wrote that through the sorting process "the city becomes a mosaic of neighborhoods, 'communities,' and little cultural worlds."[30] This is still true in 1980. Community is partly an element of choice and partly a constraint. We can acknowledge only that the neighborhood helps set some of the conditions of social life for the average urban resident, and that it continues to play a role in illustrating the patterns of social differentiation in society. The mosaic of social worlds provides a range of communities from which the prospective resident can choose.

Over time the neighborhood pattern has shifted, and we have tried to outline the elements of that change. For one thing the metropolis appears to be organized less simply and less compactly in 1980 than in previous decades, a process we described as population diffusion. We identified a ladder of residential segregation, in which separation of neighborhoods by housing characteristics and race were most prominent, followed by socioeconomic status, and life cycle characteristics. Our results suggest that neighborhood evolution may become more independent of geographic position than traditional views would imply. In sum, immediate neighborhood is still very important, for reasons of community, of property values, of favorable and sinister sources of homogeneity and exclusion, although the traditional organizational glue that once controlled metropolitan structure has begun to break down. The mosaic of social worlds is still very much a part of the reality of everyday urban living; however, the pattern of tiles in the mosaic has become a bit blurred and the picture is a little bit more difficult to discern.

[30]Harvey W. Zorbaugh, *The Gold Coast and the Slum* (Chicago: University of Chicago Press, 1976 [1929]), p. 234.

APPENDIX A:
QUALITY OF SMALL AREA DATA
IN THE 1980 CENSUS

T HE 1980 CENSUS, perhaps more than any other, was plagued with controversy about the accuracy of the data, the undercount, and its differential impact on population groups and places in the nation. The controversy itself, which began before the enumeration and continues, has received book-length treatment.[1] Discussions of the accuracy of the count itself and the differential impact of underenumeration on the individual municipalities, specifically with reference to revenue-sharing funds, have also appeared.[2] Several major cities claimed that they were severely undercounted. Sections of some cities were reenumerated; Detroit filed suit to have the official census figures adjusted for undercount.

The objective of an accurate and complete census is generally agreed upon. However, little consensus exists on how best to improve quality of census information, and even more specifically, where the most payoff will be for a given expenditure of funds. The 1980 census

---

[1]Ian I. Mitroff, Richard O. Mason, and Vincent P. Barabba, *The 1980 Census: Policy-Making Amid Turbulence* (Lexington, Mass.: Lexington Books, 1983); William Alonso and Paul Starr, *The Politics of Numbers*, The Population of the United States in the 1980s: A Census Monograph Series (New York: Russell Sage Foundation, 1987).
[2]Jeffrey S. Passel, Jacob S. Siegel, and J. Gregory Robinson, "Coverage of the National Population in the 1980 Census by Age, Sex and Race." U.S. Bureau of the Census, *Current Population Reports*, 1982, pp. 23–115; Arthur J. Maurice and Richard P. Nathan, "The Census Undercount," *Urban Affairs Quarterly* 17 (1982):251–284.

cost over $1 billion, or about five dollars per person enumerated. Discussions are already well underway about how to improve processing, reduce costs, and increase accuracy for the 1990 census.[3] Procedures that would improve accuracy and/or productivity at less relative costs are being sought. Since taking the census is, by nature, a geographically coordinated project, we examine geographic variation in the quality of the data in this appendix.

Traditionally, formal demographic concern with the accuracy of the census has focused on the underenumeration of the population. By means of postenumeration surveys or coordination with other sources of demographic data, estimates of the degree of undercount by age, sex, and race have been developed. For recent censuses (1960, 1970), coverage ratios have been published which allow one to reinflate (or with some groups, deflate) the population to a best estimate of the true resident population. Similar efforts have also been made for early periods of time in an attempt to produce more accurate estimates of the range of demographic processes.[4]

Most information about the accuracy of the census takes this form. Despite the controversy over data quality in the 1980 census, coverage probably improved over previous censuses, although the Census Bureau has not been able to develop exact estimates.[5] We may be observing, then, more the growth of an audience concerned about census accuracy than an increase in inaccuracy. The demographic differentials in this undercount are substantial, ranging from negligible values in certain age-race-sex groups, up to a preliminary estimate of 16 percent for black males aged 34 to 44. Whites and females usually have much better coverage. The presence of a substantial undocumented alien population (many of whom are Hispanic) has complicated the development of precise estimates.

There is considerable geographic variation in the coverage of the census and even of the accuracy of the information that is collected. Much of this variation is related to socioeconomic factors which, as we have tried to show in this volume, are distributed differentially through space. We expect areas with greater concentration of uneducated, poor, fearful, illiterate, and mobile populations to have less accurate statistics and poorer coverage. But variation in the administration and field work in the census exists as well. This may reflect quality of training census field staff and/or the labor pool from which the census can draw, as well

---

[3]U.S. General Accounting Office, *The Census Bureau Needs to Plan Now for a More Automated 1990 Census* (Washington, D.C.: General Accounting Office, 1983).

[4]Ansley J. Coale and Melvin Zelnik, *New Estimates of Fertility and Population in the United States* (Princeton, N.J.: Princeton University Press, 1963).

[5]Passel, Siegel, and Robinson, "Coverage of the National Population."

as interaction with morale and the type of community served. Processing errors can also be geographically concentrated.[6] Whatever the source, the impact of data problems on individual neighborhoods can be enormous. For example, and to foreshadow our analysis to come, we found that data for three neighborhoods in the Chicago metropolitan area were based on 100 percent substitution, that is, information on the neighborhood population was not supplied by the residents themselves but by an imputation procedure. A description of the extent of such imputation, and its correlates, is the subject of this appendix.

Explicit measurement of small area variation in data quality has rarely been undertaken. This appendix focuses specifically on the extent and correlates of imputation for the neighborhoods in the twenty-one SMSAs. We comment also briefly and qualitatively on the accuracy of the data themselves from our experience in working with them. We hope that this will be of help to users of the 1980 census and planners of future censuses.

Methods

A variety of nonsampling errors can damage the utility of the census. These include errors of coverage (undercount), noninterview, respondent error, and processing error. (Enumerator errors are possible in certain cases). Coverage is inherently difficult to assess because of the simple fact that no information is directly collected from the omitted population. Most other research on coverage accuracy employs other sources of data (vital statistics, follow-up surveys, etc.) to develop the estimates. Such estimates, though, cannot generally be developed for small areas.

Allocations and substitutions, two forms of imputation, result from noninterview, omitted, or inconsistent responses on the mail form, and from processing errors. Imputation is one form of data deficiency itself worthy of examination. To the extent that imputation is correlated with undercoverage, our analyses may shed light on the intrametropoli-

[6]The best example of administrative sources of variation comes from income data in the 1980 census. Income information was sometimes miscoded, causing grave discrepancies in the reported incomes for some enumerated individuals, affecting about 0.5 percent of the nation's 300,000 enumeration districts. Tabulations of this problem show great regional disparity, with the heaviest incidence in the South. The net effect in the state of Georgia, for instance, was $140 per capita, and within the state ranged from 0 percent in Richmond County to 8.6 percent in Treutlen County.

tan distribution and socioeconomic correlates of undercount for neighborhoods. (It is not clear that imputation and coverage are correlated, since occurrences of the former can stem from several problems.) The Census Bureau maintains strict guidelines for allocation and substitution, and publishes the extent of these two events along with the other data for tracts.

The Census Bureau defines the substitution procedure as follows:

> When there was indication that a housing unit was occupied but the questionnaire contained no information for all or most of the people, a previously processed household was selected as a substitute, and the full set of characteristics for the housing unit and each substitute person was duplicated. These duplications fall into two classes: (1) persons or housing units "substituted due to noninterview," for example, when a housing unit was determined to be occupied but the occupants could not be found at home during repeated callbacks; and (2) persons or housing units "substituted due to mechanical failure," for example, when the questionnaire page on which the housing unit or persons are listed was not properly microfilmed.

Substitution of housing units is handled in a parallel fashion.

Allocation, on the other hand, involves not the entire data record for the person or housing unit, but rather pertains to specific items:

> After the information on the questionnaires was computerized, any missing characteristics for a person or housing unit were supplied by computerized allocation. Allocations, or assignments of acceptable codes in place of unacceptable entries, were needed most often when an entry for a given item was lacking or when the information reported for a person on that item was inconsistent with other information for the person or housing unit.
>
> As in previous censuses, the general procedure for changing unacceptable entries was to assign an entry for a person or housing unit that was consistent with entries for other persons or housing units with similar characteristics. Thus a person reported as a 20-year-old son of the householder, but with marital status unreported, was assigned the same marital status as that of the last son processed in the same age group. Bureau statisticians believe that this procedure for assigning information in place of blanks or unacceptable entries enhances the usefulness of the data.

Tabulations of extent of allocation are made for specific items, and there is also one tabulation of whether an individual or housing unit has had any information allocated. The Census Bureau believes that imputation is the best solution to the missing data problem. Leaving the data items blank or inconsistent would lead to more processing difficulties by subsequent users, and would result in more bias than the assignment of information from nearby persons of similar basic characteristics. When possible the assigned information in allocation comes from someone else in the dwelling unit, but a substantial fraction of the imputed information comes from another individual in the census distribution.

Table A.1, taken from 1980 census printed reports, gives an overview of the problem spots. The incidence of processing errors (mechanical failure) is about 1/1,000 and is fairly constant across states and other large geographic units. Most of the substitution (where an entire individual record is assigned) arises from noninterview. The incidence of any allocation is much more extensive, and varies significantly by subject. On the complete count form, Spanish origin is allocated five times more frequently than sex. With the exception of race, the majority of these allocations come from individuals not in the household. (For age it is 100 percent since direct within-household inference is not possible.) Several of the sample characteristics have a much more serious incidence of imputation. While almost all (99.2 percent) of the sample census forms have at least two items per person reported, slightly less than half (44.9 percent) have at least one other item allocated. Income has always been troublesome, both in sample surveys and the census. About 17 percent of households have allocated income. Several of the items of information requested toward the end of the census schedule (disability status, first marriage, journey to work) also seem to suffer more allocation. The figures in columns 2 and 3 of Table A.1 indicate that the extent of imputation in SMSAs (where about three-quarters of the enumerated population lives) is nearly identical to the nation, and that central cities generally have higher rates of these types of data deficiency.

We analyze here substitution and allocation as general indicators of data quality for small areas. Of course, the figures represent tabulations for people and dwelling units known to exist. Through an ecological analysis, they can tell us something about the neighborhoods where such data deficiency occurs most frequently. We analyze the extent and distribution of allocation and substitution problems in the SMSAs of the study and then provide regression equations which predict from other tract characteristics the fraction of allocation and substituted persons. This statistical analysis is restricted to the complete count information from Summary Tape File 1, and focuses on the population tabulations.

TABLE A.1

Percent of Substitution and Allocation by Type and Size of Place

	United States	SMSAs	Central Cities
COMPLETE COUNT DATA*			
Substitution			
Mechanical Failure	0.1	0.1	0.1
Non-interview	1.4	1.4	1.8
Allocation			
Any Characteristic	10.2	10.1	11.8
Characteristic			
Relationship to			
Householder	2.1	2.1	2.5
Sex	0.8	0.8	1.0
Age	2.9	2.9	3.5
Race	1.5	1.5	1.7
Spanish Origin	4.2	4.1	4.8
Marital Status (15+)	1.3	1.3	1.8
SAMPLE DATA†			
Persons with 2+			
Characteristics Reported	99.2	99.2	98.9
Persons with 1+			
Allocations	44.9	45.0	48.3
Characteristic			
Place of Birth	4.9	5.0	6.2
Residence in 1975	8.0	8.2	9.6
Educational			
Attainment	2.9	3.0	3.6
Occupation	6.7	6.8	8.3
Household Income	16.8	16.9	18.1

*General Population Characteristics, U.S. Summary PC80-1-A, Table B-4.

†General Social and Economic Characteristics, U.S. Summary, PC80-1-C1, Table C-1.

Results

Table A.2 (panel A) contains descriptive statistics for basic measures of allocation and substitution for the overall sample of census tracts, with low-count tracts and crews of vessels eliminated, as in Chapter 2. Naturally, there are many more tabulated allocations (of any item) than substituted individuals. Of the nearly 6,000 census tracts in this study, the typical (median) value on substitution of persons was under 1 percent. That is, half the tracts had a higher fraction of the tract population substituted, and half a smaller proportion. In the typical

TABLE A.2

Descriptive Statistics for Incidence of Imputation for Census Tracts

SMSA NAME	Minimum	Lower Quartile	Median	Upper Quartile	Upper Decile	Maximum	Mean	Standard Deviation	No. of Tracts
A. FOUR MEASURES OF IMPUTATION: 21 SMSAs POOLED									
Population with Allocated Information (%)	0.0	7.5	9.5	12.7	16.5	59.0	10.6	4.5	5917
Population Substituted (%)	0.0	0.4	0.9	2.3	5.0	100.0	2.1	3.7	5917
Housing Units with Allocated Information (%)	0.0	10.9	14.3	18.6	23.6	100.0	15.4	6.6	5980
Housing Units Substituted (%)	0.0	0.6	1.3	3.0	6.1	100.0	2.6	4.7	5911
B. PERCENT POPULATION SUBSTITUTED, BY SMSA									
Allentown	0.0	0.2	0.4	0.7	1.2	10.4	0.6	1.1	155
Amarillo	0.0	0.3	0.7	1.1	2.5	7.4	1.0	1.2	63
Atlanta	0.0	0.6	1.2	2.3	3.9	16.6	1.8	2.0	352
Bangor	0.0	0.1	0.4	1.3	2.1	3.6	0.8	0.9	28
Birmingham	0.0	0.7	1.3	2.3	3.9	33.3	2.0	2.9	202
Boston	0.0	0.4	0.9	2.1	4.0	36.1	1.7	2.8	580
Chicago	0.0	0.7	1.9	4.8	9.5	100.0	3.8	5.8	1,486
Flint	0.0	0.4	0.8	1.8	3.4	18.2	1.7	2.6	124
Indianapolis	0.0	0.4	0.6	1.2	2.4	9.0	1.0	1.1	269
Lexington	0.0	0.6	0.8	1.6	3.1	7.2	1.4	1.5	79
New Bedford	0.1	0.2	0.6	1.1	2.2	3.7	0.9	0.9	44
New Haven	0.0	0.3	0.6	1.2	2.0	4.8	0.9	0.9	93
New Orleans	0.0	0.8	1.4	2.5	4.0	13.6	2.0	2.1	318
Newark	0.0	0.3	0.8	3.0	7.6	26.4	2.5	4.1	462
St. Louis	0.0	0.2	0.6	1.8	4.0	17.9	1.4	2.1	435
Salt Lake City	0.0	0.2	0.3	0.5	0.8	3.5	0.4	0.6	189
San Antonio	0.0	0.6	1.0	1.7	2.9	32.5	1.5	2.6	197
San Diego	0.0	0.3	0.5	1.0	2.2	7.9	0.9	1.1	379
Seattle	0.0	0.5	0.8	1.4	2.3	50.3	1.3	3.0	353
Sheboygan	0.0	0.1	0.2	0.3	0.5	4.4	0.4	0.9	24
Stockton	0.0	0.3	0.6	1.1	2.0	6.2	0.9	1.0	85

neighborhood nearly 10 percent of the population has had some short form item allocated, a figure that approximates the individual national average in Table A.1. The housing data have higher incidence of both allocation and substitution. This is partly due to assignment of information for vacant units and perhaps also to the fact that many housing questions appear at the end of the form. The upper percentiles of the distribution indicate that a small minority of census tracts have very great data deficiency. About 500 tracts (10 percent) have over 5 percent of the population substituted, and there are three instances (all in Chicago) of tracts with 100 percent substitution. In this small minority of census tracts, the information available may indeed be quite unreliable, but for the bulk of neighborhoods the incidence of these two types of data deficiency is rare enough to introduce little bias or instability into calculations.

Panel B of Table A.2 presents the distribution of population substitution in the 21 SMSAs. Although the median substitution proportions are all under 2 percent, there is great variation among SMSAs with respect to this value. The gap between Sheboygan (least substitution) and Chicago (most substitution) represents a factor of ten. There appears to be a tendency for the level of substitution to increase with city size and perhaps with location in the South. In Atlanta, Birmingham, Chicago, New Orleans, and San Antonio more than half the census tracts have over 1 percent substitution.

The circumstances for the other three variables (in tabulations not shown) is broadly similar. For population allocation, the median is again lowest in Sheboygan but is highest in New Orleans (13.3 percent). Substitution of housing units, as would be expected, is more severe than population, with three metropolitan medians over 2 percent. The average extent of allocation is in only one case lower than 10 percent and in several SMSAs reaches 15 or 16 percent. These four measures are not equivalent, however. The correlation (on 5,917 tracts) between substitution and allocation (any item) of population is .51, and that between population substitution and housing substitution is .56. The pairwise correlations of age, race, and origin allocation are all over 90 percent.

It is clear from Table A.2 that for the substantial majority of census tracts in these metropolitan areas, tabulations derive from information almost all collected from the original individuals. A few SMSAs contribute most of the tracts found in the most problematic group. It is here that the geographic disparity in quality of the data begins to emerge. In the larger cities particularly the top decile has a sizable fraction of substitution. Several metropolitan areas hover near 4 percent; in the Newark SMSA it is over 7 percent. In the Chicago SMSA, for example, nearly 150 census tracts have substitution rates above 10 percent.

Higher rates of imputation threaten the reliability of tabulations, especially from the sample data. Six SMSAs have at least one tract of 30 percent substitution, with 17 cases in Chicago. Depending on the accuracy of the assumptions underlying the imputation procedure, significant bias or increased sampling error may be introduced in data collected for these tracts. If, for example, the true instance of plumbing deficiency were double that assumed by the imputation procedure, the result might be enough to raise a calculated mean for a census tract with 30 percent substitution from 5 percent to nearly 7 percent.

The effect on sample data is complex, again depending on the representativeness of the population substituted. In a tract with 3,000 persons of age 25 and over, educational attainment (a sample item) would be based on about 600 individuals. With a 30 percent substitution rate these calculations would be based on complete information for about 400 persons and imputed information for 200 others. If one were to treat the sample size as 400 instead of 600 (taking only information for the complete information individuals), the standard error would be some 20 percent higher. For other items where rates of allocation are high (such as income, disability status, journey to work), the parallel circumstance occurs. Since the incidence of allocation is usually higher, the issue is more germane.

The geographic concentration of substitution within metropolitan areas is of particular interest. A simple measure of unevenness is provided in Table A.3 with the index of dissimilarity, as in Chapter 4. About four in ten of substituted "persons" would have to be relocated in order for the fraction in every census tract to be equal. This concentration is particularly apparent in Newark and Sheboygan. This level of segregation corresponds roughly to that separating owners from renters. The incidence of allocation, on the other hand, is more dispersed with calculated values of D only about one-third that for substitution.

Table A.3 also reports the mean level of substitution and allocation for tracts within four rings surrounding the city center. (Each ring contains about the same number of tracts, defined by distance quartile.) Imputation is by no means even with respect to distance, nor is the pattern consistent by city. In most cities, but especially evident in the big northern industrial SMSAs, substitution is most extensive in the core ring. (In Newark, it is over twelve times higher.) In a few areas (Allentown, Indianapolis, New Orleans, San Antonio, Salt Lake City, Seattle) the pattern is inverted. In every SMSA but one (Allentown) allocation is more frequent in central tracts. It is also clear that age allocation exceeds 20 percent in many inner ring neighborhoods.

The fact that the inner city areas of larger SMSAs have the greatest

TABLE A.3

Spatial Concentration of Imputation: 21 SMSAs

SMSA Name	Substitution (%)					Age Allocation (%)				
	D	RING 1	RING 2	RING 3	RING 4	D	RING 1	RING 2	RING 3	RING 4
Allentown	40	.38	.64	.68	.77	12	8.31	7.94	8.09	8.94
Amarillo	34	1.89	.47	.89	.78	17	12.32	9.05	6.76	6.55
Atlanta	35	2.30	1.65	1.45	1.86	15	15.66	11.16	8.14	9.48
Bangor	40	1.03	1.24	.86	.34	13	10.03	8.16	7.45	8.77
Birmingham	33	2.71	2.59	1.42	1.40	15	14.51	11.88	10.79	9.60
Boston	43	3.69	1.44	.93	.84	15	15.40	11.27	9.29	7.77
Chicago	46	8.98	2.58	2.15	2.59	19	15.71	12.42	10.89	8.11
Flint	44	2.97	2.39	.90	.47	10	12.25	9.69	8.44	8.82
Indianapolis	36	1.42	.80	.62	1.17	11	10.62	9.00	7.71	8.10
Lexington	38	4.64	.87	1.14	.92	11	12.89	9.44	8.76	10.25
New Bedford	34	1.49	.93	.41	.69	13	13.24	9.39	9.56	7.47
New Haven	34	1.50	.63	.36	1.09	15	18.42	11.00	8.81	8.06
New Orleans	33	2.19	1.78	1.62	2.44	12	17.28	17.29	13.05	12.63
Newark	56	7.08	1.93	.85	.58	17	15.12	11.53	8.79	7.75
St. Louis	49	2.68	.91	.53	1.66	18	17.07	10.57	7.42	7.68
Salt Lake City	29	.36	.38	.49	.55	12	11.08	7.58	6.99	9.38
San Antonio	33	1.85	1.10	.87	2.28	11	10.95	8.82	7.52	8.94
San Diego	41	1.79	.75	.55	.53	14	11.92	9.21	8.12	9.11
Seattle	36	1.20	.79	1.16	1.95	12	14.67	9.28	8.43	11.43
Sheboygan	55	.18	.87	.17	.33	7	8.27	6.14	6.52	6.13
Stockton	39	.94	1.06	.66	.98	15	13.99	12.17	9.84	11.64

NOTE: Index of Dissimilarity; see Chapter 3 for definition.

incidence of substitution will come as no surprise. (The level and range of substitution may be news.) Can we predict the extent of allocation and substitution in the cities and nationally? Ability to predict data deficiency and the degree of consistency across the various kinds of deficiency have implications for identifying the location and social correlates of individuals who are entirely missed by the census and for the geographic distribution of effort to rectify errors in coverage.

In Table A.4 we present regression equations for imputation of nearly 6,000 census tracts, pooled across the twenty-one SMSAs. The regressors were chosen to represent a variety of demographic and housing characteristics thought to be related to imputation. In the first equation we predict percent of the population substituted. Using eleven tract characteristics, we can explain over two-thirds of the variation in substitution. The urban dummy variable is a very strong predictor by it-

TABLE A.4

Regression Analysis on Substitution and Allocation, Pooled (N = 5,993)

	Tract Population Substituted (%)	Tract Persons with Age Allocated (%)
Tract Proportion Urban	1.14 (.02)	1.02 (.02)
SMSA Size (millions)	.35 (.002)	
Owner Occupied	−.02 (.0002)	
Median Education	−.13 (.03)	.31 (.03)
Black %	.02 (.002)	
Group Quarter %	−.04 (.004)	.06 (.005)
Female %	−.09 (.01)	−.06 (.01)
Vacant %	.04 (.005)	.06 (.007)
Tract Population (1,000s)	−.14 (.02)	
Median Housing Age	−.03 (.005)	
"Other" Racial Category	.04 (.008)	
Crews of Vessels		21.5 (1.06)
Families in Poverty (%)		.06 (.006)
Median Rooms		−.62 (.07)
Movers		−.09 (.004)
Length of Residence		−.27 (.03)
Foreign Born		.04 (.006)
Unemployed (tract %)		.04 (.009)
South (= 1 if in South)		.48 (.14)
Constant	8.05 (.56)	7.91 (.65)
R^2	.69	.70

NOTES: Standard errors given in parentheses. All coefficients significant at $p \leq .001$.

self and indicates that tracts that are rural in character, generally at the periphery of the metropolitan region, have almost no substitution.[7] Larger SMSAs exhibit higher levels of substitution, even after controlling for these other characteristics. Socioeconomic status and population stability, as indicated by owner occupation and educational attainment, are negatively related to substitution. Tracts with high percentages of blacks, males, and persons of "other" racial classifications, that is, not white, black, Indian, or Asian, have a higher incidence of substitution.

At least as interesting are the variables that did not enter this prediction equation. Age and family status composition, Spanish origin, and location of the SMSA in the South are of no additional help in predicting population substitution for census tracts.

In the case of allocation we have focused on age, an item that, when left blank, must be filled in from information outside the household, and so is a potentially more serious problem. The best predictions of age allocation are for the most part not the same as the predictors of population substitution. (Population substitution and age allocation correlate at .56.) Understandably, the strongest effect of age allocation is in crews of vessels tracts. Information about these cases is obtained by special procedures in the Bureau. Neighborhoods with higher SES (less poverty, more rooms per home) tend to have less allocation, yet after controlling for these characteristics education works in the opposite direction. Neighborhoods with longer-term residents, fewer foreign born, fewer group quarters, and located in southern metropolitan areas also have less allocation. Overall we can explain also about 70 percent of the variation in this characteristic.

We have repeated the regression analysis of population substitution for individual cities, except that we have limited the included variables to the four tract-level characteristics that best predicted substitution in the combined analysis. Results for the twenty-one SMSAs are presented in Table A.5. Even though these characteristics explain two-thirds of the variation in the combined analyses, the SMSA-specific R^2 covers nearly the entire range from zero to 100 percent. Tract educational attainment (an SES indicator) is negatively related to substitution in most SMSAs, but interestingly is never significant in the Deep South or West. Tract percent urban is a statistically significant predictor of substitution in about half the areas, but the sign is not consistent. As one might anticipate from Table A.3, rural tracts have more problems in

---

[7]In the census, the urban–rural classification is independent of metropolitan classification, and is based on density of settlement. Some metropolitan territory, usually at the outskirts of large, diverse counties, is rural.

TABLE A.5

Regression Results on Population Substitution, by SMSA

SMSA	Constant	Median Education	Proportion Urban	Percent Black	Percent Owner	Adjusted R^2
Allentown	.94	−.07	−.12	.08†	.01	.05
Amarillo	4.01	−.11	−.76	.03†	−.02†	.39
Atlanta	2.23	−.03	−.67	.00	.01†	.07
Bangor	−3.49	.09	.03†	.42	1.94†	.46
Birmingham	5.68	−.19	1.09†	−.04†	−.01	.87
Boston	2.19	−.08	.05†	.98†	−.02†	.78
Chicago	10.21	−.49†	1.12†	.01	−.05†	.61
Flint	12.15	−1.07†	.02†	.00	1.06†	.95
Indianapolis	2.42	−.05	−.95†	.02†	−.01	.24
Lexington	9.83	−.91†	2.44	−.02	.00	.15
New Bedford	1.61	−.07	.13†	−.49	.00	.16
New Haven	1.07	.00	−.19	.01†	.00	.09
New Orleans	5.21	−.07	−2.39†	.00	.00	.06
Newark	7.03	−.31†	−.41	.04†	−.03†	.38
St. Louis	2.52	−.20†	.99†	.02†	.00	.86
Salt Lake City	3.17	−.13†	−1.05†	.00	−.03*	.18
San Antonio	4.14	−.06	.01	.00	−2.14†	.05
San Diego	−.06	.02	.04†	−.01†	.96	.98
Seattle	1.74	−.16	.01	.01	.99†	.86
Sheboygan	−1.89	.14	.47	−.02	.01	−.15
Stockton	−.07	−.06	−.01	.01	.99†	.99

*Significant at $p \leq .05$.

†Significant at $p \leq .01$.

New Orleans, Salt Lake City, and Indianapolis. In most locations, tracts with higher proportion black and more rental housing units usually have a higher incidence of substitution.

In no metropolitan area were all four of these variables statistically significant. Some indication of the magnitude of these variables can be seen in a sample calculation from Chicago. An all-white exurban tract (50 percent urban), whose adult population had thirteen years average education and in which four-fifths of dwellings were owned, has a predicted substitution level of .4 percent. An all-black urban tract composed of persons with nine years of education and all renters would have a predicted level of 8 percent.

In another analysis (not shown) we explored a wider array of characteristics with stepwise regression for each SMSA. Again R^2 varied widely. These four variables were generally important, and the importance of other measures was specific to the individual SMSAs.

Conclusions

It is difficult to develop a criterion that would allow one to decide that a particular level of deficiency in the data was acceptable or beyond the range of tolerance. We can, however, offer an interpretation of some aspects of these results, operating on the assumption that allocation and especially substitution are summary indicators of data quality. Hence tabulations of allocation and substitution can provide a window on the geographic incidence of data quality problems.

The overall level of substitution of persons and housing units is quite modest nationally. The incidence of data deficiency is, nevertheless, not even across cities nor especially within cities. A large majority of census tracts or neighborhoods have negligible data problems; however, in some metropolitan areas, especially the larger ones, a small fraction of census tracts have levels of deficiency that cannot be termed negligible. In certain neighborhoods the fraction of population substituted exceeds one-third. Incidence of housing substitution and allocation (persons and housing) are generally higher.

We can summarize the geographic concentration of data deficiency as follows:

1. About 11 percent ($N = 650$) of all census tracts account for one-half of all the tabulated occurrences of substitution in the twenty-one metropolitan areas. Just 50 tracts of the nearly 6,000 contain 11 percent of the cumulative incidence of substitution.

2. Within metropolitan areas, tracts with serious data deficiency are more likely to be found in the inner core. In a few SMSAs, however, the problems occur at the periphery.

3. Our regression analysis shows that tracts with higher proportions blacks, renters, and the less educated are predicted to have higher levels of population substitution. Rural (peripheral) tracts usually have lower levels. Size of SMSA also exerts an independent effect on the probability of data deficiency. While these characteristics predict well in a national sample, the predictability of substitution (overall and by characteristic) can vary greatly.

4. In most cities the level of housing substitution is slightly (about 1 percentage point) higher than population substitution. Incidence of allocation (of any item) to population or housing data is much higher, often a factor of 10. (Allocation of individual items is much lower.) The correlation among the four types of data deficiency specifically examined here is modest.

Two considerations derive from this analysis. The first concerns the present 1980 census and its use. In most instances the census tabulations can be taken as given, as if the incidence of undercount and data deficiency were very small. For the nation and the SMSA as a whole, little overall error is probably introduced. The Census Bureau's "hotdeck" procedure matches information for person or item based on known characteristics and information from a person previously processed. This procedure, which may be the best available and most reasonably accurate, allows fewer individuals to stand for many. The potential unreliability (or sampling error) of data for many small areas is higher than usually imagined. In intensive analyses of subsections of a metropolitan area, particularly neighborhoods in core areas of the largest metropolises, the researcher may be advised to check beforehand on the extent of data replacement as a general caution to the validity of inferences that can be made for the specific location. This admonition applies more strongly to the analysis of items that have a very high incidence of allocation. The Census Bureau's imputation procedure probably introduces much less bias than would omission of "bad" tracts from the data set. For our own part, we have used in the monograph the census data as given. Imputation is not serious for most census tracts, and the Census Bureau procedures provide the best means for working with the data under the least bias. We have, though, tended to favor variables with less imputation (for example, education) over those with greater incidence of allocation and more likely to be subject to misreporting (such as income). Overall we find that the variation across neighborhoods is so large that it dwarfs the inaccuracies introduced by imputation.

The second consideration pertains to census taking. No census can be perfect, and the 1980 census has come close to its objective of finding each resident individual and recording basic demographic information. Our results give information about the geographic incidence of problems in collecting and maintaining data and the social characteristics of places where these problems are most likely to occur. To the extent that actual undercount and incidence of substitution are correlated, our analysis (together with other independent analysis) provides some indirect indication of whom the 1980 census most likely missed. (Without question there is some error and bias in any such inference.) A more refined analysis of the type we provide might prove even more fruitful. It would be possible to introduce relevant, more detailed, even cross-tabulated characteristics and thereby home in on the influence of demographic composition more precisely.

Equally important, our results shed some light on where effort might be concentrated to improve coverage of the 1990 census. The 1980 census cost approximately $5 per person, or about $20,000 per census tract. Since a small fraction of census tracts account for a disproportionate share of the missing data (and probably uncounted persons), a cost-benefit analysis may suggest some redistribution of effort in the fieldwork of the next census. No amount of effort can secure the cooperation of all persons, but as the problem in this century has shifted from a dispersed rural coverage to a concentrated urban one, it may be possible to take advantage of intrametropolitan geographic disparity to improve future censuses.

APPENDIX B: GEOGRAPHIC CONCEPTS AND DATA SOURCES

T HIS APPENDIX contains background material regarding small area data in the 1980 census. The appendix presents (1) an overview of geographic concepts related to our analysis; (2) a discussion of the theoretical principles for defining census tracts, with tabulations of how well they were actually upheld in the twenty-one metropolitan areas of this study; (3) the results of my survey of the study cities to see how they actually carried out the tracting process and used small area data; and (4) a brief description of where small area census data may be found.

Census Geographic Concepts

The 1980 census makes available information for a very large range of geographic areas, some of which are competing and even overlapping. The census geography for states and counties is straightforward for most people, but confusion often arises as to the exact boundaries and purposes of some of the larger, statistically defined areas, as well as the smaller, local areas for which tabulations are available. In principle—except for suppression—all census tabulations are available for every level of geography. We concentrate now on the discussion of the two census units that have been most relevant to this study, the Standard Metropolitan Statistical Area and the census tract.

The Standard Metropolitan Statistical Area (SMSA) is the official 1980 census designation for a metropolitan region. The concept has been in use since the 1950 census, although the definition has undergone some change in the intervening years, and continues to evolve.[1] The Census Bureau provides the following description of SMSA:

> The general concept of a metropolitan area is one of a large population nucleus, together with adjacent communities which have a high degree of economic and social integration with that nucleus. The standard metropolitan statistical area (SMSA) classification is a statistical standard, developed for use by Federal agencies in the production, analysis, and publication of data on metropolitan areas. The SMSA's are designated and defined by the Office of Management and Budget, following a set of official published standards developed by the interagency Federal Committee on Standard Metropolitan Statistical Areas.
>
> Each SMSA has one or more central counties containing the area's main population concentration: an urbanized area with at least 50,000 inhabitants. An SMSA may also include outlying counties which have close economic and social relationships with the central counties. The outlying counties must have a specified level of commuting to the central counties and must also meet certain standards regarding metropolitan character, such as population density, urban population, and population growth. In New England, SMSA's are composed of cities and towns rather than whole counties.[2]

In 1980 there were 318 designated SMSAs in the fifty states. The nearly 6,000 neighborhoods of this study are contained within twenty-one SMSAs. It is important to bear in mind that SMSAs are constructed from building blocks of counties, and that they may cross state boundaries if the neighboring counties fit the criteria for inclusion. Sometimes one or two of the peripheral counties include a large area and a spread-out population. It is even possible for the metropolitan area to include rural population according to the Census Bureau's independent definition of urban. In fact, for our twenty-one SMSAs a small minority of our neighborhoods (tracts) have populations that are over half rural.

The geographic definition of metropolitan area can change from

---

[1]Subsequent to the 1980 census, the designation was changed to Metropolitan Statistical Area. In 1950 the term was Standard Metropolitan Area.

[2]U.S. Bureau of the Census, Census of Population and Housing, 1980, Appendix A, "Area Classification" (Washington, D.C.: U.S. Government Printing Office, 1982).

census to census as counties are added, or occasionally dropped, and as the requirements change. For instance, the Atlanta SMSA consisted of five counties for the 1970 census but by 1980 had added ten more. New SMSAs are added as settlements grow to a point where they reach qualification. Bangor, Maine, and Sheboygan, Wisconsin, are two SMSAs that qualified for the first time in the 1980 census.

The Urbanized Area is a competing geographic concept, which can and has been used to represent the urban region. Urbanized areas share many of the same principles as SMSAs, but exclude low-density "rural-looking" portions of the region that may well be integrated into the metropolitan system, as well as some distant satellite settlements and the "truly" rural population itself. Since so much of the United States statistical system is based on counties, urbanized areas are sometimes not as convenient as SMSAs. In practice it appears that the SMSA as regional entity has gained prominence.[3]

Within the Standard Metropolitan Statistical Area several urban subareas can be defined, for which data are available. Some are primarily political or administrative units; others are analytical or statistical units. Figure B.1 presents an outline of the geographical hierarchy of the census. There are competing geographical organizations of the population. Blocks nest into block groups which nest into tracts, which in turn nest into counties, and several counties comprise the SMSA. On the other hand, political units such as central city, village, and census designated place may not nest so neatly. Neighborhood areas (not shown) may also exist within the SMSA.

We have chosen to work almost exclusively with tracts and tract data. Tracts have a number of advantages over the other subarea data available to us. Since they form the unit of analysis for our research, and because of their broad use, we devote a short discussion to the definition of tracts with some attention to changing historical conceptions and alternative urban small area data.

Census Tracts: The Idea and the Reality

According to information printed for the 1980 census by the Census Bureau, tracts are defined in the following way:

> Census tracts are small, relatively permanent areas into which metropolitan and certain other areas are divided for the purpose of providing

---

[3]More extensive discussions of the definitions used by the Census Bureau are contained in "Area Classification."

FIGURE B.1

Geographic Hierarchy

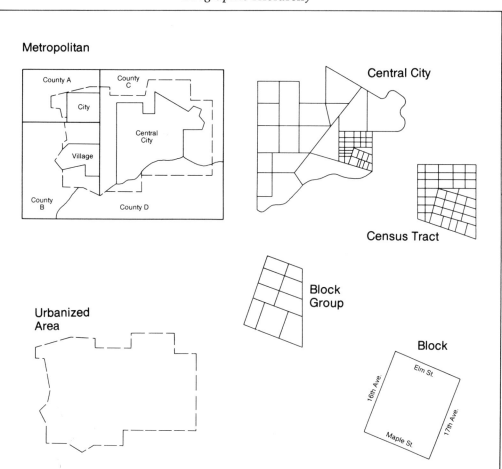

SOURCE: U.S. Bureau of the Census, *1980 Census of Population and Housing: User's Guide* (Washington, D.C.: U.S. Government Printing Office, 1982), p. 57.

statistics for small areas. When census tracts are established, they are designed to be homogeneous with respect to population characteristics, economic status, and living conditions. Tracts generally have between 2,500 and 8,000 residents.[4]

Census tracts have, in theory, a number of advantages. First, tracts are exclusively and exhaustively defined. With the exception of a few

[4]Ibid.

new SMSAs for the 1980 census, all of the metropolitan population lives within tracts. This nice feature holds for SMSAs but not necessarily for urbanized areas; that is, some tracts may be partly in and partly out of the urbanized area.

Second, tracts are designed to be relatively permanent. They are the main unit of small area geography that should be available for comparisons from census to census. This principle goes back to the very origins of the census tract concept around 1900, when the need for subcity statistics became apparent.

Third, the definition of tracts has an advantage from the viewpoint of social science concepts. They are designed to be relatively homogeneous with respect to the socioeconomic status and lifestyle. They are consistent in size and so can be used as the unit of analysis in comparative studies.

Fourth, tracts are a very useful size for statistical purposes. They are small enough to provide a wealth of information about the population and housing characteristics of areas within the cities, since all tables are replicated at every level of geography. Equally important, they are large enough to avoid problems of data suppression.

A comparison of tracts to some of the other popular types of metropolitan subarea statistics may be useful. Blocks are the smallest geographic unit for which information is available, but they have three problems. They do not cover the metropolitan area in general, being limited only to the built-up core region. Since blocks are defined by the notion of a physical city block, they may themselves vary greatly in size, from a high-density apartment block of several thousand persons to a low-density block of well under one hundred. Small blocks are very often subject to suppression of information about the social and economic information of residents. (Information is suppressed when the confidentiality of respondents' information might be compromised.) This can occur especially in cross-tabulated information, such as income by race or tenure by condition of dwelling unit. In major metropolitan areas the large number of blocks also can make data processing unwieldy and expensive. Block data have proven most useful in the analysis of racial segregation, where it has a long history. (Race is also an item that is not suppressed.) Block groups (formerly also enumeration districts) are aggregates of blocks smaller than census tracts. As such they provide a finer-grained population and housing relief than tracts. On the other hand, they are devised as an administrative convenience for the current census only; they can be more often subject to suppression, and no printed reports are made available for them. Municipalities and places have the advantage of corresponding to territory with familiar names around the metropolis, but they too suffer from widely varying sizes, and need not exhaustively cover the SMSA.

Perhaps the most direct alternative to the census tract as the basic, workable unit of census small area geography are the neighborhood areas, developed for the Census Bureau's new Neighborhood Statistics Program. Since this work is about neighborhoods, it is reasonable to ask why not use these neighborhood statistics in the analytical work. Indeed, this was an appealing option.

The Neighborhood Statistics Program (NSP) involved a new set of tabulations designed for use in the 1980 census. The program was instituted partly as a response to the demands from municipalities for small area statistics matched to program and policy activity within their jurisdictions. As I mentioned at the outset, many policies call for a specific subcity delineation for the focus of public sector activity. Neighborhood statistics would provide data for urban renewal areas, targeted community development block grant activity, and the like. In addition, the neighborhood movement in many cities had taken on a more organized and formal structure, to the point where in some municipalities neighborhood organizations were recognized to have a legal or quasi-legal status. There was no guarantee, of course, that the boundaries of these designated areas would correspond to preexisting census geography. Thus, the NSP was formed to provide tabulated census data for these areas.

At the inception of the NSP, only neighborhoods with some form of officially recognized status were allowed to be included, but the rules were eventually relaxed so that most municipalities could develop neighborhood statistics if they so desired. The local area constructed its neighborhoods by aggregating city blocks into the recognized neighborhood unit, following the general guidelines supplied by the Bureau. Once approved by Washington, the neighborhoods became part of this geographic system. Participation in the Neighborhood Statistics Program is optional; consequently, within many metropolitan regions some communities are participating (usually including the major central city), but many others are not. Since the NSP is an "extra," a special tabulation is called for, after the standard round of tabulations for the conventional statistical geography is completed.

The NSP will undoubtedly have considerable utility to the municipalities that participate, both because it can provide statistics for program and policy areas and because it provides community groups who are organized into neighborhoods with specific information pertaining to them. We have elected not to rely on the NSP for several reasons. First, it does not provide the sort of comprehensive statistical geography that the census tracts themselves do. Since participation is optional, some municipalities are delineated into neighborhoods, while undefined areas are lumped into a "balance" tabulation. Second, the defined neighborhood areas are less uniform with respect to size. (On the other hand, some would argue that the neighborhood areas are more homogeneous with respect to social characteristics and certainly have a more coherent community identity.) The NSP is disadvantaged when one desires a systematic set of urban subareas for comparative analysis.

Criteria for Census Tracts

We have presented above the standard published definition of a census tract familiar to most users of census tract statistics. Now we provide further information on the guidelines provided by the Census Bureau for the delineation of census tracts within metropolitan areas. Since we have also surveyed relevant agencies in our twenty-one SMSAs, we follow this presentation with a discussion of some of the strategies and problems involved in developing a census tract system mentioned by these officials.

There were several steps in the basic procedure through which 1980 census tracts within metropolitan areas were established for tabulation. The Census Bureau first developed guidelines to be circulated to the local areas involved. Within the metropolitan areas, census tract committees were formed to oversee the delineation. They submitted tract maps and boundary descriptions at mid-decade for approval. Once approved, official maps were made by the Census Bureau and the areas incorporated into the tabulation scheme. For many metropolitan areas, this process involved only revision of a handful of the 1970 census tracts to reflect changes in the physical landscape and shifts in population. The Census Bureau issues the *Census Tract Manual* and its updates to guide the local area committees.[5] A new guide is being prepared as part of the *Geographic Areas Handbook* for the 1990 census.

For insight into the origin of census tracts and their applicability to the study of small area social phenomena within urban areas, it is important to understand exactly what characteristics apply to their definition. We quote directly from the supplement to the *Census Tract Manual* printed for the 1980 census:

Criteria for Defining Census Tracts

In order that census tract data may be useful to and useable by as many interests as possible, the Census Bureau has found certain criteria

---

[5]U.S. Bureau of the Census, *Census Tract Manual* (Washington, D.C.: U.S. Government Printing Office, 1966).

should be followed when delineating census tracts. These criteria, in the order of importance, are:

1. Boundaries should follow permanent and easily recognized lines in order to facilitate the allocation of house number ranges as well as enumeration.
2. Population should range from a minimum of 2,500 to 8,000 or more. Overall the tracts should average around 4,000.
3. The census tract should be as homogeneous as possible.
4. The census tract should be a compact area, if possible.
5. Consistent with the above criteria, the fewest number of tracts should be delimited.

So the criteria of homogeneity and an average population size are maintained.

In its guidelines, the Census Bureau goes on to develop a few points in more detail. The Bureau argues that tract boundaries should not follow municipal or political boundaries such as wards, where changes due to annexation or redistricting are likely. Rather, the tracts should follow permanent physical features. The Census Bureau stresses the need for stability in census tract boundaries. When tracts are permanent, the change in population, housing, and socioeconomic characteristics for these small subareas can be accurately studied. In certain regions where boundaries of minor civil divisions are virtually permanent, these may be used for tracts.

With regard to population size, the Bureau states that while the recommended range is 2,500 to 8,000, "a tract may contain upwards of 15,000 persons if the population is homogeneous and there is no need or benefit in further subdividing the tract."[6] The Bureau argues strongly against census tracts of under 2,500 population, with the exception of occasional areas that are distinctly different in social and economic characteristics. On the issue of homogeneity, the recommendation is that "Census tracts should contain, as far as is practicable, people of similar characteristics and with similar housing."[7] The Bureau also acknowledges the desire to establish separate census tracts for institutions and military installations of over 1,000 population, because the government and market research firms wish to exclude these populations. The system also recognizes in each SMSA one or more Central Business District (CBD) tracts. We have used these tracts in our analysis to form to first approximation to a central focus for the metropolitan area.

---

[6]U.S. Bureau of the Census, *Census Tract Manual Supplement* (Washington, D.C.: U.S. Government Printing Office, n.d.), p. 8.
[7]Ibid., p. 9.

The work of defining and delineating census tracts falls to the Census Tract Committee of each region. The head of this committee is the Census Tract Key Person. The committee is generally composed of civic leaders, planners, sociologists, business users of census statistics, and geographers, and is charged with producing the list of tracts and the preliminary map for the bureau. The advantage of a local committee for the delineation is that its members (and any staff they so designate) are generally very familiar with the local territory. The disadvantage is that they may not understand the Census Bureau's guidelines or may even be unwilling to follow them, or they may not have sufficient resources to produce an accurate and satisfactory delimitation. The Census Bureau argues that it is even more important today that constancy of boundaries be maintained than in the early periods of the census tract program. Minor civil divisions and other political boundaries are undesirable because they are difficult to maintain over time.

Redistribution of the population within the greater urban area will result in changes in the tract system. The simplest change is the addition of another peripheral county to the SMSA, which then needs to be tracted. Of more concern is the growth or decline of population within existing tracted areas. "Growth tracts" can be split when their 1980 population (pre-census estimate) will be over 8,000 persons. Such "split tracts," very common in suburban areas, are given special numerical suffixes which link them to the former single tract identification, and the new tracts can be easily reaggregated into a parcel that is completely comparable with the prior census(es). Conversely, the Census Bureau here recommends that tracts that have declined to under 1,000 persons be combined with an adjacent tract, "preferably with one of lower than average population and of similar characteristics."[8] Strict temporal comparability can be achieved only by combining census tracts for the earlier census. Failure to consolidate low population tracts may result in the loss of information anyway, due to suppression of information for confidentiality reasons or procedures for weighting sample data.[9]

Census Tracts in Practice

This is the ideal. What are the actual characteristics, census tract size, and distribution in the twenty-one SMSAs under study here? How

[8]Ibid., p. 20
[9]The weighting procedure is designed to give counts for sample items that equal 100% data. In smaller population units (including some tracts) data may be pooled with another entity for weighting. The result may be counts that are in slight disagreement or, on occasion, wholly anomalous. The User's Guide provides more detail and examples.

closely do they match up with the guidelines promulgated by the Bureau of the Census? Did the local area census tract committees successfully follow the guidelines established and circulated by the Census Bureau? We investigate these questions here by examining the statistical characteristics of population size for our tracts and by evaluating the responses to the questions we posed to the local area committees in the various metropolitan areas.

Figure B.2 presents information about the size of census tracts in our metropolitan areas. The modal value is near 4,000, but have a tendency to pile up on the low end of the scale, while there are a few extremely large tracts. Fully 70 percent of tracts are within the Bureau's recommended (2,500–8,000) size range. A handful of tracts, mostly in depopulated older cores, have no population. Another small fraction (.3 percent) are small enough to be subject to suppression. About one-fifth of tracts fall under the Census Bureau's recommended minimum. Because 10 percent of tracts have populations above the recommended 8,000 maximum, and because a few of these are huge, the mean tract population size in this group of nearly 6,000 is over 4,600 persons.

In most analyses we have taken the tract as the unit of observation. Our argument was a conceptual and theoretical one: tracts have been designed to be distinct, relatively homogeneous communities. We have elected generally not to weight for differential population size, precisely because these tracts should represent neighborhoods and communities as entities within the metropolis. We can see from the histogram that most tracts fall within a fairly well defined band, and thus a researcher can feel a bit more confident about taking such a tack. Differential weighting would change results very little; some previous empirical tests have shown this to be true. Many segregation formulae, most notably the index of dissimilarity and the entropy calculations used here, do implicitly weight for parcel size by construction.[10]

Survey of Local Committees

We also surveyed the census tract statistical committees and the planning boards of the respective central cities to determine how the administrative system for delineation of tracts worked in practice and how many neighborhoods participated in the Neighborhood Statistics Program. We were particularly curious about whether the guidelines formed by the Census Bureau were followed and how local practition-

[10]We excluded crews of vessels tracts from our analyses, but not from Figure B.2. Tracts with small population sizes tend to be omitted in the analysis due to missing data.

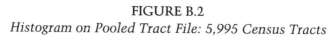

FIGURE B.2

Histogram on Pooled Tract File: 5,995 Census Tracts

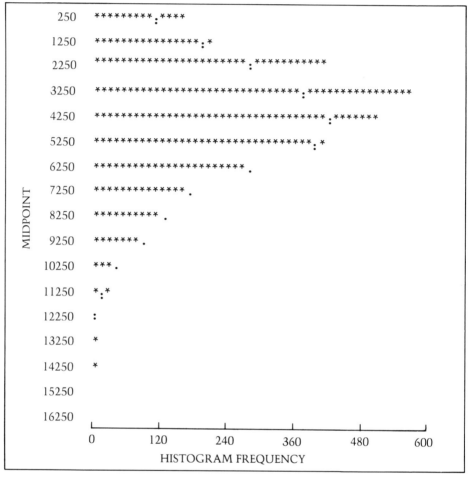

ers, who make the most extensive use of census small area data, perceived the utility of the different statistical systems. The following is a summary of our information gathering. The structure and level of activity of census tract committees does appear to differ from SMSA to SMSA. The most common affiliation of the census tract key person (and often the site of much of the detailed work) was a regional planning agency. In some cases the committees were very active, even forming subcommittees for tracting outlying areas as recommended by the bureau. But in many cases (although I did not inquire specifically) the work fell to one small staff, or even one individual. Often this individual had been involved in the tracting procedure in the previous census and was knowledgeable about both the city and the requirements.

I queried the key persons about their actual delimitation criteria. Almost every metropolitan area acknowledged that the "sourcebook" for the tracting was the Census Bureau's *Census Tract Manual* and its updates. The responses also confirmed that, in accord with the criteria, physical boundaries took precedence over political boundaries in the delimitation. Some respondents mentioned explicitly trying to use the concept of "ecological areas" as a model for tracts. There were some notable exceptions. In at least one SMSA, there seemed to be a great amount of confusion as to the priority for boundaries. The local area wished to emphasize political boundaries, and found itself in conflict with the Census Bureau. It is my interpretation that in this and other cities, the purpose of census tracts was not as well comprehended, and so the local committee preferred to delineate a set of boundaries of practical importance for political or planning purposes as of 1980. Conversely, in older areas with stable population and municipal boundaries, tracts have a relatively long history, and have often earned a prominent place in the local statistical geography. In such cases, little reworking of the boundaries was desired or necessary, and the 1980 delimitation proceeded quickly and without incident.

How stable in fact are census tract boundaries, and what kinds of changes do take place? The Census Bureau Geography Division has looked at this question for the nation's 37,821 census tracts for 1980 within 1970 areas. About one-quarter experienced some sort of change, but the majority of these were simple splits due to population growth, and slightly less than 5 percent were renumbered. The fraction of "significant" splits, revisions, and combinations, those with over 100 persons affected, was under 5 percent.[11]

About three-quarters of our metropolitan areas maintain some form of participation in the Neighborhood Statistics Program. The number of neighborhoods and their average size vary widely, and delineation is far from comprehensive across the metropolis, and indeed, even across the city itself. In general, neighborhood areas seem to be smaller than tracts, but in the major cities they are larger. The criteria for the boundaries of the neighborhood are quite varied as well. Planning areas not coterminous with census tracts are sometimes used; in other cases formal neighborhoods with their quasi-legal status are defined. Most cities acknowledge that neighborhood boundaries do not respect tract boundaries; in general they are small areas, determined more by planning is-

---

[11]*Census Tract Comparability Listings,* unpublished. This information was compiled from unpublished listings supplied to the author by the Bureau of the Census.

sues and community groups' geographic self-recognition. A useful distinction made by one respondent is that tracts are reserved for long-term geographic comparability, and neighborhood areas tend to be strictly short-term planning or community response delimitations. Interestingly, though, in a few of our cities, the neighborhood areas are aggregates, or near aggregates, of tracts.

From this analysis we can offer some conclusions. First, the Census Bureau must inform places about the purpose and utility of tracts, especially so in newer, growing areas. The desire for administratively convenient boundaries poses a challenge to the integrity of the tract concept. In particular, many of those involved in the delimitation process do not understand the importance of maintaining a minimum size greater than 2,500. Second, several cities (agencies) exhibit a lack of understanding of the statistical rationale pertaining to tract size and the virtue of comparability. Third, the bureau's guidelines are generally clear, and a revised manual is likely to be part of the *Geographic Areas Handbook* for 1990. Some advice on how to develop population projections for small areas would also appear to be very useful to localities that are growing and in the process of redelimiting. Fourth, neighborhood statistics may be very useful in their own right, especially for programmatic needs, but they cannot supplant tracts. Fifth, the homogeneity issue arises time and again. It is possible, using currently available data and statistical techniques, to make some quantitative assessment of the degree of homogeneity achieved in the tracting process. Such an assessment touches on the very definition of neighborhood, as discussed in Chapter 1.

Are tracts neighborhoods? In theory, many of the organizing or conceptual principles are similar, yet in practice the system of census tracts conflicts with the system of neighborhoods. One respondent stated: "Most tracts in their own way defined neighborhoods."

Small Area Census Data Sources

All population and housing data for census tracts used in here came from STF1A and STF3A. A computer tape extract for twenty-one SMSAs was provided by the Donnelley Marketing Company of Stamford, Connecticut. Tracts split by higher geography had been reaggregated. (Occasionally suppression influenced the tally, as discussed in Chapter 4.) Geographic coordinates and tract areal data (not census products) were purchased from Geographic Data Technology of Hanover, New Hampshire, and merged with the population and housing information. There is an overwhelming variety of information produced by the Census Bureau for areas below the county or municipality. Here we give a very quick overview of how to access that material. We divide our discussion into access to data on computer tapes (machine readable form) and access to data in the various printed reports. A complete discussion of data products is presented in the *User's Guide* prepared for the 1980 census.[12]

Information on census tracts is available in both printed and machine readable form. The printed reports for census tracts are contained in the series PHC80-2 *Census Tracts*. These reports contain statistics for most of the population and housing subjects covered in the 1980 census; some tables show complete count data, while others present sample data. Portions of tracts split by municipality boundaries are also shown. Many basic statistics are presented separately by race and Spanish origin for groups within tracts of sufficient size. The amount of detail in the printed volumes is necessarily more limited than that available on computer tape.

The most complete census tract information is available in the Summary Tape File (STF) series, magnetic tapes issued for data processing. There are four basic Summary Tape Files. (They correspond roughly to the four "counts" of the 1970 census tape file series.) STF1 provides 321 data items of complete count population and housing information. STF2 is the detailed tabulation and cross-tabulation of the complete count data, containing 2,292 cells of information for the total population and housing, some of which is repeated separately for the race/Spanish groups of sufficient size within the tract. STF3 is the sample tabulation analog of STF1, and includes 1,126 cells of information. STF4 presents the very detailed information for sample data. It is a huge file, with thousands of cells of information, and like STF2 repeats for population subgroups. The sample files (STF3 and STF4) contain information on income, labor force participation, and many other tabulations based on questions that appeared only in the sample "long form." The analyst should be aware that these tape files are issued on a state-by-state basis, arranged hierarchically by level of geography. For the individual who desires a data file of census tracts (or blocks or municipalities) within a metropolitan area it is necessary both to extract the records for the particular level of geography of interest and to merge across state tapes, where the statistical area of interest (for example, SMSA) crosses state boundaries. The Census Bureau's packaged computer programs and those made available by other vendors will. gen-

---

[12]U.S. Bureau of the Census, PHC80-R1-A, *Users' Guide* (Washington, D.C.: U.S. Government Printing Office, 1982).

erally perform this readily. A final problem with regard to the STFs is that they are released in three versions, each with a different geographic emphasis. Anyone desiring to use the machine readable forms of the census should consult the *User's Guide* before obtaining the data files.

Data for other small areas in the census are much less comprehensive or consistently available. Generally, block groups and enumeration district data are available on computer tape. Block data themselves are available on the computer tapes, under the same organizational framework as census tracts, although block information is not included on the tabulations for sample data. Printed reports of block statistics (organized by metropolitan area and state) are also available, although the level of detail of characteristics is limited. Again the *User's Guide* presents a complete description of what kind of information is available in what places and forms. It should be evident that for the study of urban differentiation, census tracts have a number of practical advantages.

Bibliography

Included here are studies of the theory of residential differentiation, segregation, and urban and neighborhood policy.

Albrecht, Roger S., and James V. Cunningham *A New Public Policy for Neighborhood Preservation.* New York: Praeger, 1979.

Alonso, William *Location and Land Use.* Cambridge, Mass.: Harvard University Press, 1964.

Bell, Colin, and Howard Newby *Community Studies.* New York: Praeger, 1972.

Berger, Benet *Working Class Suburb.* Berkeley: University of California Press, 1971.

Berry, Brian J. L. "Internal Structure of the City." *Law and Contemporary Problems* 30 (Winter 1965):11–119.

_____ "Islands of Renewal in Seas of Decay." In Paul Peterson, ed., *The New Urban Reality.* Washington, D.C.: Brookings Institution, 1985.

_____, **and Quentin Gillard** *The Changing Shape of Metropolitan America.* Cambridge, Mass.: Ballinger, 1977.

_____, **and John Kasarda** *Contemporary Urban Ecology.* New York: Macmillan, 1977.

Bogue, Donald J. "Ecological Community Areas." In Donald J. Bogue and Michael J. White, eds., *Essays in Human Ecology II.* Chicago: Community and Family Study Center, 1984.

Bourne, Larry S., ed. *Internal Structure of the City,* 2nd ed. New York: Oxford University Press, 1982.

Burgess, Ernest W. "The Growth of the City." In R. E. Park and E. W. Burgess, eds., *The City.* Chicago: University of Chicago Press, 1967.

Clark, W. A. V. "Residential Mobility and Neighborhood Change." *Urban Geography* 1 (April–June 1980):95–117.

Clay, Philip L., and Robert M. Hollister *Neighborhood Policy and Planning.* Lexington, Mass.: Lexington Books, 1983.

Committee on National Urban Policy *The Evolution of National Urban Policy 1970–1980.* Washington, D.C.: National Academy of Sciences, 1982.

Crenson, Matthew *Neighborhood Politics.* Cambridge, Mass.: Harvard University Press, 1983.

Danielson, Michael N. *The Politics of Exclusion.* New York: Columbia University Press, 1976.

Downs, Anthony *Neighborhoods and Urban Development.* Washington, D.C.: Brookings Institution, 1981.

Duncan, Otis D., and Beverly Duncan *The Negro Population of Chicago.* Chicago: Aldine, 1965.

Duncan, Otis D., and Stanley Lieberson "Ethnic Segregation and Assimilation." *American Journal of Sociology* 64 (1959):364–374.

Edmonston, Barry *Population Distribution in American Cities.* Lexington, Mass.: Lexington Books, 1975.

Farley, Reynolds "Residential Segregation in Urbanized Areas of the United States." *Demography* 4 (1977):497–518.

Fischer, Claude S. *To Dwell Among Friends.* Chicago: University of Chicago Press, 1982.

Goetz, Rolf, and Kent W. Colton "Dynamics of Neighborhoods: A Fresh Approach to Understanding Housing and Neighborhood Change." *Journal of the American Planning Association* 46 (1980):184–194.

Harris, Chauncy D., and Edward Ullman "The Nature of Cities." *Annals of the American Academy of Political and Social Science* 142 (1945):7–17.

Hatt, Paul "The Concept of Natural Area." *American Sociological Review* 11 (August 1946):423–427.

Hoover, Edgar M., and Raymond E. Vernon *Anatomy of a Metropolis.* New York: Doubleday-Anchor, 1962.

Hoyt, Homer *The Structure and Growth of Residential Neighborhoods in American Cities.* Washington, D.C.: U.S. Government Printing Office, 1939.

Hunter, Albert *Symbolic Communities.* Chicago: University of Chicago Press, 1974.

—— "The Urban Neighborhood: Its Analytical and Social Contexts." *Urban Affairs Quarterly* 14 (March 1979):267–288.

Jacobs, Jane *The Death and Life of Great American Cities.* New York: Random House, 1961.

Janowitz, Morris *The Community Press in an Urban Setting.* Chicago: University of Chicago Press, 1967.

Kain, John F. "The Journey to Work as a Determinant of Residential Location." In *Essays on Urban Spatial Structure.* Cambridge, Mass.: Ballinger, 1975 (1968).

Kasarda, John D. "The Implications of Contemporary Redistribution Trends for National Urban Policy." *Social Science Quarterly* 61 (December 1980): 373–400.

Keller, Suzanne *The Urban Neighborhood: A Sociological Perspective.* New York: Random House, 1968.

Kornblum, William *Blue Collar Community.* Chicago: University of Chicago Press, 1974.

Kotler, Milton *Neighborhood Government.* New York: Bobbs-Merrill, 1969.

Laska, Shirley, and Daphne Spain, eds. *Back to the City Issues in Neighborhood Renovation.* New York: Pergamon Press, 1980.

Leven, Charles L., ed. *The Mature Metropolis.* Lexington, Mass.: Heath, 1978.

Lieberson, Stanley *A Piece of the Pie.* Berkeley: University of California Press, 1980.

Logan, John R. "Industrialization and the Stratification of Cities in Suburban Regions." *American Journal of Sociology* 82 (September 1976):333–348.

——, **and Linda Brewster Stearns** "Suburban Racial Segregation as a Nonecological Process." *Social Forces* 60 (September 1981):61–73.

Long, Larry, and Diana DeAre "Repopulating the Countryside: A 1980 Census Trend." *Science* 217 (September 1982):1111–1116.

Massey, Douglas S. "Effects of Socioeconomic Factors on the Residential Segregation of Black and Spanish Americans in U. S. Urbanized Areas." *American Sociological Review* 44 (December 1979):1015–1022.

———, **and Brendan P. Mullan** "Processes of Hispanic and Black Spatial Assimilation." *American Journal of Sociology* 89 (1984):836–873.

Mills, Edwin. S. *Studies in the Structure of the Urban Economy.* Baltimore: Johns Hopkins University Press, 1972.

Murdie, R. A. "Factorial Ecology of Metropolitan Toronto, 1959–61." Research Paper No. 116. Chicago: University of Chicago, Department of Geography Research Series, 1969.

Muth, Richard *Cities and Housing.* Chicago: University of Chicago Press, 1969.

National Academy of Sciences *Rethinking Urban Policy.* Washington, D.C.: National Academy of Sciences, 1983.

National Commission on Neighborhoods *People, Building Neighborhoods.* Final Report to the President and Congress of the United States. Washington D.C.: Superintendent of Documents, 1979.

Noyelle, Thierry J., and Thomas M. Stanback *The Economic Transformation of American Cities.* Totowa, N.J.: Rowman & Allanheld, 1983.

O'Brien, David J. *Neighborhood Organization and Interest-Group Processes.* Princeton, N.J.: Princeton University Press, 1975.

Park, Robert, and Ernest Burgess *The City.* Chicago: University of Chicago Press, 1967.

Rees, Philip H. *Residential Patterns in American Cities.* Research Paper No. 118. Chicago: Department of Geography, University of Chicago, 1979.

Schoenberg, Sandra, and Patricia L. Rosenbaum *Neighborhoods That Work.* New Brunswick, N.J.: Rutgers University Press, 1981.

Segal, David, ed. *The Economics of Neighborhood.* New York: Academic Press, 1979.

Solomon, Arthur P., ed. *The Prospective City.* Cambridge, Mass.: MIT Press, 1980.

Sumka, Howard "Neighborhood Revitalization and Displacement: A Review of the Evidence." *Journal of the American Planning Association* 45 (October 1979):480–487.

Suttles, Gerald D. *The Social Order of the Slum.* Chicago: University of Chicago Press, 1968.

Tiebout, Charles A. "A Pure Theory of Local Public Expenditures." *Journal of Political Economy* 64 (October 1956):416–424.

U. S. Department of Housing and Urban Development *The President's National Urban Policy Report.* Washington, D.C.: Superintendent of Documents, 1983.

U. S. President's Commission *Urban America in the Eighties.* Washington, D.C.: U.S. Government Printing Office, 1981.

van Valey, T. L.; W. C. Roof; and J. E. Wilcox "Trends in Residential Segregation: 1960–1970." *American Journal of Sociology* 82 (January 1977):826–844.

White, Michael J. "Racial and Ethnic Succession in Four Cities." *Urban Affairs Quarterly* 20 (December 1984):165–183.

Yin, Robert K. *Conserving America's Neighborhoods.* New York: Plenum Press, 1982.

Name Index

Subject Index